LOUISA

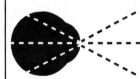

This Large Print Book carries the
Seal of Approval of N.A.V.H.

LOUISA

THE EXTRAORDINARY LIFE OF MRS. ADAMS

LOUISA THOMAS

THORNDIKE PRESS
A part of Gale, Cengage Learning

Farmington Hills, Mich • San Francisco • New York • Waterville, Maine
Meriden, Conn • Mason, Ohio • Chicago

GALE
CENGAGE Learning

LIBRARY OF CONGRESS CATALOGING-IN-PUBLICATION DATA

Names: Thomas, Louisa, author.
Title: Louisa : the extraordinary life of Mrs. Adams / by Louisa Thomas.
Description: Large print edition. | Waterville, Maine : Thorndike Press, 2016. | ©
  2016 | Series: Thorndike Press large print biographies and memoirs
Identifiers: LCCN 2016008070 | ISBN 9781410488145 (hardcover) | ISBN 1410488144
  (hardcover)
Subjects: LCSH: Adams, Louisa Catherine, 1775-1852. | Presidents' spouses—United
  States—Biography. | Adams, John Quincy, 1767-1848.
Classification: LCC E377.2 .T48 2016 | DDC 973.5/5092—dc23
LC record available at http://lccn.loc.gov/2016008070

Published in 2016 by arrangement with Penguin Press, an imprint of
Penguin Publishing Group, a division of Penguin Random House LLC

Printed in the United States of America
1 2 3 4 5 6 7 20 19 18 17 16

FOR MY GRANDMOTHER
Osceola Herron Freear

CONTENTS

8

INTRODUCTION

Louisa Catherine Adams waited at the doors. She was easy to overlook — small and slight and nearing fifty, with shadows beneath her large dark eyes. But that night, January 8, 1824, she stood where she would be seen, and all attention was on her.

"Have a beautiful plan in my head," she had written in her diary three weeks earlier. She had cleared four rooms of her house in Washington, then eight. Chandeliers were hung, doors taken off their hinges, and pictures of eagles and flags chalked on the ballroom floor. Fifty-four bonfires were lit lining the road. In the end, newspapers reported that about a thousand guests had come. It was "as splendid an assemblage of beauty and fashion as we have ever witnessed," the *Richmond Enquirer* would write. All the members of Congress (except two Virginians who had been obnoxious to her husband, John Quincy) were in attendance. The department heads, the diplomatic corps, and all the leaders of Washington society were there. Only President James Monroe and his wife were absent, as was their custom. It was the tenth anniversary of victory at the Battle of New Orleans, and this ball was in Andrew Jackson's honor. It was Old Hickory's day and it was his time; his candidacy for president of the United States was starting to surge. But one thing was already clear: though it was Andrew Jackson's day, it was Louisa Catherine Adams's night.

A little after eight o'clock, a carriage made its way through the throng, and Jackson emerged. Louisa was there to meet him and lead him through the rooms. Her spangled silk dress shone in the lamplight. "In her manner she unites dignity with an unusual share of ease and elegance; and I never saw her appear to greater advantage than when promenading the rooms, winding her way through the multitude by the side of the gallant General," read one of the dozens of accounts of the ball published in newspapers around the country. When supper was called, Jackson raised his glass and drank to her. Then he left, but it did not matter. The guests stayed, and the dancing went on.

Louisa and John Quincy were not merely throwing a party that night. They had an aim in mind: Jackson's ball would become the Adamses' ball. It was a bid to establish John Quincy Adams as the front-runner for the presidency. She had been preparing for this moment not for weeks but for years. She called her parties "my campaigne."

John Quincy did not like to think that throwing a ball could help him become president. He had served his country since he had been a boy, shaped by the Revolution. He had seen dead and bloodied soldiers, had stood on a hillside and watched the Battle at Bunker Hill across the bay, and had felt the shudder of a cannonball blasting through a ship's wall. His mother had made herself a model of American motherhood, and his father was an instrumental figure in American intellectual and political life. As an adult, John Quincy had been minister to Holland, Prussia, Russia, and England. He had served as a senator from Massachusetts, had negotiated the treaty to end the War of 1812, and now held the prime post, secretary of state, in James Monroe's Cabinet. He was the architect of the Transcontinental Treaty with Spain and had helped devise the Monroe Doctrine, a foreign policy that would guide the country for a century. He had done his duty at every chance. He would rather believe, or at least pretend, that he did nothing to position himself for the presidency — that if it came to him, it came to him simply because he deserved it, not because he begged for it. He feared ambition, thought it craven. The great-

11

ness of the republic depended on that disinterest. This was what his parents had taught him, and his parents, John and Abigail Adams, had done as much as anyone to invent the United States. John Quincy had grown up in their shadow. Yet he was also their great hope. If the republic was to last, it would be up to the second generation, he was constantly told: it would be up to him.

The United States were turning out not to be quite the country the founding father and mother had envisioned. The virtues that the Adamses so strongly stressed — education, duty, deference to the public good — were not held with the common commitment they had assumed. Commercial interests, political factions, and private concerns were growing more powerful. More men were getting the power to vote, and fewer had studied Seneca and Tacitus. Sectionalism, undergirded by slavery, was pulling the country apart. Power would not merely come to John Quincy; he had to pursue it. He had to make promises, impressions, and friends. Relationships governed politics then, as they always have. Adams did not have the support of the larger public that a man like Jackson had, but that was hardly decisive — the masses did not choose the president, at least not yet. "The only possible chance for a head of a Department to attain the Presidency is by ingratiating himself personally with the members of

Congress," he wrote in his diary. This, he added, "leads to a thousand corrupt cabals." Terrible at currying favor, he made a show of his distaste for flattery. But John Quincy knew he would fail without friends. Knowing that it was his wife, not he, to whom people were drawn, he endured and encouraged their social life. In fact, this ball for Jackson had been his idea.

Louisa Adams understood him. Sometimes she thought she could see through him. Certainly, she could see politics for what it was, and she knew at that moment there was a part she could play. She was a wonderful hostess, generous and outgoing, though she called herself shy. As young women in London, she and her sisters had entertained a steady stream of visitors by singing, hoping to demonstrate the depths of their souls with the range of their voices, or by playing the harp, hoping to flatter their shapely arms. The courts of Prussia, Russia, and England, where the Adamses lived when John Quincy was a diplomat, had taught her when to compliment and when to gossip, what to watch for and what to overlook. While John Quincy studied laws and treaties, she studied people, wrote letters, and read books. By befriending royalty, by whispering with whatever dignitary she was seated with at supper, by being the one the king asked to dance to open a ball, she had made herself into an asset for John Quincy abroad. And by being the social presence he refused to be, she was integral to his efforts at home. She knew she should not be proud of this, though sometimes she could not help it. She knew that women were supposed to be selfless. She also knew that an Adams — an American — was supposed to build a sturdy, dutiful life instead of a searching one.

She saw the new nation a little differently than an Adams did. She saw herself as different, too.

After all, she was born in London on February 12, 1775, a time before the city of Washington even existed. The Revolutionary War would begin only months after Louisa Catherine Johnson's birth, but more than three thousand miles away. Louisa's father was a proud, patriotic American merchant; her mother was vivacious, charming, socially ambitious, and English. Her parents had secrets, some of which Louisa may have sensed. She spent the American Revolution as a young child living in an opulent mansion in Nantes, France. When the war was over, she returned with her family to London, where she was taught to be lovely and ornamental. Her family lived in a gracious house on Tower Hill, above the Thames, where there were fine oil portraits on the wall, a harp in the parlor, and a neat carriage and stables.

For the most part, Louisa was raised as young, pretty, wealthy English girls were raised — only she was told to consider herself an American and, more important, to marry one.

One problem was that John Quincy was supposed to marry an American, too, and Louisa was not quite one. Another problem was that Louisa perplexed him. It was unclear to him how his self-mastery and his responsibility to the public and to his parents could coexist with his desire for her. In Louisa — and in a life that revolved around the parlor, not the public — he found an alluring alternative to the life for which he had been trained. Their courtship was spirited and contentious. In 1798, when they wed, he made it clear that he was committed to his country, and in marrying Louisa, he committed her to his country, too. In more ways than one, then, she had to leave the Johnsons behind in order to become an Adams.

She tried at once to conform and to resist. Wherever she was, she was caught between roles. After their wedding, she and John Quincy moved to Berlin, where he was tasked with negotiating a treaty and she with negotiating a royal court as a republican who had never been in a republic, representing a nation she had never seen. Louisa was twenty-six and newly a mother when she stepped onto American soil for the first time. Navigating Quincy, Massachusetts, and the fine social distinctions of "democratic" Washington — not to mention her relationship with the Adams family — would turn out to be much harder than dancing with a king. There was a model for an American woman — she thought of her mother-in-law, Abigail Adams — and Louisa knew she did not fit it. She often felt misunderstood and unsure of where she could call home.

There were apartments, hotels, houses, dachas, cottages, the White House; ships, carriages, sleds, coaches, trains, steamboats. It might not be too much to say that for long stretches, she lived in trunks and traveling cases. But there were also rare opportunities and extraordinary experiences. At a time when limits were the norm for women, her life was wide ranging. Her experience was the ground from which she grew.

This book follows Louisa from London, to Nantes, to Berlin, to the United States. It then takes her to St. Petersburg, Russia, where, for six years, she was moored in gaudy loneliness and buffeted by grief, and where she made herself indispensable. From there, it follows her on a dangerous and difficult journey with her eight-year-old son Charles across Europe, from St. Petersburg to Paris, where her husband was waiting. England came next — a stretch of domestic tranquility. Then the family returned to Washington, where the pursuit of power began. There would be costs. In the White House, she found only sadness. John Quincy was stymied as a leader, Louisa was isolated, and they fought; their children struggled; their family began to fall apart. Within a few years, she would bury two sons. When she and her husband returned to Quincy, she believed they had come to live out their days, weary and bereft. But their last and greatest act had not yet begun. While her husband became one of the first great antislavery leaders in Congress, Louisa wrestled with what it meant to be free. Women should cast off "the thraldom of the mind," she wrote to her daughter-in-law, "which has been so long, and so unjustly shackled."

Louisa accepted many of the conventions that constrained her, but she sometimes resisted what those conventions implied. And in doing so, she both witnessed and helped shape the new nation. When John Quincy died, some said that in his life one could find the history of the country's first half century. Something like that could be said of her. When she was born in England, her king ruled the colonies. When she first reached the United States' shores, federal power passed peacefully to the opposition for the first time. On the day that her daughter died in St. Petersburg, Moscow was set on fire. When she traveled across Europe through the wreckage of war, she converged on Paris with Napoleon, newly escaped from Elba. When she died, the United States were only a few years away from civil war.

Wherever she lived, she was always pressing her nose against the glass, not quite sure whether she was looking out or looking in. She was certain she would not be remembered like her husband, John Quincy, or her father-in-law, John Adams, or her son, Charles Francis Adams, men who considered themselves architects of American history. The only history Louisa could claim was personal history, but even there, she sometimes wondered whether she had the right. She started three memoirs for her family, but she gave them shy titles: "Record of a Life"; "Narrative of a Journey"; "The Adventures of a Nobody." She felt she was misunderstood.

But she did something extraordinary with her self-doubt: she explored it. That was unusual. The idea that a woman should wonder about her independent identity — apart from her husband, apart from her son, apart from her family — was hardly prevalent or desirable during the era in which she lived. It could be painful, but there was also a kind of freedom in it. The other members of the Adams family took their identity and the expectations it implied for granted. Because she did not have to speak for the ages, she could speak for herself. It became her habit, even her strategy, to define herself as not like them. And yet in some larger sense, the Adams family helped instill in Louisa what it helped instill in the young republic: a concern for the value of the individual; a fascination with human nature in its manifold forms; an awareness of selfish instincts; a suspicion of power; a respect for traditions; and an invitation — almost an imperative — to scrutinize people, including oneself. She did not always know what to say, and she sometimes doubted whether women should speak at all. Still, there was something singular in the way she related to the world. "Now I like very well to adopt my husband's thoughts and words when I approve them," she wrote to John Quincy at the age of seventy, "but I do not like to repeat them like a parrot, and *prove myself* a nonenity. . . . When my husband married me, he made a great mistake if he thought I only intended to play an echo."

She was not a modern woman, but she had a kind of modern voice.

For two centuries, Louisa Catherine Johnson Adams has been treated mostly as another name on the well-examined Adams family tree. There were times when she saw herself that way too — as a nobody. She figures only indirectly in the history of men's great deeds. I do not pretend that she held some secret political power, though her help was crucial for her husband's career. Her real power is in the story of her life, and in her efforts to learn, to feel, to think, to understand, to have faith, to find what to live for and why. This book tells that story. It is also a story about a transforming country in a transformative age, and a story about what it means to be a woman — a question that had different answers in the nineteenth century but that still resonates today.

"In the entire span of the Adams dynasty, no figure is more central than the wife of the second Adams statesman, John Quincy Adams," wrote the first editor of the Adams Papers, Lyman H. Butterfield. "And yet none is less known or more elusive." She was unknown because, for two centuries, she was seen to exist outside the bounds of history — those great tracts of men, deeds, and laws. She was elusive, too, because she was contradictory, left false trails about her family's background, demurred and denied her merits, and was quick to describe her doubts. Her character was quicksilver, and the roles she held were unofficial. She was also an American who was foreign born, a first lady in a country that was not entirely her own, and a mother who survived all but one of her children. She was torn between cultural and familial ideals and strong instincts that she could not ignore. She was sunk by despair and lifted by laughter.

Her biography cannot be told like her husband's. It is a history of feelings as well as facts, of questions as well as answers, of doubt as well as certainty. It is a record of a life, a narrative of a journey, the adventures of an extraordinary woman. And her story begins where, as a young girl with a romantic imagination, she might have assumed it would happily end: at the moment she met the man whom she would marry.

■ ■ ■ ■

PART ONE:
FRAUGHT WITH BLISS

London, 1775–1797

■ ■ ■ ■

1

The first time Louisa Catherine Johnson saw John Quincy Adams, she thought that he looked ridiculous. When he came to dinner at the Johnsons' house in London, on Wednesday, November 11, 1795, the young American diplomat was dressed in a strange boxy Dutch coat so pale that it appeared, absurdly, almost white. Watching him talk at the table, though, she did like him. He seemed spirited, showing no signs of exhaustion after a long and difficult journey from Holland, where he was the United States' representative. He was handsome, with penetrating, dark round eyes under a pair of peaked eyebrows, and a mouth that was full and strong. He liked a good story and a good glass of wine. Only twenty-eight years old, he was already a high-ranking diplomat — and the son of the vice president of the United States. No one who met him could miss his intense intelligence. Still, after John Quincy had gone, the girls sat in the parlor and joked a little about his unfashionable attire. They were drawn to men who wore well-cut jackets, men who arrived at dinner looking ready for a gallop. John Trumbull, an artist and frequent guest at the Johnsons', who had brought John Quincy to dinner, tried to convince them that Mr. Adams was "a fine fellow and would make a good husband." The sisters laughed.

More than a month passed before John Quincy came back, and Louisa did not miss him. She was twenty years old, clever, and charming, though she could be shy, and she and her sisters were accustomed to being objects of admiration. There were seven daughters in all — beguiling, lively, and lovely — and their mother, Catherine, knew how to exploit their good looks. (An eighth child, a son named Thomas, was at boarding school and then across the Atlantic at Harvard.) Catherine was petite and pretty, with a sparkling wit and a talent for putting guests at ease while keeping them on their toes; she was, Louisa remembered, "what the French call spirituél." When they were little, Catherine had dressed her children in matching clothes and marched them into church by twos. "We were objects of general curiosity and permit me to say admiration to the publick," Louisa would remember with a touch of unembarrassed pride. When they were older, the girls had ostrich feathers for their hats, buffons of starched muslin, and hairdressers to curl, sculpt, and powder their hair. They ordered gloves by the dozen. The three oldest — Nancy was twenty-two, two years older than Louisa, and Caroline eighteen, two years younger — had already been introduced to society, and society was happy to be introduced to them.

There were frequent visitors to entertain them, dinners with dignitaries, merchants, scientists, ministers, British abolitionists, wealthy American plantation owners, young men and old. Their elegant house, No. 8 Cooper's Row on Tower Hill, perched above the Thames and the Tower of London, was known as a welcoming place. Visitors from the United States were treated especially well. Louisa's father, Joshua Johnson, a merchant from Maryland, was the American consul in London, appointed by Secretary of State Thomas Jefferson in 1790. He interpreted his responsibilities liberally. (Perhaps a little self-interestedly, too, which was not uncommon for a consul.) His ships carried Americans' mail to and from the United States; he found them a doctor when they were sick; he pled their case when they were in trouble; he offered his house as their haven. Americans came to Cooper's Row to collect their letters and stayed for tea. They came to discuss a trading scheme and found themselves at dinner. After dinner they would linger for card games, conversation, and music in the parlor.

They came for the comforts of the sofa in the parlor, the oil paintings on the walls, the cook in the kitchen, the harp in the corner, and the eleven servants who would suddenly appear at their elbow to whisk away their finished plates or materialize in the drawing room with a glass of good brandy. They also came, perhaps, for the women.

Louisa barely noticed John Quincy's reappearance at the dinner table in December, but he returned and returned again. He could be found on Tower Hill almost every night. He would linger after dinner with the sisters to watch their skits, play their games, and listen to their laughter. He teased them and was teased; they called him "Mr. Quiz." He sat on the sofa next to Louisa and held the end of a string as Louisa threaded spangles on it for her embroidery. He loved watching them perform — Nancy played the pianoforte, Caroline the harp, and Louisa sang. "Evening at Mr. Johnson's. His daughters pretty and agreeable . . . Late home," he would record in his small, strict handwriting, logging his visits to the Johnsons' night after night.

He was drawn to them, this warm feminine circle — to the sound of a soprano voice, the mellifluous laughter, the suggestion of a life not of strain and hardship but of modestly easy luxury. It was so different from the atmosphere of expectations in which he'd

28

been raised, so different from what he told himself he wanted. He noted the difference and it disturbed him; yet he could not seem to stay away.

The Johnson sisters could sense the increasing attention from this almost-stranger, serious and somewhat supercilious, though not unable to smile. He was unusual — but then, there were ways in which they were unusual too — and perhaps Louisa most of all.

She was almost an outsider by birth. At the time the American Revolution broke out across the Atlantic, when she was only two months old, her father was the buyer for a firm based in Annapolis. He was a proud American patriot unafraid to show his allegiance, which meant that it became neither safe nor profitable for him to live nearly in view of the Tower of London. When Louisa was three, her family moved to Nantes, France, where Joshua worked for a time as an agent for the nascent American government and tried to establish his own business. His house there, on L'Île Feydeau, in the middle of the Loire River, the part of town fashionable among the newly rich, became a frequent meeting point for Americans passing through — Benjamin Franklin, Thomas Jefferson, John Paul Jones, and dozens of others, including John Adams, perhaps with his middle son in tow. They came for business, and perhaps for pleasure; Joshua Johnson projected a sense of living well. His apartments were in a mansion called "Le Temple du Goût" — the Temple of Taste. Rows of wrought iron balconies curved and curled into delicate tendrils; long windows opened like doors; the fireplaces were made of marble; and the ceilings soared. Later, Louisa blamed Le Temple du Goût for encouraging a certain showiness and ruinous cupidity in her mother, but it molded her own aesthetic as well. Long after she had been to the Hermitage, to the Tuileries, to Peterhof, to Sans Souci, she would remember Le Temple du Goût as a singular marvel, elegant and perfect.

She remembered her childhood, she would later say, like a dreamscape. She wouldn't remember the revolutionaries who came to tea, though — they meant little to her then, and anyway, she often wasn't home. Her parents sent her to a Roman Catholic boarding school located in Le Temple du Goût, up the mansion's spiral staircase. The Johnsons weren't Catholic, and Joshua probably wasn't too interested in formally educating his tiny children at that point. (Americans in France sometimes enrolled their children in Roman Catholic schools; Thomas Jefferson — highly skeptical of religion — sent his daughter Patsy to a convent.) But Catherine was frequently pregnant, all the Johnsons often sick, and Joshua prone to feeling over-whelmed. The school left an impression on Louisa, though the only nun she could later recall was the one who brought toys. What she would remember were the trips to con-vents and cathedrals, where she would stand in the tinctured light and then drop to her knees to pray before the cross. She was imprinted with a certain sacerdotal sensitiv-ity, an openness to awe. She also would remember the French she learned.

The school was only upstairs from her parents' family, but to judge from how much she liked to come home — even if it meant falling sick — it felt far away. With her mother, the lessons were of a different order. Louisa learned to dance on top of a table. Catherine dressed her children in the latest French fashions, in silks and tiny hoops, and took them to children's balls, where they were exhibited, admired, and "perfectly ruined by adulation and flattery." One of Louisa's earli-est childhood memories, a kaleidoscope of colors and textures, was of a party — in fact, a wedding. Late in her life, she could still picture the bride of her father's coachman: the flowers on her dress, the flowers in her hands, the flowering flush upon her cheeks. The bride opened the ball, Louisa wrote in 1825, "with all the gaiety of French sprightli-ness."

In 1781, Joshua rejoined his old partner

Charles Wallace and another Annapolis merchant, John Muir, to form Wallace, Johnson & Muir, focusing on commission trade with Europe. Two years later, when Louisa was eight, with the end of the Revolution imminent, the Johnsons returned to London. They moved into the graceful mansion on Tower Hill, a short walk from the fortress and the long artery to the sea below it. Louisa and her sisters were sent to a boarding school in Shacklewell, near Hackney, about four miles north of Tower Hill. The school aimed at preparing middle-class English girls to become marriageable young women; it was run by a headmistress named Elizabeth Carter, who was well read, somewhat narrow minded, and very fat. Students were taught drawing, needlepoint, how to play the harp, and sloppy French — all considered necessary adornments for a wife.

Louisa was young and shy, which at times could make her seem haughty; the other girls called her "Miss Proud." Later in her life, she would remember a persistent feeling that she did not fit in. She had arrived at school wearing a stiff silk dress, as was the style in France, and chattering with her sisters in French only to find her schoolmates wearing high-waisted frocks with pretty sashes and flowing chemise skirts, speaking in proper English idioms coded with signals of birth and bearing. Louisa and her sisters, she wrote in "Record of a Life," "became objects of ridicule to the whole school." But Louisa *was* also proud. Being different might mean being something more than ordinary. There was power in that. She had an innate flair for the dramatic. A story about the first time she went to a church service with her schoolmates in Hackney is telling: when a teacher told her to kneel to pray, she "fell as it were dead upon the floor." Echoing what she'd heard from the nuns at the Catholic school she had attended at Le Temple du Goût, she declared that she was surrounded by *"hereticks."* Likely, her fear of heresy and hell was real and overwhelming; young and impressionable, she had been influenced by what the nuns had told her. But her response was assertive and perhaps a little strange, since her own parents went to an Anglican church (and, when she was home, she likely went with them), and since her sisters seem to have had no similar trouble. She was sensitive, and she had a sense that those around her believed and behaved unlike her.

What happened next, after the fainting, was also characteristic: Louisa fell so "ill" she had to be removed from school. This time she did not go home. Instead, her parents, distracted by the demands of their growing family, their own frequent illnesses, and the vagaries of a merchant's business, sent her to stay with family friends, John and Elizabeth Hewlett.

Parents could be remote, if not seemingly indifferent, in the eighteenth century; nonetheless, sending Louisa to friends seems harsh. Yet Louisa came to see it as a blessing. It shaped her independence and intellect at a very early age. Elizabeth Hewlett was the widow of another American merchant who had remarried a young, bold-minded Anglican minister named John. Louisa's father, Joshua, deferred to John Hewlett in religious and educational matters — not so much, it seems, because he admired Hewlett's renowned scholarship as because he admired his connections. Anglicanism made sense for a socially ambitious family in England, and Joshua did not care what dogma his daughters actually believed. He had been raised on a Chesapeake plantation, where women were worshipped but not for their independent minds. What mattered was that his daughter not make a fuss. A lady was not supposed to disagree with the minister's creed, much less faint upon the floor. Joshua asked John Hewlett to coax Louisa into line. "As in regard to women he always said there was little danger in believing," Louisa later wrote of her father, but "there was destruction in doubt."

John Hewlett did bring her around to a more or less conventional religious view (although, she would write in 1825, "I am not quite sure that some people do not think me a little of a fanatic even now"). But he did something that Joshua did not intend when he asked John to minister to Louisa: he listened to her, talked with her, recommended books for her to read, and treated the child with unusual respect. On her visits over the years, he and Louisa would engage in "serious conversation." His wife, too, treated her with unusual attention and care. Elizabeth Hewlett was "a very eccentric woman of strong mind and still stronger passions." She was a woman for the age of sensibility — but also a counterpoint to the woman Louisa would have encountered in popular advice manuals of the day. Elizabeth was not quiet and delicate; she did not blush and fade. So forceful was her personality that her neighbors, including the formidable Mary Wollstonecraft — the author of *A Vindication of the Rights of Woman* — found her bossy and intimidating. (Wollstonecraft, at the time a local schoolmistress, complained of Elizabeth's power over John Hewlett: "How he is yoked!")

John Hewlett, Louisa wrote, "led me early to think." Thinking was not something that most young women were encouraged to do. John Hewlett was something of a radical. He ran a boys' school in Shacklewell and was a sizar of Magdalen College at Oxford, and he would go on to have an illustrious career as a scholar and preacher, but in the 1780s and 1790s, his friends included famous dissenters and writers, and he had unusual ideas about the education of young women. Even as he was encouraging Louisa, John was urging Mary Wollstonecraft to write an essay about her ideas about the education of young women, which he carried to the publisher himself. Though *Thoughts on the Education of Daughters* was less explosive than Wollstonecraft's more famous work, it still had an incendiary message: a woman should learn to think for herself.

So Louisa began to imagine she might have a mind of her own, which further set her apart. "At school," she later wrote, "I was universally *respected,* but I was never beloved." While she was there, she and her best friend, Miss Edwards — another misfit, "an East Indian very dark, with long black Indian hair; not handsome, but looked up to by all the teachers as a girl of uncommon talents" — were the "decided favorites" of a teacher named Miss Young. By conventional definitions of the time, the Miss Young she described was hardly a woman at all. "Her uncle had her educated with boys for many years; and obliged her to wear boys clothes: and in this way she had in a great measure acquired something like a classical education," Louisa wrote in "Record of a Life." In Louisa's world, there was nothing natural about a lady who acted like a man, and Louisa would routinely express her uneasiness with women who did. Yet in the same breath, she would often also express her admiration. Miss Young was, Louisa wrote, "a most extraordinary woman." She was the kind of woman — strong, forceful, unconventional, educated, "masculine" — who would always both impress and confound her. Louisa flourished under her attention. Miss Young "conversed freely with us upon the books we read," and taught her and Miss Edwards how to recognize "the most beautiful and striking passages." She took the lessons to heart. When her father gave her a guinea, Louisa used it to buy the kinds of books Miss Young and John Hewlett had encouraged her to read: Milton's *Paradise Lost and Regained* and John Mason's *Self-Knowledge: A Treatise, Shewing the Nature and Benefit of that Important Science, and the Way to Attain It.*

Louisa was pulled, then, between seemingly incompatible imperatives. A woman should not think for herself, because a woman pursued knowledge at the cost of a husband. When she recalled her purchase — as she did more than once, even into old age — she said she regretted buying those books and studying them closely. "How often since that time have I thought it injured me; by teaching me to scrutinize too closely into motives, and looking too closely at the truth," she wrote. *Too closely at the truth!* Understanding the truth was not the goal of a young woman's education. A wife did not need self-knowledge; she needed self-effacement. As Hannah More, the most popular author of her day, had written in *Essays Addressed to Young Ladies,* "Girls should be taught to give up their opinions betimes, and not pertinaciously to carry on a dispute, even if they would know themselves to be in the right." Lady Mary Wortley Montagu, another author whom Louisa read, taught herself Latin and Greek in secret and urged her daughter to teach her granddaughter how to hide a good education. Book learning, Lady Montagu wrote, should be concealed "with as much solicitude as she would hide crookedness or lameness."

When Louisa was around fourteen, she was taken out of school, and the point of her schooling was made plain: she had been educated to be married, not to learn about Milton's poetry or the science of self-knowledge. To this end she was brought home to finish her education — her embroidery, her dancing, her painting — under the half-mindful eye of the younger children's governess. Before long, she was introduced into society — which is to say, she was brought into the marriage market. The search began, as it were, for a man in possession of a fortune and in want of a wife.

What Louisa called "work" was mostly embroidery, stitching that was elegantly useless. Her daily tasks were made easy by the assistance of a team of servants — servants to wake her in the morning, to cook her food, to carry her plates, to drive the carriage to the theater or the park. In her spare time (and all of her time was spare), she painted or drew, or visited acquaintances, or received verses from admirers, or played games and gossiped. Some evenings, at parties or in the parlor, she danced. Some afternoons, she read novels that taught her to waste away from love.

Louisa romanticized her childhood, but imperfectly. As she herself evocatively put it, her youth was "fraught with bliss." She was, she would later say — protesting a bit much, perhaps — happiest at home, among her siblings and parents, singing to calm her father at the end of a long day, or perhaps rolling up the carpets and dancing. At parties and balls, she was "timid as a hare."

She had to be careful, too, because at those parties — at the Johnsons' rich friends the Churches, say, or the Pinckneys or the Copleys — she was tasked with remembering that she was different: she was an American. Learning to be an American, of course, was not exactly on the curriculum at Mrs. Carter's school, and it was hardly an identity her mother could impart to her. She had missed the critical experience of the first generation of those growing up in the United States, the

Revolution itself. Most of her sense of it was formed, it seems, by whatever story or testimony she happened to hear from Americans visiting for tea or dinner, and from her father's stories, which generally played up his daring and dangerous actions on behalf of the rebels during the Revolution. He would describe visiting Americans in prison, or General Washington, "of whom he spoke with a degree of enthusiasm which fired our young hearts with the purest love and admiration." He would tell them how, on learning that he held Benedict Arnold's pen in his hand, he had picked up the pen with a pair of tongs and thrown it in the fire. He had named Louisa's younger sister, born in 1776, Carolina Virginia Marylanda. All of this made its impact, and it didn't. The girls were British by their habits. As a child, Louisa's favorite game was "duchess"; she answered only to Your Grace. But their Americanness was forcefully impressed upon them after Lord Andover took a liking to Caroline: the girls were told they must marry Americans.

Joshua planned "to get them to America before they fix their affections on any object here," he wrote to his brother Thomas, the first Revolutionary governor of Maryland, but business kept him in London. It helped that if Joshua could not bring them to America, he could bring Americans to them.

2

Joshua would have preferred that his daughters marry Southerners, but he could not afford to be too choosy. Every American bachelor who walked through the door was a potential suitor. The stakes were high. For the girls, it was such anxious business that it was better treated as a game. They made bets among themselves that would be settled only at an altar. Those who joined in the girls' jokes were favored. Colonel William Smith, General Washington's dashing former aide, was their "model" for a fashionable, daring, desirable man. Walter Hellen was good for a game of battledore. David Sterrett called Louisa his "little wife." After a French servant botched an introduction at a party, Peter Jay (son of the statesman John Jay) and Colonel John Trumbull were forever known as "Mr. Pétéràjay" and "Colonel Terrible." When young Thomas Adams came to the house for dinner while visiting London, Nancy nicknamed him, for some reason, "Uncle Abel."

After that, his absent brother John Quincy was known as "Cain." Louisa had no idea then, of course, of the significant roles both those men would come to play in her life.

The American men who visited her father were not in England to find wives. They generally planned on living well and then leaving. In fact, already Nancy had one engagement slip away when her intended partner returned to the United States. There were other, more dangerous aspects of marriage that a young woman was not supposed to acknowledge. A woman was not supposed to think about what marriage might entail. She was not allowed to dwell on the idea of separation from her family or the dangers of childbirth — or above all sex. She could not dismiss the overt attention of any bachelor, even if that bachelor was "old enough to be my father," as Louisa once described Colonel Trumbull (or "Colonel Terrible"). Yet she had to deny it, even if "he took every opportunity to mark the distinction between myself and my sisters," and even if he confessed his ardor to her, as Trumbull once did. She was supposed to be demure, pleasing, passive, and agreeable, to blend in, and yet also to be the one chosen. She was encouraged to expect a man's attentions and accept his proffered verses but to be "very much surprized" when he compared her to a cherub. Chastity and the appearance of spotless modesty were paramount. The girls were, Louisa wrote, "never permitted to be out of sight a moment."

All games have rules. One was that the Johnson girls could not admit to being pursued. When her sisters decided that William Vans Murray was chasing Louisa, for instance, she professed perfect innocence. "I was perpetually quized literally without knowing what it meant," she later wrote, "for my heart was as free as the roving birds who spreads in wanton sport his plumage to the garish sun." Another rule was that bachelors were always in pursuit of the sisters. "A man old or young who visits frequently in a family of young ladies must be supposed to be in love," Louisa would remember. Another rule was that love had an object. "When a young man frequents a family on terms of great intimacy where there are young ladies," Louisa wrote, "one of them must of course be selected as an object of preference." And who selected who was the object of preference? The sisters did.

And so when John Quincy became a fixture at the Johnsons' dinner table on Tower Hill, as 1795 turned to 1796, they decided that he must be in love with one of them. And in fact, he was. But they were wrong about which one.

One night at the Johnsons' house on Tower

Hill, just after the New Year, 1796, Louisa turned to John Quincy and, in her mellifluous voice, teased him. She had heard that he was a poet, she said, and she wanted him to write her a song. Her demand became a running joke, part of the "perpetual banter" between them. He took the challenge seriously, though, as he took every challenge. John Quincy actually did consider himself something of a poet, and throughout his life nothing made him want to rhyme like the presence of a pretty woman. So at dinner one evening soon after, he reached across the table and slipped Louisa a sealed piece of paper. She opened it immediately, found the promised song, and started to read it aloud. But she had made it through only a few lines when the younger Johnson girls' governess snatched the paper from her hands and whispered in her ear to stop — as if to say the sentiments in the poem were meant for Louisa alone.

A fluster of feeling inside Louisa echoed the fluster at the table. She would later insist that she was sure the poem wasn't private, and that the sentiments it expressed weren't genuine. She would later say that the governess's imagination was overwrought, and that the whole situation was based on a mistake. It was her older sister Nancy, not her, whom John Quincy was courting.

But in that moment, as she would remember it, something happened. The suggestion that he looked at her differently made her look at him differently. There was a surge of emotion, and then a change between them. Was this love? She had her doubts.

What did John Quincy see when he looked at Louisa? There was a portrait painted of her at around the time she met him. In it, her skin is the same color of the milk-pink roses that she holds in her fingertips, and her hair is powdered and piled on top of her head in a nebula of curls, as was the fashion. A baby blue sash encircles her narrow waist, pale where it catches the light and then darkening as it curves into shadow. A black velvet ribbon wrapped around her wrist, startling in its simplicity, is her only adornment. But what makes the painting so striking is the directness of her look. It is not at all the expression of a vain and vapid girl, of a pleasure seeker. It is not the face of some of the other girls John Quincy spent time with in London, like the rich Kitty Church, "a sweet girl entirely engrossed with pleasure, and formed to give as well as to enjoy it." Louisa's dark gaze is intelligent, her smile small and assured. She is beautiful.

Louisa would always insist that her looks were unremarkable. She claimed that she could not compare to her sister Nancy, who had auburn ringlets, a dimpled smile, and hazel eyes — "a perfect Hebe." Nor did she think she rivaled Caroline, whose "form was light her complexion dazzling her manners arch and playful and her disposition sweet." Her mother, Catherine, had been a Venus, and "was at this time very lovely, her person was very small, and exquisitely delicate, and very finely proportioned." Louisa probably looked at herself and catalogued faults, as young women often do: a long face, a nose that swept a little upward. She was slight, usually thinner than she wanted to be. And it was true, she was not someone whose appearance radiated in the air around her, not someone who stopped the conversation when she walked into a room. Her face was singular, her prettiness more subtle than conventional. But she also may have deprecated her own appearance and insisted upon her modesty a little much, especially when she was fifty years old and writing a memoir for descendants in a family that frowned on superficiality, because she knew good looks were not a simple blessing. Even the Johnsons, despite their expensive tastes and interest in the *mode du monde,* knew that while beauty may have made a woman seem special and desirable, modesty was supposed to be the greater virtue. So Louisa both celebrated beauty and, with a little note of falseness, denied its importance. "Accustomed to consider both my sisters superior to myself; surrounded by a beautiful growing family, and remarkably handsome parents, it never appeared to me to possess intrinsic value; and though I ranked it high among the blessings which I had received from heaven, it seemed *too natural* to excite a puérile vanity in my mind." She knew she was beautiful — or at least that others thought she was. "In my own eyes I never possessed beauty," she wrote; "and yet strange to say, I was so familiarized to the idea of possessing it."

So there was something unusually attractive about her, with suggestions of unmentionable desires. But there was something else, something that could only be glimpsed in the serious set of her mouth and in her eyes. She was different from other girls, different even from her sisters. Louisa's mother would later tell her that she had been "thoughtful or grave" as a child, yet also "a creature of ardent affections and strong impulse." She still was. She had an untutored, solemn intelligence, a watchfulness that had earned her the nickname "Cassandra" within her family. But her seriousness enlivened into wit when she was at ease. She had a sense of humor, a teasing and testing nature. She thought of herself as timid, but she was contradictory by nature. Confident that she had nothing to gain or lose from John Quincy — since, of course, he was supposed to be Nancy's suitor — she had "rattled on" to him without reserve.

■ ■ ■ ■

At the end of January, with Louisa's birthday approaching — she would turn twenty-one on February 12 — her father, Joshua, threw her a ball. (Perhaps he held it to help her find a husband, perhaps not — either way, the goal was likely never far from her parents' minds.) The house was filled with guests; the musicians played and the dancing continued long past midnight into morning. John Quincy stayed until three a.m. "Evening very agreeable," he wrote in his diary afterward. He paid the guest of honor more than the usual attentions. Those at the party whispered that his preference for the second Johnson daughter was "decidedly publick." His obvious interest, Louisa would remember, "brought much trouble on my head."

Nancy was furious. She was the one whom the sisters had designated as the chosen one. The unspoken rules of their game were broken. Marriage was the best viable opportunity open to a woman, but society dictated that she could not openly pursue a man. She was the passive player; she had only veto power over the choice of a mate. If John Quincy wanted Louisa and not Nancy, Louisa it would be, and "the whole family [was thrown] into confusion."

Louisa might have tried to defer or to stop

John Quincy right there. But now in the superior position, she refused to refuse him. For weeks the sisters fought. A cold silence fell between them. Even John Quincy — not much disposed to note the moods of women in his diary — registered that something was wrong. "Nancy very much affected, I know not at what," he wrote in his diary. "Louisa pretended a head ache for the privilege of being cross."

Despite how close the sisters were — or, more probably, because of it — their relationship had never been perfectly easy. Louisa was not the much-wanted son, nor the oldest or youngest or neediest — in fact, her father treated her as more independent and capable than the others, which made her a target of her older sister's envy, and so she found it "painful." There had always been little sharp jokes and pranks between the sisters. Louisa would never forget the time her sisters slyly cut her hair short and curled close to her head; once they had powdered it, she looked awfully like a lamb. Louisa and Nancy had been introduced into society at the same time, had access to the same small pool of American men, had the same pressures placed upon them. And if they shone brighter for the combined lights of their beauty and accomplishments, then it was also because their competitiveness generated so much heat. The way Louisa describes a music performance with Nancy is telling, despite her claims that "no jealousy was excited" between them. "On the contrary each endeavoured to add lustre to the other," she insisted, before describing in a backhanded way how their competitiveness drove each of them to perform. "My natural timidity which was excessive, often proved almost insurmountable; but she would say something to me when sitting down to the instrument which would pique me, when she was particularly desirous that I should shine; and then I would sing at her and by pointing the words of the songs I selected; give them an expression of which I was unconscious but which generally produced the happiest effects on my auditors."

It was, in fact, probably her singing that most powerfully brought her to John Quincy's attention. She had a pliant voice, and she knew its power. As a student at Mrs. Carter's boarding school, she had enjoyed her "great reputation" as a singer. Singing brought her pleasure, and it brought her a complicated kind of attention — attention both sought and feared, attention that could be neither acknowledged nor denied. It had given her even a hint of John Quincy's interest; she had noticed that when she began to sing the songs "which he knew to be favorites of Col. Trumbull," John Quincy would pick up his hat and leave. (Later, John Quincy confessed to Louisa that he had noticed that Colonel Trumbull was trying to woo her. "By my Gods — Wish'd him at the D——" John Quincy later wrote to Louisa, "Innocent as he was of all I feared.") John Quincy often recorded the Johnson sisters' musical performances in his diary, and he noted in particular when Louisa sang. He enjoyed watching her perform for him, and she enjoyed performing. Their evenings became part of a larger performance, a courtship. She began to assume the role her life had prepared her for, a lover. But she found that her lover wouldn't follow the same script.

3

The winter of 1796, cold and wet, began to warm into spring. The days grew longer quickly, and the gardens showed budding signs of life. John Quincy adopted a routine not only of dining with the Johnsons but also of taking daily walks with the ladies in the park. It was customary for John Quincy and Louisa to break away — not out of sight of their chaperone, and certainly not out of mind, but out of hearing. The two lovers would stroll beneath springtime's budding boughs, the picture of romance, discussing "philosophy."

Philosophy, John Quincy told Louisa, was not so much about theory as an attitude, not something you developed through thought but a character trait, something you had or you didn't. Its attributes were patience, restraint, and endurance. Louisa was impatient, hardly knew the meaning of restraint, had never had reason to endure — but she wanted to be taken seriously. She was, after all, a girl who had used her guinea to buy *Self-Knowledge* and *Paradise Lost*. She had, clearly, a conventional and sentimental conception of romance, but she fashioned herself as his student. So she listened and would speak often of "my philosophy" — which was, anyway, pretty romantic itself: desire was sharpened by fortitude; love went hand in hand with pain. Love was confusing. Its source seemed uncertain, and her lover seemed not entirely convinced.

He was alternately direct and evasive — and not only to her. Writing to his younger brother Thomas, who was also his secretary at The Hague, where John Quincy was stationed as the American minister, Louisa's suitor was playful but coy. Thomas was teased into replying, "But tell me a little, *who* among this *most attractive society* has most 'charms' for you?" To his mother, John Quincy was suggestive but vague: "At present without having any thing to do, I find it extremely difficult to snatch so much as a quarter of an hour to write ever so short a letter. Perhaps I may tell you the reason of this at a future day; or perhaps you may guess at it without being told." In his diary, though, he was perplexed and anxious. "Customary day, dull and dispirited . . . Wrote scarce anything," John Quincy wrote on February 1, less than a week after the birthday ball where he danced with Louisa. "Dine out almost every day, and pass the evening at Mr. Johnson's. Health low. Spirits lower still. This must be reformed almost entirely." His misery and his displeasure with himself were constant themes during his months in London. "Scope for reflection," he wrote another day. "The life I am leading totally dissatisfactory."

He was silent in his diary about his love, and nearly as silent about his lover. In John Quincy's famously massive diary — some fifteen thousand pages in fifty-one volumes — Louisa appears very little, even when he was pursuing her. Except when she was ill, he rarely recorded anything particular about her — not the way she looked, or the things she said, or the way she made him feel. She was merely marked as present or absent, sick or well. This doesn't mean he didn't think of her — indeed, his silence was often telling; it may suggest he thought of her much more than he wanted to admit. He was oblique and contradictory about his feelings. He wrote that pleasure made him miserable. After recording walking with the Johnsons, "reflections perplexing," he actually skipped a day in his diary — which was unheard of for him. March 2, 1796, followed February 29; March 1 followed that with the parenthetical "(omitted above)." "The regular day as objectionable as before," he wrote of March 1. "Very little different from the last, excepting that it is still more marked with the character of indolence & dissipation. Can find no time to write, none to read, But much to dross and dross over again to visit and be visited, to lose my home, and to find pernicious passions. O rus (/) quando te aspiciam." *O country / when will I see you.*

Passions were pernicious; his time was tyrannized by his attraction to Louisa — and to the whole way of life on Tower Hill. He was drawn to her in ways that he could hardly understand, and perhaps in ways that made him question what he wanted. Writing home, he told his father that a man in service of his country must think only of his duty, at the cost of "love of ease, or the love of life, or the love of fame itself." At the Johnsons', though, he found ease, he found life, and he found flattering attentions — and there he found himself, night after night.

His career was drifting. It had taken him twenty-eight days to travel from The Hague to London, twenty-eight days of frustration and despair that ended in failure. His task, the formal exchange of the ratification of a treaty between the United States and Britain, had already been completed before he arrived. What was worse, he had known it would be. His instructions were very clear. He was given a deadline of October 20 to complete the task; if he could not reach London by then, then William Allen Deas, the secretary of legation, would do it. Weather had trapped John Quincy on the coast of Holland, in Helvoetsluys; he would not reach London until November 11. He could have turned around and returned to his post at The Hague. But he was bored there, restless and brooding, anxious about his future and unhappy with his past. So he came. It was more than a pointless exercise; it was self-inflicted frustration. The treaty was a sign of closer amity between the two nations, resolving contentious issues left over from the Revolution and laying the groundwork for trade, but it was loathed by some in the United States (especially followers of Thomas Jefferson), who foresaw the dangers of subservience to Britain. John Quincy Adams was hardly a Jeffersonian, and he was cautiously in favor of the treaty, but he hated any suggestion of servility to the British, and once in London, he found himself continually ignored or insulted by British officials. "I have been accustomed all my life to plain dealing and candour, and am not sufficiently versed in the art of political swindling to be prepared for negotiating with a European minister of state," he wrote in a dispatch describing a meeting with Lord Grenville, the minister of foreign affairs. He became so incensed by the perceived insults that some started to worry he'd provoke a rift.

For nearly two years he had been living in Holland, on the edge of Europe, watching the convulsions and aftershocks of the French Revolution rock the continent, but always as an observer. He wrote brilliant dispatches to the secretary of state as the destruction of France's monarchy transformed the continent, and he also wrote, more intimately, to his father, dispatches that were highly valued. George Washington read them while composing his famous Farewell Address, warning the United States against involvement in European conflicts — and expressed his admiration. Still, John Quincy called himself an exile.

He was used to being far away, thousands of miles from his home. He had the example of his father, who had left the farm in Braintree, Massachusetts, in order to join the Continental Congress when John Quincy was only a child, telling his tiny oldest son that he entrusted the family to him. Abigail was more than up to the task — she was an extraordinarily capable farmer, manager, teacher, and mother — but Johnny remembered his father's words and knew what was at stake, saw the soldiers and the distant flash of guns. He had accompanied his father on two diplomatic missions, serving as a secretary though he was only a boy. On two voyages to France he brushed up against the war, watched a surgeon saw off the leg of a wounded man, and nearly died in a shipwreck. At times without a formal school to attend, he taught himself Latin and learned to play alone. His father sent him to Russia to serve as the American emissary's private secretary when he was only fourteen. He knew what patriotism entailed and what incredible sacrifices were expected of Adams men — especially of him. Raised to live for his country, he had been taught that his life was not too much to offer. "At a very early period in life, I devoted him to the publick," Abigail Adams told Martha Washington.

It might have been easier if the Adamses truly had conceived of their family as a monarchical dynasty, as their critics charged. Then there might have been some support in the sense of a birthright — that rulership came naturally, divinely. But the dynasty that John Quincy was supposed to be a part of was one based on merit. Nothing would be given; everything had to be earned. And everything *would* be earned — if only he lived according to strict and steady virtue, according to the expectations of his parents. The pressure was enormous. From London now, he told himself (and his parents) that he was ready to pay any cost when "my duty commands me to act." But how should he act? What could he do? He waited for his orders.

He went to galleries, read plays (*The Wheel of Fortune* and *First Love*), and went to the theater at Drury Lane. He wrangled with the British foreign secretary's office over protocol, becoming absurdly agitated about matters of deportment. He told himself that he was in London against his wishes, consoling himself with a lecture about duty. "The die is cast," he wrote in his diary. "Here I must be, spite my wishes and endeavors. My duty to the best of my judgment shall be done: the result must be left to Providence." In fact, he had come knowing the ratification had already been exchanged, but he wrote as if he had no choice.

He carried his loneliness with him. "There is something so dissipated and yet so solitary in the residence of a city like this, that I have never found in it either the pleasures of society or the profits of retirement," he wrote to his mother two weeks after he arrived in London. "There is a continual flutter, an agitation of the spirits excited by the multitude of objects that crowd upon the senses at once." He had made it his habit to call solitude bliss, but now that same solitude was "the craving void." The city was also, he admitted, full of beautiful women, which shook him. His opinion had not much changed since he was eighteen, when he had written, "I consider it the greatest misfortune; that can befall a young man to be in love."

He had been in love, and in pain, when he left the United States to go to the Netherlands. In Massachusetts, he had wanted a woman, Mary Frazier, but she was too young to marry and his law career was not established. A sense of responsibility — and the foreboding of his parents' disapproval — had led him to break off the relationship, even if he could not completely bury his love. Leaving Mary Frazier was, he wrote to his mother bitterly, "voluntary violence" to his feelings.

Marriage had been on his mind while he waited in Helvoetsluys, Holland, for the wind to turn so that he could leave for London. After hearing that his older brother Charles had wed, he waxed lyrical that he was "buffeted about the world in solitary celibacy." To his mother, he was mournful and even angry, writing her a long and unusually open and emotional letter about Mary Frazier. He had done his duty, he told her, sacrificing his passion for "prudential and family considerations" — but it had cost him dearly. He now had, he said, a "widowed heart." He met Louisa Johnson only four days later.

His parents' goal for him was nothing less than greatness. "Let your ambition be engaged to become eminent," Abigail wrote to him when he was still a schoolboy. Eminence to the Adams family was not what it was to the Johnsons; it was not the kind of greatness that could be gauged by the quality of a coat or popular opinion. "Nothing great or valuable among men, was ever achieved, without the counterpoise of strong opposition," John Quincy wrote to his father, repeating his father's lesson, "and the persecution that proceeds from opinion, becomes itself a title to esteem, when the opinion is found to have been erroneous." Instead, greatness adhered to civility, disinterestedness, independence, and thrift. Abigail pushed the point. "Justice, humanity and benevolence are the duties you owe to society in general," she wrote to her son. "To your country the same duties are incumbent upon you with the additional obligations of sacrificeing ease, pleasure, wealth and life itself for its defense and security." Johnny was thirteen years old.

John Quincy had tried hard to live up to his parents' warnings and expectations, disciplining himself from the earliest age. "I make but a poor figure at composition," he wrote to his father when he was nine.

My head is much too fickle, my thoughts are running after birds eggs play and trifles, till I get vexed with myself. . . . I own I am ashamed of myself. I have but just entered the 3d volume of Smollett, tho' I had designed to have got it half through by this time. I have determined this week to be more diligent. . . . I wish, Sir, you would give me some instructions with regard to my time, and advise me how to proportion my studies and my play, in writing, and I will keep them by me, and endeavor to follow them. I am, dear Sir, with a present determination of growing better, yours.

His self-assessment in London, at the age of twenty-eight, was still as damning, and his determination to be more diligent, to be more resolved, to be better, was just as strong. Only the nature of the distractions had changed. Instead of birds' eggs and trifles, beautiful women were the sirens, pulling him from the path. They stirred feelings in himself that he could hardly contain. To put distance between him and them, to flee, was the only way he understood how to maintain his perfect self-control. John Quincy called relaxation a "hard word." Social gatherings were always "dissipations." He was wary of his feelings; he wanted to dislike what he liked.

When he was only eleven, Abigail had written of her fear of what exposure to life in Europe would do to him. "To exclude him from temptation would be to exclude him from the world in which he is to live," she had said, "and the only method which can be persued with any advantage is to fix the padlock upon the mind." But the padlock Abigail tried to place on his mind would not protect him. He would later write of London as "a luxurious and splendid metropolis, where all the energies and powers of man are combined to vary the scenes of delight, and multiply enjoyments, where sloth allures to beds of down, and pleasure beckons with swimming eye, and enchanting smiles, he retained the firmness and resolution of devoting his time and attention to those objects, which were to mark the usefulness of his future life." John Quincy associated London with danger — pleasure and enchantment. The problem wasn't that he wasn't enjoying himself; the problem was that he was.

Instead of attending to Tacitus, instead of reflecting on the dramatic changes taking place in Europe and the formidable challenges the nascent United States faced, John Quincy was walking in the park with the Johnson girls. He was horrified by his own pleasure. He had not gone to the Johnsons' house in the hopes of coming away with a wife. But he was drawn to their manner of life, the animate warmth of the parlor, the refuge from the English winter evenings he spent alone. He had become a part of the household at Cooper's Row, not merely an observer but a participant, already almost part of the family — a family so unlike his own. The terse, self-critical, agonized John Quincy that appears in his diary is not the John Quincy that Louisa met at her house. He knew it as well as she. In fact, he sketched the scene himself in a letter to her:

I see you sitting on the sopha with the table before you, working at a Vandyke, and

Caroline at the other end with her silken network pinned before her, while Nancy calls the very soul of harmony from the forte-piano. I place myself between you, I run a file of spangles upon a needle; I urge you, though without success to produce the long-expected harp, or to give the graces of your voice to the shepherds charming "pipe upon the mountain." From thence we pass to the opposite room, where the humorous additions to the dictionary from one sister, and the unfilled outlines of imprecation from another, delight and charm though they cannot inspire the inflexible dulness of gravity, at your Mamma's left hand; and at length when the hour of midnight sounded from the unrelenting monitor of the moments past, in spite of reluctance commands my departure, then is the moment for the illusion to vanish, and leave me to that solitude which the pencil of Fancy herself can no longer colour.

It was very unlike the house where he had grown up in New England, where the snowdrifts piled against the house and the cows grew lean in winter. He tried not to enjoy himself, but he could not help it. "Wherefore must this be so pleasing?" he wrote, resisting and acquiescing at once. The contrast between this letter and his writing in his diary is almost tragic. He both wanted to be with her and wanted to run from her.

"Solitude is the only source of my valuable enjoyments," he wrote on another day. "This day was however remarkable pleasant. — That indeed is the greatest objection against it for what will be tomorrow?"

A maelstrom of emotions and self-reproaches was raging within the heart and mind of Louisa's suitor, behind the wall of the stony expression he had learned to practice as a boy. She did not know about Mary Frazier, or of the expectations of the Adamses. She did not know that when he looked around the Johnsons' parlor — when he heard the soft, slippered whisper of the girls' silk skirts and saw the harp in the corner — he might consider the comforts she took for granted to be evidence that she was not in his eyes "*wholly* American." She had no idea of Quincy, no conception of the Puritan inheritance, no real understanding that John Quincy, like his forebears, distrusted happiness and was prone to punish himself. But she could sense that something was not right.

What Louisa could see was that her suitor was fickle and uncertain — and she was not so sure either. That it was not "love at first sight," she later wrote, she was convinced. But she told herself it could become real "affection," which could last "much longer."

John Quincy was a good match for her. It was not easy to come across a young American man from an illustrious family and with bright prospects while living in London — not least when one had to compete for attention with sisters such as hers. She might not do better. It's likely that she also faced some pressure from her parents to make the match. Catherine openly advocated for John Quincy, and Joshua had more than the usual reasons for a father to want his daughter to find a husband. His business, highly leveraged and always uncertain, was going badly, and he was fighting over profits with his former partners back in Maryland. He was not the kind of man who would discount that a marriage between his daughter and the son of the vice president of the United States might help his own reputation — and perhaps bring him good connections. But Nancy was unhappy, and the discord between the sisters continued.

Louisa felt herself withdraw "in a sort of consciousness of something wrong without knowing [how] to find the error." Instead of feeling the kind of passion that she had encountered in plays and books, she felt insecure and somber around her lover. "Love seemed to chill all the natural hilarity of my disposition," she said in "Record of a Life" — written at a time of sadness decades later, to be sure, but it may have been true. After all, John Quincy had made his attentions to her clear, but not yet his intentions. They were not engaged, and he would not be staying in London for much longer. He was indecisive. There were "asperities" between them. Both had tempers, both were sensitive, and neither was adept at soothing bruised feelings.

John Quincy wrote about the situation in his diary as if he were helpless to affect it. "Reflections perplexing," he wrote at the end of February. "Ring from Louisa's finger. — Tricks play'd, a little music and dancing. — Placed in a very difficult dilemma," he wrote two days later. "Know not how I shall escape from it." *Ring from Louisa's finger? Tricks play'd? Placed in a very difficult dilemma?* It was as if he were a completely passive, helpless agent. Perhaps, as one historian wryly noted, the ring just jumped.

If his real desire was to escape the Johnsons, then he was making a debacle of it, because he was spending more time with them, not less. Day after day, his diary records dinner with the Johnsons, walks with the Johnson sisters, card games at the Johnsons', music at the Johnsons'. A month later, he recorded his daily schedule: "Walk or ride with the Ladies from 2 till dinner time. Evening at Mr Johnson's and very often dine there. Home between midnight & 1 in the morning, abed between 1 and 2." He wrote of being unable to get away. He practically called himself kidnapped.

John Quincy was waiting for orders to return to The Hague, apparently half hoping they'd force him to escape. The Johnsons were waiting for a proposal to marry. Neither was quick in coming. Finally, on the morning of April 13, Louisa's mother, Catherine Johnson — not Joshua, and not Louisa — took matters into her own hands. She sent the withholding suitor a note at his hotel, the Adelphi. The language was "partly apologetic and partly spirited." Catherine had seen enough. She demanded a meeting. And so John Quincy went to Tower Hill and gave her a "full explanation of my views and intentions . . . upon the subject which was interesting to her."

The subject of John Quincy's intention to marry Louisa was more interesting to Catherine than John Quincy could have known. Catherine was aware of what was at stake — all too aware. She had once been in a similar position to her daughter's. She, too, had been a young woman who attracted the amorous attentions of an American man living near Tower Hill. She, too, had been petite, stylish, and beautiful. She had been desirable, and Joshua Johnson had desired her. In early 1773, Joshua made Catherine pregnant. But that did not mean he married her.

4

Joshua Johnson had arrived in Britain in 1771, two years before his daughter Nancy was born. The eighth of twelve children (including one who died young), he had left his father's plantation in Calvert County, Maryland, eager to make money, to enjoy himself, and to become a man of some reputation. He went to Annapolis first, where he was apprenticed in the countinghouse of a Scotsman named Charles Wallace, and then started a business importing goods and selling them to the growing class of rich tobacco planters. He did well, accumulating enough wealth to build a showroom and residence in the market facing the docks, where he could see the ships sail to and from London, leaving laden with tobacco and returning loaded with luxuries — linens, shoes, rugs, dresses, tea, sweets.

Since those goods were generally bought through British merchants, with money changing hands at each step, his old boss

Charles Wallace sensed an opportunity. Wallace approached Joshua and proposed forming a firm based in Annapolis, with a man in London. The plan, hatched at Wallace's house on cheerful nights with drinks in hand and feet up on the jamb, was to have a buyer on the spot, at the center of the mercantile world. They would cut out the middleman, avoiding his onerous fees, and negotiate credit with London sellers on better terms. Joshua and Charles Wallace joined a third, John Davidson, a trader and deputy naval officer of the port of Annapolis, to form the firm of Wallace, Davidson & Johnson. Joshua left for London in the spring of 1771. He was twenty-eight years old, handsome, and confident. His brows were arched, his nose long and fine, and his slight smile suggested an enigmatic knowingness, secretive or supercilious. He sailed with £3,000 capital, and a wealth of self-importance. He arrived in Bristol and immediately bought new clothes.

Early success made him bold. Soon, he was telling correspondents to address his letters "simply to J. J., Merchant, London, as I am become of that consequence that they will readily come to hand." But being of consequence was costly. The prices in London made him despair. He was given £30 a year for rent, but laundry alone, he reported, would cost him £20. "I am frighted at the expense attending one's living here," he wrote to his partner at home. "O Joney, you have no idea of it." When he arrived, Joshua rented two rooms on Fenchurch Street, not far from alleyways and rookeries where light never penetrated, streets with names like Idle and Seething. He used the smaller of his two rooms, the "closet," for his bed; in the front room, the papers piled so high that there was no place for a visitor to sit. It offended him to live so low; he described his situation with drama and elaborate shame. Often sick, he wrote mournful letters home describing his ailments — the festering leg, the cough he feared was consumptive, the inflamed lungs — but during his first year, at least, his real underlying illness may have been homesickness. News of a smallpox outbreak in Maryland sent him sympathetically to bed in London for a week. He worried that he would be forgotten by his friends. He wrote that he yearned for letters, though they sometimes contained unwelcome news. His partners were unhappy with the quality of his first shipment; there were troubles collecting remittances; bills of exchange were protested and unpaid. He had arrived just in time for a financial crisis in London, when some of the most reputable banks went belly-up. His British contacts were less helpful than he hoped. The system of credit and payment by bills of exchange meant that men had to be able to collect in order to pay — and sometimes they couldn't collect. Every ship that sailed was a gamble, a game of trust. Ships sank and cargoes rotted. Remittances were slow in coming, and profits bled quickly into debts. Small bills that went unpaid could send a man to debtor's prison. Joshua feared for his fate. His capital was sunk. When a ship was late, he feared the dun. If his partners could not come up with money fast, he warned them more than once, "expect to hear I am fast in some damned dungeon living on musty mutton chops."

Business was volatile. When Joshua wasn't fearing debtors' jail, he was flush. After Wallace, Davidson & Johnson moved into the tobacco trade, they dominated the Maryland market — accounting for as much as 70 percent of Maryland's exported tobacco business between 1773 and 1775. Charles Carroll, one of the Chesapeake's wealthiest planters, brought his business to Joshua; others followed suit. Joshua assumed more than an intermediary role. He explained how the system of credit, purchasing, and exchange rates worked in London. He advised his partners on favorable deals and told them which firms to trust and which to avoid. He gossiped and complained. He rewarded himself whenever he could.

In 1773, he moved into better lodgings on Swan Street. Even when money was tight, he went out of his way to appear successful.

When his partners grew nervous about his lifestyle, he defended himself. "It is a maxim with me that I had rather sink the profits of my labour than to diminish my partners and self in the good opinion of the world," he wrote. The house a respectable merchant needed, he wrote to his partners in November 1773, had to be large enough to include a "dwelling house, counting house, and sample house" for business. He did not mention that it also needed to be large enough for a woman and infant to live with him. Nor did he mention that, in that very house, that very month, Catherine gave birth to Nancy, their first child.

Joshua and Catherine did not marry before Nancy was born. Nor did they marry a year later, around the birth of Louisa. They were not married in 1777, at the birth of Caroline, nor in 1778, when their fourth child was born, nor in 1779, when they had their fifth, or in 1781, when Catherine gave birth to their sixth child. For years, Joshua kept Catherine's existence a secret from his correspondents across the Atlantic. In a time of trouble, when he suggested leaving London in secret should the need to escape his creditors arise, he did not mention that he might bring a woman with him. Nor did he mention a family when he talked of plans to return home to fight during the Revolution, including when Louisa was one month old.

The first reference we have to Catherine in one of his letters — and careful copies of much of his correspondence have survived — is from 1776. It is a request to a ship captain to buy Mrs. Johnson some lace.

After that, and without extant explanation, Mrs. Johnson begins to appear in his letters very often. In London, "the Johnsons" seem to have passed for married from the start. No rumors of any taint seem to have circulated among the expatriate community; no gossip kept distinguished visitors from their table. Indeed, they may have considered themselves married. "Catherine Johnson" and Joshua baptized all their children as legitimate — a fraud with consequences were the true facts found out. By the time they moved to Nantes, in 1778, Joshua was not shy about referring to his family in letters home. The opposite, in fact: when he needed money, he claimed it was because he had so many mouths to feed.

Since he kept her a secret at first, and since any account of their relationship she may have written has been lost, we don't know when or how Joshua met Catherine Newth. Since Joshua was a merchant, they may have met at her father's shoe shop. Martin Newth was a shoemaker, a good one — a Citizen Freeman Cordwainer, nominated to be an arts-master, whose work, according to court records, was good enough at least for a thief to steal — and Joshua was always on the lookout for fine shoes to ship to America. Or Joshua may have simply seen Catherine on the street or in the neighborhood. Around the time he moved to London, she lived only a few steps from where he settled. She was known as beautiful, "very small, and exquisitely delicate, and very finely proportioned." Pretty as she was, she may have caught Joshua's eye.

So why did they remain unwed, even as their lives grew intertwined — and their attraction became, apparently, love? That was how their adoring daughter remembered it, at least. "My father seemed to hang on every word she uttered and gazed on her with looks of love and admiration," Louisa wrote. Her mother was "his pride his joy his love." This is idealized, but perhaps not by too much. Joshua spoke of "Kitty" to correspondents in a tone that was often playful and intimate. He was quick to defend her, and she was quick to defend him. When the other was sick, both were affected. Where she was not welcome, he told a friend, he would not go. He doted on her, tried to buy the luxurious and pampered life that she wanted. He cut her meat when she was sick, and he wrapped the handles of her forks with a paper and warmed them by the fire.

It is possible, though unlikely, that remaining unmarried was not Joshua's choice. Catherine could have been wary of marrying an American who occasionally found himself threatened with debtor's prison. There is also a little evidence to suggest that Catherine's father forbade the marriage. Joshua and Martin Newth disliked each other; Louisa later spoke of "some misunderstanding" that ended all communication between the two after the death of Catherine's mother while the Johnsons were in Nantes. Louisa wrote that Joshua (without mentioning Catherine) "loved and respected [Mary Newth] to the hour of his death and always spoke of her to us, as an example of exalted goodness." But Martin Newth was presented to the children as a man "whose character was I am sorry to say very indifferent." Whether that was true, it was certainly convenient for Joshua to think so — especially if the cause of the rupture was Martin's anger toward Joshua for impregnating his unwed daughter. Or perhaps Martin didn't want his daughter to marry an American patriot, one who would go on to petition the House of Lords in support of Boston after the Boston Tea Party, one who would turn rebel. Martin does seem to have given Catherine some money, which suggests that he distrusted Joshua to provide for his daughter. Had Joshua and Catherine been legally married, Catherine's money would have been absorbed into Joshua's estate by the laws of coverture, which subsumed a wife's legal status to her husband's. She invested it, shrewdly, herself.

It is, of course, possible that the decision not to marry was mutual. Unusual family arrangements were not entirely uncommon in eighteenth-century London. In fact, after low rates of prenuptial pregnancy in the seventeenth century, during the second half of the eighteenth century it became increasingly common for women outside of the social elite to give birth within eight and a half months of marriage. But the Marriage Act that came into force in 1754 restricted clandestine marriages, and if it did not immediately change behavior, it at least influenced attitudes toward it. The middle classes became more concerned about sexual permissiveness and mores as the eighteenth century went on — and showed a titillated interest in prominent cases of adultery, written up in magazines like *Town and Country* and *Bon Ton,* which reported misbehavior among the elites as a kind of sport. The fact that all of the Johnson children were baptized as legitimate means that the Johnsons went out of their way to appear married; it mattered to them.

The ruse worked. Society accepted Mrs. Johnson as a married woman. She was listed as Joshua's wife in the annals of the Maryland state legislature when she and the Johnson children were naturalized as citizens of the state. Perhaps being legally married seemed beside the point. Perhaps no one was aware that they were not. Whether or not anyone else knew it, though, Catherine did. Lesser sins could set off scandals. Marriage was one of the fundamental bonds of polite society. Indiscretions happened, but they were not openly tolerated in the Johnsons' circle. Joshua's friends and acquaintances included more than a few who were committed to disrupting the social order — American patriots, British abolitionists, and self-described freethinkers — but there were certain aspects of society even the iconoclasts did not openly question, and the institution of marriage was one of them. Catherine's unwed status made her vulnerable. She had more to lose than he.

And he seemed willing to risk it. Joshua wrote home about his bachelorhood with bravado. In March 1773, nine months before Catherine gave birth to Nancy, Joshua wrote to Maryland to snuff out rumors that he was going to get married. "It is the least of my thoughts," he wrote to a friend, "and if I continue in the same mind I believe I never shall." Then, in November 1773, just before the birth of his first daughter, Joshua wrote to another friend: "You say that you have heard I was to be married. I pawn my honor to you that there is nothing in it." He did "not even dare to form any acquaintance," he added. He admitted to one friend that he "worshipped at the Temple of Venus" but regretted too much carousing. In the fall of 1773, with Catherine about to give birth, he wrote to a friend that "a man must possess true courage indeed to engage the matrimonial way in these hard times." True courage, apparently, that Joshua lacked.

It would have been natural for Catherine to wonder who might find out. After all, even if she had been legally married, her position was already precarious. Joshua openly participated in pro-American activities when it was dangerous to do so in a hostile country. The British government was reading his letters, and spies kept him under watch. The rift between him, if not also her, and her parents would have affected her. And she was as sensitive as she was sharp. When Joshua's female acquaintances were cold or distant to her, she reacted badly. There was gossip of "a terrible row" between Catherine and the wife of one of Joshua's friends. Another wrote that Catherine's manner was "very flighting disrespectful." Later in her life, she would often feel a sting where none was intended. And marriage meant something important to her, clearly — because eventually, they did marry.

Joshua Johnson and Catherine Newth were wed on August 22, 1785. By that time, they had had six children (five still living). The event took place at St. Anne Soho, in Westminster. Secretive arrangements were made. The parish register described Catherine

Newth (not Nuth) and Joshua Johnson as living in the parish of St. Anne Soho, even though they did not. It said they were married by banns (an announcement read out on three Sundays at the church, to allow for objections), even though they do not appear in the banns book. One of the witnesses was a man named Joseph Palmer. To judge from the number of times his signature appears as a witness in the register, he was not an acquaintance but somebody regularly on hand at the church. Perhaps he played the organ or swept the floor. The other witness was Catherine's friend Elizabeth Hewlett, the one Louisa described as "a very eccentric woman of strong mind and still stronger passions."

Catherine had her own strong independent streak. Some found her dazzling, and some found her difficult to describe. She enlivened teatime; she made a simple dinner of roasted oysters and cider an occasion worth commenting on. Women gossiped about what she wore. When people tried to capture something of Catherine's character, they tended toward contradictions. "So much spirit and so much gentleness are rarely united," wrote one who knew her. Another described her as "lively, sedate." She was applauded for her mildness and discretion and yet criticized for having too biting a wit. She was "free and chatty." The woman who summoned John

Quincy to explain himself was not a woman to be trifled with.

How much of her parents' history did Louisa know? There's no way to say for sure. It's doubtful that she was told of their wedding in August 1785, when she was ten years old. She may not have been in London when it happened; she and her siblings were at Ramsgate, a popular seaside resort in east Kent, for at least part of that month. But there are some signs that, as she grew older, she at least sensed something out of the ordinary. Among the many romantic stories she told about her parents, for instance, there was no account of how they met and married — a curious omission for one who liked to tell wedding stories throughout her life.

Most tellingly, she was hazy and misleading about her mother's origins — so much so that Catherine Johnson's identity was a mystery. For more than a hundred and fifty years — in fact, until now — the Adams family and historians alike thoroughly misinterpreted her background. Even her maiden name was invented: she was called Catherine Nuth, instead of the name she was born with, Catherine Newth.

"All families are not as indifferent to their maternal connections as ours are," Louisa later wrote self-pityingly to her son Charles, but she was the one largely to blame. About her maternal grandfather, she was vague. The story she told was strange and full of holes. Her grandfather's "name was Nuth . . . I do not even recollect his Christian name and am not sure that I ever heard." He "had a place like that of Charles Lamb mentioned in his memoirs of a writer I think it is termed in the India House." He married a woman named Mary Young, with whom he had "twenty two living children born but only reared two." Her grandfather, she added, "died at the age of 96 — I think when I was about 12 or 13 years old — He lived in Camberwell and left at his death the sum of 500 sterling to my Mother which my Father permitted her to use as her own." The only other information she offered about her mother was an age. Catherine was, Louisa wrote, "not one and twenty" when the family moved to Nantes in 1778 — which would have made her fifteen when Nancy was born.

Louisa's descendants in fact were quite interested in her maternal connections — but when they tried to reconstruct the story she had given them, they were left with more questions than answers. The great nineteenth-century historian Henry Adams, Louisa's grandson, was among those who tried to track down Catherine's origins and failed. He joked that his great-great-grandmother's existence was "one of the deepest mysteries of metaphysical theology." He hired a genealogist in London to comb through parish registers, looking for her; for two years he searched "everywhere he could think, but not a trace has he ever found of Nuth or Young or Johnson, in marriage or out." Later, historians who normally knew enough to squint hard at Louisa's careless use of numbers and dates found a scandalous version of Catherine's past, without contrary evidence, irresistible. In the story they told, Catherine's parents were unmarried and her grandmother was possibly a prostitute who left a steady stream of children at the foundling hospital. In this version, Catherine was hardly more than a child when she met Joshua, and possibly a disreputable one. In one historian's telling, "it was a cold fact" that Catherine "had been the fondling sort."

But Catherine Newth's parish birth record does exist, and it is now possible to create a map of Catherine's family background. No one can say for certain what Catherine did in bed, but the real story of her birth is more quotidian than the one that has been told until now, and it changes our understanding of Louisa's background. Her grandfather, Martin Newth, was married to a woman named Mary (née Young). There may have been many Newth children — there are several extant baptismal records of children born to Martin and Mary (if not twenty-two), but the burial records suggest that the children were not abandoned; they died. Catherine was not "not one and twenty" when she moved to Nantes; she was not one and *thirty* — she was born in 1749.

Many of Louisa's facts were confusing, misunderstood, or wrong. Most of her errors are probably innocent. The biggest, of course, is her mother's maiden surname. "Nuth" sounds like "Newth." Louisa may not have ever seen the name in writing, and she had a habit of using phonetic spellings in any case. Because of the breach between Joshua and Catherine's father, she spent very little time with her grandparents, and it's unlikely she heard much about them. As for Catherine's age, Louisa may have made a meaningless mistake when she wrote that Catherine was twenty instead of thirty, or it may have been a telling slip: Louisa herself was twenty-two when she moved from England to continental Europe. Describing the fear her mother must have felt moving to an unknown city in a strange culture, she may have put herself in her mother's place. Or she may have wanted to put the emphasis on her father's ancestry, since she was proud that Joshua Johnson descended from aristocratic stock. Martin Newth's humble profession of a shoemaker may have been something to hide.

But whether she knew of her illegitimacy and how it influenced her are open questions. In the United States, rumors of impropriety in Catherine and Joshua's union circulated first in Maryland and then more widely — indeed, they would become widespread. There is a good chance that, at least by the time Louisa wrote her second memoir sketch, "The Adventures of a Nobody," those rumors reached her. Again and again, she dwells on her insecurity and her sense of illegitimacy in the Adams family — her sense of not belonging. It's tempting to wonder whether she had some sense that she had been an illegitimate child.

Whatever Louisa discovered about her parents, this much is certainly true: a sensitive child intuits more than she knows, and Louisa was a sensitive child. From the earliest age, Louisa had learned to read those around her. "My disposition inclined me to read the countenances of all who approached me with extreme care," she later wrote, "and my judgment of character was almost immediately stamped upon this investigation." She grew up in a household where there were secrets.

Catherine's meeting with John Quincy to learn of his intentions toward Louisa was one more thing that happened without her knowledge. But the meeting did not remain a secret for long.

In his diary, John Quincy wrote that Catherine "declared herself satisfied." (Presumably, he told her he planned to marry.) But Louisa was not — perhaps not with the meeting at all. Her mother had intervened in an unusual way, she was still fighting with Nancy, and John Quincy's hesitation no doubt hurt her in the first place. "Something uncommonly out of course," John Quincy wrote in his diary two days after his conversation with Catherine. The next day: "Required an explanation of last evening's singularities, from Louisa." He got it, or gave it, two days after that. "Conversation with Louisa. Was explicit with her, and obtained her acquiescence. The same with him" — presumably, consent from her father.

She admitted to him that she felt uncertain. She wasn't sure of his affection and his desire to marry her (an admission she would later regret). Her humiliation was probably worse because she knew there were reasons John Quincy might be wary, and they may have talked about them. There were problems. John Quincy could easily guess that his parents would disapprove of his choice. He almost disapproved himself. She had been naturalized by Maryland, but she was still half British by birth and British — even French — by her upbringing. She could not possibly declare her American patriotism in a way that would erase his impression of her un-American life. Money was another issue. John Quincy was still not in a good position to support a wife, and a quick glance around the nice house on Cooper's Row gave him some indication of what kind of style Louisa would expect to maintain. At Harvard, John Quincy had once given a speech about marriage. Beauty fades, passion fades, people fall out of love, he declared, and so a sound republican marriage (a citizen's duty, he liked to say) was based on procreation, companionship, and economic security. Presumably, Louisa would bring some money to the marriage, but he had some intimations that Joshua's finances were not nearly as good as the graceful mansion and presence of servants suggested. When he and Louisa spoke, it seems they talked about money; she let on that her father was facing difficulties that would soon force him to return to America. But the promise was made.

Faced with an engagement or losing Louisa, John Quincy chose the engagement. But the problems did not disappear — least of all the tension over money. A marriage was an agreement, a contract. Along with his permission, Joshua promised a dowry: £5,000 sterling. There was only one point of lingering contention: John Quincy insisted that he would return to The Hague unmarried, and they would not marry until he was in a position to resume his law practice and support her. He would serve out the remainder of his diplomatic posting alone. He could not say how long it would take. She would have to wait.

Louisa was devastated. Their bond already felt strange and fragile, and she worried that time and distance would weaken it. She worried, too, about the effects it would have on her reputation — not unreasonably. Women in limbo — betrothed but unmarried — easily became jokes, exposed to humiliating "banter and jests." Long engagements were considered unnatural, uncertain. She begged him to let them be married before he left London, she later wrote, so that she might at least take his name. In fact, that might have been ideal: she could become a bride, the great goal of the young Johnson girls' lives, and at the same time, nothing would change. She could remain with her parents and sisters. She could become a wife and remain a child. But John Quincy was inflexible. With no other choice but to accept his conditions or to call off the engagement, Louisa gave in.

Orders arrived for John Quincy to return to Holland in May, and they faced the prospect of a separation. She was uneasy. He had committed to marrying her, and yet he insisted on delay. She was not sure whether she had fallen in love or had been convinced. She was not entirely sure what he felt at all. She saw signs that he loved her, and signs that he did not. The burden was on her to mold herself to his wishes, while she could not expect the same of him.

She did try, once, to change his behavior. It was a springtime evening, warm and suggestive, and they planned to walk the next day in the fashionable pleasure gardens of Ranelagh. Teasing him, she told him that he must dress very handsomely for their excursion, "as dashy as possible." His clothing was a sensitive subject — the one subject (besides his engagement, that is) that he fought with his mother about — and he stiffened. He distrusted fine things and disdained the conventions of lovers. But he did not like to be made fun of, and he wanted to please her. So he showed up the next day wearing a new Napoleon hat, "very handsomely dressed in blue," looking as wonderful as she had hoped he would. She was delighted and charmed. They entered the Rotunda, broke away from the others, and took each other's arm. Lovers were blooming like flowers. She complimented his excellent appearance — but instead of accepting her praise, he turned on her. He "assured me that *his* wife must never take the liberty of interfering in those particulars, and assumed a tone so high and lofty and made so serious a grievance of the affair, that I felt offended and told him that I resigned all pretensions to his hand, and left him as free as air to choose a Lady who would be more discreet." She pulled away from his arm and went to join her mother and sisters. She had heard the lesson behind his words — he would try to change her, but she was never to try to change him — and she was stung. That night they made up, but the wound was fresh, and it refused to fully heal. It seemed to her to portend something terrible. Later, she wrote that she felt within her "a secret and unknown dread of something hidden beneath the rosy wreath of love."

They said goodbye to each other at the end of May. To his father, John Quincy expressed relief at returning to The Hague. "At length I have been released from a situation, equally remote from all public utility and all personal satisfaction," John Quincy wrote. To his mother, he was more honest: "Albeit unused to the melting mood, I found the separation not a little painful."

To Louisa, he was tender, and so was she to him. She gave him a miniature to remember her by, along with the promise of her love. "An evening full of delight and of regret," he wrote in his diary just before leaving. "Took my leave of all the family with sensations unusually painful."

So he went. He had been stringent and clear; she would have no say about when their separation would end. She did not know whether she would marry him "in one year or in seven." She was left to wait.

5

Their betrothal was neither an end nor a beginning. Louisa drifted through the days. A storm blew in just after John Quincy sailed for Holland, and she was left to wonder whether his ship had wrecked. A portrait, which he had spent his final hours in London sitting for, arrived at Cooper's Row; he had wanted to give her some reminder of him. But the presence of the painting only made her more nervous. He had left her in doubt, and her doubt colored what she saw. She studied his portrait and thought the image did not match the one in her mind — his complexion was wrong, his body too large. In his expression, she thought she could detect some misgivings.

His first letter came soon after the portrait, and it offered her the tenderest expressions of his devotion. He described his reluctance to go, how it tore at him — how he was "half anxious" to reach his boat and "half fretting, at the consciousness of an involuntary wish that I might be too late." In tones that seemed to mean it, he reassured her that their separation would not be long. In fact, he would give up his public career and devote himself to her and their home. He would take, he wrote, "the earliest opportunity" to write to America. "If I can procure any prospect that will enable me to indulge the wishes of my heart, I shall cheerfully resign a career of public life which can offer nothing satisfactory to ambition, and which forbids the professions of that private happiness, the first object of my hopes and which you only can confer."

He said everything kind. She should have been calmed, but instead she was stricken. It wasn't what he said that so upset her; it was that he had written at all. A letter from him required her to respond with a letter of her own. "Terror which assailed me at the idea of answering it," she recalled. She had no experience with writing, and no real desire to gain any. Nothing had happened in her life since he left, she thought, and she had no art with which to say it. She could bring herself only to tell him that she was persuaded that her letters would be boring. It was torture even to say that. She was embarrassed. "I felt my folly and my insignificance," she would remember.

Her memory did not exaggerate. She waited a month after his departure before sending her first words. When she finally wrote, the rush of her words produced the tremulous high note of a vibrating nerve. The opening sentence of her second letter (the first letter has been lost) read:

So totally incapacitated do I feel myself for writing were it not through fear of giving you pain I certainly should indulge my avowed aversion to it and decline the task but judging of your feelings by my own think it incumbent on me to avail myself of every opportunity of testifying my affectionate esteem for you I yesterday received yours of the 17 instant in which you desire my opinion of your picture I approve the likeness tho' the complexion is much too dark and the figure altogether too large I have lately been introduced to a Mr. and Mrs: Gore of Boston who say they should never have known it but I cannot allow them to be such competent judges as myself who finds the original too deeply engraven on my heart to admit of a mistake in the likeness Oh Philosophy where art thou now without thy aid my present sensations will carry me beyond myself and far exceed the limits of my paper.

The second sentence was: "I will therefore quit this subject."

But she did not know what else she was

supposed to say.

It had been six years since she had left school. She may have tried reading John Milton's poetry as a child, but her reading now was ranging and undisciplined. She was, it's clear, well versed in the conventions of popular die-for-love stories, and in the epistolary conventions those encouraged. So was the younger children's governess, a devotee of romantic novels — many of them written in the form of correspondence — who buffed and polished Louisa's letters to make them "most elegant." The result was an inelegant mess; the language was stilted and formal, and at first tight and childish. Louisa's favorite subject, indeed her only real subject, was how much she hated to write.

But she tried to mold herself into whatever he wanted. She studied his letters for clues of what he expected from her. She parroted his lessons about fortitude. "As I have very little *natural philosophy* I must copy yours," she wrote. She repeated what he said about the corrupting influence of Europe, correcting her course as she went in order to conform to his little lectures. "Kindly undertake to teach your Louisa, how to avoid such errors in future," she said.

She was determined to learn. She intended to start reading, too, so that she might "lessen the immense distance" she sensed between her mind and John Quincy's. A woman's education, however, was not supposed to look like a man's. Her father rented a small house in Clapham Common, a fashionable area dotted with pretty parks south of London, and sent Louisa, along with the youngest children, the governess, and two servants, there to practice running a house — ordering servants, presiding at dinner. (It may also be that her parents wanted to separate their spirited and rivalrous older daughters, perhaps for their own sanity.)

There was no way for her to bridge the distance between Clapham Common and Harvard. Nor was it possible for their correspondence to make Louisa and John Quincy truly intimate. She had yet to find her own voice, and he did not know how to adapt his to address her. There were misunderstandings. When she congratulated John Quincy on the probability that his father would be elected president of the United States that November, for instance, he responded by confessing the pressure he felt. "The more conspicuous he becomes in the world, the more incumbent it will be upon me to prove myself not unworthy to be his son," he wrote and added, "I *must* not be unworthy of my father or of my Country." She took his forthright words as a rebuke against herself for asking the question. Too wound up to grasp the poignancy of his situation, and by extension her own, she could only see herself blunder. When he was honest and revealing about himself, she took it as a reproach against her own conduct or character. And he, in turn, quickly became more distant, more didactic, and more stern.

Still, the two maintained the conventions of lovers' correspondence. They sent each other the regular expressions of swooning love and tender devotion. They were trying. Then something upset the routine, the fiction that all was fine. John Quincy was appointed minister to Portugal. She heard the news before he did, near the end of July, because it came through her father. She was, in fact, the first to tell him. She pretended to congratulate him, but her tone was anguished. Another appointment meant more years apart. Portugal meant a longer distance. Joshua's plans to return to the United States soon meant that she would have to go with her family, putting an ocean between her and her betrothed. If he planned to travel through London on his way to Lisbon, she wrote to him, she wanted him to take a different route. She could not stand the idea of seeing him and then separating again.

The news shook him out of the fantasy he had been constructing of moving back to America quickly and abandoning his public ambitions. He had provocatively told his parents that he would relocate south for a life of literature, leisure, and domestic bliss (not unlike a Johnson). But he was not willing to give up the dream altogether. He told Louisa that he would take her with him to Portugal, instructing her to prepare for the trip and to be ready to leave quickly. The Johnsons flew into activity. She needed passports. He wanted a ship. She must have a trousseau. Yet there was also a hint in his invitation that all was not well between them. He cautioned her that when she went to a European court, she would have to "suppress some of the little attachments to splendor that lurk at your heart, perhaps imperceptibly to yourself." She heard in those words the suggestion that he thought she was vain, impressionable, shallow. She was hurt and said so. She was not wrong about his suspicion — though in fairness, neither was he wrong; she did like luxury. But she knew what he was implying: he wasn't quite sure that she was fit to be a republican American minister's wife. The insinuation riled her, which he disliked. Their correspondence grew sharper — softened only slightly by offering surrender. "Between us two, my lovely friend let there be peace," he wrote.

"If possible teach my rebellious heart gently to acquiesce without murmering," she wrote to him.

It wasn't possible. The insinuation against her character and her overwrought response was a scratch, another small wound, another reason for her to nurse her sense of being slighted and for him to have reservations. Soon he was backtracking, mentioning vague complications that would keep him in Holland for months longer. With sadness, and with some private relief, since she had been scared to leave her family and move to a strange place, she packed away her new gowns. Then John Quincy backtracked further. In fact, he wrote, he would be compelled to go to Lisbon without her. His tone grew distant, and the little homilies about correct conduct and republican principles grew longer and more persistent. She read these as signs that he did not trust her; he thought she would embarrass him.

She tried to convince him he was mistaken: "I knew not why of your having erroneously supposed me dazzled with what you style rank." But she vacillated between being indignant and suspecting she'd done something to deserve it. Anxiously, she studied herself — her actions, her faults, her memories of the conversations that had passed between them — to see what she had done wrong. It was true that when they had sat together on the sofa, they were surrounded by the kinds of fine things that you would find in a prosperous merchant's house. It was true that she wore silk sashes and ostrich feathers, gloves and curls, and that she had told him he must dress handsomely for her.

Now he appeared to hold those things against her. Luxury was corrupting, and she would be corrupted. She would be impressed by titles. The lifestyle that she would want would be expensive to maintain. She tried to persuade him that she preferred "domestic felicity to the alloy of *ambition* or *parade,*" but nothing she said could convince him that she was not delighted by balls, duchesses, and pretty things. To defend herself, she fired off an accusation that he was the one who was ambitious. The misfire was bigger than she could have known. To an Adams, ambition was craven, and to be accused of it, especially in the context of a European court, was a grave insult. She might as well have called him un-American.

Meanwhile, John Quincy's parents were launching salvos against Louisa from the United States, and those shots started hitting their mark. Abigail was bewildered by his choice of bride. Louisa was accomplished in "music dancing French &c.," Abigail — the self-proclaimed "farmeress" — unflatteringly conceded. She was pretty. She was lovely! But was she an *American*? "Some fair one has shown you its sophistry, and taught you to admire!" Abigail wrote. "Youth and beauty have penetrated through your fancied apathy, and you find yourself warmed by one and invigorated by the other; as you tell me that the enthusiasm of youth has subsided, I will presume that reason and judgment have taken its place. I would hope for the love I bear my country, that the siren, is at least *half blood.*"

John Quincy still blamed his mother, though, for her role in forcing him to leave Mary Frazier. Her words may have had the opposite of their intended effect — he would defend his heart's right to choose. He pointed out that if he waited for a choice that would satisfy all her requirements, "I should have been certainly doomed to perpetual celibacy."

The elder Adamses shifted their approach. Louisa was surely a worthy woman, they wrote — they thought of her as a daughter already — but John Quincy must not bring her to Portugal. A European court would ruin her. She would be unfit to be a wife when it came time to return to the United States. Their motivation for saying these things was not punitive, and actually, they would change their minds and urge him to marry before he went. Their advice reflected their own experience. John Adams had been a foreign minister in Europe, and its corrupting influence was a common attack against him. He was called a monarchist, a lover of courts and court style, a corrupted republican. It was a devastating and unfair charge (though it was true that he had a taste for titles), and it was deeply damaging to his political career. Despite this — perhaps because of this — they turned around and made the same charges against Louisa. "Is there not great danger of her contracting such inclinations, and habits as to endanger her youth and inexperience, as to unfit her for the discharge of those domestic duties?" Abigail wrote. "Who can answer for her after having been introduced into the dissipations of a foreign court?"

"A young lady of fine parts and accomplishments, educated to drawing dancing and music, however domestic and retired from the world she may have been in her fathers house, when she comes to shine in a court among the families of ambassadors and ministers of state, if she has not more discretion, prudence and philosophy than commonly belong to her sex, will be in danger of involving you in expenses far beyond your appointments," wrote John Adams. "I give you a hint and you must take it."

John Quincy took the hint. At The Hague, he slipped back into his scholarly routine. He had too little time for sociable frivolity. For companionship, he had his brother and his books. He had his work, which grew more interesting. Events in Europe were accelerating. While he whiled away his days threading spangles in the Johnsons' parlor, a French general named Napoleon Bonaparte had been winning battles and amassing power, and now France had command over much of the continent. The country was using its control of ports to control commerce; it was bullying representatives from the United States while preparing for war with England. John Quincy saw how easily the United States could be swept into wars that were not its own, and he felt the weight of his responsibilities.

That November, John Adams was elected president of the United States. The burden grew. John Quincy's every move would be watched especially closely, his every word scrutinized. So would his wife's. He had been inside enough European drawing rooms to understand — even if he would never say so — that a diplomat's wife is also watched, listened to, judged. The childish tone Louisa sometimes adopted in her letters did not help her cause. His own tone became condescending. John Quincy counseled Louisa not only to take comfort but to find pleasure in resignation to their distance. There was a finality and self-satisfaction in the way he spoke. In his heart and mind, he was moving on.

6

Louisa grew desperate, the more so because her family's preparations to move to the United States were under way at No. 8 Cooper's Row. If she was not married by the time the Johnsons left, she would be going too. What hope could she have that her engagement to John Quincy could survive across the Atlantic? It hardly seemed possible when it was so hard with only the Channel between them. There was, she wrote to John Quincy, "a feeble ray of hope" that they might see each other before she sailed for America, however. The Johnsons would travel aboard one of her father's ships, and she happened to know he had one in Holland. She would ask if the Johnsons could leave for America from there. She feared that if they did not see each other at all, their relationship would not survive.

Her youth, her inexperience, and her lack of reassurance exaggerated her natural fears — and her family surely heightened them.

Her sisters mocked her for seeming withdrawn. As an engaged woman, she was restricted in her company. Neither married nor unattached, she was not allowed to do anything that might attract reproof — even speaking to bachelors at balls. She was isolated and insecure. Considering that Catherine had intervened to pressure John Quincy when he had been in London, Catherine was probably also expressing her anxiety about John Quincy's intentions in some way at home. Joshua, too, had something at stake in ensuring the marriage came off, more than his daughter's happiness. His finances were under extreme pressure, which could have brought the engagement contract into danger. Joshua followed Louisa's letter with one of his own, suggesting that the family might stop at The Hague on the way to the United States in order to restore his daughter's happiness. John Quincy was quick to read between the lines. He responded to Joshua coldly and accused Louisa of conspiring with her father to be left behind with him in Holland while her family went to America.

It was a cruel thing to say. He made no allowance for the idea that Louisa might miss him, or that she might want to strengthen their attachment by seeing him before a longer separation. Nor did he acknowledge that Joshua had made no explicit mention of hurrying the marriage in his own letter. But his paranoia was not completely unfounded. Joshua probably did have ulterior motives. He was in trouble.

John Quincy did not know just how bad Joshua's problems were. Joshua could not hide his debts for much longer; they were spiraling out of his control. Money had been a recurring problem for him since his arrival in England twenty-five years before. The life of a merchant was unpredictable. The system of credit and payment by bills of exchange meant that men had to be able to collect in order to pay — and sometimes they couldn't collect. Shipping was risky in the best of times. A sunk cargo could mean ruin. Joshua was not cavalier. He had advised his partners and instructed them intelligently on how British and European trade operated. He had won business and earned respect. He did operate in the margins of his accounts sometimes, as many merchants did, and his bookkeeping grew increasingly disordered as business grew more complex. He had been criticized by some of his associates. But he was still trusted by many.

Joshua had dark eyes — the same eyes as his daughter Louisa — and a piercing gaze. His friends knew him for his ardent feelings and his calculating mind. He inspired at once confidence and wariness in men who met him. "Mr. Johnson seems cool, collected, and decided, a most valuable friend or a dreadful enemy," wrote one acquaintance. "I hope to know him only as the former." There were men who would know him as the latter. He was self-interested and self-preserving. But Louisa did not misjudge his character when she later said that he was too optimistic, too trusting. He was also quick to panic, abandon friends, and to protect himself when things went wrong. He had a tendency to enter trading arrangements with the highest hopes, and was crushed when they failed. In the late 1780s, the firm of Wallace, Johnson & Muir was so deeply in debt that he had to put the account books in the hands of the firm's major creditors in order to avoid bankruptcy. By the time John Quincy knew him, his finances were a mess. Wallace, Johnson & Muir had dissolved effective 1790, but it had taken years for the business to unwind, and he was still fighting not only those former partners over his share of the profits but the widow of John Davidson, from his first firm, which had ended before the Revolution.

His latest problem centered on a scheme to enter the brandy market with Colonel John Trumbull. In November 1795, at just the time that Trumbull brought John Quincy to dinner at the Johnsons' house, Joshua and Trumbull had hatched a plan to export brandy to the United States. Joshua lined up backers in London and handed the colonel instructions, along with a stack of letters of introduction. Joshua wrote to the Hennessys, whose brandy house had just begun selling to the United States, and to Mr. Turner, the mayor of Cognac, and to his contacts in France. He gave Trumbull a bill of remittance for £5,000. "As the advantage promises to be considerable, I hope the quantity will be large," he wrote to Trumbull, and told him to "get all the rum you can lay your hands on." But within months, the familiar pattern began. Joshua's soaring self-confidence gave way to doubt, then panic. Orders were rejected for poor quality. A ship was wrecked in Guernsey Roads, when the tide went out and several pipes of cognac shattered on the rocks. "I am sorry to tell you our ill luck continues," Joshua wrote Trumbull when he reported yet another disaster. Money was scarce, and Joshua had to rely on massive lines of credit. In May 1796, just as John Quincy was packing to return to The Hague, Joshua asked one investor alone, his friend Frederick Delius, a merchant in Bremen, Germany, to extend Trumbull's credit — on Joshua's account — to £40,000. "Had it not been for this friendship and genteel behavior our whole scheme must have been defeated," Joshua confessed to Trumbull, adding that he was desperate to get a ship with a full cargo of tobacco to Delius to make up some of the difference. The situation had not improved over the summer and fall. In December, Joshua was writing to Trumbull of a shipwreck — six or eight pipes of brandy lost. His creditors were having trouble paying their own debts. To satisfy his hungry investors, and to pay that promised dowry to John Quincy, Joshua needed to return to the United States and lay his claim to everything he could.

John Quincy had some hint of Joshua's situation from Louisa and perhaps from others. He acknowledged to his mother that he suspected that the Johnsons' wealth was not as great as their fine lifestyle suggested. His suspicions only went so far — he did not doubt that the dowry would be there, and in his daydreams, he was living on the Johnsons' southern land. But John Quincy had friends in London who did business with Joshua and may have heard something from one of them, or he may have merely surmised. Joshua was open about his struggles with his former partners in Maryland and his need to wrap up matters in person. One of his letters to John Quincy contained a disconcerting line: "I am in hourly expectations of letters from my late partners, they will be interesting, and as then rec[eive]d, I will come to a decided resolution will then communicate to you my planns without guile or reserve." John Quincy read guile and reserve straight into his words, guessing at a plan to leave Louisa in Holland so that he would have to fix the wedding date.

Maybe that really was the plan. Maybe Joshua knew, too, that if his financial situation grew much worse, it would be that much harder for him to marry his daughter off. He had once been a young man with a cavalier attitude toward marriage himself. Perhaps he saw John Quincy's reluctance and decided to apply some pressure himself.

Whatever the truth, John Quincy responded to Louisa in the worst possible way. "You will be sensible what an appearance in the eyes of the world, your coming here would have; an appearance consistent neither with your dignity, nor my delicacy," he wrote to Louisa, accusing her of conspiring with her father. Impugning a young woman's "dignity" and "delicacy" — which she rightly read as *her* modesty, not his — was as bad an insult as he could have made to a young woman. Her suggestion that a betrothed couple facing a long separation might welcome a reunion was treated as disgraceful. He tried to soften it by saying, "Let us my lovely friend rather submit with cheerfulness to the laws of necessity than resort to unbecoming remedies for relief," but that just made matters worse. John Quincy was calling her virtue into question.

She recoiled from his response. "Believe me I should be sorry to put it in your power, or in that of the world, to say I wished to force myself upon any man or into any family," Louisa retorted, as angry at his innuendo as she deserved to be. She had done nothing, she added, to deserve such "mortification" as his letters brought. So began a period of angry, passionate attacks. While couching their words in claims of total devotion and love, they hurtled shots across the Channel fast and thick. She criticized his excessive attachment to his books. With careless cruelty, he scorned her choice of reading — and so the quality of her mind. She was, she could easily infer, no match for him.

In truth, his insult had a liberating effect. She wrote, for the first time, without the help of the governess. She would not let herself be so easily dismissed, so rudely pushed around. Her writing grew in confidence, style, and wit. It is remarkable that, in so short a time after writing such cringing, pathetic letters, she started to find a voice. It was immature, and not as strong and vivid as the one she would later develop, but it was her voice nonetheless.

They engaged in a series of small skirmishes — feinting with this one, pulling back with the next — that led to passion and flirtation, and also to anger and misunderstanding. It was a charged correspondence, in which the heat emanated from both their attraction and their fury. She used sarcasm. He found her tone unattractive. "Let us understand one another, Louisa," John Quincy wrote to her (on her birthday, no less). "I never thought your disposition deficient in *spirit,* and that I am fully convinced you have as much of it as can be consistent with an amiable temper, but let me earnestly entreat you never to employ it in discussion with me, and to remember that it is in its nature a *repellent* quality."

She found his peremptory style offensive. He detected "suspicion and distrust" within her.

He accused her of "childish weakness or idle lamentations." She was incensed by his sanctimony and turned on his "philosophy." She did not pause to punctuate all her lines. "Ah my beloved friend, this boasted philosophy that I have heard so much of is indeed a *dreadful* thing. . . . Delusive as may have been my imagination, I have never dreamt of *cloudless* skies Yet did I not expect that *you* would have been the person to have strewn my path with needless *thorns.*"

They were at cross-purposes, even when it came to names. He called her Louisa, and she addressed him as "my Adams," which must have sounded rather romantic. John Quincy bridled. "I have endeavoured to habituate myself to it, because you appear fond of using it; but it looks to me more and more uncouth and awkward," he wrote to her. The address seemed to him "too much like that of novels." She learned the lesson a little too well; after that, she did not address him by name in her letters at all.

They would apologize and try to soothe each other's hurt feelings, calling each barb a proof of their care. Sometimes their apologies would work; their letters, even the harsh ones, were little grappling hooks binding them together. They could not efface their attraction; they did in fact care. But mail took time to travel, and before one conciliatory letter could arrive, another hurtful missive was already en route, slashing open the wounds before they could heal.

"I am so miserably dull, stupid, and cross, that I have gained the appellation of the Nun," Louisa wrote.

"I will freely confess a material change which absence has produced," John Quincy replied. "It is the restoration of sober reason, and reflection, which alas! if they did not abandon me were without all the influence they should have, during the latter part of my residence in London. It was indeed a time of delight; but a time of too much indulgence. . . . I am the man I was when you *first* knew me" — which is to say, the man who had not returned to the Johnsons' right away. "My lovely friend, *that* man, is much more estimable, and much more respectable than the man I was for two or three months before I left you." He could not have been more provocative. He was not the man who had fallen in love.

They were pushed to the brink. With quiet sadness, with philosophy, she saw that they might have gone too far. "Let us mutually forget the past," she wrote. "Our departure for America is fixed." The Johnsons were to leave England in three months. She would, she wrote, "indulge the pleasing idea" that he would follow them soon, and when he did, she would be happy to "share the simple fortunes of my dearest friend." Only then, "should this happen," when he was "divested of rank," would she be able to prove that he, not his station, was what drew her to him — "that it was not your situation, but yourself that I loved."

It nearly ended there — almost in heartbreak. She felt she had to prove herself and her affections to him. She felt him slipping away. "Should this happen," she had written, because there was doubt. Though anguished, she was ready to let go. Gracefully, she was saying goodbye. But John Quincy changed course once more. He pulled her back.

On April 13, 1797, he wrote to her that circumstances had changed. It *might* be possible to come through London, *if* he could travel by an American ship (such as one, incidentally, that Joshua owned), and *if* he was able to come to London, then he would marry Louisa and bring her to Lisbon.

He gave Louisa a chance to call off their

engagement. He spoke honestly. They knew each other now; they knew not only their attraction to each other but also their capacity to repel. "You know the Man you have chosen, for the friend of your life," he wrote to her.

You know him the better, for that absence, which has at once shewn you a trial of his affection and of his temper. — He has disguised to you none of his failings and weaknesses. You know the chances of hardship, inconvenience and danger, which you may be called to share with him. You know his inviolable attachment to his Country, and his resolute determination not to continue long his absence from it. — You know that upon his retirement, the state of his fortune will require privations, which will be painful to him only as they may affect you. Choose, Louisa, choose for yourself, and be assured that his Heart will ratify your choice.

Her opportunity to withdraw was real. Women could, and did, end engagements. It was the brief window in which women were allowed, in theory, to be masters of their fate. She could not ask for marriage, and she could not escape from it; once vows were exchanged, she was subject to her husband's authority. But she had the freedom to say no, up until that point at the altar when she submitted herself to his control.

That she would be submitting herself if they married, he left no doubt — and not only to him, but to his country. In his life, he wrote to her, she would always come second. There was sadness in that — but perhaps there was also something stirring about his dedication, something pure and clear in the clarion call. "I may therefore own to you," he wrote to her, "that my duty to my Country is in my mind the first and most imperious of all obligations; before which every interest and every feeling inconsistent with it must forever disappear."

She could have told him to leave for Lisbon without her. Instead, she told him to come.

7

John Quincy arrived in England with his brother Thomas on July 12, 1797. She knew he was in London, and she expected him to come to her right away. Night came and he did not. He appeared at the Johnsons' door the next day, finding "my friends there and particularly my best friend, well." Either she hid her disappointment that he had not hurried to her, or he chose not to see it. She, meanwhile, could do nothing but sense his misgivings. Her insecurity worked as a magnifying glass. When John Quincy asked her to set a wedding date she replied that she wanted to marry as soon as possible — "naturally supposing that it was what he most desired." When she saw the startled expression on his face, she felt she had done something wrong.

In fact, the wedding could not come soon enough for the Johnsons, who were hurriedly packing to leave for the United States in early autumn. It's no wonder that she wanted to be married fast. Not only had John Quincy kept her in wait, but the ground kept moving beneath her. News arrived that President Adams, his father — and his commander — had changed his son's appointment from Portugal to Prussia. John Quincy was furious; it was one thing for George Washington to give him a large commission and another for his own father to do it. It was nepotism, and he felt ashamed. He wrote to his father of "the degraded and humiliating aspect in which it places me personally" and considered asking for a recall. He would accept the new position, he wrote to his father, for two reasons — both revealing. The first was "parental authority." The second was "that the new destination, will be so much more inconvenient and troublesome to myself." He had already shipped his beloved books to Portugal, at high expense. Characteristically, he managed to turn annoyance into a virtue. Anything that required a significant sacrifice on his part was easier to accept.

It's unlikely he kept secret from his bride-to-be how upset he was; already, she was sensitive to his dark moods, no doubt especially in the days leading to their union. The switch in destinations wouldn't have been easy for her, either. Portugal had promised warmth, proximity to the ocean; it would have brought her as close to her family, once they had sailed for the United States, as possible while remaining in Europe. Prussia meant long nights and cold winters. It meant the guttural sounds and glottal stops of German. It meant an extra 1,400 miles between her and her family. It was another swerve, another hard adjustment, another lesson that in her husband's life, she would never have a say. It was a reminder that John Quincy's first devotion was to his country, his second to his parents, and his third to his books — he was insistent about the books. She could expect a share of his attention and his affection, but it would be only a share. He had said this explicitly. It would help if she could learn to love his country, his parents, and his books; but that summer, 1797, in London, his country was abstract, his parents unknown, and she could not understand his attachment to his books. She thought too much reading injured his health.

Despite all this, their wedding day was a happy one. The ceremony was small. It took place at eleven on Wednesday morning, July 26, at All Hallows Barking, around the corner from the house on Cooper's Row. Louisa's family, John Quincy's young brother, Thomas — his secretary at The Hague — and two of John Quincy's friends were there to witness. Rev. John Hewlett, the man who had taught Louisa "early to think," performed the service.

She walked out of the dark stone church

into the bright sunlight as a wife. It was a hot and cheerful day. The Tower of London lay below them, and lighters and skiffs crowded the Thames. For the next month, Louisa's days were filled with celebrations: excursions to the countryside, dinners and parties hosted by friends for the bride and groom. Late mornings followed the late nights — the loss of sleep while in bed, as John Quincy wrote in his diary with a touch of circumspect pride, coming "from an inevitable cause."

Louisa was happy. She had her family around her and her husband with her; she had everything she wanted and every hope for the future. "At this moment," Louisa wrote in "Record of a Life," "every thing seemed to combine to make my prospects brilliant."

The celebrations for the newlyweds culminated in a large ball thrown by Joshua at the Johnsons' house on Tower Hill on August 25. The party was a triumph; the last guests, flushed from pleasure, dancing, and drink, did not leave until four in the morning. But for Joshua, the ball must have been torture. Earlier that day, letters had arrived from America with news that a ship he needed in order to cover a bill for £500 would not arrive. He was broke. He knew that the bills for the flowers, the food, the musicians, the flowing wine would come soon, and he knew he could not pay them. The worst was to come. He did not, it seems, tell his daughter.

Louisa and John Quincy left the Johnsons' house and moved into the Adelphi Hotel, where they planned to live until leaving for Berlin in October, while the Johnsons continued their preparations to move to America. The plan was for Catherine, Joshua, and the other Johnson sisters to go in mid-September. On the night of September 8, 1797, Joshua, Catherine, and Louisa's six sisters came to have dinner with Louisa and John Quincy at the Adelphi. It turned out that they were coming to say goodbye.

Unknown to Louisa, two days earlier, on September 6, Joshua had a bill due to Frederick Delius, U.S. consul and a merchant in Bremen, Germany, who had generously and riskily extended credit to help fund Joshua's brandy scheme. On September 8, an independent reviewer of Joshua's accounts gave his books to one of Joshua's other creditors, Jonathan Maitland, with whom Joshua had three accounts. Maitland was claiming that Joshua owed him money, too. Joshua's response was to run. The hope — fervently held, grasped at, promised to anyone who would listen — was that Joshua could claim more of his old firm's profits in person than he could from abroad. The Johnsons left the Adelphi and then went to meet a ship at Gravesend under the cover of the dark.

Before daybreak, they were bound for the United States. In her memory, it happened all at once and without warning. As she told it, she woke and found them gone. She was "the most forlorn miserable wretch that the sun ever smiled upon." That wasn't quite true. But it had been a brutal night for her. "After supper we had a distressing scene, while the whole family took leave of Louisa," John Quincy wrote in his diary of that night.

The story she would later tell was that her father was wronged. He was taken by surprise; he was the victim. He had been unlucky, as any honest merchant could be, and then he had been betrayed by his creditors. There had been a wreck, a cargo of brandy lost. A ship had not arrived from the East Indies, a remittance hadn't come in, and "he was obliged to stop payment for the sum of five hundred pounds." The missing remittance, "the sum which had been destined to settle all my fathers current debts; every one of which it would cover," had arrived just after he'd left, and it had been stolen by his creditor "the villain Maitland." In Maryland, his former partners cheated him out of his fair share of his old firm's profits. In his daughter's view, Joshua had merely suffered the vicissitudes of a merchant's life. For that bad luck and badly placed trust alone, the Johnson name — the name she had just given up — would be slandered.

She had small details right: there was a brandy scheme, a wreck, a missing remittance, a bill for £500, and a creditor named Maitland. But she could not admit that she also had at least a dim sense of the larger picture. She had known that it was imperative that her family return to the United States as soon as possible. Much was masked by the Johnsons' fine lifestyle, but Joshua was not calm or quiet about his financial troubles. "Several of my family are unwell, nor can they be better until I am relieved from the pain I labor under," he had once written a correspondent during a time of financial distress. But her father was her idol, and she could not see clearly or accept the poor choices that had combined with bad luck to lead to his ruin. She could not see that, at least to an extent, he was at fault. To be fair, no one in or out of chancery courts in London and the United States could untangle the books. (Merchants from Fleet Street and the Strand and Maitland would still be arguing over the remnants of Joshua's estate in chancery court a decade later. The verdicts have been lost.) She had been raised to defer to him absolutely. He was not a despot; he was an affectionate father, as fathers in her time and class were supposed to be; but he ruled.

There were betrayals. What she could never admit was that she was one of the ones betrayed. Her father had not only left her, but he also left her in the most vulnerable position. When he fled, one of the promises he left unfilled was Louisa's dowry. Only a few months before, Joshua had reaffirmed her dowry of £5,000 sterling to John Quincy and to Louisa as well. It wasn't a great fortune, not by the standards of the aristocracy, but a dowry was no idle inducement. A marriage was not just a religious sacrament, and it was not just a union of two people in love. (The notion that romantic love should govern the decision at all was an idea only then gaining purchase in Britain's upper middle class.) It was a contract. If a bride's father could not produce the bridal portion, the groom would have legal grounds to abandon the bride. Joshua's bankruptcy made his daughter vulnerable. John Quincy would have been justified in leaving her.

The thought did cross his mind — if only to be rejected. John Quincy met with Maitland and others who had studied Joshua's books. "Find the affairs of Mr. J. more and more adverse," John Quincy wrote in his diary a few weeks after the Johnsons were gone. He would not help his father-in-law by lending money. "This trial is a strong one — more so indeed than I expected — and I expected it would be strong. — I have done my duty — rigorous, inflexible duty." He acknowledged in his diary that he would be within his rights to leave Louisa. But he was dutiful by nature, and he had made his vows. "No event whatever shall convince me that by pursuing a more interested and less faithful course I should have been rewarded with greater success," he wrote.

The more interested course would have been leaving his new wife. There is no evidence from his diary or letters to anyone else that he said anything like this to her. But even had he been a saint, she would have heard accusations and threats in his voice. Money was already a difficult subject between them. He had been explicit about his sense of probity and his determination to wait until he could marry on sound financial footing. He had already accused Louisa and Joshua of conspiring to accelerate the marriage and to leave her in Holland while the rest of the family made it to the United States. He had made it clear to Louisa that money would be tight and that they would be pressed to the edge of their means. He would not live like the Europeans in court — he would not go into debt.

John Quincy loathed debt — and feared it. In that, he was like the leaders of his country, including those (Thomas Jefferson, Alexander Hamilton, and many others) who were so deeply in debt they would never emerge from it. Debt was thought to undermine republican liberty. A man in debt could not be independent; he could not be free to act according to his own will. A debtor not only threatened his own freedom but the freedom of the United States. "A nation of men, each of whom owned enough property to support his family, could be a republic," the historian Edmund Morgan has explained. "It would follow that a nation of debtors, who had lost their property or mortgaged it to creditors, was ripe for tyranny." For John Quincy, Joshua's failure followed on the heels of a crisis in the Adams family — some of which affected John Quincy directly. John Quincy had left his savings of $4,000 with his younger brother Charles to invest. Charles had speculated with it, lost it, and then more or less cut off contact with his family. John Quincy answered a six-month silence from his brother with sternness. "I hereby withdraw all power and authority that I have heretofore given you to draw for money in my behalf," he would write to Charles a year later. Meanwhile, his sister, Nabby, had married a man — Louisa's old friend the "dashing" Colonel William Smith — whose debts were so massive that he had abandoned his family to the care of Abigail and John Adams.

To Louisa's humiliation, and no doubt to John Quincy's indignation, men clutching Joshua's bills came to their hotel room. "Every rap at the door," she wrote, "made me tremble." They wanted John Quincy to pay, and he refused. The debts were not his. But she felt they were hers. She knew how things looked: her father had married off his daughter under false pretenses and then left her new husband in the lurch, and she'd been in on the scheme.

In October, Frederick Delius sent John Quincy a damning letter, impugning Joshua's character while implicitly and insultingly suggesting that John Quincy was privy to the truth. "It is impossible for me to describe to you the horror I feel at such a low mean and unpardonable conduct which has done more injury to my credit and reputation than Mr Johnson and his family can ever make good again," Delius wrote. (*And his family* — how those words must have stung.) "I have been very much mistaken in Mr Johnson's character," Delius continued. "I always took him to be open, upright and candid and without any deceit whatever, but his present conduct towards me shews what he meant by all his affectionate and tender expressions."

John Quincy passed Delius's letter along to Joshua, in Washington. "The turn of affairs here has not been such as your friends could have wished," John Quincy wrote. "Appearances and allegations are advanced which bring in question something more than merely your credit." And John Quincy gave it to Louisa to read, too.

Years later, recounting the moment, she

defended her father by saying that his "misfortunes were as unexpected as they were sudden." Really, she was defending herself. She knew how things looked. "Every appearance was against me; actions proceeding from the most innocent causes looked like deliberate plans to deceive; and I felt that all the honest pride of my soul was laid low for ever," she wrote nearly thirty years later, the pain fresh. She marked that moment as the one that changed her — that broke her. The timing couldn't have been worse. She was discovering a terrible truth about her family at the same moment she was forced to join a new one, turning a natural break into a traumatic rupture. And it was the worse, because she felt her husband judge her.

There is little evidence that John Quincy was anything but patient with her. But no record exists of what he said to her behind closed doors. Most likely, she wanted him to defend her "beloved father," which he would not do. Whatever he said, or whatever she imagined him saying, burned her. "It was strict and rigid justice and I had nothing to complain of — Such was my honey moon."

Louisa saw her character and position called into question. The question of money became a question of standing in the marriage, and she had lost her claim. For years, it would weigh on her. She would refer to it constantly, especially during times of stress.

She could not buy her son a present because she had no money. She could not defend herself against John Quincy's reproaches about "strict economy" because her father had gone bankrupt. "Beggar as I am," she would write. She would consider herself poor, even when her husband was not.

The memory of her father's fall would haunt Louisa for the rest of her life, especially when she felt most vulnerable. She used it to mark the moment that divided her life: she had been a Johnson, and now she was an Adams. She had been a child, and now she was a woman. She had been innocent, but now knew shame. "It has been forty three years since I became a wife," she would write when she was sixty-five years old, "and yet the rankling sore is not healed which then broke upon my heart of hearts. . . . It has hung like an incubus upon my spirit." *An incubus.* A demon that has sex with sleeping women. This was the level of her fixation, her terror, her sense of powerlessness — her loss of innocence.

The timing was unfortunate for another reason. On October 18, Louisa and John Quincy left London for Berlin. She was already pregnant.

■ ■ ■ ■

PART TWO:
LIFE WAS NEW

Berlin, 1797–1801

■ ■ ■ ■

1

They arrived at Gravesend on Wednesday, October 18, 1797, after night had fallen, and discovered that the *Frans,* the ship they planned to take to Prussia, had already gone. They were late and despairing; there had been some confusion about the passports, and John Quincy was upset that the documents were still not right. After some inquiries, they learned that the ship had anchored for the night about ten miles downriver, at a place called Hope. They would have to row to meet it.

Louisa was exhausted. Night after night, the rowdy cheers of men lighting bonfires and shattering glass in the name of the king, celebrating Britain's recent victory over the Dutch fleet, allies of France, had kept her and John Quincy awake. Perhaps those boisterous shouts were also a hint of what she was about to face — a continent roiled in conflict. Only two years earlier Prussia had been at war, part of the coalition of European

131

monarchies that had united against Revolutionary France and its charismatic general, Napoleon Bonaparte. For John Quincy, at least, the clamor would have been a troubling reminder of the dangerous and difficult situation he was in, as a diplomat representing a new nation that had too often been treated as a pawn by the old great powers in their own conflicts. No doubt Louisa tossed and turned with her own fears of the unknown — the alien country to which she was headed; the dangers of pregnancy, which she faced without a friend; the almost-stranger to whom she had united her fate; and the trauma of her parents' and sisters' flight to the United States.

There would be no turning back, and no relief. At eight in the evening, the five members of their group — Louisa and John Quincy, John Quincy's brother Thomas (who would serve as his brother's secretary, as he had at The Hague), and two servants, Tilly Whitcomb and Elizabeth Epps — stepped into a rowboat. The pilot pushed off, and the boat whispered through the quiet Thames, as the river widened toward the sea and opened into darkness. The moon that night was only a sliver; what little light there was came from lamps and distant stars. The air, though mid-October, was almost warm, and the travelers marveled at the fineness of the evening. It took two hours for the rowboat to reach the

Frans. As soon as Louisa climbed on board, the water moved and the ship rolled. She felt ill right away.

She was sick all eight days at sea, and she was scared. When huge gales blew through, Louisa became convinced the boat would sink. Passengers took turns at the pumps. The ship heaved and plunged. "Almost sick myself," John Quincy wrote in his diary. The ship was dirty, "very disgusting," he thought. There was little relief when she stepped onto firm ground at the harbor at Hamburg, on October 26. She hardly knew what to make of the country that would be her new home: the unfamiliar lattice of canals and narrow streets, the smell of peat that made her nauseous, the sound of water as it sluiced through rooftop gutters and shattered on the ground.

From Hamburg they traveled south toward Berlin, their English carriage lurching over the rough Prussian roads. Everything was strange and horrible. She found the inns almost uninhabitable. "The house was dirty, noisy, and uncomfortable — The beds miserable; the table execrable; the manners of the Mrs of the mansion" — the only women she would have contact with on the road — "coarse though kind, and between *us,* no means whatever existed of communication, which would have made my situation more agreeable." Probably, nothing would have made her situation agreeable. She was home-sick, and her mind was still fixed on her family's "downfal."

Still, she marveled at what she saw. At her father's dinner table and in the parlor, she had heard about the extraordinary travels of captains come recently from the West Indies, envoys to Europe, and traders who trafficked in China, and she thought that she knew something about the world. So she was surprised by how much surprised her. She watched, fascinated, as the ship's crew passed around a string with a cube of sugar tied to the end, which they sucked as they drank tea. There was something fresh about those experiences, something that made her mind reach even as she recoiled. She could not help but be curious. Later, she would insist that during those first few months of marriage, she spent her time mourning for the life she had lost. And yet, even then, she looked at the world and was amazed by what she saw. She may have thought her life was over, but when she arrived in Berlin, she discovered that it had just begun. She was twenty-two years old, weary, pregnant, and worried. And yet she was enchanted. "To me," she wrote a quarter century later, looking back, "life was *new.*"

A lieutenant stopped Louisa, John Quincy, and their group at the gates to the city. The official looked at the travelers, studied their papers, and questioned them, suspicious "until one of his private soldiers explained to him, who the United States of America were," wrote John Quincy in his diary. John Quincy made no more comment — but the situation was enough to make any man wry and despairing. He was representing a nation that did not exist in the minds of many. What was worse, the traditional great powers of Europe generally treated the young nation as an annoying child.

The tired travelers went to find lodgings at the Ville de Paris, where they were turned away, and then to the Hotel de Russie, at the end of Unter den Linden. And there, finally, they were able to stop and look around. John Quincy knew something of what to expect from the city. He had been to Berlin before, when he was fourteen years old, on his way to St. Petersburg to serve as secretary to the American envoy Francis Dana. The city had impressed him. It conformed to his ideals, his desire for order and structure. The land was flat. The streets ran parallel or met at right angles, so unlike the tangled cowpaths of Quincy. "It is the handsomest and the most regular city I ever saw," the boy had written in his diary. At thirty, not everything about Berlin would please him. The roads would turn to clouds of dust in summer, unless it had rained, when they were bogs; the climate was oppressive; finding and furnishing a cheap apartment was hard. But he had routes for his walks, and a place to arrange his books.

What Louisa thought when she saw Berlin is surprising. Many foreign visitors found it ugly. They looked at the windy plain and saw desolation; they looked down the wide avenues and saw absence. It was an old city, a settlement dating to the twelfth century, but most of the construction was recent, and its grand proportions were optimistic. To those who liked the look of history, the brick and plaster buildings looked unused, too large and low slung against the open sky. It strained for magnificence. Louisa, though, thought the city "beautiful." It was November when they arrived, and the days were already short. But the late-autumn sun was incandescent; it could edge statues with fire and make creamy walls blush. Their hotel was situated near the winding river Spree, at the end of the long boulevard of lime trees. The open, blank plan of the place was so unlike the stacked and crowded old cities that were her reference. Here was a place that looked toward its future instead of back at its past.

It was a good place, then, for a young woman who had experienced something she wanted to forget, and who was newly married and pregnant. But almost immediately Louisa fell ill. Two days later she was up the whole night "in the most excruciating pain," John Quincy wrote in his diary. She was starting to miscarry. The pregnancy was not far along, but there must have been severe complications; it took more than a week to discharge the fetus, and she lost a lot of blood. At one point, she heard Thomas's voice through the haze of her pain asking the doctor if she was still alive. He had heard a rumor spread through the hotel that she had died.

The recovery was slow and painful, not only physically but emotionally. She wanted her mother, or at the least a woman to talk to, and there was none. Her maid, Elizabeth Epps, was seventeen years old and as frightened as Louisa. Louisa needed more than a doctor, someone who could heal more than her body. She had lost her parents and sisters, and now she had lost the hope of a child.

She was mortified, too, because she sensed herself violated. Strange men surrounded her bedside and took off her clothes. Most likely, until her wedding night only months before, no man had ever seen her naked. The attendants at the hotel were unblinking when they saw her. A German professor arrived at her bedside to poke and probe her; she came to hate him so much that she later refused to let him back into her sight. "It is almost impossible to imagine a situation more truly distressing for a woman of refinement and delicacy than the one into which I was thrown," she later wrote. She was "shocked by the disgusting and to me indecent manners" of those who attended her. Only a kind Scottish doctor, Charles Brown, the king and queen's physician, treated her with a gentleness and understanding that made her feel safe.

At least her husband was by her side, day after day and night after night. He was tender and attentive to her, as he had not yet been and as she might not have expected. He shared her agony, and in his diary, his normally stiff tone gave way to sadness and sympathy for her pain and for the loss of her — and his — child. Under the pressure of his distress, the abstract platitudes John Quincy had once used to describe Louisa to his mother now turned to real — if pointed — expressions of affection. "My wife is all that *your* heart can wish," he wrote to his mother.

But as he returned to his work, her husband was not always all her own heart could wish. Louisa had the company of Elizabeth Epps and often Thomas Adams, but sometimes she felt abandoned and alone — the more so after the Adamses moved from the Hotel de Russie into apartments over the guardhouse at the gigantic Brandenburg Gate. On one side was the Tiergarten, Berlin's great park, which stretched all the way to the king's palace at Charlottenburg. Once she could rise from her bed and step outside, she could walk along paths past lovely ponds, espaliers, and neat little forests. But on the other side of the gate, below her bedroom windows, stood a soldiers' parade ground. Every royal personage or ambassador — and there seemed to be countless of them — who passed through the gate received a noisy presentation of arms. Berlin had had a large garrison since the days of Frederick the Great, even if, for the past decade, the king (son of Frederick William II) was better known for his courtesans than commanders. To Louisa's horror, "few days nay even hours passed without my ears being assailed and my eyes shocked by the screams and blows" when an unruly soldier was beaten or dressed down.

She was not locked in a fortress, but it could seem that way. "I felt that I was an exile," she wrote. While her husband met people and made connections, she was isolated in the guardhouse, unable to leave with no carriage, no escort, nowhere to go. She was frightened at the thought of entering the royal court, but it was worse to be excluded.

Finally, Miss Dorville, the daughter of the master of ceremonies to the first wife of Frederick William II, appeared at her door, curious to see the reclusive new arrival. Miss Dorville was a tall and self-assured beauty, and she had eyes that seemed to price a person at a glance. Louisa, still weak, shrank as she felt herself sized up — and with reason; she would later hear that Miss Dorville reported that she had "a face like a horse." But the second visitor was a godsend. Pauline Neale was eighteen years old — only a few years younger than Louisa — and a lady-in-waiting to the queen and the maid of honor to Princess Radziwill (also known as Princess Louise). Pauline swept in, "full of animation and esprit," exuding at once sympathy and a bracing confidence. Pauline was born in Berlin (her father had been the chamberlain and at one point "grand cupbearer" to Frederick the Great and Frederick William II, and her mother was the mistress of the household to Prince Ferdinand), but she had Irish ancestry, had been to Britain, and she spoke English, which put Louisa at ease. Louisa could not have dreamed of a better friend — nor a more necessary one, because when Miss Dorville came back to while away the hours before husband-hunting began, she very casually (and no doubt with a hint of malice) asked when Louisa expected to be presented at court. There were rumors, Miss Dorville continued, about the delay; indeed it was wondered whether the Adamses were really married.

So arrangements were quickly made. On January 20, John Quincy came home from a ball and told Louisa, who had been at home, that Sophie Marie, Countess von Voss, the queen's *grande gouvernante* — the woman charged with enforcing where to walk, when to sit, and how to bow in the presence of a queen — had scheduled Mrs. Adams's presentation for the next day.

There was hardly time to prepare. Louisa needed a dress. She needed instructions in protocol. She needed the right gossip so that she would not blunder. She needed to learn names and titles, which was hard, because the family tree was confusing. There were three layers of royal families — the current king, Frederick William III; the family of Frederick William II, who had just died; and the people attached to Frederick the Great. It was all the more difficult to sort out because in the Prussian court, wives were known by their husbands' names if the men's ranks were higher. On the other hand, many of the women were named Louise or Luise — pronounced, more or less, "Louisa" — including the queen. Little else was easy. Pauline Neale materialized and fed her the necessary gossip, taught her the rules, helped her find something to wear and something to make it special (Louisa bought a blue satin robe), and smiled reassuringly.

Before Louisa could give way to her fears, it was seven o'clock in the evening, and she was quivering in the queen's private apartments. Countess von Voss was the first woman she saw, and the sight of the *grande*

141

gouvernante made her freeze. Countess von Voss, nearly seventy, stood rigid, a hoop skirt encircling her skeletal frame. A train of brocaded silk lay over her petticoats; her bodice bristled with ruffles and jewels; a little cap sat on the back of her frizzed hair. At the sight of this person, so "stiff and formal," Louisa began to tremble, her knees turned weak, and she found herself unable to walk when Queen Luise appeared.

The queen, though, was kind. She waved away the rules and went up to Louisa instead. "Never shall I forget with what inexpressible admiration I saw the Queen of Queens," Louisa later wrote. She was not alone in her devotion. Queen Luise had been a monarch for only a month, but already she was a legend — famous for her charisma, her intelligent and passionate nature, and especially for her fair skin, her heart-shaped face, her little red mouth, her blond curls, her limpid blue eyes, and her body, which was painted, sculpted, worshipped. She was called a muse, an angel. When she wore a headscarf around her neck, women wore headscarfs around their necks. When she wore gauzy gowns with empire waists, chemise dresses became the fashion. These dresses suited her, because she was tall, five foot eight, and had the body of a figure painted by Botticelli. No one could overlook her erotic appeal. The clothes she wore were sometimes so thin and low cut that they seemed only to outline her sylvan form; a statue of her and her sister by Johann Gottfried Schadow, in which she stands with her arm wrapped around her sister, wearing a suggestion of a dress and looking more like a nymph than a mortal, was deemed too dangerous for public view. Yet Queen Luise was also known for her modesty, generosity, warmth, and domesticity. She was a woman who represented, it was agreed, all a woman should be. Thousands of stern Prussian hearts had softened when, upon arriving in Berlin from Mecklenburg as a teenager to marry the heir apparent, Luise broke protocol to embrace and kiss the child who greeted her with verses on Unter den Linden. The king was known as her husband. She was known as the Queen.

It was not out of character for her to break protocol to approach Louisa and smile sympathetically. It was typical, too, for her to inquire kindly about Louisa's health, since Queen Luise — although a year younger than Louisa — was already the mother of three and pregnant again, and since Dr. Brown, who had nursed Louisa after her miscarriage, was also the queen's own doctor. She watched Louisa sensitively, cut the interview short, and invited the American minister's young wife for supper later that night — without her husband, as was customary, as diplomats were not permitted to dine with the monarch.

None of this treatment was unusual for Queen Luise. But to Louisa, the kindness was extraordinary. It put her at ease. Queen Luise embodied an ideal, a union of spirit and humble affability, modesty and allurement, power and grace. She was a fantasy, of course, something out of a fairy tale — the Queen of Queens. But for a young woman who felt alone, who was in search of a model, Queen Luise became the measure.

After her presentation to the queen, there were countless lesser royal households to meet. Louisa was inspected, questioned, studied. She passed the tests. It helped that she spoke excellent French, the language of the court, and that she wanted to please. It probably helped, too, that — notwithstanding Miss Dorville's whispering — she was pretty. The invitations for the Adamses piled up, and she was "launched in the giddy round of fashionable life." She was dazzled, but not afraid or intimidated by the grand personages she met. Some of them delighted her, some impressed her, some made her scowl, some summoned a smile. Nothing could have prepared Louisa, for instance, for the sight of the queen dowager, who wore a twilled robe and skirt, her hair "scratched out on each side" "a la Crazy Jane" and overlaid with diamonds, all hooded by a black veil that fell to her feet. "It was with the utmost difficulty that I kept my *sérieux,* with the dignity suited to the Wife of a foreign dignitary," Louisa wrote.

"When I got home [Thomas Adams] laughed with all his heart at my recital of the Scene, and the gravity assumed by Mr A. who terribly dreaded some indiscretion on my part, could not controul our mirth."

2

John Quincy was anxious for a reason. Some Europeans considered Americans hardly more than upstart rebels; some, as he was reminded by that suspicious lieutenant at the gates of Berlin, had not heard of the United States at all. The old great powers routinely violated American sovereign rights, carelessly insulting ships and disrupting trade, aware that there was little worry of repercussions from the United States' infant navy — the first American warships had been launched only the year before. The United States had the luxury of an ocean to separate itself from the "vortex" of Europe, but American ships on that same ocean made it vulnerable. Both the French and the British routinely disregarded American maritime rights — because they could, and because they had bigger worries than American grievances. Just as John Quincy and Louisa were arriving in Berlin, Napoleon was headed to Paris as a conquering hero, and his gaze was fixed on Britain.

Prussia watched nervously.

John Quincy was determined that neutrality in European affairs was the best path for the United States to adopt. That course would not be easy to maintain. Caught between Britain and France — with partisans of both in Congress working hard to ensure their favored nation's advantage, even at the cost of war — the United States was in a delicate position. "Of all the dangers which encompass the liberties of a republican state," John Quincy had written in 1793, "the intrusion of a foreign influence into the administration of their affairs, is the most alarming." George Washington, who would soon write his Farewell Address counseling the country to avoid becoming involved with foreign powers, read those words and was deeply impressed. Prussia, although under pressure to join an alliance with or against France, was intent on maintaining its neutrality. A close and friendly relationship with the United States made sense. Renewing the expired treaty would be easy enough; the harder task was to analyze the situation in all of Europe.

To do that, John Quincy needed to cultivate contacts and sources. And to do that, he needed to attend dinners and balls. In his diaries and letters, he called these entertainments tiresome distractions, but he knew they were required. In a European court, the crucial business of making relationships happened in the social realm. Men stood in for states; diplomacy masqueraded as civility. Civility was not his strong suit.

Here is where his wife — ignorant of all the machinations, and blithely assuming she would and should remain so — came in. His posture of dismissing this society as frivolous was partly republican and partly defensive. He knew that as a courtier, he would not shine. "The jealousy which I marked in his temper and the suspicious turn of mind have already disgusted those whom he had to do business with," wrote the American Gouverneur Morris when he saw John Quincy in London two years before, adding that his hot temper would "do mischief here." Morris was biased toward the British and probably somewhat jealous of John Quincy, but John Quincy himself acknowledged that he had bumbled badly in his diplomatic efforts in London. In Berlin, he needed to ingratiate himself while always keeping his distance, as a republican should.

The balance was even harder for his wife, though she had little inkling of it at the start. She would be judged — by John Quincy as well as by others. John Quincy had little appreciation for women at court. He found them frivolous and shallow. "Political subserviency and domestic influence must be the lot of women, and those who have departed the most from their natural sphere are not those who have shown their sex in the most amiable light," he had written in his diary while in the Netherlands. Out of context, John Quincy's contempt for women in the proximity of power is curious, in light of the forceful presence and curiosity of his mother. After all, he should have appreciated better than anyone that wives could be smart and invaluable advisers: he had his own mother for a high counselor. But he considered Abigail the exception that proved the rule, and even in her case, she could never aspire to more than to remain behind the scenes. The Adamses shared the view that courts threatened masculine mores. In England, John Adams once wrote, "luxury, effeminacy, and venality are arrived at such a shocking pitch." The country had become, he added, "the residence of musicians, pimps, panders, and catamites."

The American Revolution had been a rebellion not merely against a particular king but against an idea about kings and their inevitable corruptions — corruptions that were often presented in terms of gender. The physical presence of women during political discussions was constantly held up as evidence. Thomas Jefferson, for instance, had been shocked when he saw how women "mix promiscuously in gatherings of men" in Paris. "I have ever believed that had there been no queen there would have been no [French]

Revolution," he wrote. When Philadelphia was the capital of the United States, a political cartoon lampooned its politics by personifying it as a transvestite prostitute. Female courtiers were suspected of being capable of ruining a country, both morally and financially, seen at once as too weak and too dangerously powerful, capable of "omnipotent influence," in the words of one founder. They were assumed to make men effete and susceptible. The Adamses were more enlightened; they were less inclined to put women on a pedestal and then shut the door and lock the key, but they were not feminists. Assumptions of Abigail Adams's political power, in fact, tend to be anachronistic. John Adams spoke to her frequently and openly about his work, and he took into account her advice, but she was not the power behind the throne. Nor did she want to be. She did not see herself as effaced by her husband. Believing that her proper place was in the home, she never questioned her supportive role. When Abigail famously told her husband to "remember the ladies," she was not calling for voting rights but for legal protections against abuse, and even then John laughed her off. Abigail did speak her mind about the great political events of the day, and to an extraordinary degree she was a valuable adviser to her husband, but she also made it clear: she was in charge of the children and the chickens, not the capital.

John Quincy did not push his wife to play an active public role in Berlin. Being Abigail Adams's son did not mean that he thought women should move in realms outside the home. In fact, he discouraged his wife. "I knew so little concerning politicks, I seldom heard, and never enquired what was going on," Louisa wrote of her time in Berlin forty years later. "I only knew that it was a period of great events, which I did not understand; and in which I individually took no interest — Mr Adams had always accustomed me to believe, that women had nothing to do with politics; and as he was the glass from which my opinions were reflected, I was convinced of its truth, and sought no farther." All the same, it would help him to have a partner — preferably a much-admired one, one who could dazzle on his behalf — and it would hurt him if she stumbled. So those presentations to the queen and the royal family mattered. She could help unlock doors for him — but a gaffe on her part might keep them both on the outside.

John Quincy did not need to worry. The presentations went off "with more success than could possibly have been anticipated." The members of the court looked over the American minister's wife, with her fragile aspect, her smile, her simple dress, her white satin shoes. They said, *"Elle est jolie."*

That March, 1798, the Adamses moved from the Brandenburg Gate into apartments on Behrenstrasse, around the corner from the palaces lining Unter den Linden, a more fitting address for a diplomat and one far from the soldiers' constant drumbeats. There, Louisa moved between a world in which she was privileged and a world in which she sharply felt her disadvantage. The rent was too high for John Quincy to furnish the place decently — Congress, suspicious of foreign courts, appropriated far less than other countries for the salaries of its ministers plenipotentiary — but he and Louisa managed to gild a few rooms to fool exacting guests. Those who did catch a glimpse of the bare backstage raised their eyebrows. One good friend, Louisa remembered, "taxed us with *meanness.*" In John Quincy's library, some comforts were considered necessaries: a carpet sewn from scraps covered the floor, and the writing desk was built of mahogany. Louisa's chamber was inferior — *"no carpet,"* coarse cotton curtains, and a rough wood table. She kept a plain mirror on the table. When she looked in it and saw her long, pale face and large, dark eyes, she saw a wife, though not a mother. A woman who answered to "your *Excellency*" in palace drawing rooms but who shivered in her own bedroom for want of a fire.

It was not easy to maintain the appearance

of a Princess Royal at balls and a poor republican at home. The counts, bankers, and ambassadors who lived in the neighborhood offered standing invitations to their suppers and parties. Invitations required reciprocation, which was expensive, and sometimes her cook was drunk. The schedule was repetitive, a "tread-mill round of ceremonious heavy etiquette" during the winter season. There were layers upon layers of the court, each with its own rules of custom and deference. Gambling was common, and it was a grave affront to decline a spot at the table. On Mondays she had to go to Prince Henry's, where the "harpies" — fixtures of court life, minor members of the aristocracy bearing titles of various rank and stripe — would descend upon her and lead her to the whist table, where they would pick her purse of the few gold pieces John Quincy had allowed her to carry. On Tuesdays, Thursdays, and Saturdays, she and her husband visited royal advisers, or princesses, or one count or another. Wednesday was reserved for the old king's widow. Fridays offered some relief, when Louisa went to the home of Luise, known as Princess Ferdinand, where the dinners were a little less pretentious, and where Princess Ferdinand's sister, the Landgravine of Hesse-Kassel, "the most elegant woman I ever beheld," made Louisa feel "at *home.*" On Sundays, John Quincy and Louisa joined the company of the king and queen.

She was supposed to dislike being part of the "elegant mob." She and John Quincy had already argued during their engagement, after all, about her impressionability, the lures of luxury, and the corrupting influence of a court. She was wise, then, to bemoan the "almost constant dissipation." And it was true: the treadmill of court parties would become "very irksome." She had to settle into a chair without shoving her hoop into the knee of the prince sitting next to her, and to demurely deny a baron's request that they breakfast in his garden tête-à-tête. She had no choice of where to go, nor what to do once she was there, except when she was sick (and, in fact, she was often sick). If there were games of cards, she played cards. If summoned by royalty, she stepped forward. If she was dismissed, she had to figure out how to walk away without turning her back. It was exhausting, to be out past midnight night after night, rarely in perfect health, and to eat rich meals she did not enjoy. She was not completely lying when she wrote, to satisfy those who suspected her of harboring a fondness for silks and quadrilles, that "these duties were a torment." She grew sick of the quivering joints of meat marbled with fat.

Her frequently poor health gave her a reason and excuse to form real and deep relationships in more intimate places. Away from the court, she learned who her true friends were. She would go to the house of her physician, Charles Brown, a few doors away from her apartment, for suppers of bread and cheese without ceremony. The Browns' house was a refuge, "the resort of all the English foreigners of distinction." It was familiar to her — a glimpse of Britain in Berlin. Charles Brown was Scottish and his wife Welsh. Their children were not so unlike her own siblings, and the family had a hum she would have recognized. There was bookish Margaret; little golden Fanny; William, "very handsome and very wild"; and pretty, sweet Isabella, who worshipped her.

Louisa also spent countless hours at the home of Countess Pauline Neale, who welcomed her into her large circle of intimates. The young women drank tea, half attended to their embroidery, chatted about "the scandal of the town," or amused themselves by "satirizing the vagaries of the court belles, or the follies of the court dowdies, or the prank of the young foreigners." They gossiped about the secret marriage of the queen's sister ("her brute of a husband said to receive all his officers while in bed with her, at five o'clock in the morning, smoking a Meerschaum"); they talked about the *roué* British ambassador, Lord Elgin, who made a deal with Miss Dorville: a pair of diamond earrings in exchange for a very public kiss. On inky winter nights they told ghost stories. Pauline was "highly educated; remarkably well read; enthusiastic in her religion; was full of German mysticism in its most exaggerated sense; and a sincere and true believer," by which Louisa meant she believed in ghosts. It was the age of the great gothic novel, of *The Mysteries of Udolpho,* Friedrich Schiller's *The Ghost-Seer,* Matthew Gregory Lewis's *The Monk,* the novels of E. T. A. Hoffmann, and Mary Shelley's *Frankenstein.* When Louisa heard a story that had "artificial colouring," she could easily dismiss it. "It is good! but it is not life!!!" Stories that were more roughly told, though, could produce "that electric surprise" that made her hair stand up. The "suppressed fear" would send a shudder through her and send her home in a "fever of excitement." No one was better at telling these stories than her best friend. Sometimes Louisa would protest and try to "banter" with Pauline, but the young woman would stop, turn "instantly pale," and glance nervously around, and Louisa's heart would race. "Living in a school like this; sickly and weak both in body and mind," Louisa later wrote, "can you wonder that my mind became tainted, and infected by a weakness, of which I have tried to be ashamed; but which still clings to me as if it was a part of my nature?" And why not? Strange things happened, and even the most well-trained minds were susceptible. The "dread of things unknown," she wrote, "palsies the mind with fear."

While her husband was reading the newly published essays of Immanuel Kant on *Sinnlichkeit* and *Verstand* (and sending the philosopher's works to America), Louisa was forming her own untutored thoughts and doubts about the dichotomy between reason and sensibility. What could "the cold and artificial presumption of what we term reason" do to explain "the mysterious realities of our actual being?"

Her husband was interested in names, dates, countries. His diary teemed with information, carefully noted. Facts never meant that much to her. "As I write without attention to dates many errors will be found in my relation of events as to the exact time of their occurrences," she said in "Record of a Life." The territory that she was curious about, the one she mapped in her memoirs, was different. She was mapping a psychological and emotional landscape.

It was a peculiar education that she was receiving. She saw the world and painted it in high color, but she was also learning to give it structure, shape, and shadows. She was drawn to stories. On evenings when they were at home, she and John Quincy read aloud: Spenser's "The Faerie Queen," Shakespeare, Milton. In his inimitable way, he hatched a plan to read to Louisa "the whole collection of British poets," and began with Chaucer's *The Canterbury Tales.*

The reading was a habit they would keep throughout their life. Louisa and John Quincy grew closer as the months in Berlin passed into years. They took walks in the Tiergarten together, sometimes twice a day. They needed each other more after John Quincy's brother Thomas, who had been a friend to them both, left Berlin to return to the United States in the fall of 1798. "You cannot conceive Mr. Adams's disappointment on opening your letter and finding it directed to me," Louisa wrote to Thomas that October. "*I* was so agreeably surprized that I absolutely kissed it."

Louisa and John Quincy celebrated their first anniversary on July 26, 1798. It came at a difficult time. Louisa lay in bed, suffering through another miscarriage that devastated them both. John Quincy was anxious, worried about money and struggling to defuse the potentially explosive conflict between the United States and France, a conflict that threatened to sink his father's presidency. He felt listless in Berlin. A week later he noted that he had quit studying German and had become "careless about every other study — of what good is it all?"

"The external occurrences of the year have not been fortunate," he wrote in his diary on that first anniversary. For once, though, he acknowledged that there was a brightness in the dark. "But from the loveliness of temper and excellence of character of my wife, I account it the happiest day of my life."

Still, there were differences between them. He could not make up for what she had lost: her parents and siblings. She was separated from the Johnsons not only by four thousand miles but by an emotional breach. Though Louisa later wrote about her family in highly idealized terms, in the years following their separation, while the Johnsons were in Georgetown and she was in Berlin, she was rarely in contact with them. The few letters that were sent and survive sound strained. The distance made correspondence difficult — it could take six months for a letter to arrive. Letters sent by a circuitous route were easily and frequently lost — and Louisa excused herself by claiming how much she hated to write. Still, the silence on both sides says much. The gulf between them was hard to cross. What Louisa did write to them was stilted and perfunctory. She did not — and apparently, at that point, could not — describe much of her life with the animation and observations that would characterize her later prose. Instead, her brief letters were mostly filled with formulaic apologies for the inadequacy of her words. "As I am certain you must be extremely tired of this letter," she wrote in one short letter to Nancy, before bringing it to a quick close. "I am sure you will have the goodness to excuse my inability to write any thing amusing," she wrote to Abigail.

When the rare letters did arrive from Georgetown, they tended to bring her pain. Not long after his arrival in Georgetown, Joshua learned that the settlement with his former business partners would not be what he had counted on. He continued to fight for more money, and the acrimony grew intense. Louisa heard the news in bitter reports. "The letters from America weighed me down with sorrow, and mortification," Louisa later wrote. Her life was now in Berlin, and theirs was now in the United States, a place that she had never even seen. She had found some success; they reported only their difficulties and failures. There was an ocean between them, in more ways than one. At one point, after John Quincy had passed along Delius's accusatory letter regarding Joshua's failure to pay his debts, Catherine sent a furious response, angry at John Quincy's tacit insinuation. Louisa wrote to Nancy that John Quincy's letter had been "misunderstood." "You know Mr. A's manner of writing," she wrote. Those harsh letters she had received during her courtship had been shared throughout the family. "I am now fully convinced [they] were never intended to give me a moment's pain." She knew how that letter would read, even as tentative as it was: as taking her husband's side over her parents'. Soon after, she wrote a panicked letter trying to take her words back — as if even the slightest defense of her husband had been a betrayal of her family. She was caught between them.

And there was that old and pernicious problem: John Quincy's suspicion that she would be corrupted by the glamorous court. She claimed to have hated the extravagance and expense, the hollowness of the aristocracy, but her exhilarated descriptions of it undercut her complaints. The princesses and barons flattered her, and she enjoyed being flattered. It pleased her to say that she was *"respected";* she underscored the word. And she was "extravagantly fond" of dancing. At her first ball, John Quincy joined the noblemen and left his young wife to fend for herself. But his playful younger brother Thomas led her onto the floor for an English country dance. "Strangers were forgotten and he danced so well and with so much spirit," she remembered, "I was quite delighted." Prince Radziwill appeared before her to ask for a dance, and Prince Wittgenstein followed, and on and on, until suddenly it was two in the morning. "I became a *Belle.*"

Her success at court was reported back to John and Abigail Adams as flattering to the

United States and not to herself. "She is neither dazzled by the splendor nor captivated by the gaiety of the scene in which she finds herself placed," John Quincy reassured his mother. That was true to an extent — she could laugh at anything, including herself — but not quite true enough for her to escape trouble. There was, for instance, the matter of rouge.

The conflict arose when the king wanted to open a ball by dancing with her. She had planned to decline all dances that evening — she had worn a long train to signal her intent — but when Countess von Voss, the queen's *grande gouvernante,* appeared in front of her to announce the king's desire, she knew she had no choice but to stand up, gather her dress, and take her place on the floor across from King Frederick William. She nearly fainted under the hot spotlight of attention. The queen saw the blood drain from Louisa's face, looked at her kindly, and spoke to her with concern. To put her at ease, she told Louisa that she would give her a present to help her hide her nerves: a box of rouge. In the United States, "paint" was associated with the debauchery of brothels and — not incidentally — European courts. It suggested the sins of Versailles. (Of course, even a quick glance at portraits from than the pious sermons allowed.) Louisa knew that John Quincy would never let her accept it, and so she protested. But the queen was persistent. "She smiled at my simplicity, and observed that if *she* presented me the box he must not refuse it, and told me to tell him so." Before Louisa could say anything more, the dance began. Louisa was elated when she returned to her chair alongside the visiting British Prince Augustus and his suite after the dance was done. The prince and his companions, her "accustomed *partners*," flattered her with "encouraging" attention and smiles, exclaiming over "the marked distinction" that the king had shown her and complaining that she had accepted him when she had already turned them down. But her husband was unhappy about the promise of the rouge.

The gift arrived, and she hid it away. But one day she felt particularly pale. It was Carnival, which meant masked balls. The custom was for a woman to wear a black dress with deep décolletage, a black Spanish hat, black shoes, and black feathers — a stunning look if you could offset the dark cloth with flush cheeks and the glitter of diamonds but a difficult look if you couldn't. Knowing that the black dresses made pale faces "look cadaverous," and tired of feeling "a *fright* in the midst of the splendor," Louisa brought out the forbidden rouge. When it was time to leave for the ball, she rushed past her husband, calling to him behind her to put out the lights. He sensed something suspicious in her quick step and stopped her before she went down the stairs. When he saw the blush on her cheeks, he led her to the table and sat her on his knee. He picked up a towel, "and all my beauty was clean washed a way."

All was forgiven, for a time. "A kiss made the peace" between them, and they drove off to the party. But all was not really forgotten. John Quincy did not need to ask himself what John and Abigail Adams would have thought about the queen's present to Louisa, or her succession of "princely partners," or the invitations to the visiting sons of the tyrant King George III to their house for boisterous meals. Unlike Louisa, he was not pleased when she was "the only foreign lady" offered a part in a quadrille at court. When he learned that the quadrille depicted the marriage of Queen Mary and Philip of Spain, and that it required six weeks of rehearsals, and that performers made liberal use of crown jewels, and that costume painters studied paintings from the era to create the most accurate costumes possible (perhaps snipping off the stitches here and there — "the ladies could not adopt the dress of that period so far as to cover their bosoms," John Quincy sniffed in his diary), he told Louisa to decline the invitation. She was told to say she was sick. He needed her to be admired but not adored. She had to fit in but could never belong.

3

At the start of 1799, illness was a credible excuse. She was often sick. Reports of her illnesses, often unnamed in nature, appear again and again in letters and John Quincy's diary. From the regularity of them, it seems she may have suffered from debilitating menstrual cycles. But there was sometimes another cause: she was often pregnant. Almost immediately after recovering from her miscarriage at the end of 1797, she believed she was pregnant, but in February their hopes were "severely dashed to the ground." She was certainly pregnant in March. Her body reacted violently to the change; she was often sick through the night and into morning. Before long, she was showing signs that she would lose the child. "My prophetic heart! I have no doubt of the cause," John Quincy wrote in his diary. "The cup of bitterness must be filled to the brim and drank to the dregs." In July, he wrote of despair: "I cannot even form an hope with impunity." His anguish was palpable. "The tortures of Tantalus have been inflicted upon me without ceasing."

The exact number of Louisa's miscarriages is impossible to know. John Quincy and Louisa, in keeping with custom, were circumspect about her pregnancies. In their writings and letters, they usually referred to pregnancy as an "illness" and made only opaque hints about her condition. There may have also been times when she thought she was pregnant and turned out not to be. But it appears likely that she miscarried four times between 1797 and 1800. Discharging the fetus was brutally painful for her, often taking several days unless a doctor intervened, and that was perhaps more traumatic. She complained of being "roughly handled." She lost dangerous amounts of blood. Doctors could do little for her; medicine in those days was less a science than an art. After a young man dropped dead at a ball, for instance, doctors concluded that "his death was owing to the excessive tightness of his clothes, and perhaps to his having drank several glasses of cold limonade, while heated with dancing," John Quincy wrote in his diary. When she was ill or pregnant, doctors plied her with powders, emetics, and laudanum; they bled and blistered her. No doubt the remedies further damaged her health.

Her body baffled her and others. Along

with the complications from pregnancy, she suffered from headaches, influenza, fainting spells, and other vaguely described ailments. Dr. Brown thought her "in a deep consumption." She was almost surely anemic. The frequency with which she was bled by doctors didn't help. It's no wonder that she wanted to wear rouge and became obsessed with her pallor.

It wasn't only her body, though, that perplexed Louisa. She could never untangle the connection between her physical ailments and her mind. The discourse about diseases around 1800 made much of the disturbance of nerves. Even where the etiology of an illness was known, emotional and mental stress were thought to play a part — especially in women. Louisa was convinced that the slightest agitation would send devastating tremors through her body that would leave her pitched and prostrate. A distressing sight or overstimulation could make her fall ill. "From eight o'clock in the evening until midnight she had a continual succession of fainting fits, and cramps almost amounting to convulsion," John Quincy wrote in his diary after Louisa came home and fell ill after helping a woman who had broken a leg.

When it came to the miscarriages, of course, her emotional pain was as bad as the physical trauma. John Quincy felt it too, and showed it — which only made her feel worse.

Every hope was a harbinger of disappointment.

April 27, 1798
Mrs. Adams went with Mrs. Brown to Charlottenburg in the morning. Was taken unwell in the afternoon. It is of no use, but rather a misfortune to foresee evils which can neither be remedied nor prevented.

July 17, 1798
A dreadful night. Mrs. A. soon after going to bed was taken extremely ill, and between 12 and 1 o'clock was in such extreme pain, that I sent for Doctor Ribke. He was at Charlottenburg. So was Dr. Brown. [. . .] The case appears in almost every point similar to that of last November. Patience and resignation is all that we can have. Was up all night.

December 1799
Monthly Summary
The year would in general have been a pleasant one, but for the state of my wife's health which has been almost continually bad, and concerning which I am even now deeply concerned. The subject presses upon my spirits more than I can express.

My wife's health is now the object of my greatest concern.

After yet another one of Louisa's prolonged illnesses, they spent the summer of 1800 traveling throughout Silesia, an area in central Europe (mostly in what is now Poland). They had taken a similar trip, to the baths in Töplitz, to help her recover from a debilitating miscarriage in the summer of 1799, after John Quincy completed the renewal of the commercial treaty between the United States and Prussia. They spent their days wandering through the art galleries in Dresden, visited with friends from Berlin who crossed their path, and, when Louisa was strong enough, took long hikes. They visited textile mills, hiked in the mountains, and carved their names in the walls of a ruined castle. They studied a moving model of the solar system at a weaver's workshop, and at a carpenter's, they were moved to tears by an ingenious puppet show. They went to glassworks in Bohemia, coal mines in Walenberg, the theater everywhere. In Silesia, they bought three sketches of the picturesque countryside, which they later kept hung in their bedroom — three small but transporting reminders of their time there together. She benefited from the fresh air, simple food, and good exercise to a degree that startled John Quincy. "It would astonish you, as it does me, to see how she supports the fatigues of this journey," wrote John Quincy to his brother. One difficult hike that she completed, he continued, "is considered as so much beyond the strength even of the strongest women, that our guide, who has followed this business these twelve years, assured me he had never conducted but one lady before upon this tour." On the trips to both Silesia and Töplitz, she became pregnant again: despite the danger to her health (she'd miscarried after Töplitz), their sexual attraction clearly had not waned.

He was tender with Louisa, and she felt it. Still, there were distances between Louisa and John Quincy that were difficult to bridge. She wanted to be needed; he wanted to be alone. She could be flighty. He could be intransigent or remote. She had once called herself "the spoilt child of indulgence." He had been schooled by his parents in stoicism — although his strong feelings sometimes forced open a vent, with eruptions of anger and frustration.

She bore the burden of his frustration and felt the blowback of his stormy moods. At times, a sense of futility tortured John Quincy. From a distance, he watched his father's presidency founder. He also missed his parents; he missed his brother after Thomas had returned to the United States. Louisa told Thomas that the sound of his name brought tears to John Quincy's eyes. It was not easy to be an Adams, gifted to America from birth, then sent into the world for the sake of America. In February 1801, John Quincy learned that his brother Charles had died at the age of thirty, probably of cirrhosis from alcoholism, after years of trouble. He had stopped responding to John Quincy's letters, which were increasingly curt and frustrated inquiries about his investments. The two brothers had lived apart for most of their lives, and John Quincy had not seen him for seven years.

He heard the news of Charles's death the first week of February 1801, within twenty-four hours of learning that Thomas Jefferson had defeated John Adams in the presidential election of 1800. The effects on John Quincy's own life were inevitably profound. He would be recalled from Europe; any political prospects he had were likely over; worst, his brother was dead. But in his first letter to his mother — he waited until March 10 to write — he tersely expressed his grief at Charles's death and his father's defeat, then moved on. "Political disappointment is perhaps one of the occasions in human life which requires the greatest portion of philosophy," he wrote to Abigail; "although philosophy has very little power to assuage the keenness of our feelings, she has at least the power to silence the voice of complaint." Then he turned to foreign affairs. "The North of Europe, and the views, interests, and relations of the several states it contains, are indeed becoming an object of no small concern to our commerce," he continued. His diary shows signs of a great struggle to manage his sadness — long walks at the park, excuses sent to parties, days at home. "In the evening read the first canto of Savage's *Wanderer,*" he wrote a few days after hearing of his brother's death and father's loss to Jefferson. It was, he wrote, "a poem the object of which is to prove that 'the sons of men may owe / The fruits of bliss to bursting clouds of woe.' "

He was already preparing himself for his recall to the United States and a return to private life when he wrote that. In Berlin, his primary task, the renegotiation of the commercial treaty, was done, completed in the summer of 1799. He had been able to use his vantage point to advise the American minister to France, his friend William Vans Murray, and his father, the president, on the perilous situation between the United States and France, helping to avert war. He had time to take his walks, to learn German, to translate *Oberon.* He sometimes despaired of what his future would be when he returned to the United States and resumed a life of drudgery as a lawyer. He was not suited for the law, he admitted, but he had no choice. He had a wife to support. And he could not be sure that he had been right in telling his mother that his wife was uncorrupted by a royal court.

There were signs that there would be trouble between them when they went to the United States. She had made a home for herself in Berlin; he tried, ungently, to remind her that his home was very different. That winter, 1801, Louisa had tried to wear the rouge again. This time, instead of trying to sneak past her husband, "I walked boldly forward to meet Mr. Adams." John Quincy told her to wash the makeup off, and she refused "with some temper." He turned on his heels, went down to the carriage, and left for the party without her. She cried "with vexation" for a few minutes, took off her gown, washed off the rouge, put on something simple, and went over to the Browns' for the evening. By the time her husband picked her up, she was smiling, and the two were "as good friends as ever," she later wrote. In 1801, "anger seldom lasted with me more than ten minutes, and once over all was forgotten" — or almost, since, writing nearly forty years later, the scene and its humiliations were still fresh in her mind.

It was only a little makeup. Behind it, though, was a serious issue. It had to do with the queen. John Quincy could respect the king well enough, because the king was trying to remain neutral between France, Great Britain, Russia, and Austria, and because the king rose at six in the morning and famously disliked parties. But the queen made him uneasy. She had a frank willingness to command. She was a queen, and a forceful one. She tried to command even him, the republican. "If *she* presented me the box he must not refuse it," she had told Louisa. It was a royal order he could not stand.

Six years later, the Prussian army was crushed by Napoleon at Jena. When Queen Luise went herself to make a personal appeal to the emperor, she was mocked: Napoleon responded to her pleas for mercy on behalf of her country by inquiring about the fabric of her dress. John Quincy read the reports of the conflict and took some pleasure in her fate. "The vicissitudes of the world have reached many of our old acquaintance there," John Quincy wrote to Louisa, thoughtlessly — or pointedly — telling her the news of Prussia's defeat, "and the beautiful and thoughtless queen whom we were accustomed to see so splendid has been brought to dance something less delicious and more vivid than a waltz."

Queen Luise was and would remain an angel in Louisa's mind, whatever John Quincy thought. But it was another woman who exerted an even more powerful influence upon her, a woman who had the kind of fascinating attraction Louisa was drawn to throughout her life. In 1800, a new British ambassador, Lord Carysfort, arrived in Berlin, and he brought with him his wife. Elizabeth Carysfort was a forceful, even dazzling figure. It was Louisa's opinion, at least, that Lady Elizabeth Carysfort "did most of the diplomacy" on behalf of her husband, and even John Quincy, who was not inclined to compliment anyone's intelligence too highly (let alone a woman's), was impressed by Elizabeth's mind. Lady Carysfort was, John Quincy wrote to his brother, "a woman of a remarkable fine understanding." Educated like her brothers (one of whom was Lord William Grenville, Britain's foreign secretary), she was, Louisa wrote, "one of the finest women I ever knew — of very superior mind and cultivation." This was a fault, even as it was a strength. In the same breath, Louisa betrayed her sense of conflict. She wrote that Elizabeth was "very plain in her person; somewhat masculine in her manners," and she had a tendency to make other women "timid and afraid."

Louisa was drawn to such "masculine" women (her teacher Miss Young had been another), even though she believed that she should be repelled. And they were drawn to her. However Louisa described their gender, what these women seem to have offered her was a kind of mothering. Lady Carysfort "took a fancy to me," and in return Louisa loved the older woman "as if she were my own mother." Louisa would visit Elizabeth in her boudoir, "a sort of sanctum sanctorum," where the British ambassador's wife would talk about books, her thoughts for the future, death, and how her faith in God wavered. "Here she sometimes gave way to her private sorrows — and here only she could talk to me of her private history; of her afflictions; of her own peculiar opinions; both religious and literary," Louisa wrote.

This idea that a woman's "private history" might have value, that she might have a rich inner life shaped by deep emotions, strong beliefs, and personally formed opinions, was crucial. When she was older, it would mean more to her, but the seed was planted when she was young. And her time with Lady Carysfort helped her in a more immediate sense. It gave her strength. At the start of 1801, she needed it. She was pregnant again.

She and John Quincy hardly let themselves hope, not even writing to their parents about the possibility of a child. Lady Carysfort refused to let Louisa submit herself to her anxiety. Instead of letting her lie on her sofa, weak and reclining, Lady Carysfort would appear at her door and demand that they go riding. She would send an invitation for dinner and refuse to take no for an answer. And so Louisa rode out into the bracing air, or spent evenings in *"a perfect gale"* of laughter while sitting next to some "German lump of obesity," or listening to the king of England's son play the piano while a Frenchwoman sang "God Save the King."

In mid-April, Louisa entered her confinement. The king, she later said, ordered the street outside the Adamses' apartment blocked, so that the clatter of traffic would not disturb her. On April 12, she went into labor. The pain was intense, the German male midwife drunk, and Louisa's left leg temporarily crippled. But a son was born, breathing. They named him George Washington Adams.

A high fever gripped Louisa after the delivery. Puerperal fevers were common; doctors, drunk or sober, were not always in the habit of washing their hands. John Quincy was anguished and scared. When he wrote to tell his mother about the birth of her grandson, he added that he was waiting a few days to tell Catherine Johnson: he was afraid to write immediately, since he might have to follow the good news with a letter saying that her daughter was dead. But his responsibilities to his country remained foremost in his mind. Two weeks after the child was born, John Quincy received his recall to the United

States, and he wanted to leave without delay. One of John Adams's last acts as president had been to summon his son home. On the day John Quincy received his recall, Louisa, who had been slowly improving in health, was "continually seized" with "sudden faintings." John Quincy despairingly wrote in his diary that she was "immovable," unable even to shift from one side of her bed to the other. She lay there for weeks, her baby suckling one breast while a borrowed infant nursed the other, since Dr. Brown feared that excess milk would spread her fever to her brain.

But she could not convalesce forever — however much some part of her, consciously or not, might have wanted to remain right where she was. John Quincy prepared to leave Berlin at the earliest possible chance. There was not even time to wait for the child to be vaccinated by traditional methods; a faster, experimental one was done instead. By the time Louisa managed to limp across the room with assistance, arrangements had been made to sail to the United States. She still could not climb the stairs. On June 17, she was lifted into a carriage, and she, John Quincy, their son, and their two servants, Whitcomb and Epps, left Berlin. Saying goodbye, she cried "bitter tears."

The son she held in her arms was her solace. What she thought of his name is unknown. Perhaps it was a chance to prove her American patriotism. Perhaps she was just glad that the name was not an Adams name, that it was not John. (Presumably, the disgraced Joshua was not an option.) Perhaps she didn't care. What mattered was the existence of the child in her arms. It was her triumph, the redemption of what she saw as her failures so far. "I was a *Mother,*" she wrote.

They went first to Hamburg, where, on July 8, they boarded a ship. It was called the *America.* Its deck was as close to America as Louisa had ever been.

■ ■ ■ ■

PART THREE:
MY HEAD AND
MY HEART

Washington and Massachusetts, 1801–1809

■ ■ ■ ■

1

The *America* floated into the harbor of Philadelphia on September 4, and John Quincy's brother Thomas stood on the dock to meet it. When he caught sight of the travelers disembarking, he was shocked to see Louisa, his dear friend, still fragile and limping after her difficult delivery of George followed by two months at sea. The evident distress on Thomas's face at the sight of her made her self-conscious. She was uncertain of the ground beneath her feet, about to see the country she was supposed to consider her home, and painfully aware of how she looked after the taxing voyage.

The prospect of other reunions stood before her. She would be reunited with her parents and siblings for the first time since their sudden flight. It had been four years, almost exactly, since the night Louisa's family had left her at the Adelphi Hotel in London; four years since her "beloved father" had given her a "worse than broken-hearted look" and then fled. In that time, Nancy had married Walter Hellen and had a child. Her brother, Thomas, a schoolboy when she'd seen him last, was already practicing law. Even the youngest, little Adelaide, who had been eight when Louisa last saw her in 1797, was no longer quite a child. She would also meet John Quincy's family, which loomed so large in his life. And she would be judged, scrutinized, compared to others. She was already doing it to herself. In "The Adventures of a Nobody," she would remember that trip as the time when John Quincy told her — in some detail — about his thwarted love for Mary Frazier. The "elaborate but just account which I heard of her extreme beauty; her great attainments; the elegance of her letters; altogether made me feel *little,*" she later wrote.

But the city of Philadelphia, despite an intense late-summer heat wave, revived her. The former capital had a tidy, reassuring appearance: two miles of wharfs crowded with ships and shallops, a forest of masts with furled topgallants; neat brick buildings flush against the foot-walks and tidy streets; the optimistic edifices of the State House and Carpenters' Hall; shops displaying familiar French brandy and French shoes; gentle gardens. During a week spent in the city, she grew physically stronger and more confident, despite round after round of introductions, dinners, and excursions. But the day before she was supposed to head south to see her parents and John Quincy was to head north to his, she fell ill. In his diary, John Quincy attributed her illness to the weather — it was a drop in the temperature, he wrote, that brought it on. It's likely that there was another factor, one that he would not have wanted to acknowledge: Louisa and John Quincy would be separated for the first time since their marriage, and Louisa would have to face her family, which had been through so much that pained her, without him. She wanted him to come. Despite her cough, they followed his plan and went separate ways, he to Quincy and she to Washington.

She was not alone. Her baby, George, and their servants Elizabeth Epps and Tilly Whitcomb, were with her. Still, she felt abandoned, lost, and confused in the country that she'd been instructed to consider her home. The trip was "tedious and dangerous." Aboard a series of stages, she passed through a landscape that invited brooding: dense, dark forests and scrubby fields, past shacks and shanties, past slaves working in succulent tobacco fields, through overgrown forests and barren stretches of land, empty but for the clouds of insects humming sawtoothed songs. They reached the Chesapeake Bay and drove into Maryland, that mythical place in her father's stories. But her reflections on the reality of what she saw were curt and unhappy. She was, she described herself, "a forlorn stranger in the land of my Fathers."

They crossed the limits of the Federal City, though it would have been hard to notice; the wild landscape hardly changed. Oaks and pines, dusty turnpikes and cratered roads, muddy creeks and churning rivers; a few scattered clusters of dwellings amid broken plaster, kilns, and weedy fields were all that existed. They passed the two wings of the headless Capitol and the President's House, which John Quincy's parents had so unhappily inhabited. They passed little clusters of boardinghouses where members of Congress sat in their smoke-filled messes, divided into fractious camps. "Mrs. Adams is going to a place different from all she has ever yet visited, and amongst a people where it will be impossible for her to be too gaurded," Abigail warned her son the day after Louisa had left Philadelphia. "Every syllable she utters will be scaned not with loss of candour, but carping malice; such is the spirit of party."

The spirit of party — in those days, the United States *were,* not *was,* and the collective was riven, as men tried to work out the mechanics of power. Their ideals of harmony ran up against the realities of personal ambition, divergent interests, distrust, and differing ideologies. Louisa would not be able to escape the nasty business of gossip and intrigue even at home. Georgetown, where the Johnsons lived, was a small outcropping of civilization on an escarpment above the Potomac — but it was hardly a place of civility. Joshua's troubles had followed him from London. The fight with his partners had become public — as Louisa had dreaded — and his debts were now known. "I doubt not she will be prudent," Abigail continued to John Quincy, "but her family have been very basely traduced."

Did Louisa know the details of her father's financial situation? It would have been impossible to remain entirely ignorant of his reputation: the gangrene of gossip had spread. Joshua Johnson couldn't have hidden much anyway. He was doing everything he could to search for money to pay off his debts. He was suing the widow of one of his former partners; he was being sued by his creditors in courts in both Britain and the United States; he was in a fight over ownership of land in Georgia; he was suing Wallace and Muir. Wallace and Muir were circulating a handbill defending themselves against his attacks. As a final blow, President Thomas Jefferson had removed Joshua from his post as superintendent of stamps, which deprived him of a $2,000 salary. (In fact, Joshua owed the post to Jefferson in the first place; the vice president had cast the deciding vote for his confirmation in a deadlocked Senate.) The removal was simply a part of the sweeping changes Jefferson was making in the federal government, but the Johnsons took it personally. However much Louisa knew, she knew enough to be angry and ashamed. "Your father . . . is obliged to sue every man to realize one shilling," Catherine had written to her in Berlin. "Such is the honor of honesty of this part of the world."

When Louisa arrived at the house in Washington, Joshua was standing on the steps waiting for her. His appearance shocked her. His handsome looks were gone; pain lined his face. She assumed that her own worn, wretched appearance was the cause of it. "He kept exclaiming that 'he did not know his own child,' " she would remember. But really, he was the one who was altered. Once, a portrait painter had depicted him wearing an immaculate lace cravat, holding a stack of papers, with a gleaming stylus, ink pot, and little handbell by his side; smiling slightly, giving him an enigmatic knowingness — a man of business, a man of purpose. Now he appeared broken. Only the baby George and his other infant grandson, Johnson, could make him smile.

The morning after her arrival, Louisa woke with a high fever. The doctor declared that she had to wean the child, which she did "with great bodily suffering," submitting herself to the care of her mother and sisters.

It was a relief to be back among her family, but it was also awkward. They had expected her husband to come down to Washington in order to accompany her to Quincy. She did not tell them that he expected her to make the journey alone.

She tried to lure him south, stressing how much she liked Washington, and how it was "very well worth coming to see." "I am quite delighted with the situation of this place," she wrote when she arrived, "and I think should it ever be finished" — here she hedged — "it will be one of the most beautiful spots in the world." Repeatedly, she pressed her purpose. "I only want you here to be completely happy," she wrote three times in two weeks. She wanted him to come, and she wanted them to stay in Washington.

He responded to her first desire, at least, right away. How much he missed her, and in different ways, is clear. "Our dear George — how I long to kiss even *his* slavering lips!" he wrote in one. "As for those of his mother I say nothing. Let her consult my heart in her own and all that pen can write or language express will shrink to nothing." He had not seen his own parents since leaving the United States in 1794, and in his absence his parents had suffered painful losses. It was natural that he would be eager to see them upon his return. But no sooner did he arrive in Quincy than he agreed to leave. He took a fast route, riding "the whole night through," and arriving in a week, on October 21. His plan was to turn around almost immediately. Winter was coming; the roads would become dangerous. But politics drew him in, even though, after his father's defeat, he'd called it a dirty business. He went to dinners and meetings, connected with his contacts, with congressmen, Cabinet members, the president. "He has no propensity to engage in a political career," his brother Thomas had reassured their mother, Abigail, after seeing him in Philadelphia. Anyone watching him move through Washington, visiting all the right people, might have heard that and laughed.

Louisa was in no hurry to leave either. On October 30, the day before their planned departure, Louisa "caught a violent cold," pushing back their departure by several days. But she couldn't delay it forever. Finally they set out, traveling in a large group: Louisa, John Quincy, George, Elizabeth Epps, and Tilly Whitcomb, along with Louisa's parents and three younger sisters, who accompanied them as far as Frederick, Maryland.

They had only just left Washington when Joshua fell ill, in pain "of more excessive violence than I have ever witnessed," John Quincy wrote in his diary. As soon as Joshua could be moved — the attack appears to have been kidney stones — the group made its way to Rose Hill, the large estate where his brother Thomas Johnson lived. Thomas's reputation and fortunes were as good as Joshua's were bad. He had been the one to nominate George Washington as commander in chief of the Continental Army. He had been the first Revolutionary governor of Maryland. He had served as a judge on the U.S. Supreme Court. Through his friendship with Thomas Jefferson and John Adams, and because of their mutual regard for him, he had been an important link between the North and South. He had also been an investor and (sometimes critical) adviser in some of Joshua's business ventures. Joshua had always written to him in a deferential, even nervous tone. The lively "little old man with sharp bright gray eyes" gently took in his ailing brother. The prodigal had come home to die.

Before that day would come, but with it looming, Louisa would have to leave him. Winter was fast approaching, and the journey to Quincy was growing more difficult with each passing day. After a week by her father's bedside, Louisa was pulled away, not even allowed to say goodbye for fear of upsetting them both. The reduced group traveled at a relentless speed to make up for lost time, twice setting out on the road at two a.m. They would push onward until Louisa or the child could go no farther. They had to stop to rest. "It is I find, utterly impossible, travelling with such a family, to fix a day when I can expect to reach any given place," John Quincy wrote to his mother.

He thought the group was dragging; she thought they moved at a punishing pace. George, teething, was "constantly shrieking," and suffering from diarrhea. The turnpike was rough and jarring. The stagecoach was crowded with strangers. In Philadelphia, Louisa fell ill, had a day to rest, and then rose to move out before dawn. In New Jersey the roads were slowed by drenching rains. The Hudson was rough with storm, the boat to cross it open and flat-bottomed. Louisa shivered in her thin, lace-trimmed, blue satin pelisse.

No carriage was there to meet them on the far shore. They had no umbrella or roof to keep them dry. When they reached the house of John Quincy's sister Nabby in New York, Louisa collapsed. "More depressed in her spirits than really ill," John Quincy wrote in his diary. As they traveled north, the rain turned to snow. They reached Boston on November 24, missing the day's last stagecoach to Quincy. After breakfast the following morning, in cold, clear weather, they took their final stage, traveling south along the edge of the steely bay, to the Adamses' house. In Louisa's eyes, everything was strange and grim.

2

"Quincy! What shall I say of my impressions of Quincy!" Louisa wrote in "The Adventures of a Nobody." "Had I stepped into Noah's Ark, I do not think I could have been more utterly astonished." November in Quincy was a month of black bark, brambles, and dead leaves, of mossy weather and low, smoky skies. The day after their arrival was Thanksgiving. Everything about it was strange and astonishing — the holiday itself, the church, the congregation. With her Anglican sensibility, she found the place bleak, the singing plain, and the people appallingly "snuffling through the nose." She remained quiet, feeling "so much depressed, and so ill," which she'd later think a blessing, because otherwise she would "certainly have given mortal offense."

Writing in 1840, she painted herself as naive. It was as if the United States were her first foreign land and not the fourth country in which she had lived. It was as if she had never met a stranger until she arrived in Quincy. It was as if she'd never submitted to an unfamiliar custom until she had to sit through church (or "meeting," a term that sounded odd to her). It was as if no one had ever looked at her curiously until the relics of John Quincy's childhood peered at her. "Dr. Tufts!" she wrote. "Deacon French! Mr Cranch! Old Uncle Peter! and Capt Beale!!!" She had already lived in three countries, but she had never felt herself as much a foreigner as she was in her husband's hometown.

The shock she felt when she arrived at the Adamses' house was real, common, and comic: she was meeting her in-laws. She saw in them what she wanted to see, and they saw in her what they wanted too. Where another woman might have looked around the Adamses' clapboard mansion and seen the English cut-glass candelabras, Louis XV chairs, and a Chippendale-style sofa, Louisa saw a farm. Where another woman might have looked at Abigail and seen a woman who had lived in Paris and London, who had charmed generals and dignitaries, she saw a thin-lipped woman who boasted about waking at five to milk the cows. For her part, Abigail wasn't more charitable. The mother-in-law regarded the young woman with a critical eye. Quincy women didn't wear satin coats in the cold rain. Louisa saw the gaze, felt the judgment, and saw herself as someone who was set apart. John Adams took "a fancy to me," she wrote pointedly in "Adventures," but "he was the only one."

The person who unsettled her most was Abigail Adams — the matriarch, the authority, the *real* Mrs. Adams. Abigail had planned a special welcome for Louisa. The newcomer was given a separate dish at dinner. "Every delicate preserve" was offered to her alone, every kind attention paid. Louisa responded to the attention mutely, which appeared to others as ingratitude, though it sprang from shame. She was too aware that the special treatment "appeared so strongly to stamp me with unfitness," Louisa wrote.

No doubt Abigail intended well. She was determined to accept her son's wife, as she had already accepted the others in the Johnson family — writing them often, inviting them to visit in Philadelphia, welcoming Louisa's brother Thomas for dinner when he was at Harvard, lobbying for Joshua to get a government job, and showing the whole family unstinting generosity. But she had also seen them in London, and had observed the way they lived: the servants, the paintings, the harp. She damned Catherine with her praise, calling her "conspicuous" for her "taste of elegance." Abigail had a hard time overcoming her early and instinctive aversion to Louisa. From the start, she had imagined Louisa as a flighty, spoiled, sickly, English child, a half-blood siren not made of the right stuff to be her son's wife. Even before seeing her, Abigail fretted about how caring for a "poor, weak and feeble wife and boy" would affect her John Quincy. Although she called Charles's widow "Sally" and the woman Thomas would marry "Nancy," she called Louisa "Mrs. Adams" — except when she referred to her as *"Madam."*

Abigail heard her daughter-in-law's hacking cough and looked at her thin pale frame, her delicate wrists, and her large, grief-worn eyes, and predicted to Thomas that Louisa would probably soon die: "I have many fears that she will be of short duration." Then she added that John Quincy's "helpless family" was a terrible burden to him. "The constant state of anxiety which has harassed his mind upon her account," she wrote, "has added a weight of years to his Brow, which time alone could not have effected in double the space."

But this, as unfair as it was, accounts for only half the story. Louisa did not make her acceptance easy. She was as determined not to adapt to Quincy as Abigail was to prove her unfitness. If Abigail was unsympathetic, then so was Louisa. Abigail, after all, was not as one-dimensional as Louisa made her out to be. The wife of John Adams had lived in Paris and London, had charmed every kind of statesman. She was proud, even aristocratic, a woman who had ordered the Quincy coat of arms painted on her carriage when she went to New York. Abigail was also, in the fall of 1801, suffering, which Louisa seems not to have seen. Louisa arrived in Quincy at a difficult time. John Adams had been humiliated during the presidential election of 1800, repudiated not only for his politics but — as a pamphlet by Alexander Hamilton too thoroughly spelled out — for his vanity, splenetic temper, jealousy, and incapacity. The Adamses had retreated to Quincy shamed by failure and furious with the country. Greater misfortunes, which they could hardly bear to speak of, followed them home. Charles had died only the previous winter. His parents had watched his decline with anger and overwhelming anguish. To John Adams, Charles was "a mere rake, buck, blood and beast . . . I renounce him." Abigail wrote to John Quincy about her eldest son with unreserved anguish. Charles wasn't the only source of deep grief. At just the moment Charles had died, Abigail had learned that her daughter Nabby's husband, William Smith, had abandoned her on a farm in upstate New York. Now her prized son, her hope for the nation, appeared with a wife as pale and fragile as porcelain.

So there was a chasm between them, and neither of the women helped the other cross it — or made much of a meaningful attempt herself. "I longed for my home, with an impatience that made me completely dis-agreeable," Louisa later wrote. "In short I was in every respect any thing but what I should have been."

Relief came when John Quincy and Louisa left the elder Adamses' home, Peacefield, and moved into a house on Hanover Street in Boston just before Christmas 1801. But that relief was short-lived. No sooner had Louisa begun to settle in than she realized that she had no idea how to run a New England household.

Everything seemed to go wrong all at once. She was expected by tradition to handle the household accounts, but she could not match John Quincy's exacting standards. He counted the cents in her purse, let her know that shopkeepers viewed her as an easy mark, and resumed control of the books himself. She was expected to manage the laundry, the stove, the huge copper pots, but her experi-ence had been largely limited to baking cakes under the watchful eye of the Johnsons' cook and learning how to manage a team of servants. In America, she found that she was expected to "*work* as they call it" — not hid-ing well her disdain. Growing up, "work" had meant embroidery. A wife was expected to pick up where a mother left off, but what had her mother taught her? Her mother had taught her how to instruct the maids, how to charm a parlor, how to dance. Where, Louisa wondered, was she supposed to have learned to milk a cow? On Tower Hill in London? At the whist table in the Prussian court? In Berlin, Louisa lived less luxuriously than those she socialized with, but she still had servants and a cook, and John Quincy and Whitcomb had controlled the accounts. "The qualifications necessary to form an accomplished Quincy Lady, were in direct opposition to the mode of life which I had led — and I soon felt, that even my husband would acknowledge my deficiency, and that I should lose most of my value in his eyes."

She heard the way other women talked, saw how they acted, and watched how they taught their daughters. Her self-assessment wasn't absurdly harsh. Running the household was considered to be not only a New England wife's responsibility but also her divinely ordained role. Even women who studied political debates, managed money under their control, and were not shy about speaking their minds were convinced that their domain was their household, and that their domestic role was intended that way by God. It was a matter, they thought, of biology and theology. Most women accepted it; they assumed that a flower does not wish to be a bee. Abigail herself succinctly and uncomplainingly described the dominant view: "I consider it as an indispensable requisite that every

American wife should herself know how to order and regulate her family; how to govern her domestics, and train up her children," Abigail wrote to her sister in 1809. "For this purpose, the all-wise Creator made woman an help-meet for man, and she who fails in these duties does not answer the end of her creation."

For the most part, New England women did not complain about their positions. They did not consider their work trivial or degrading. They may have found themselves, when circumstances required, with expanded responsibilities, but they did not argue for alternatives to their traditional positions; they did not push to become lawyers or doctors or presidents. The role they played was important, not only within the family but in the republic. They were considered the protectors and promoters of virtue, the first educators, the paragons of the values on which the republic was based. So when Louisa bungled the accounts, or came home from shopping and was shown to have been cheated, or when she burned the cakes and spoiled the meat, her shame ran deep. She did not rebel against the conclusion that she was failing in the only role that she had been given the opportunity to fill. "Accommodation to her husband," Catherine Johnson had written Louisa, "is the only basis on which we women ought to build."

Louisa tried, but she could not be "useful." "I hourly betrayed my incapacity," she later wrote. Abigail tried to teach her, but Louisa was an inept student, which only made her more insecure — and in turn more hopeless in her tasks. To Abigail, "equal to every occasion in life; I appeared like a maudlin hysterical fine lady, not to be the partner of a man, who was evidently to play a great part on the theatre of life." Abigail was hardly sympathetic. When Louisa asked her to help find a cook, she responded, "I have not the least chance; we do not have any such persons" — drawing a pointed contrast with the serving class in London and the Prussian court. Perhaps, Abigail wrote, Louisa could find "a young girl of ten or eleven years old" to run after the baby George.

The atmosphere around the house was tense. It grew worse when John Quincy, anxious about money, fired their servants. He may have regretted it when he found that he, not his wife, would have to do most of their work. "I find myself burdened with the minutest and vilest details of our domestic economy," John Quincy complained to his brother Thomas. One can only imagine what he said to his wife. He not only kept careful note of how many cents she paid for every purchase, but for several weeks, he also kept a tab of how much cash she carried in her purse. For her part, she noted his "cold

201

looks" and, in her insecurity, saw his every moment of annoyance as a reflection on her.

Louisa did not see much of her husband once they moved to Boston. Occasionally, they spent evenings at home together, reading aloud Shakespeare or works on pedagogy (John Quincy was, as Louisa sardonically noted, "in the fervour of a lately acquired parental duty; our son being eighteen months old"), but John Quincy went to Quincy most weekends to be with his parents. He left his wife, often ill, behind. "Constant faintings and violent attacks of illness short in their duration," Louisa wrote in "Adventures," were quite curiously timed: they "prevented my visits to Quincy."

Joshua died that spring, having lingered for six months after Louisa and John Quincy left him ill in Maryland. It was a painful time, and she withdrew further from the Adamses into her private mourning. Her mother and siblings were destitute. Joshua's assets were in orphan's court, his suits were still in chancery, Catherine was without a cent. Now completely reliant on the support of others, Catherine and Louisa's younger sister Caroline came to Boston for an extended stay.

Despite their sad circumstances, they brightened Louisa's mood. Catherine was still sharp and defiant, and Caroline, now twenty-five years old, was spirited and happy, a universal favorite. Caroline had her own preparation to be a "fine lady" on Tower Hill in London, but she was much more capable with housework than her older sister, and her assistance put the house in good order. Able to relax in their familiar company, Louisa started to like Boston. The city had an unstrained elegance that appealed to her, a shinier gloss than Quincy; the men still wore waistcoats and long boots, ruffled shirts and wristbands. Its residents found her appealing, too. Her time in London and Berlin had given her a patina that was considered aristocratic in the Adamses' small town but admired in Boston. In the state capital, her British upbringing hardly hurt her; in fact, it probably helped. She was young, only twenty-seven, polished, and pretty. Invitations to parties and dinners started to arrive. "I met with the most decidedly flattering reception," she later recalled. She found herself in a position she was used to: dressing for dinners and dances. In January, she hosted her first ball. It lasted until one in the morning. "I danced myself the whole evening," John Quincy wrote afterward. There was more to her days than dinners and dances, though. She made friends, as she always had, easily, and some of them were among the more educated and literary women in the United States — women who would talk of writers like Rousseau in "rapt effusion." Louisa found these women intimidating and wasn't sure such subjects were appropriate for women, but she enjoyed these visits and these conversations, and was proud of her participation almost despite herself.

As Louisa spent more time with her mother, sister, and friends, pulled back into the life of the Johnsons, John Quincy was retreating into the world of his parents. But he was restless. He filled his time as if time were a larger void. Strange to say, he had a harder time adjusting to life in the United States even than she. After seven years away from the bar, he had opened a law practice with dread and felt himself sinking beneath it. At one point he proposed to Thomas, who was working at a magazine in Philadelphia, that they move to the frontier in New York, in search of "independence, thrift and sport." With bravado, he wrote, "Why should we wither away our best days, and sneak through life, pinched by penury and yawning off existence?" The plan, such as it was, went nowhere. Without a sense of greater purpose — a sense of being instrumental to his country — he wondered what in his life was worthwhile. "I enter this day upon my thirty-seventh year with sorrow to think how long I have lived, and to how little purpose," he wrote in his diary on his birthday.

He was drawn to politics, which seemed now forbidden. His father's adversary Jefferson was in power and the Adams name was impugned. Abigail and John had adopted the habit of referring to the political arena as a den of thieves or snakes, of party intrigues and venal men; John swore it would have been better to have been an honest shoe-maker, like his own father, than president. John Quincy swore off politics in his diary, declaring that he wanted to serve his whole country, and politicians now served only their own narrow interests. Yet his whole life had been oriented toward public service. Politics gripped his attention, no matter his claims otherwise. As a boy he had lived through the Revolution and witnessed the political machi-nations that had led to the founding of the United States; as a young man in Europe, he had traced the titanic struggles, the move-ments of armies, the shocks of revolutions, the compromises and betrayals of statesmen, the seismic vibrations of regimes forming, power shifting everywhere — while having enough leisure to translate German poetry on the side. Now back in Boston, he was more of an exile from the center of power than ever. One winter evening, before head-ing home for the night, John Quincy walked through the cold grass in the park half a mile from his house. Above him in the dark towered the great dome of the statehouse, which had been built while he was gone. He was pensive. "I feel strong temptation and have great provocation to plunge into political controversy," he wrote in his diary afterward. "But I hope to preserve myself from it, by the considerations which have led me to the resolutions of renouncing." His resolution would not last. That spring, his name was put forward for the state senate. He did nothing to swat it back. At the end of May, he was sworn into office as a representative of Suffolk County, which included Boston.

But even that was not enough. His diary groaned with activity. By the end of 1801, he was also on Harvard's Board of Overseers, in various clubs and societies, and was the corresponding secretary of the American Academy of Arts and Sciences — to name only a few extra activities. In a letter to his brother he enumerated the obligations that swallowed up his days: his law work, his science club, his work as a state senator, his responsibilities as Massachusetts bankruptcy commissioner (until President Jefferson eliminated the position — an act the Adams family, probably mistakenly, would always take personally), speeches on civic issues, "unavoidable encroachment of dissipation" (those dinners and balls with Louisa), weekly trips to "the paternal mansion." He promised to give Thomas the remnant of his time, telling him that he would write essays for the *Portfolio,* a publication that Thomas was involved with. He mentioned his wife and son nowhere in his letter about his commitments, except perhaps obliquely, when he referred to the unavoidable encroachment of dissipation.

"Of course with so much business," Louisa simply noted, her husband "was not much at home."

That fall, 1802, John Quincy's name was put forward to represent his district in Congress, and again he did nothing to stop the movement. When he lost the race, he consoled himself by saying that he had not wanted to win — even though he recorded the tallies of ballots in his diaries and privately scorned his allies for letting rain showers keep them from the polls. But on February 8, 1803, a divided Massachusetts state legislature appointed him to the United States Senate. It had required a deal cut between his supporters and the high Federalists. John Quincy, kept apprised of the maneuvering, remained demure and circumspect. In his diary he recorded the event but without his own reaction at the election, as if his name belonged to someone else.

When Louisa heard that she would be moving to Washington, she was furious. She had begun to imagine herself at home in Boston, and it was "painful" for her to leave it. "I surely did not behave with either the fortitude or the patience, which might have been expected," she would recall. What was more, she was pregnant again. "She is very well for so feeble a body as she is," Abigail wrote to Thomas, not bothering to disguise her point. "When you take a wife, it must be for better or for worse, but a healthy and good constitution is an object with those who consider, maturely."

Louisa was stronger than her mother-in-law gave her credit for. Louisa's water broke on July 3, while she was having tea with friends. Fluttering about their delicacy, the women scattered, leaving her and her sister alone. John Quincy was out at Peacefield visiting his parents. The doctor could not be found; even George's nurse was out. She and Caroline managed, and finally the doctor was located. On July 4, John Quincy came home to find that he had another boy. This one they dutifully named John Adams. As soon as she could rise from her bed, she lifted the lids of her empty trunks and opened her packing cases to prepare to leave for Washington. She was "a wanderer" again.

3

They drove through the woods into Washington on October 20, 1803, through the descending dusk. The coach clattered past unfinished federal buildings. The sandstone was already beginning to crumble, and the young city looked like it was in ruins. Where roads should have been, there was a vast web of sight lines. Where carriages were promised, there were cows and fowl. The carriage passed the huddled boardinghouses where most senators and congressmen lived, the mess halls where rough allegiances and enmities were formed, and drove on. It passed the Capitol, which was still hardly more than an idea, bare without its columns and flat without its dome. Tree stumps studded the rutted way. The area was "a scene," Louisa wrote, "of utter desolation."

They were exhausted from the journey. Louisa, John Quincy, two-year-old George, three-month-old John, the children's nurse Patty Walin, and Louisa's sister Caroline had been on the road for twenty days — three miserable weeks. On the ship to Newark, George had thrown the keys of all their trunks into the sea, along with his shoes. They had to take a creeping route around New York and Philadelphia due to outbreaks of yellow fever. In New Jersey, the group was forced to stop because Louisa fell ill. When the doctor came to take her pulse, he told her to stretch out her arm; he thought she had yellow fever and was too afraid to come close.

Now, because they had waited for her to recover, they were late. The Senate had convened early in a special session to consider the ratification of the Louisiana Purchase, an acquisition that would add 828,000 square miles to the United States. But Louisa's illness and the long route had slowed them too much, and the opening of the special Senate was over. As their coach lurched over Pennsylvania Avenue, another carriage came into view, coming from the direction of the President's House. Inside sat Samuel Allyne Otis, the secretary of the Senate, a Federalist, and an old Bostonian. The two carriages stopped. Otis had a bit of news for John Quincy: he had just delivered to President Jefferson the Senate's ratification of the treaty that brought the United States the Louisiana Purchase. The treaty had passed 24 yeas to 7 nays. Those friendly toward the French — Jacobins, the Federalists called them — were "caballing," Otis wrote to John Quincy later that night, "and I expect will attack me tomorrow when I shall want the aid of all my friends. I hope you will not be too fatigued to attend." He did not suspect that John Quincy, nominally a Federalist, was not on his side; John Quincy wanted Louisiana, wanted France out of a position to meddle, and wanted passage to the west. He also wanted the chance to prove that he was no party loyalist, no man's friend.

He planned on keeping himself apart. To economize, the family was to live in Georgetown with Louisa's brother-in-law, Walter Hellen, who also housed the rest of the Johnson family. They didn't have much choice; they needed to save money. In April, a London banking house that John Quincy had advised his father to use had failed, just at the moment when John Adams needed the funds after buying more family land. John Quincy had stepped in to cover the loss. Now, with his law practice suspended, he would be relying on a senator's per diem: $6 a day while Congress was in session. The decision to live in Georgetown was financial, then, but the distance from the other members of Congress suited John Quincy's sense of independence. Most senators and representatives left their families at home and lodged at boardinghouses on Capitol Hill, often blocking with regional and ideological friends. John

Quincy, meanwhile, would make the long walk from the Capitol, eat his meal, and then shut himself in his room with his books, his diary, and his pen.

The arrangement should have suited Louisa, too; it was almost a return to the house on Cooper's Row. She would be able to live with her mother and six sisters — Nancy, Caroline, Harriet, Catherine (Kitty), Eliza, and Adelaide. But at the start, it was strange. Her sisters were adults now, and almost strangers. It startled her to see them "with all the pretensions of belles, fond of society, without means to keep up the appearance to which they had been accustomed; and without the protection of *father* or *guardian.*" The absence of her father was ever-present. Her mother, Catherine, was forced to rely entirely on the largess of Walter Hellen, and was keenly aware of her diminished station, struggling to reconcile herself to life in the southern United States.

Louisa, too, had to adjust to the strangeness of a city under construction in almost every way. For the first time in her life, she was also not only confronted by the reality of slavery but party to it. She arrived in Washington "with English feelings," which is to say, antislavery beliefs. Louisa had a "dislike of a system, to give it no harsher name harassing, distressing, and degrading to all the finer feelings of the heart," she wrote years later. But her beloved father was a slaveholder before he died, and Louisa was silent about the presence of the slaves who served her in Walter Hellen's house and the slaves who surrounded her in Washington. She was not, of course, alone in that; her husband, who would become an antislavery crusader, didn't mention them either. (In theory, John Quincy was already against slavery. But his antislavery convictions did not stop him from living with the Hellens, or even from voting against a measure that would have gradually abolished slavery in the Louisiana territories.) In 1801, Washington was a southern town, a slave city, inhabited by roughly 2,500 whites, 120 free blacks, and 600 slaves; slaves built the federal offices, staffed the boardinghouses, drove the carriages, served the dinners, performed every manner of task. Often called servants, they were rarely remarked upon, even by those who opposed slavery; it was as if they couldn't see the presence of six hundred people in their midst.

So life was different at the Hellens' from what it had been on Tower Hill. Louisa was an Adams now. Still, she was a Johnson again, pulled back into her old family's orbit, just as her husband was in Massachusetts. In Washington, she had her family for company, and John Quincy had his work. John Quincy walked the five-mile route from Georgetown to the Capitol each day. Sometimes he read "to the ladies" in the evening, but mostly he stayed at his desk or in his room. He spent his time making an index for his diary, keeping the household accounts, writing a list of people in power: *President of the United States Thomas Jefferson. . . . Secretary of the Navy Robert Smith. . . . Senator from New Hampshire William Plummer. . . .* He studied laws, worked on his speeches, read Herodotus. He was on special committees to deal with revising the articles of war, appropriating money for roads, New Orleans territorial legislation, revision of Senate rules, the Library of Congress, Georgia land claims, the impressment of seamen — and so on. The kind of closeness he and Louisa had enjoyed in Berlin was a distant thought. Louisa grew half accustomed to his absence. "Mr. Adams is so much engaged he scarcely allows himself time to eat, drink or sleep," Louisa wrote to Abigail in the spring. Sometimes, she went to parties without him. "He stays at home and sends me out to make his apology."

She went to Congress or the Supreme Court occasionally, because it was theater. One visitor called it "as good as going to a play." She wasn't interested in the politics, but she was interested in the people. Her vision was stereoscopic; she saw the good and bad in people, and merged the contradictions into a single character. Eccentrics fascinated her. John Randolph of Roanoke "was to Congress what Shakespeare's *Fools* were to a Court" — brilliant, mercurial, impulsive, uncontrollable. She was wary of — but quite susceptible to — the charismatic. She watched Aaron Burr control the noisy spectators at the Senate with awe. "The little hammer in his graceful little hand," Louisa wrote, "would startle them into silence." Other men repulsed her. The French minister, General Turreau, was famous in France for his brutality on the battlefield and famous in Washington for beating his wife. As she watched him one night at the President's House as he amused himself by galloping back and forth across the room, she wasn't charmed; she didn't forget the abuse.

She came to think that what she saw during those first few years in Washington reflected a fundamental truth of human nature, the grasping for special privilege in a society that only pretended to award none. She found the suggestion that there were no classes in Washington to be ridiculous. She saw how men inevitably generated distinctions. The pretense of equality made relationships unpredictable, capricious, or confused. In England and in Berlin, the protocol was clear. Each person knew what to do. Mistakes were pointed out, corrected, more easily fixed. In Washington, men formed little tribes and suspected one another of conspiracies. Hierarchies sprang up like weeds, were flattened, sprang up again. Slights were not misdemeanors but personal affronts: a man, distracted, might fail to return another man's bow, and for this he would be blackballed. There was a code of honor, loosely codified, but it could be stupid — leading to challenges, duels, and sometimes deaths. She was more meritocratic than she might have seemed to some; she had an idea of a true aristocracy. She was drawn to "kind friendly excellent people" who had risen to high station, people like Secretary of War Henry Dearborn and his wife, Dorcas, with their "real genuine pattern of unsophisticated democracy," and their "social virtues of benevolence, sincerity, and natural goodness of heart." What she hated were the "affected blandishments" of those who made grand claims for the equality of Americans. The worst offender, to her mind, was President Thomas Jefferson.

She disliked President Jefferson with a special animosity. He was "the ruling Demagogue of the hour," a man of "peering restlessness," so adept at "drawing out *others* and at the same time attracting attention to himself." She was prepared to dislike him. It was personal. The Jefferson name had not only become a dirty word among the Adamses after the mudslinging of the 1800 presidential campaign, but because Jefferson had also stripped Joshua of his post, she also seems to have partly blamed him for her father's death.

She even disliked the way Jefferson looked: tall and ungainly, with a habit of wearing old red britches while uniformed French servants (and slaves) staffed his house. She distrusted his self-fashioning as one of the people, a common man. She saw him as canny, always superior, calculating. His egalitarianism struck Louisa as a show, and not an earnest one. She had occasion at a few dinners to appreciate that his table — the food, the wine, the servants (though slaves) — would not have been out of place at any European court. She probably would have liked the courtliness had it been matched with sincere politeness. Instead, she found him disingenuous and sometimes rude. She was immune, it seems, to his famous charm — though of course, he may have purposefully tamped it down. After dinner one night he led his guests into a cold room, where a tiny fire licked a few coals; Louisa's teeth chattered; another guest joked that he could have entertained himself by spitting out the flame. Jefferson leaned back in his chair, not hiding his impatience for them to leave.

She may have felt personally dismissed. Louisa was stained by her British birth and her time in a royal court — cardinal sins in

Jefferson's view. Jefferson so hated the idea of courts that he had made a point of insulting the British minister, Anthony Merry, and especially his wife, Elizabeth, who Jefferson sneered was too aristocratic to have a place in the United States. It wasn't only her diamond jewelry that Jefferson objected to; it was her presumption of some power, her force of character, and her obvious assumption that the social sphere was also a sphere of power politics — as it was in Europe, and in fact as it was in Washington, but only in a tacit and taboo way. Jefferson called Elizabeth Merry a "virago" — a mannish woman, a woman who was a threat to the purity of the republic. Of course, when it was in his interest to flatter a British minister and his wife, he would do that too. His dining table might have been round — in the republic of equality, there would be no head — but when Louisa sat at his left hand, he kept himself turned toward his right. His interests at that moment, in 1807, determined that the British minister's wife next to him was worth his attention, and the Massachusetts senator's wife was not.

Louis a was in a difficult spot, then: a city where protocol was never clear. Women were supposed to remain innocent and ignorant of the affairs of men, and yet, as Margaret Bayard Smith, a Washington social doyenne noted, "the house of representatives is the lounging place of both sexes, where acquaintance is as easily made as at public amusements." Women were supposed to stay away from public life, and yet, as one who saw the treatment of Elizabeth Merry — or, for that matter, anyone who saw the senators and officers pay deference to Dolley Madison, who was quickly establishing herself as the leading hostess — could see, politics and socializing were closely intertwined. Women were present and absent at once.

Louisa claimed to have nothing to do with her husband's career. "I knew nothing of politics, and of course was without ambition: and domestic life seemed to be the only life for which nature had intended me," Louisa wrote in "The Adventures of a Nobody." The "of course" is telling: this is what a woman was supposed to say. It does not completely describe Louisa's attitude. She listened to her husband practice his speeches and gave him advice; she was especially good, the prolix orator told her, at knowing what to cut. She took note of politicians' rifts and alliances. When they were apart, she made John Quincy promise to write her about politics. "I have not forgotten," he later replied. When he suggested that he might resign from public office and find contentment in focusing on his private life, she urged him not to. But when John Adams expressed his displeasure at John Quincy's votes, Louisa made a point of reporting to her husband that she had disclaimed any influence or, for that matter, awareness at all. And she viewed his public position as an unbearable burden on them both.

It was hard for any woman to find her way, acknowledging one conviction and acting according to another. (Even Smith wrote candidly of her struggles in revealing letters and diaries.) It was perhaps even harder for Louisa than most. There were few women to whom she could turn to find out the correct way to behave, no Pauline Neale to sweep in and whisper when to curtsy. She had her sisters, of course, but she found even those relationships fraught with unspoken difficulties. At the Hellens', she watched her own family watching her, discerning the fine gradations and distinctions that marked her as a boarder versus those that marked her as a senator's wife. With no carriage, she had no mobility to seek out friends of her own. With her husband determined to keep to himself and demonstrate his independence, she had little opportunity or excuse to establish herself well in the social scene. With a Federalist for a husband and the Republicans in power, she was of the wrong party, anyway. She was of the wrong birth, and perhaps the wrong temperament. Dolley Madison, society's reigning queen, always regarded her a little suspiciously. She was no longer an object of curiosity; she was no longer the delightful republican in a royal court, so pretty, so *"jolie."* This may have been how she wanted it — she claimed to prefer the small and intimate gatherings in the Hellens' parlor, with one sister at the piano and another at the harp, with a few guests and a little cake and tea — but it was one more reminder that her range was limited. Georgetown was not her home.

Quincy was not her home either. That had been painfully apparent. So she was startled when John Quincy told her that spring, 1804, as they prepared to head north for the summer break between sessions of Congress, that he would be returning to Washington for the next congressional session without her, leaving her and the children in Quincy with his parents. That arrangement was typical; senators tended to live and work in boardinghouse blocks, without their wives. But she was horrified by his pronouncement and refused to head north. If she could not travel back and forth with him, she told him, then she would stay in Washington. If she had to choose between "five dreary winters in Quincy" and Washington, between her family or his, she chose her own family. She was still furious when he left her with their two small sons, charging him with "coldness or unkindness."

"Our separation was very much against my

inclination, but it was your own choice," he responded. She replied that given the options, it was no choice at all.

He explained that he could not support the great expense — not to mention the miserable trials — of traveling back and forth with a wife of fragile health and two small boys. The appeals to his poverty hurt her, as they always did; reflexively, she would bring up the lost dowry. "I brought you nothing and therefore have no claim on you whatever," she wrote in cringing response. "My life ever has been and ever must remain a life of painful obligation."

He was the one who seemed to suffer, though, at least at first, from the costs of their separation. "I feel already to use a vulgar phrase, like a fish out of water, without you and my children," John Quincy wrote to her, "but I will not complain." He spent the summer punishing himself. He studied the U.S. Code and all U.S. Supreme Court decisions. He berated himself for accomplishing nothing during the Senate session except alienating everyone. He had been the only Federalist to support the acquisition of Louisiana, but he had failed in his efforts to pass a constitutional amendment in support of it. He had given long speeches, but he was not happy with his performances. His days lacked purpose. "Irregular and indolent," he summarized the month of August in his diary.

The dark maw of feeling that he struggled against his whole life threatened to overwhelm him. There was an inherited component to this; compulsive disorders and depressive tendencies ran in his family, on both sides. Thomas, his younger brother, also had trouble fighting off punishing self-doubt, and Charles, of course, had helped hasten his own death by drinking. John Quincy's self-analysis was constant, and his diary became at times a record of pain and self-loathing. "My self-examination this night gave rise to many mortifying reflections. . . . Pride and self-conceit and presumption lie so deep in my natural character," John Quincy wrote, "that, when their deformity betrays them, they run through all the changes of Proteus, to disguise themselves to my own heart."

He was also lonely. He was lonely anywhere, but being apart from Louisa appears to have made the loneliness worse. He missed her. "Good Night my best beloved. *Je t'envoye les plus tendres baisers de l'amour,*" he wrote.

But her anger with him burned a little longer. She could not, she wrote, understand why he missed her in Quincy, because they were so rarely together in Quincy. She wanted him to return to Washington early, "before *Congress* takes you from me." Some of her letters were short, perfunctory, and passive-aggressive. "George is very angry with you. He says you are very naughty to go away and leave him." As for herself, she reported, "I never was so well in my life."

Her sisters, her mother, a stream of visitors, and her children kept her busy. John fussed at teething, and George was a precocious troublemaker. "He destroys all Mrs. Hellens chickens, drives the ducks to death, gets down to the wharf and plays such pranks I am obliged to keep a person constantly running after him," Louisa wrote to her husband. "In fact he is one of the finest children I ever saw but much too clever or wise for his age." She told John Quincy that she was "studying" the Scottish Enlightenment thinker Elizabeth Hamilton's work on education, which argued for the equal capacity of the female intellect and the importance of its instruction to cultivate the mind, imagination, and heart. "I admire her more than any author I have yet seen," Louisa wrote. "Had I a daughter it is the only system I would wish to adopt." Then, typically, she retreated: "but it requires a mother of a superior cast to be able to undertake it and do it justice."

She had her arias, her gossip, her health, and her books in Washington. Still, her days became "interminable." The river moved slowly around Georgetown's gentle bend, and restless storms swept through each afternoon. The air turned hot, Southern hot, and Louisa's letters turned pensive. Her irritation with John Quincy sometimes flared, but her frustration with him became something more complex. Her letters with John Quincy reflect a marriage far more multifaceted and dynamic than any glimpse of it from his coolly dispassionate diary or from her forlorn memoir sketches, written much later, ever could. Their words were inflected with concern, anger, boredom, irritation, desire, humor, and intimacy. They give us a glimpse at how they communicated, perhaps also in conversation in person. They were, then, as many husbands and wives are, married in heart and mind through their contradictions, not only in spite of them.

"I shall know neither happiness or peace till you return," Louisa wrote him. Yet divorce, in fact, was also on her mind. That summer, she brought up the subject cautiously to John Quincy. She mentioned it in order to reject it emphatically — but she did mention it. She had read Madame de Staël's book of letters, in which de Staël makes an argument in favor of divorce if a husband and wife "find that their dispositions do not accord," Louisa wrote to her husband, and asked him to read it himself. "This letter is I am told very much admired. I think I must have misunderstood it very much for it appears to me calculated to destroy every moral principal, to destroy every tie which binds society together." She wanted to know what he thought.

He responded caustically — "After having sacrificed all decency as well as all virtue in her own conduct, it is natural enough to find her torturing her ingenuity to give infamy itself a wash of plausibility" — and then blamed the French Revolution for de Staël's argument. Louisa was not going to divorce her husband — there was no question, even though it was becoming clear that their dispositions did not in fact accord. Divorces happened, but only in extreme cases and attended by scandal. She thought about it with a tentative kind of curiosity mixed with apprehension. That summer, Louisa learned that her acquaintances the Laws were separating. "This is setting the opinion of the world at defiance," she wrote. "I never wish to court it but I should dread it too much ever to set it at defiance."

Still, she described her inner life as like a battlefield. "Formed for domestic life my whole soul devoted to you and my children yet ambitious to excess," she wrote to John Quincy in August, "my heart and head are constantly at war."

"It grieves me to see him sacrificing the best years of his life in so painful and unprofitable a way," she wrote to Abigail soon after he arrived back in Washington. "It would however cause me infinite pain to see him give it up."

4

In the summer of 1805, Louisa and the boys came to Quincy with her sister Eliza, moving into the small saltbox cottage where John Quincy had been born near Penn's Hill, two miles away from the elder Adamses' mansion. Washington may have seemed remote from cosmopolitan life, but Penn's Hill was set in farmland and woods. When they arrived, Louisa and Eliza had to milk the cow themselves, laughing "heartily" at their failure.

But her good humor quickly soured. Although she liked rambling in the fields and forest with George and John and occasionally John Quincy, who would try to teach his "unfruitful scholars" to distinguish the blooming peach trees from the plum, she disliked living in the woods after a life spent in cities. She felt at once claustrophobic and exposed, worried about "two or three insane persons" at loose in the area, and trapped in the tiny farmhouse — four rooms downstairs and three small rooms above, too small for three adults, a few young servants, a toddler always up to mischief, and a baby just learning to run. When she had more space, though, after John Quincy began to spend more time at his parents' and Eliza went to Boston for parties, she felt no better; she felt alone. It was hard for them to be together, hard for them to be apart.

It would have been hard to be around John Quincy, in any event, that summer. He lashed himself in his diary for his "mental imbecility." "My prospects are again blasted, and I have nothing left before me but resignation," he wrote. Abigail wrote to Hannah Quincy that she was worried about John Quincy's "depression of spirits," but did not know what to do. "There are some malidies so deep rooted," Abigail wrote to Eliza Susan Quincy, "that the most delicate hand dare not probe. The attempt might fix an incurable wound." She took him to Dr. Cotton Tufts, in hopes that he could prescribe a pill.

An offer from Harvard to be the first Boylston Professor of Rhetoric partly boosted his spirits, but it produced new tension with his wife. Louisa didn't like Harvard; she thought that the school was more concerned with its own wealth and power than with its students. But it was not her decision. He took the job, teaching during summers when Congress was not in session. His spirits rose — but hers dropped as he became even more pre-occupied with Cicero. He spent his days preparing his lectures and had no time for anything but teaching — certainly not for her. She found the whole thing "odious." "Having relinquished almost all claim to [your presence] in the winter . . . I am the less willing to give it up in the summer," she wrote to John Quincy. But what she was willing to tolerate didn't much matter.

So they tried different arrangements. They split up, shuttled back and forth, and made unhappy compromises. When Louisa and John Quincy returned to Washington in the fall of 1805, they left George, now four years old, and John, now two, behind at John Quincy's insistence and by Abigail's arrangement. Louisa protested, which the other Adamses considered unreasonable. It was common for members of the extended Adams family to share in the education and care of one another's children. Abigail grew tired of Louisa's self-pitying, forlorn letters about missing her children: "I believe they are much better off than they could have been at any boarding house in Washington, where they must have been confined to some degree, or have mixd with improper persons" — harsh words, since the "boarding house" in question was the home of Louisa's own sister.

"Nothing but compulsion would have

induced me to leave them," Louisa responded.

Her husband or her children; her children or her husband. Having her children meant no husband, but having no children meant, it seems, the chance to grow closer to him. During the winter they spent together without George and John, 1805–6, they were moody — at times short with each other, and at times more tender and affectionate. She was pregnant, and its effects were violent. "My health was particularly delicate and my spirits worse," she would remember. Yet she was able to write to Abigail, "I have enjoyed almost perfect happiness."

The following summer, 1806, he left her in Washington, pregnant. His departure left her bereft. "The loss of Mr. Adams's society is to me irreparable," she wrote to Abigail. "I already look forward to his return with the most anxious impatience." John Quincy had been in the habit of measuring the temperature each morning; in his absence, she rose at sunrise to do it. In his letters to her, he was intimate. She was "dearest Louisa"; she was sent kisses *de l'amour.* She was sweetly teased. "George appears to have lost none of his sensibility, but has a placidness and ease of temper, which must have come to him I think from some of his *remote* ancestors," John Quincy quipped after he was reunited with his sons. "He resembles you more than formerly. Not however so much as John, who seems a little miniature of yourself."

"I can believe that George grows like me but Johns round face and deep dimples must I think be infinitely more like his father," Louisa responded, "who has ever been celebrated for this to *me* fascinating beauty."

Their separation was the more difficult because of the complications from pregnancy. She was confined to her room in the suffocating heat, suffering from abscesses in the throat and ears, her legs badly swollen. She could hardly stand. Even so, when she learned that her sister Harriet's son was dying, she made the hot mile-long walk to her sister's house. That night, with the temperature at 100 degrees, she went into labor and gave birth to a stillborn child.

The tragedy, for a while, seemed to make them realize their closeness. When John Quincy heard the news from her, he staggered. "Her letter affected me deeply in its tenderness, its resignation, and its fortitude," he wrote in his diary. In his room, by himself, he "yielded to the weakness, which I had so long struggled to conceal and restrain," and he cried. For his part, his response was balm to her. "My heart swelled with gratitude and love," she wrote to him, "and I almost ceased to think the strike so bitter which proved to me how dear I am to your heart."

It was never that simple, though. They loved

at a distance; proximity was harder. So was the long separation from her children. She was furious when she learned that John Quincy had taken a room for himself in Cambridge instead of spending time with the boys. By the time she reached Massachusetts in August 1806, she had not seen them for nine months. When Louisa arrived in Quincy, her children "recieved me as a stranger," and little John cried that he wanted to return to his grandmother. John Quincy was almost as fractious. The solicitude and tenderness he'd shown toward his wife in her absence evaporated. Louisa was overwhelmed; the little saltbox cottage was as crowded as ever. When they tried to have company at the house, Louisa burned her cakes and greeted guests with soot on her face. John Quincy retreated into his irritation. "This is no longer the studious life of the two former months," he wrote in his diary soon after Louisa arrived. "I have wasted the past week, and fear I shall waste the next. Nothing can be more fatal to study than petty avocations continually recurring."

The following winter, 1806–7, she stayed in Boston with the children in a boardinghouse on the outskirts of the city, a lodging so grim that even Abigail thought it "cold and bleak." Louisa would remember John Quincy's decision with bitterness. "Everything as usual was fixed without a word of consultation with the family," she later wrote. The pattern in which she was excluded from major decisions about her children's life and in fact her own was growing stronger; when she looked back, she could see it too clearly. At the time, though, it was something she could neither accept nor refuse. Contradictions animated her marriage. "I already long for your return," Louisa wrote to John Quincy in Washington. "But so it is, I can neither live with you or without you."

"The last paragraph of your letter I do not fully understand — I will not say I can neither live with you or without you," John Quincy responded, then dismissed it with a joke, thinking of his empty bed: "but in this cold weather I should be very glad to live with you." He was not shy about his sexual ardor for her — nor simply his sexual ardor. After observing at a party, with wry appreciation, how little women's fashion left to the imagination, he sent his wife a poem that did the same. "When the Serpent's subtle head / Had brought her to disgrace; / When Innocence and Bliss were fled — / The fig-leaf took their place," he wrote, before calling on "Dear Sally" to "Fling the *last* fig-leaf to the wind, / And snatch me to thy arms!" "My heart throbs to behold you," she wrote to him a few days later.

As it happens, Louisa was pregnant again. In August 1807, after yet another trying summer in the small cottage on Penn's Hill, the

Adamses moved into a house in Boston on the corner of Boylston and Tremont streets, bought by John Quincy as an investment (and perhaps with an eye toward the end of his political career). Only two weeks later, Louisa gave birth to another son, Charles Francis. It was, as usual, a brutally difficult labor — Charles was born breech and seemed at first not to breathe. She had hardly recovered before making the trip back to Washington that fall, this time with her newborn. In yet another disappointment, the older children were to stay behind in Massachusetts. Six-year-old George would board with Abigail's sister Elizabeth Peabody in New Hampshire; four-year-old John would live with Abigail's sister Mary Cranch. Louisa never reconciled herself to these separations. Perhaps because she did not know her own grandparents, she never accepted Abigail Adams's insistence on the primary right of grandparents.

Louisa did not share the Adamses' view of communal child rearing. She believed that "incessant love" was as important as the "advantages of education, of accomplishment, of morals, and of virtue." She herself had attended boarding schools at young ages, but she had never been more than a few miles from home — and even then, it seems to have been an unhappy experience; many of the memories she would most cherish were of periods of sickness, when she'd been brought home or to the Hewletts'. To a degree that was unusual for her time, she thought that parents had an "absolutely essential" role to play in their children's development. But Louisa did submit. She wrote sad, beseeching letters. "Kiss my darling children for me over and over again," she would write, "and remind them constantly of their mother whose every wish on this earth centres in them." She worried over their little illnesses and scrapes, writing anxiously with instructions and prescriptions — "five drops of spirit of Turpentine upon a lump of sugar every other morning" — and advice on what to feed them.

Partly, no doubt, her intense affection and interest in her children came from the difficulties of having them; they were triumphs hard won. "With what ardent love I regarded this my first born child," she later wrote about George, "and with what earnest anxiety I watched his growth." She "traced each little thought or expression" with inexpressible joy. She sometimes wondered whether she had the qualities that she needed to be a good mother. Later, she would wonder whether the worst mistake she ever made was not demanding the chance to be with them as they grew up.

When she reached Washington in the late fall of 1807, she could tell that something had changed — in the political climate, and in the Adamses' own situation. All the talk in the city was of war. For years the United States had been caught in the struggle between France and England, provoked and carelessly insulted, its sovereign rights disregarded. Now the conflict threatened to escalate. But there was no army, hardly a navy, and not much of a national will. Louisa did not pay much attention to the back-and-forth; she was unconcerned with Napoleon's illegal closure of continental Europe to British ships, and with Britain's retaliation by blocking commerce with French-controlled countries except by ships that passed through British ports and paid a license fee and a toll — which was more or less robbery from American ships. Nor did she care about the details of England's practice of essentially kidnapping thousands of American sailors suspected of being British deserters in order to man its ships during the Napoleonic wars. In 1803, the peace following the treaty of Amiens — the brief cessation of fighting in Europe sparked by the French Revolutionary wars and Napoleon's successful coup — had ended, Britain and France were once again at war, and the reverberations were felt even across the vast Atlantic. But Louisa was more worried about whether her son John, up in Massachusetts, had hives.

"Mr. Adams was so deeply engrossed with

business that he had scarcely time to speak to the family; and we had but little conversation on any subject," she remembered. That was harsh — it's unlikely she had wanted to know the details of his work, the way his mother did. But it was impossible to ignore the larger situation, not least because of how it affected her. British ships routinely lurked off the shores of the east coast in order to stop and search vessels. Crisis was only a trigger-pull away. On June 22, 1807, the British warship *Leopard* fired on the USS *Chesapeake* after its commander refused to hand over alleged British deserters. Three of the *Chesapeake*'s crew were killed (another died later in Norfolk), eighteen wounded, and four were captured by the British and tried as deserters. Three of them were American-born free black sailors who had escaped impressment, having been seized and forced into the British navy. One was an actual deserter; the British hanged him. In response to the incredible affront to American rights, Jefferson tried an experiment. With anti-British feeling high on one side and a stubborn pro-British faction on the other, Jefferson had no good options. He was absolutely opposed to going to war, but he could not afford to let the crisis pass. He proposed a shipping embargo, which he hoped would be war by pacific means, and he turned to John Quincy to help him.

The senator from Massachusetts was an

improbable ally for Jefferson. The animosity between John Adams and Jefferson had grown so deep that they were not speaking, and the Federalists in Boston were rabidly pro-British; the economy of New England depended on British trade. John Quincy's constituents would bear the burden of a commercial retaliation disproportionately. Indeed, his fellow Massachusetts Federalist senator, Timothy Pickering, was plotting disunion and scheming to undermine John Quincy specifically. But John Quincy was offended by the affronts from Britain. The scenes of the Revolution he had witnessed as a child remained, always, fresh in his mind. He was determined to prove that he was no one's man, and he was willing to risk his own comfort at a chance to prove his patriotism. It did not escape Jefferson that John Quincy was trying to distance himself from his supposed allies, nor that John Quincy could be counted on to act as he felt right, even if — or especially if — the action was wrong for his career. John Quincy knew he had more or less deserted his supporters altogether when he agreed to consider Jefferson's proposal. Jefferson appointed John Quincy and four Republican senators to a committee to consider his confidential recommendation for a general embargo. John Quincy was cynical about the measure's efficacy. But with reluctance, and while proposing terms to amend it, he gave it his support.

So the embargo passed Congress, and John Quincy's Senate term was sunk. He may not have minded, anyway, losing his seat. He was frustrated by his work, and he probably gambled that his help for the other side might lead to new opportunities. In fact, he may have cannily taken a longer view: there was little future for him among Federalists anyway. His move meant political suicide in the short term, but it was politically expedient in the long. He was sending signals to the Republicans that although he would not ask for one, he might be interested in some plum post as a reward. The feud between John Quincy and Pickering spilled into the newspapers. In Washington, Federalists considered him a turncoat, while Republicans distrusted him but called upon him constantly. "Since the Commencement of the present Session I have been placed upon every Committee of national importance, and made the reporter of several," John Quincy wrote to his father. "Without having the weight of a single vote besides my own, in point of personal influence, I find myself charged with the duty of originating — and conducting measures of the highest interest — I am made a leader without followers." There was frustration in this — but also some peculiar note of pleasure.

His wife was less pleased. She was also

isolated in Washington, not by her choice. "Our situation here this winter is not very pleasant as it is universally believed your son has changed his party and the F[ederalists] are extremely bitter," Louisa wrote to Abigail.

He shut the door to his room and worked in silence. She was aware of the anger and distrust that her husband aroused. "In private," Louisa wrote to Abigail, his opponents "circulate reports very much to his disadvantage." For the sake of a president who had humiliated his father, and for a measure he did not believe would really work, John Quincy defended the embargo. He signaled his break with the Federalists altogether when he attended the meeting of the Republican caucus that nominated James Madison for president in January 1808. At the end of May, the Massachusetts legislature voted him out of office ten months early, effective when his term expired, and the state senate issued instructions that he must vote for the embargo's repeal. It was a vote of no confidence. He resigned his Senate seat immediately.

So Louisa packed up her trunks again, and the Adamses returned north — this time, she thought, for good.

When they reached Boston, where they planned to live permanently, John Quincy and Louisa found themselves ostracized.

Even John and Abigail were upset; in caucusing with the Republicans, John Quincy hadn't simply turned against his own party, but allied himself with the one that had so savaged his father's reputation. Papers accused John Quincy of being a "party scavenger." Anonymous letters called him Lucifer. Some Federalists were openly encouraging merchants to break the embargo; some were secretly corresponding with the British. Louisa, loyal to her husband, was disgusted. "With all their boasted independence [they] hang on the skirts of Great Britain, as child clings to its nurse," she wrote. But she could console herself that she was unpacking her bags once and for all, that her husband was done with public life.

Perhaps anticipating the premature end of his Senate term, John Quincy had bought a house on Nassau Street and Frog Lane the year before, and they had already partly moved in. The house was hard to heat and drafty in winter, and smoke filled the rooms when it snowed, but it was theirs — it was home. Louisa quickly embraced it. She had her sister Catherine ("Kitty") for company, and began to entertain once more, learning that not everyone planned to stay away. "The mere commonplace routine of every day life suits me very well," she wrote in November. She was pregnant again but complained less frequently of illness. She had her husband

241

home and her children back. "Once again," she later remembered, "we were a family."

And then, once again, he was gone.

He would make only a short visit to Washington, he reassured her. In January 1809, with James Madison set to be sworn into office in March, John Quincy accepted three cases before the Supreme Court — cases he was confident he would lose — and went to Washington until the court adjourned. He claimed he needed the money. Though he would never admit it, those who knew him suspected that he wanted to be in Washington when Madison was making federal appointments. John Quincy had risked and lost his political career to support the Republicans Jefferson and Madison. There might be a reward.

Louisa and John Quincy fought just before he left. The immediate cause isn't clear, but the arc of their correspondence suggests that she knew he was positioning himself for more than a trip to argue a case before the Supreme Court. "I forgive you though you did part with me very *cavalierly*," she wrote.

"I do not know whether I have yet *forgiven you* —" he responded. "I am sure I have not yet got over it."

A few weeks later she slipped on some ice, struck her back on a street curb, and miscarried. John Quincy, normally so attentive to her when she suffered a miscarriage, responded coolly, even cruelly. "As to the disappointment which we suffer from it," he wrote, "I certainly can bear it without complaint, and you must reconcile yourself to it by the reflection how much of pain and suffering it may relieve you from."

She was caustic in her own letters. "It is here said you are nominated for the War Department and have accepted to walk in the steps of the God of War I make no comments," she wrote. A week later, she told him that if he planned on staying in Washington for any longer, he should consider himself too busy to write to her again.

On February 26, John Quincy told Louisa to ignore "the ridiculous reports" that he was to be offered a federal appointment. "There is not the slightest foundation for any one of them." Hardly a week later, James Madison summoned John Quincy to his office and offered him the position of minister plenipotentiary to Russia. "How long will the mission probably continue?" John Quincy asked.

"Indefinitely," Madison answered.

John Quincy immediately accepted.

But the following day, the Senate rejected the nomination, saying it was "inexpedient" to send a minister to Russia. John Quincy waited two more days, until March 9, to tell Louisa of the nomination and its rejection. "I believe you will not be much disappointed, at the failure of a proposition to go to Russia."

It took no imagination to believe so.

She might, then, have considered herself out of danger and settled. But on July 4, while listening to the Fourth of July oration at the Old South Church in Boston, John Quincy was informed that Congress had reversed course and accepted his nomination. He was the new minister plenipotentiary to Russia.

He might have left his wife behind, as his father had done when he crossed the Atlantic, and as many diplomats did when they were posted abroad. The journey to Russia would be long and extremely dangerous. St. Petersburg would be cold, dark, expensive. He could not be certain of how the United States would be received; after all, when he had made the trip to Russia as a boy, accompanying the envoy Francis Dana, Dana had been entirely ignored. And there was, of course, the matter of their three young boys.

If the thought of bringing all the children or leaving Louisa behind with them even crossed his mind, there is no record of it. John Quincy seems to have wanted his wife with him, even where wives were not often found.

But the children were another story. The two older children, John and George, would stay in the United States, boarded with Abigail's sister Mary Cranch. Later, Louisa would claim that she wasn't involved in the decision. There is no evidence to contradict Louisa's own memory of how that decision was made, and it is in keeping with how the family tended to work. When John Quincy weighed the factors for going to St. Petersburg, he included his job at Harvard, the president and his countrymen's faith in him, the old age of his parents, the young age of his children. Nowhere, it appears, did he consider his wife. Nor did he acknowledge her resistance, even if the anguish she later described was amplified by tragedy and time. John Quincy's exercise of his power in deciding to leave George and John behind would become an inextinguishable source of her fury. "I had been so grossly deceived!" she would write. Again and again, and when it mattered most, Louisa was absent in the major decisions that involved her life and the lives of her children.

John Quincy and Abigail made the arrangements for George and John to live with John Quincy's aunt and uncle, the Cranchs. "I think I could not consent to part with them all," Abigail wrote to her sister. The boys' mother was apparently not given that choice. As Louisa would tell it, Thomas was the one who broke the news to her. Not even John Adams was told ahead of time, for fear that she would "excite his pity and he allow me to take my boys with me." Abigail was the one who suggested that Kitty Johnson accompany Louisa, and Charles, not even two years old, would also come. The details were managed; the trunks were packed; passage was arranged; in all of these discussions and arrangements, she would later insist, and John Quincy's diary at the time would suggest, she was nowhere to be found.

Just before they left, John Quincy and Louisa had their silhouettes cut by an artist for their children. If George and John could not remember the color of her eyes and the feel of her cheeks, then at least they would know the slope of her nose, the curve of her small chin. Then at noon on Saturday, August 5, 1809, a group consisting of John Quincy; Charles, only two weeks from his second birthday; Louisa's sister Kitty, who was vivacious, charming, and "entirely dependent without one sixpence in the world"; John Quincy's twenty-two-year-old nephew William Steuben Smith, who would serve as his secretary; Martha Godfrey, Louisa's chambermaid; Nelson, a free black from Trinidad who would serve as John Quincy's valet; and Louisa boarded the ship *Horace* in the Charlestown harbor. Waiting for them were two young men, Alexander Everett and Francis Gray, who were going to Russia as diplomatic attachés at their parents' expense. As the church bells in Boston and Charlestown rang in one o'clock in the afternoon, the ship left its mooring. By the time night obscured the view, land was almost out of sight.

What Louisa thought as she fell asleep that first night at sea is impossible to know; she left no contemporaneous record. None of her letters from the time survive, save for a stiff thank-you to Dolley Madison for the honor bestowed on John Quincy. But in Louisa's late accounts of that moment, she insisted that it had not been her choice to leave her children. At the time, she felt no choice but to do as her husband wished; he was her authority. Later, she would wish she had resisted. She would struggle with her desire to submit and her desire to revolt for the rest of her life. "A man can take care of himself: — And if he abandons one part of his family he soon learns that he might as well leave them all," she wrote in 1840, as she furiously raked over John Quincy's decision not to bring her sons to Russia. Immediately, she pulled back. "I do not mean to suggest the smallest reproach."

In 1840, she would know what she could not have known at the time — that she would not see her sons for six years, and that she would lose them well before their time. In retrospect, she was certain that it was wrong to be separated from her sons. "Oh this agony of agonies!" Louisa wrote in "Adventures." "Can ambition repay such sacrifices? never!!"

■ ■ ■ ■

PART FOUR:
THE GILDED
DARKNESS

St. Petersburg, 1809–1815

■ ■ ■ ■

1

The voyage took eighty days. Aboard ship, the single room, shared by seven adults and a boy who turned two on the voyage, was rife with tension. Everyone became seasick. Charles was "fractious," wrote his frustrated father, and the three young men working for John Quincy immediately formed rivalries. Kitty, unwillingly or not, put herself at the center of them. There was no escape, nothing to do but endure. "I found the power of self-abstraction fails," John Quincy wrote in his diary, a mild hint of his hot temper. Louisa watched it all unfolding and felt despair, "miserable, *alone* in every feeling." And she was afraid. The *Horace* sailed past blockades and privateers, British warships and Danish gunboats. The Napoleonic Wars made every whisper of low white cloud seem like the apparition of a vessel on the horizon, and every vessel was a potential threat. The *Horace* was halted eleven times, boarded by armed men who questioned the sailors and scrutinized their papers. Near Copenhagen, three ships manned their guns and opened fire. The threat of an enemy was actually the least of the dangers, though. The weather was lethal. The storms grew more severe with each passing week; winter was coming on too fast. The waves rose like walls pulled up by ropes, and the ship slid terrifyingly down their sides. One gale snapped two of the ship's three anchors. By mid-October, in the middle of the squally Baltic, the captain of the *Horace* wanted to turn back to Copenhagen and wait until spring to sail. Louisa heard what the captain said about their chances of making it safely. "I had no hope," she would remember. "I knew that Mr. Adams would never give up." She was right. John Quincy overruled the captain's decision, and they sailed on.

The ship clawed into the Gulf of Finland, curved north toward Stockholm, and then cut east, passing barren gray shores, moving through empty waters. Finally, on October 22, the thin boundary between sea and sky became land: Russia.

They sailed into Kronstadt first, an island fortress of granite ramparts at the entrance to the harbor of St. Petersburg. Invited to a salon at an officer's house, Louisa and Kitty donned enormous brown beaver-fur bonnets that they had bought in Copenhagen, assured they were the fashion in St. Petersburg. When they entered the room, the other women, wearing stiff silk dresses and dazzling with diamonds, turned and stared at the Americans, "aghast." In the horror on their faces, Louisa saw the image of herself reflected back. It was "too ridiculous." She couldn't help but want to laugh.

Their situation was less funny in the morning. While the group had slept on the island, a storm had blown the *Horace* off its moorings and out to sea, with their trunks on board. Louisa had only the thin white cambric wrapper she wore and that ridiculous fur hat. Still, they had to board the small boat that would carry them into the city. It was a long day, a rough crossing in open water followed by hours of slow drifting through shallow channels, past vacant imperial summer palaces and weather-beaten birches. By the time they reached the quay in St. Petersburg, at four in the afternoon, the light was too dim to see the bulbous domes and tapered spires, the gilding, the statues, the vast squares, the gigantic edifices, the monuments that had been built to overwhelm them.

The travelers found a room — a "stone hole" — at the Hotel de Londres, on the Nevsky Prospect. At night Louisa could hear rats scurrying on top of the bedside table by her head, scratching and fighting. Within days, everyone in the group had diarrhea from the water (locals called the illness "seasoning"). When their trunks were finally returned, the group discovered their baggage had been plundered. The temperature outside slipped toward zero, and the sun hung over the horizon for only a few hours, leaving the day with wan, gloomy light. The serfs in town traded wool kaftans for sheepskins, and the nobles had their double windows sealed. Within three weeks of the Adamses' arrival, the bridges over the canals that laced the city together were removed, before ice coursing down from Lake Ladoga could sweep them away. Then the River Neva froze, and ice locked the harbor. It would be May before ships could go.

When the cold stone hole became intolerable, the Adamses moved to another hotel, the Ville de Bordeaux, where the walls were so thin that Louisa could hear the man in the apartment next door instructing his servant to dress him. The neighbors on the other side would cry *Brava!* when Louisa sang as she sewed. John Quincy looked for a more permanent place, but he found nothing he could afford. When they finally settled into their own house in mid-June, on the corner of New Street and the Moika Canal, it took more than his salary just to furnish it. That was before their other expenses. A Russian household required servants — lots of them. In his diary, John Quincy counted fourteen in his house — and this for a lifestyle that earned the Adamses a reputation as cheap. Wealthy families commonly had fifty or a hundred servants; three hundred was not unknown. If the servants had children, the children needed to be housed and fed. The accounts of one cook came to nearly a quarter of John Quincy's salary, and that was what was aboveboard. The steward, as a rule, could be expected to steal the best wine and pocket some of the money for bills. Supplies were regularly pilfered; at one point, John Quincy discovered that 373 bottles of wine — including the best — were gone. None of this could be stopped, only managed. In the system of servitude in St. Petersburg, thieving was greeted with a shrug. After the tsar hired away John Quincy's valet Nelson — Alexander I liked to keep a corps of richly attired African guards — John Quincy had trouble finding a manservant he could trust.

Among American government officers, John Quincy's $9,000 salary was second only to the president's, but that sum required even the stingiest diplomat in St. Petersburg to be tight and mean. In Russia, there was no virtue in thrift. The French ambassador, Armand-Augustin-Louis de Caulaincourt, the highest-ranking diplomat, set the style and tone. Caulaincourt held dinners for hundreds, serving his guests rich meals on Sèvres china. There were damask napkins at his table, and twenty footmen in silk stockings who simply lined the stairs. The French ambassador's salary was fifty times greater than John Quincy's, and the tsar, as a favor to his superior ally Napoleon, had given him a palace by the Hermitage. Yet even Caulaincourt found it hard to pay his bills. "Must I sell my shirt?" the French ambassador asked Bonaparte.

John Quincy had expected St. Petersburg to be expensive, but he had not expected that his salary would be spent so many times over. He had been to opulent balls; he had met monarchs with jewels large enough to tremble the light. But the extremities of wealth in St. Petersburg were beyond his imagining — and so were the demands it placed on courtiers. "Not a particle of the cloathing I brought with me have I been able to present myself in," John Quincy complained to his mother, an extraordinary worry for one who had taken it as a point of pride never to fret about the quality of his waistcoat. The need was even worse, he openly acknowledged, for his wife. She was expected at balls and functions nearly every night, and these events were more elaborate than either of them could have dreamed. The court at St. Petersburg made the royal functions in Berlin seem bourgeois. The Romanovs liked a show. They liked their fruit washed with gold, their chandeliers to drip crystal, their balls to be a crush of bodies clothed in the finest materials. They encrusted themselves with diamonds.

Louisa and Kitty could pass for decent during the day by stitching up some muslin or gauzy cloth, but formal occasions required hoops, silks, trains, satin shoes, gloves, furs, and trims — and even all this *"luggage"* left a lady looking bare if she did not have jewels. The empress mother, who ruled in such matters, did not tolerate anything less than too much. She was rumored to have warned a lady who wore the same dress to two dances not to show up in it again, since "she was tired of seeing the same colour so often." Louisa, who could hardly afford one gown, let alone an endless supply — and more for her sister — once tried to excuse herself from one ball by claiming illness, then went instead to have tea with a friend. The empress mother discovered the trick and sent a message that if it happened again, the American minister's wife would not be invited back. Louisa tried to wear mourning, inventing a death or two, but her ruse was suspected. So she was left to cut and recut her dresses, and spent far more money at the shops than John Quincy told her they could afford. She would flinch at her husband's lectures and frowns. "Every bill that I am forced to bring in (having not a six-pence in the world) makes ruin stare him in the face," Louisa wrote to Abigail.

The constant talk of money, want, need,

and debts triggered her worst fears. In her letters back to the United States, she obsessed over her lost dowry and her father's bankruptcy, which she almost described as her own. She begged John Quincy to send her back to America, so that "he may be able at least to support the appearance that his station requires." Instead of consoling her, he made her feel worse. As she reported to Abigail, he replied that it would be too expensive to send her back, since he could not afford to support her in Massachusetts any more than in St. Petersburg.

This was simply not true; life in Quincy did not require buying diamonds and gowns. Why did he say it? Most diplomats did not bring their wives to this post on the edge of Europe — when Louisa arrived, only the Bavarian minister had come with his wife, and within two years, she was also gone. There was precedent in the Adams family for a husband to go on a mission without his wife; after all, John Quincy's own father, John Adams, had left Abigail when he went to Europe. John Quincy himself had already shown a willingness to live in Washington and Boston without Louisa. But this mission was open-ended, and those separations had been hard. The real reason was probably simple but difficult for John Quincy to admit: he wanted her with him. Perhaps, on some level, he knew she would be useful in the court, too.

So she remained — grudgingly. "I do not like the place nor the people," Louisa wrote to Abigail. Their conversations were vapid, and the women, glittering with icy diamonds, seemed cruel. The buildings were nicer on the outside, but for most of the year she was trapped inside them, inside walls that were three feet thick, with double doors and double windows, ventilated by a sickly draft that swept in through a small swinging pane. Winter meant stale heat and the smoke of ceaseless fires; it meant constant coughs, parched throats, and outbreaks of erysipelas, a streptococcus infection. When she stepped outside, the difference in temperature could be fifty, sixty, seventy degrees. On the road, horses driven hard appeared white, their coats of every color covered in frozen perspiration. Winter muted everything outside. A monochrome ceiling stretched across a desert of ice. The sun was brightest when the air was coldest. Sometimes the snow simply hung in the air, without falling, as if frozen into the void.

She had Kitty, at least, and Louisa needed her. There was no Countess Pauline to make her feel at home when she arrived in St. Petersburg, no Queen Luise, who would ignore protocol to make a new woman welcome. Instead the empress, Elizabeth Alexeievna, was beautiful and lily-like, silent, and famously sad.

On Sunday, November 12, 1809, Louisa waited in her apartment for the call to meet the empress and empress mother. She was anxious, fluttering, and "perfectly alone." Several notes had arrived from the Winter Palace changing the time of her presentation, leaving her alternately to hurry up or slow down her nerves. Her husband was at a church service. She was left by herself to fuss over her silver tissue skirt, her hoop, her thick crimson robe; to glance one last time in the glass at her hair, which was "simply arranged and ornamented with a small diamond arrow"; and to gather her fan, fur cloak, and gloves. When she finally emerged from her room to meet the two footmen who were to accompany her in the carriage, the American legation's young men "could not refrain from laughter" at the sight of her — so much equipage, so much trim, such a long train, lined white, that followed in her wake. But once she reached the palace and climbed the grand staircase, she was grateful for all the "trappings" of her dress, because she had not erred. She would pass.

A court official led her to meet Ekaterina Vassilievna, Countess Litta, "covered with diamonds," very fat and very kind. The countess, the grand mistress of the court (and niece and former mistress of Prince Grigori Alexandrovich Potemkin), told Louisa to stand in the middle of the long hall, facing west, where two Africans in Turkish costumes with drawn sabers were waiting to open the doors. She explained that Louisa should stand still while the empress moved toward her. When the tsarina reached her, Louisa should pretend to try to kiss her hand, "which her Majesty would not *permit,*" and when Louisa lifted her head, she must be very careful not to touch the royal body. Then the countess moved into an alcove, and Louisa was left to wait once more, to worry about the tremor in her knees, her gloves, and perhaps the inadequate size of the small diamond arrow in her hair.

Finally, the guards opened the doors, and Louisa could see the action repeated in a long succession of halls, two African guards at the end of each room pulling back door after door, the way opening before her. The tsarina appeared and the doors closed behind her. To Louisa's surprise, the tsarina was not alone. The tsar was with her.

Alexander was handsome, tall, resplendent, with beseeching blue eyes that tended to melt both men and women. He wore his military uniform, which had the inevitably impressive effect. Next to him, Elizabeth Alexeievna was tall, slender, delicate, graceful, and quiet. For fifteen minutes, he spoke, asking questions that Louisa answered, with the tsarina "only joining in with a word or two." Then the interview was over, the doors opened, and Louisa remained in the middle of the room by herself until the countess materialized and congratulated her on a job well done. If Louisa had heard the court gossip, she would have known that Elizabeth had watched two daughters die; that she had been unfaithful and the first child had not been Alexander's; that he did not forgive her even though his affairs were notorious from the start; that Elizabeth loved her husband and was not loved back. But in the moment, Louisa thought only of her relief.

Next came the introduction to the empress mother, Maria Feodorovna, and of the two presentations, this one may have been even more frightening. The empress mother was more exacting and formidable than either her daughter-in-law (whom she outranked) or her son. The empress mother played favorites (as the tsar's wife had learned too well). But by the end of the long walk to Maria Feodorovna's apartments, Louisa was less nervous than she had been. She was becoming practiced at this, and she was able to meet the older woman's questions with ease. Was not St. Petersburg impressive? Yes, Louisa answered. Although she "had seen London Paris Berlin and Dresden — &c.," she had been to "no city that equaled St. Petersburg in beauty."

"Ah mon dieu, vous avez tout vue!!" the startled empress mother replied. *Oh my Lord, you have seen everything!*

Louisa would remember the moment with a smile. "The Savage had been expected!"

2

The tsar paid special attention to the Americans from the moment of their arrival. Alexander had good reasons to treat John Quincy well; Russia's interests and the United States' were aligned. The United States wanted to ensure that in any general European peace settlement concluding the Napoleonic Wars, both France and Britain would respect freedom of the seas — and, because the United States would not be a party to any conference between the European nations and would not promise anything in exchange for free seas, the Russians would have to be the ones to demand it. Even more important, John Quincy was tasked with removing barriers to trade. Russia was not only a market for American goods; it made trade possible everywhere. American ships needed Russian hemp for rope, iron for chains and anchors, and flax for sails. For its part, Russia was traditionally a partner of Great Britain, but the 1807 Treaty of Tilsit had forced Alexander into Napoleon's Continental System, which forbade trade with Britain and its allies. Alexander wanted to break Napoleon's crippling hold on Russia's commercial ambitions while at the same time counterbalancing Britain's maritime prowess. He needed America's neutral ships to do it. So when John Quincy was presented to Alexander, the tsar stepped forward in a friendly manner and said, in French, "I am so glad to see you here."

Most of the daily commercial responsibilities required to protect American merchants were performed by the consul, Levett Harris, who made his living officially by his work as a middleman for merchants (and unofficially by taking a little more on the side). John Quincy spent most of his time writing dispatches to Secretary of State James Monroe, which took months to reach Washington, usually too long to be helpful. His real purpose was his presence. And there — though neither would admit it aloud — Louisa was indispensable. Being amiable and appealing was not exactly John Quincy's strong suit. How a republican who attended meetings, joined committees, and studied laws, and who hated the idleness of *ancien régimes* could succeed in autocratic Russia was not an easy problem to solve. A minister plenipotentiary met with diplomats and ministers, but he could not make an appointment to see the man who mattered. Alexander, after all, was the law, the nation — a godlike figure. Still, John Quincy managed to make time with him. Alexander had a habit of taking daily walks along the Admiralty Embankment or Nevsky Prospect, with only a guard or two nearby, and John Quincy often met him on the quay. They would talk about the cold temperature, or the long-tailed comet that was smeared across the sky, or the coming of war — with wariness, but also with warmth.

The other job of being present was done at night. "We have dinners, and balls, and suppers, and ice-hill parties and masquerades, almost without end," John Quincy wrote to his mother. "How much I am delighted by all this, is unnecessary for me to say; nor how congenial it is to my temper to find extravagance and dissipation become a public *duty*." Even more than in Berlin, it seems, he had a tendency to sit back, silent and sullen, or to drink and then talk too much. He preferred to stay at home and work on his project of comparing national weights and lengths, or write in his diary, or read his Petrarch, or pen long letters to his sons in Massachusetts, instructing them to be useful to humanity. He was half proud of his lack of social graces. Others were appalled. One young American, John Spear Smith, who came to St. Petersburg as part of the American legation, called him the "mute of Siberia." "He has no manners," Smith wrote, "is gauche, never was intended for a foreign Minister, and is only fit to turn over musty law authorities." What made John Quincy so inept was clear to Smith, and Smith was unsparing. "You would blush to see him in society, and particularly at Court circles, walking about perfectly listless, speaking to no one, and absolutely looking as if he were in a dream. . . . Dry sense alone does not do at European Courts. Something more is necessary, which something Mr. A. does not possess."

An English lord put it this way: "Of all the men whom it was ever my lot to accost and to waste civilities upon," he wrote, John Quincy Adams "was the most dogged and systematically repulsive. With a vinegar aspect, cotton in his leathern ears, and hatred of England in his heart, he sat in the frivolous assemblies of Petersburg like a bulldog among spaniels." For reasons of personal taste and politics, both of these observers were prejudiced against the bulldog, but their assessments matched others', including John Quincy's own.

So it helped that the minister plenipotentiary did not come to Russia alone. In St. Petersburg, the business of being important depended on court life even more than it had in Berlin. Others understood this. The Sardinian minister, Joseph de Maistre — a brilliant thinker and counterrevolutionary who was more at home in a ballroom than his friend John Quincy — requested that he be sent a secretary who was a good dancer and conversationalist, someone "who would serve me as informer with the women to learn the secrets of their husbands." John Quincy would have ignored the parties altogether if he could. They were "so trifling and insignificant in themselves, and so important in the eyes of Princes and Courtiers" — but the importance of princes and courtiers made the events impossible to ignore. His wife was more adept, more willing to smile at everyone and pretend to mean it. Once she had been introduced, she rode the incessant carousel of court life — sometimes accompanied by one of the American aides instead of her husband. She, after all, seems to have had the "something more" necessary to court life, the something her husband lacked.

She saw little of the day, living almost nocturnally during the winter social season. It was "customary" to eat dinner at one in the morning and to be out until four, sometimes six. She would wake a few hours later with a splitting headache, and she would have to put on a dress again. The carousel never stopped turning. The nights were monotonously splendid — glittering palaces, marble salons, exquisite French furniture, ancient vases and statues, orchestras and polonaises, aristocrats and officers, candelabras, satin and ermine cloaks, diamonds that glittered around her like so many cold stars. All of it was "too much like a fairy tale."

She was awed. How could she not be? The wonderment never quite wore off, but the weariness deepened as the months turned into years. It was unnatural, a jewel box of a life. She watched the wasp-waisted officers, their jackets so tightly laced that their chests swelled out, waltz with any willing women or run up unpayable gambling debts. She saw the false smiles of young women, beautifully idle but for their edgy, glancing looks. "Am constantly busy here without doing anything but dress, eat, sleep and go for drives," complained a Dutch woman who spent a winter as a courtier in St. Petersburg. It was, Louisa later wrote, "a killing life."

She could do it well. Louisa was thirty-four years old when she arrived — more cynical, perhaps, than she had been as an ingenue in Berlin, but also more self-possessed, better able to hold her own. One night at the palace, when Louisa was pregnant, the emperor made a show of tending to her. The master of ceremonies was ordered not to leave Louisa alone. No one could be allowed to jostle her, for an elbow could do great harm. In fact, Alexander concluded, it would be best if Louisa joined the empress on a platform in a throne. Louisa thanked him and declined. "Don't you know that no one says no to the

Emperor?" he told her.

She laughed. "But *I* am a republican," she replied. Alexander smiled at her impertinence and bowed.

What made the moment instructive was her awareness that these small gestures, this quick banter, was not just about her charm. The social encounter was part of a complex diplomatic maneuver. "The motive of all this I presume is political," she wrote in "Adventures." And indeed it was. That night, the French ambassador watched the special attention paid to the Americans, complained of a headache, and left the party. Caulaincourt was accustomed to his superior position in the Russian court, by his right as an ambassador (as opposed to John Quincy's measly minister plenipotentiary) and by virtue of his unusual closeness with Alexander. The favor paid to the United States was a slight to France. The day before the ball, Alexander had issued an ukase that raised taxes on goods coming by land (France) and lowered them on goods by sea (Britain and the United States). Napoleon's noose around Britain, his Continental System, could not survive Russia's rebellion — and so neither could the Franco-Russian alliance.

Not long afterward, John Quincy called upon the French ambassador to discuss a dispute between the United States and the French about the origin of American vessels.

(Because the British often brought in goods under the cover of neutral ships, the French routinely protested the arrival of American ships.) "It seems you are favorites here," Caulaincourt said. "You have found powerful protection, for most of your vessels have been admitted."

The tsar wanted their ships. While he was at it, he wanted something else. Alexander had met Kitty Johnson while on his daily walk upon the quay. Since he liked what he saw — her fresh looks, her vivacity, her charm — he made these meetings a habit. After a while, he began to speed up his stride when he approached them. Louisa watched this with some amusement and some alarm. At one point, she hurried Kitty into a carriage when she saw Alexander's quick step turn toward them — and saw his obvious irritation when they drove off. She tried stopping their walks until the tsar's attentions turned elsewhere; when they returned to the quay, tempted by fine weather, Alexander pointedly turned his head away. Then he addressed them with "a real imperial command in its tone and manner." He looked at Kitty directly and said he expected to meet them every day.

This was not all. At a ball at the French ambassador's house in May 1810 to celebrate the marriage of Napoleon and the Austrian archduchess Marie Louise, the tsar asked

Louisa to dance, which she understood to be a great honor. Then he asked her where her sister was, and soon he had Kitty by the hand. As they danced, Kitty — too unaware, or too uncaring, of the rigid etiquette that should have restrained her — laughed and flirted, treating the tsar like an American suitor and not a god. Charmed, he prolonged the dance, delaying the ambassador's dinner for twenty-five minutes as the pair circled the hall, sweeping past courtiers, leaving gossip in their wake. When the following winter's social season began, an invitation to the theater at the Hermitage arrived, and Miss Catherine Johnson was included. Since Kitty held no position with the legation and had never been formally presented, there was some doubt about what to do until the master of ceremonies assured John Quincy that the emperor had taken the pen in hand and written Miss Catherine Johnson's name himself. The group of Americans was also invited to use the royal entrance, normally granted only to diplomats of ambassadorial (not ministerial) rank. It was, the Monsieur de Maisonneuve said with some astonishment, "a very extraordinary distinction."

These very extraordinary marks of distinction were flattering to the United States, but not so flattering to Kitty's reputation, and they troubled Louisa. There were already whispers and wolfish grins. But she also knew, she later wrote, that there was a danger in refusing the tsar. Everything followed from Alexander: if he wanted to make Kitty suffer, the United States could suffer too. The distinctions between world politics and social contretemps were not as clear as someone like John Quincy would have liked to allow. In 1810–11, Alexander's desire for ships, his desire to send the French a message, his desire to lure Kitty into bed were overlaid. Of these, Kitty was only a speck to the tsar, only an idle desire, one passing interest among many. Still, Kitty drew the emperor's eye toward the Americans. He lingered with them, having ways and reasons to flatter them. Louisa had to be both her sister's protector and her husband's wife, and a republican and a courtier — in this instance, conflicting roles. In the end, she let the mild flirtation play out until it dissipated, as the emperor's flirtations tended to do. For as long as it was innocent, it was amusing, and perhaps it was a slight advantage.

The French ambassador Caulaincourt, whose regular mistress was the wife of a Russian military officer, once told Louisa she was too solemn for one so pretty. "When we were at Rome we must do as Rome," he said.

She coyly replied, "If I should go to Rome perhaps I might."

By May 1811, the mood had shifted. Caulaincourt was recalled to France. Napoleon was furious with Alexander's provocations against France, and a war between their countries loomed. The city's elite alternated between fervor and droll optimism as the soldiers began to muster and march. But Louisa's attention was elsewhere. In June, the tsar bought their apartment building on Nevsky Prospect from the Adamses' landlord, and so, while seven months pregnant, she had to pack up and quickly move. John Quincy rented a dacha in a profusion of flowers on Apothecary Island, northeast of the city, with views of the river and one of the tsar's palaces. John Quincy called it their "Russian Arcadia." Outside, barges floated by with musicians serenading the imperial family. Louisa kept the windows and doors open to hear it. She needed the refuge, the calm, the distractions. She was terrified at the prospect of giving birth.

Her family at home was never far from her mind. She thought of her sons constantly, and of her siblings and mother. It was all the harder because so little communication was possible. In May, when the first letters arrived from the United States since the previous fall, they brought terrible news. She walked into John Quincy's study one day and learned that her eldest sister, Nancy Hellen, had died in childbirth. "My heart collapsed in agony," Louisa wrote in her diary, and, pregnant herself, she fell in a "dead fainting fit." Unsurprisingly, she thought she was beginning to miscarry; she had already miscarried once in Russia. Only laudanum, "freely" used, calmed her down.

There was so much riding on this unborn child. In the spring, John Quincy had learned from an old British newspaper that President Madison had nominated him to the U.S. Supreme Court, and Congress had confirmed it. His parents sent ecstatic letters about the prospect of the office and his return, and formal notice soon followed. John Quincy would be freed from the ruinous expenses in Russia. He would be able to serve his country, and in a job that would allow him to rise above partisan politics. He would come home.

But John Quincy declined the appointment. He justified his decision by explaining that the choice was out of his hands: his wife was pregnant, and by the time she would be able to travel with an infant, ice would have trapped them. This was an excuse. He disliked practicing law and suspected he would be a bad judge. Privately, he admitted he might have declined the position even if Louisa were not pregnant. Still, it relieved him to be able to say that she was.

So she tried to relax, to distract herself from her fears. She took a chair to the banks of the river outside the house and went fishing with her young son Charles. She liked this "indolent sort of amusement," she wrote, "for I *do not think.*" Thinking made her "tremble."

But, for once, the birth went smoothly. On August 11, at half past seven, Louisa gave birth to a daughter. A month later, at the English Factory Church, the Anglican minister baptized the girl as Louisa Catherine Adams. There was a small celebration at the Adamses' house on Apothecary Island afterward — a collection of counts, ambassadors, Americans. The tsar had offered to stand as godfather, which John Quincy declined, though the child's parents thought the baby did merit extraordinary attention. They studied the child's soft, small body with startled wonder. "Such a pair of eyes!" Louisa wrote. "I fear I love her too well!"

"We are daily seeking for resemblances in her countenance, and associate her in fancy with all our dearest friends," John Quincy wrote to Abigail. "She has the eyes of one; the nose of another, the mouth of a third and the forehead of a fourth, but her chin is absolutely and exclusively her own."

Winter drove the Adamses off the island, back into the city, into a cramped apartment with leaky windows. The dacha was left to the wolves. Crises were coming, in both the United States and Russia. By spring, Russia and France faced a conflict over Poland. The tsar already had troops massed along the border. "Thus it ends," Alexander told John Quincy on the cold quay in March, not long before he left to join his armies. Great Britain continued to kidnap the United States' sailors and dismiss its maritime rights. War hawks and Anglophiles worked against one another in Congress, and Madison wobbled toward war. There were crises of a domestic sort, meanwhile, in the Adamses' household. John Quincy's nephew William Smith and Kitty had some sort of romantic relationship, and Kitty was ill — possibly pregnant. For whatever reason, John Quincy forced William to marry her, which he did in a small ceremony in the Adamses' apartment. (There is no record of a miscarriage, and Kitty would become pregnant a year later.) William's debts gave John Quincy plenty to abhor; the expense of St. Petersburg was not easy for William to bear, either, and he was not the type to let pleasure pass by. He was begging John Quincy to lend him $3,000 so that he could pay what he owed.

Letters rarely arrived from the United States that year, and when they did, they were almost always devastating. News came that Louisa's mother, Catherine, had died in an epidemic that had also killed her sister Caroline's husband. They learned that John Quincy's aunt and uncle Mary and Richard Cranch, who were taking care of Louisa's sons John and George, both died. John Quincy's sister (and William's mother) Nabby had undergone an excruciating operation to have her breast removed after a tumor had been found. Nabby's situation was, Louisa knew, "a hopeless illness."

At the end of March 1812 John Quincy asked Abigail to send their sons to Russia — but George and John could make the long journey, he added, only if the United States and Britain were not at war, which would make the journey aboard an American ship impossible. It was not his wish for them to come, he added, but that of their mother, who was insistent. Soon after, Louisa learned that even that hope was gone. Congress declared war on Britain in June, the culmination of a long sequence of breaches between the two countries that had been building for decades: the impressment of sailors that had prompted the *Chesapeake* crisis that had led to John Quincy's departure from the Senate, trade restrictions prompted by the Napoleonic Wars in Europe, border issues with Canada, and the sense, in the United States, of persistent humiliations and insults from its former ruler. The declaration of war took place just a week before Napoleon's troops breached Russia's borders.

All of this touched Louisa, and it didn't. She heard the bells tolling for Te Deums and saw the illuminations after the official reports of incredible Russian victories, reports which everyone knew not to credit too much. She read in the outdated newspapers of the conflict in the United States. Most pressingly, of course, the war meant a longer separation from her older sons, a separation that brought her near despair when she dwelled on it. But she still had Charles, about to turn five years old, and the new daughter, little Louisa, and she took solace in them. The baby was a kind of gift. Little Louisa grew rapidly, and before she was one she was speaking, saying *papa* and *mama.* "I wish you could see what a good natured little mad cap she is," Louisa wrote to her son George. The child brought Louisa inexhaustible delight. "She plays all day long."

Then that child, so much loved, fell sick. Louisa was filled with the terror of losing her. That summer, 1812, little Louisa began teething rapidly. Six teeth came in quickly, and then another five or six cropped up at once. Louisa weaned her in July, just before her first birthday. In the middle of that month, the baby developed dysentery. She was already small for her age, only two feet and three inches on her first birthday. She did not have much weight to lose.

For some weeks, she seemed to improve. But in mid-August, she was extremely sick. Louisa tried to begin breast-feeding her again, but it was too late. The child developed a high fever.

Outside, thousands of lamps, hung in elaborate and spectacular patterns, were lit to celebrate reports of Russia's stupendous victories over Napoleon's Grand Army, reports most knew were false. Napoleon and his army were storming toward Moscow as the Russians retreated; many predicted Napoleon would then turn north, toward St. Petersburg. An air of crisis pervaded the city. The official optimism was set grotesquely against fear.

Inside the house, there was only terrified desperation. On August 30 Louisa took the baby to Ochta, to the countryside, to see if fresh air would help. By September 8 she was back in the city. The child's condition rapidly worsened. She was seized by convulsions. "Language cannot express the feelings of a parent beholding the long continued agonies of a lovely infant," John Quincy wrote in his diary. Doctors tried to lance her gums. They gave her emetics, digitalis, and laudanum. They shaved her hair and used poultices to raise blisters on the back of her soft head.

Louisa, thirteen months old, died at 1:25 in the morning on September 15, 1812. Her mother, in the room next door when it happened, fainted when she learned the news. The "calm fortitude and pious resignation of my dearest friend has been as remarkable as her unbounded self-devotion," John Quincy wrote, reading into her reaction what he needed to see. The funeral was held in the church where the child had been baptized almost exactly a year before. Afterward, the body was buried in the Lutheran Cemetery on Vasilevsky Island. Louisa did not attend the burial. But for months, she thought of nothing else.

At the end of October, Louisa turned over the marbled paper cover of a small blank book and began to write in a small hand. She needed to distract herself, she wrote, from her morbid thoughts and acid guilt. Instead, her diary became a record of her private, crushing sadness. "My heart is buried in my Louisa's grave," she wrote in early November, "and my greatest longing is to be laid beside her."

3

On September 15, the day Louisa's baby died in St. Petersburg, Napoleon rode through the empty streets of Moscow. Small fires had already been lit throughout the city, only four hundred miles south of St. Petersburg, and soon the streets were ablaze. Moscow burned down within days. John Quincy observed the coincidence between the death of his daughter and the destruction of the city and saw that it meant nothing. Like Louisa, he was undone by his grief. For the first time in his life, a personal tragedy so far outweighed the public one that he could not even bring himself to focus on his work. His own country was at war and the country where he lived was going up in flames, and yet neither of these compared to the loss of his tiny child. When he wrote to his mother, six days later, to report the death of the baby, he did not mention the fire in Moscow, nor Napoleon's advance, nor the meeting John Quincy attended just before dispatching the letter, in which the tsar's foreign minister, Count Rumyantsev, had told him that Alexander was proposing to mediate between the United States and Britain. It was a proposal that could change the course of history: it could mean peace for the United States. But when John Quincy wrote to his mother, he said nothing about world events. He wrote only that his daughter had died. Considering the normal content of their correspondence, even in prior times of tragedy, this was extraordinary. So was the struggle — almost the rage — he expressed in response to his father's call for philosophical resignation. "My lovely flower is blasted too, and I am not permitted to enquire why?" he wrote to John Adams that October. "The desire of my eyes, the darling of my heart is gone, and unavailing sorrow, and the bitter memory of what she was, is all that is left us in her stead!"

His grief stayed with him. The knowledge that suffering was the universal fate of men, which he had so long made the basis of his philosophy, could not lessen his pain. Even a year later, his sense of loss overwhelmed him. "On the same day that my child died, Moscow was surrendered to an invader, and was consigned to the flame by its own inhabitants — Within three months after the invader himself was a wretched fugitive and his numberless host was perishing by frost, famine and the sword," he wrote to his father.

"Neither the fires of Moscow, nor the frosts which destroyed the invaders could comfort me for the loss of my child." A year after that, two years after the event, John Quincy would tell his mother that the sight in the street of a young girl was enough to make his heart clench.

But after a time, he began to find refuge in his work, his habits, his daily walks, his books. He took comfort in routine. He was the type who knew how many strides it took him to walk a street block and who had measured the length of his stride. He mourned, but his grief ran its course, and he was able to distract himself and to recover. He had a sense of incredible responsibility and obligation. It was not so easy for his wife.

He watched her wander through her days. "Our domestic condition is no longer the same as before," he wrote in his diary at the end of September, a rare acknowledgment of his wife's situation. "The privation and the vacuity are more heavily and more constantly felt by her [Louisa] . . . than by me. The maternal cares were the business as well as the enjoyment of her life." This was sympathetic, as far as it went. She was beside herself with grief — her health wrecked, her mind inflamed. With his typical mix of pedantry and kindness, he gave her a book by his friend Benjamin Rush, *Medical Inquiries and Obser-*

vations, upon the Diseases of the Mind, published in 1812. It postulated that madness came not from the liver or intestines (still theories worth refuting at the time) or from the brain itself, but from the overstimulation of blood vessels in the brain. Insanity was a circulatory problem, and it could be connected to feelings — joy, terror, love, shame, poverty, grief. Written for an audience of doctors, the book provided a taxonomy of madness, tracing its origins, symptoms, and possible cures. She read it, and she looked for herself in its pages. "A person is apt to fancy himself afflicted with every particular symptom described," she wrote in her diary, and so she saw herself in each bleak diagnosis. She wondered if she was going insane.

She had grieved before. She had lost both of her parents, her older sister, and several friends. Yet this was different. She had not only lost her daughter; she was also half convinced that she had killed her. She blamed herself for weaning the child too early. She blamed herself for falling down with the baby in her arms, "in which I did not perceive that she had met with the slightest injury but which is said to have been the cause of her death." She blamed herself for her "procrastination" when the infant had fallen ill. She blamed herself for her sins, convinced that her child had died as her "punishment." She obsessed over the "secret and bitter reproaches of my heart."

In her diary, Louisa described a nightmare that she had one night. She was playing with her healthy daughter at the dacha in Ochta, when she was summoned by her father (by then eleven years dead) to fetch wine. She asked her sister Nancy (two years dead) to go with her. At the bottom of the stairs into the cellar, Louisa stumbled over a "body newly murdered," and when she looked for Nancy, she saw a frozen woman "just risen from the grave." The dream ended with thunder and lightning and words of fire in the sky. "Be of good cheer," the words said, "thy petition is granted." Then she woke. Her only petition, her wish she wrote in her diary again and again, was to be buried alongside her daughter in the cemetery on Vasilevsky Island. She considered suicide. "In vain I reason with myself," she wrote, "but the desire is uncontrollable and my mind is perpetually dwelling on some means to procure this desired blessing."

To an extent, strong expressions of grief were expected and allowed. In her time and culture, the loss of a child was not uncommon but still no less lamented. A grieving woman could openly acknowledge the pain she felt by the black clothes that she wore. She might wear a ring stamped with a small skull and crossbones, or a bracelet made with the dead's braided hair. She could advertise her sorrow and expect to share her tears. But in St. Petersburg, Louisa had nowhere to turn but inward. Even her sister, her confidante, was almost estranged from her. Kitty had scarlet fever in the winter of 1813, and John Quincy had declared that as soon as she was well, she and her husband, his nephew and aide William Smith, would have to leave St. Petersburg. He could hardly bear to look at William, whose conduct disgusted him. (Kitty would later become pregnant, pushing back their departure until the summer of 1814.) Louisa had few other close friends in St. Petersburg. She was cut off from her family and friends in the United States; letters took six months to arrive. She had almost given up hope of seeing her two older sons ever again. Worst of all was the distance she felt from her husband. "Mr A is even more buried in study than when he left America, and has acquired so great a disrelish for society, that even his small family circle appears at times to become irksome to him," she wrote to Abigail.

"I am condemned to wear out my existence, in this horrid place, without a friend, or a single human being who can participate in my feelings," she wrote. Kitty's illness and troubling relationship with William Smith surely affected her as much as they did John Quincy, and John Quincy's sympathy had turned to skepticism, which turned her sadness into anger. Louisa punished herself, though, as much as others. She wrote, privately, that grief had warped her personality.

They fought. When John Quincy questioned her methods of teaching Charles his prayers, Louisa stormed off. He called her "suspicious and jealous." She accused him of coldness and neglect. In his diary, he was silent about these shows of anger. He never censured her. At the same time, he acknowledged that he could not always control his temper. In letters and in her own diary, she anticipated and tried to preempt his disapproval, which could be bullying. She begged him not to criticize her — only to have him respond, "If I am angry, I am sure it will be more for your sake and that of your children than my own."

She wrote in her diary, "I feel what a burthen I must be to all around me." With her own mother dead, Louisa found herself longing for her mother-in-law, forgiving and forgetting their old tensions. She found herself wishing for someone who would understand how she felt, "a comforter" and "a friend." Someone who was not John Quincy. They fired shots at each other while pretending to claim the blame themselves. For her part, she told John Quincy, she was "perfect aware" that she was not an "agreeable companion," having "too often been made sensible of my incapacity not to feel it most keenly."

There were tensions in their marriage that both had long ago realized, "differences of sentiment, of tastes, and of opinions in regard to domestic economy, and to the education of children, between us," as John Quincy had written in his diary on their fourteenth anniversary, in 1811, even as he concluded that the marriage was a definite success. "There are natural frailties of temper in both of us; both being quick and irascible, and mine being sometimes harsh." Their daughter's death deepened those differences and sharpened their tempers. Louisa's illnesses also worsened the dynamic between them. He had proved he could care for her, and she needed and craved his care. But sometimes his attention made her feel guilty and him resentful. In January 1813, Louisa miscarried yet again. John Quincy wrote in his diary that he had some sense of "duty" to be by her bedside, but added that he did not have much time to spare for it. The duty to comfort her, he wrote, "does in some degree interfere" with "other duties."

The other duties were not insignificant. The fates of Europe and the United States were intertwined, and the tsar's invitation to mediate in the war between Britain and the United States had given John Quincy an opening to play a leading role. Napoleon had fled Russia, his Grand Army routed. A coalition of the once-vanquished European powers —

Russia, Prussia, Austria, Spain, Portugal, and several German states — along with Great Britain and Sweden, were mustering over a million troops in central Europe, to pursue the Corsican; Alexander himself assumed command of the coalition army. John Quincy calculated that once the French were defeated, a peace treaty between the United States and Britain would become even more imperative. There was doubt that the United States, which had already suffered embarrassing defeats at the hands of British forces and their Native American allies in Canada and Florida, could withstand the full force of British arms freed from the fight with France. If ever there was a moment when John Quincy's country needed its minister plenipotentiary in Russia, it was now.

While her husband worked, Louisa passed much of the time in her room alone, often ill. Outside, it was cold — reaching above zero Fahrenheit only once in January. Even inside, it was almost too cold to hold a pen. She read lurid French court memoirs and books about the queen of Navarre, King Louis XIV, the Duchess de Mazarin. She took notes from a French dictionary of famous men. These sensational stories did not make her fantasize about living an opulent lifestyle; she had no reason to escape into a world she had glimpsed in real life and understood all too well. Instead, she read the books as cautionary tales. The "weakness and fragility of human virtue, unaided by an all-wise and superintending providence," she wrote in her diary, corrupted even noble ambitions. There was a fatality to this: if human nature was vain, and ambition corrosive, then even the well-intentioned individual had not much of a chance. "It has only served to convince me," she wrote after reading the memoir of a mistress of Henry II of France, "how little we can do of ourselves."

Her reading of history only confirmed her grim conviction about what was happening in the world at that moment, the great events "which I am hourly witnessing." She heard with "unceasing astonishment" about Napoleon's calamitous retreat from Moscow, his army freezing and starving and dying on the road. Her "pity and horror" were intermingled with a sense that he deserved the punishment. "We cannot trace his rise, and see his fall," she wrote in her diary, "without shuddering at the length, to which a blind and inexhaustible ambition, will lead mankind."

Napoleon, in turn, made her think of her husband. She was harsher toward him, though not by name, than she had ever been. Her anger and grief over her lost daughter — and her distance from her two young sons, who had been left in the United States against her will — wanted an outlet, and she found one close at hand. In her diary, she barely disguised the connection between Napoleon and John Quincy when she described her contempt. When a man is self-regarding, she wrote, he becomes "incapable" of being sociable in daily life. "Every thing that surrounds him must live for him." Those "who are so unfortunate as to belong to him" — harsh and telling words — are the ones who suffer the most from his self-absorption, his willingness to sacrifice their lives for his greatness. "They say I am ambitious," she wrote on August 14, two days after what would have been her daughter's birthday. But how could that be, she asked, when she compared herself "with those to whom I am the most nearly connected," by which she meant her husband. "When I see every thought devoted peace happiness family every thing neglected for this one object" — power — "my heart decidedly assures me that for this great end I was not made." The proof of her powerlessness, she claimed, was in her inability to stop her husband's ascendance. In a voice of rising pitch and intensity, not pausing for breath, she wrote, "Were I of consequence enough to be any thing I should only prove a bar in the way of attaining it No!" This was partly private venting. Her relationship with her husband, even at that time, was more complex, as her intimate correspondence with him always attested. But that *No!* was a small cry of resistance, feeble but desperate.

It is also possible that when Louisa said "they say I am ambitious," she was guiltily defending herself against her own charge. Her husband, after all, often did the same in his diary, declaring his disinterestedness even as he grasped for glory. That chance for greatness had suddenly come into reach. In Russia — in exile, as he called it — an opportunity appeared to resuscitate his moribund political career. John Quincy did not wait for approval from Washington to accept the tsar's offer to mediate between Britain and the United States to end the War of 1812, and President Madison did not wait for the British to accept the offer before sending Senator James Bayard and Secretary of the Treasury Albert Gallatin to St. Petersburg as envoys while appointing John Quincy the head of the commission. Louisa hosted a dinner for them and accompanied them to see the city's sights, but their presence meant little to her. "The arrival of Mr. Bayard, and Gallatin, my dear Madam, has made so little alteration in our situation, that I have little or nothing to write you, but complaints, of the prospect, I have of a much lengthen'd stay in this country," she wrote to Abigail.

"We must live almost by candlelight," John Quincy wrote to his mother. The sun glimmered on the snow for only a few glancing hours. Louisa's spirits were as dark. She read John Quincy's astronomy books, peering through the thick glass of the double-paned windows in a futile attempt to see the stars. She was sealed inside.

4

The British rejected the tsar's offer of mediation, believing that Alexander was biased toward the United States ("I fear the Emperor of Russia is half an American," wrote the prime minister, Lord Liverpool, to the foreign minister, Lord Castlereagh, in September). Instead, Britain proposed an independent peace conference and agreed to a neutral location. John Quincy went to join Gallatin and Bayard, who had already left St. Petersburg, and Henry Clay, John Calhoun, and Jonathan Russell, who were coming from the United States to join the peace commission. John Quincy left St. Petersburg in April 1814. He planned to go to Revel, Stockholm, and Gothenburg; he would end up adding Ghent and then Paris. He was supposed to be gone from St. Petersburg for several months, though he privately expected that he would never come back. He would not reunite with his wife or son for eleven months.

It seems that he was relieved to leave her.

Placidly, he told her that the distance would be good for their marriage. "In the affection of those who truly love," he wrote to her, "there is a fervour of sentiment when they are separated from each other, more glowing, more unmingled and more anxious, than when being together it has the continual opportunity of manifesting itself by acts of kindness."

She was having none of it. "What being on earth is so wretched as a woman without her husband, more especially in a foreign country, without knowing the languages of those who surround her," she responded furiously. With a note of arch defiance, she declared that she was fine without him. "At first it was dreadful, I am now becoming more reconciled to it," she continued. "Perhaps in time *I shall like it.*" John Quincy took her words as serious. When he applauded her fortitude but expressed his hurt at her declaration of independence, she responded in a different tone, now mournful. "I should never even in jest have hinted that I could live happily without you. There are some wounds which are not easy to heal, and forgetfulness is not my best quality."

She had not wanted him to go. She and Charles had accompanied him as far as Strelna, twelve miles outside St. Petersburg, on a cold, gusty day, where they shared a meal and then said goodbye. After the sound of the horse's bells had vanished, six-year-old Charles cried indignantly, seeing the tears on his mother's cheeks.

She was thirty-nine years old by then. Gray streaked her hair. The long winters, endless nights, sealed rooms and stoked smoky ovens guarding against the Russian cold, constant pregnancies and heartbreaking disappointments, anxieties about her children, her parents, her sisters, and money, grief for her daughter, and lonely days had left their marks. Time had loosened the skin around her chin. Her face had grown thinner. She did not know what to expect now.

For months, she had felt distant from John Quincy. He was — as he would be for much of his life — self-involved in unbelievable ways. But his absence made her miss him. And her doubts in herself, some of which he had planted, made her unsure of her capabilities without him. John Quincy had never shown much confidence in her ability to manage herself, let alone the family's affairs. He tended to lecture and chide her. He once wrote to her that he knew her "*heart* would always take the tenderest care" of the children, but he felt the need to encourage "continual reflection — if possible to prevent a *thoughtless* moment." The implication was clear: she could not be trusted. Of course, that particular admonition came after she admitted to leaving a candle unattended and nearly burning down the house. She did not always blame him for not believing in her; she often thought he was right.

So one of his first letters from the road surprised her. He said that he had forgotten to give her something important. "It is my *Will* — of which you are constituted the sole Executrix, for all my affairs out of the United States," he wrote. From a man whose affairs were so extensive, and who by nature was so controlling, this was an extraordinary task, but also an extraordinary declaration of confidence. When the document arrived, she tucked it away in a trunk and proclaimed it quite unnecessary. Actually, though, it was a gift, one of the greatest he ever gave to her. "I have been labouring for many years under a false impression so painful to my heart," she wrote to him. She had always thought that he did not trust her.

His will was only the start of the responsibilities he now entrusted her with. He sent her memoranda and lists of all his business. He told her to open his mail and judge its importance, passing on what was necessary. He asked her to send him the listed exchange rates from London, Amsterdam, Hamburg, and Paris, the values of silver rubles and ducats, and, "as often as you can conveniently get the information, the current price of the *obligations,* in the market." He told her to settle bills, keep accounts with merchants, pay interest when it came due, fire servants when they stole too much. What was more, she was expected to represent the United States in court — unofficially, of course, but in practice. John Quincy had left Levett Harris, the American consul, as the chargé d'affaires, but reluctantly. Harris was well liked, but it was no secret to anyone, including Louisa or John Quincy, that the unsalaried consul lived the lavish life of a Russian noble — elegant clothes, fine furniture, "very tasty and expensive" apartments with crimson damask walls — by accepting huge bribes. He was also, as Louisa amusedly observed, chasing John Quincy's job.

That John Quincy was willing to leave his business in St. Petersburg in the hands of his inexperienced wife and untrustworthy lieutenant speaks to what he stood to gain by going. He wanted to help end a war he thought unwise, and if he played his part right, his reward, he had heard whispered, would be the highest diplomatic post — minister to Great Britain. He would then be able to return to the United States no longer an outcast, no longer an irrelevant figure but a leading candidate for the presidency — having completed a commission with Clay and Calhoun, two of the nation's brightest young stars. Louisa saw the situation clearly. She may have written about his ambition in her diary with a dagger for a pen, but in her letters to him, she gently teased. "I feel a little anxious to know how the rival candidates for the Presidency will feel towards each other," she wrote to him.

Maybe John Quincy was right; maybe being apart allowed them to be more tender with each other. Twice a week, they wrote each other letters. His were long, full of charming and self-deprecating anecdotes and evaluations of his fellow commissioners and of himself. He would sketch a scene at supper, or assess Gallatin's considerable talents, or draw the curious comparison between himself and Clay, who was destined to become a crucial figure in his life. Outwardly, Clay seemed the opposite of John Quincy — tall and gaunt, where John Quincy was stout; a gambler, where John Quincy was at heart a Puritan. Clay would sometimes return to bed after a night of cards just as John Quincy was rising. But John Quincy sensed an unflattering kinship. He half joked about it: they shared "the same dogmatical, overbearing manner, the same harshness of look and expression, and the same forgetfulness of the courtesies of society." The two men sparred throughout the peace conference. Then again, John Quincy sparred with everyone.

Admiring Louisa's own ability to sketch a character in a letter, he could be sure that his descriptions of others and his self-analysis would interest her. It was more surprising that his letters to her were also full of news. He would report the capture of the frigate *Essex,* the threat to Sackets Harbor, the deals cut at the Congress of Vienna, and the British peace commissioner's delaying tactics. He wrote to his wife as he was used to writing to his mother. Louisa encouraged him and tried to respond in kind, though her insights into geopolitical events were never as shrewd as her insights into people, and the foreign newspapers she read were usually outdated and wrong. But she was earnest in her effort to engage him. Unlike Abigail, she cared less about what he said than about his saying anything at all. It was a measure of how badly she wanted to be taken seriously. "I have just done reading the Life of Cicero, (dont laugh) and there is a passage in it concerning the defence of republic's, that has struck me most forcibly, and is certainly the most applicable to the present state of our country, of any thing I ever met with," she would write. She was afraid of being made fun of, but the effect of their exchange was galvanizing. "You will smile at my politics but when I write you my thoughts run so rappidly, that I find my paper full before I am aware of it, and generally on subjects very foreign to my intentions, when I first sat down to write."

Her confidence in herself and her ability to manage was growing. Given the chance, she did her best, and she did well. She rented a dacha for the summer, negotiated rent for a new apartment in the city, hired and fired servants. When her carriage broke, she bought a new one. She had arrived in Russia lamenting that she could not buy a present for George and John because of her lost dowry, but now she sent each of them a watch. She spent more than usual on her clothing "on account of the fetes." "I am sorry for it," she lied.

She liked the independence, which was new to her. She claimed to hate going into public, especially without her husband. But after one ball she wrote, "On the whole I was never at a more charming party in my life." When Alexander returned to St. Petersburg for the first time since the defeat of Napoleon, she went to her first Te Deum — the great Russian Orthodox service of celebration — and joined the multitudes in watching the tsar kiss the cross. In early August, she went to a ball at the summer palace at Peterhof, where the terraces over the Neva seemed to spread in all directions, lit by lantern globes, extending even into the sea. From that vantage, St. Petersburg seemed only a slender white vision. She said she feared she would disgrace John Quincy, but in fact she was proud of how she had done. An Englishman, Mr. Bailey, "said he would astonish the world, and show them that the English and Americans had enter'd into an alliance, by dancing a Polonaise with me," she wrote. The emperor, she added, was delighted to see it done.

She now did things her way, confident in her good intentions. When Levett Harris, the chargé d'affaires, ordered her not to attend the great ball at Pavlovski (he was miffed at the form of the invitation he himself had received), she went without an escort, taking her young son Charles. They walked through the rose garden, dined with the diplomatic corps, delighted in the pleasure boats, and enjoyed a sense of distinction, after the empress received them with special notice and invited them to stay an extra night. While Charles watched fireworks, Louisa attended the empress mother's ball. "Poor I became the only representative of America," she wrote to John Quincy — quite pleased.

Charles began to appear more often in her letters and diary. He had always been a part of her life in St. Petersburg, but never before quite in this way. Before John Quincy left, Louisa's preoccupations were elsewhere, on the endless rounds of social obligations, her health, her grief, her other two sons, almost nearer to her mind by their absence. Charles spent much of his time with servants, or his friends — mostly children of expatriates — or at a little school. John Quincy, of course, superintended his education, and Louisa had long ago given up the sense that she should have some say in it. So Charles had spent his five and a half years in St. Petersburg in a strange setting — trapped inside for much of the frozen year; more comfortable speaking French or German, the language of his nursemaid (English was his third language); becoming a kind of curious appendage to the court, as they all were. He had played with the tsarina on the floor; he had been put on display at children's balls and parties, where there were "oceans of champaign for the little people." Once, at the age of three, he opened a ball with the French ambassador's illegitimate daughter. (Louisa had dressed him as an Indian chief, and when he entered — to his startled surprise — the crowd applauded. Another time, he had gone as Bacchus.) He had borne the burden of standing in for his dead sister and absent brothers. John Quincy, in fact, had measured Charles's height not only on his own birthday, but also on George's and John's.

But Louisa came to find herself fascinated by her youngest son — his precocity, his arrogance, his tenderness, and his temper, which could be as stormy as his parents'. He was seven years old and very small, with ginger hair and hazel eyes, fiercely loyal to his mother and sensitive to her moods. In many ways he was so young, a child who took delight in fantastical stories or in discovering a row of tiny cucumbers underneath the blossoms in the garden, who threw tantrums, who missed his father. He liked to test his mother's authority, but he was curious, intelligent, and could be tender. They spent endless hours together. Most unusually, he had learned to read his mother's feelings and moods. When she was grieving for her daughter, he comforted her with "little tender assiduities; attentions gentle and affectionate beyond [his] years." He had drawn her back into the world, breathing "new hope" into her. And when she found herself fully in charge, she came to see how her influence might shape him, too — not only her husband's. She was also capable of giving an education. "I found delight," she would later tell him, "in your opening mind." In Charles, she found a companion when she most needed one.

On some days, though, not even he could help her feel less alone. After Kitty and William Smith left that summer, she spent days roaming the house like a ghost. Sometimes, she could not help but cry, and when winter came, her sadness grew worse. She was "sick and weary," too keenly aware of the "gaudy loneliness" of the court. "I know not what ails me to day but these holidays do not suit me at all I feel so isolated among all the gay folks," she wrote to John Quincy, "and it makes me feel our separation more keenly than ever."

"Mama is a great amateur of cards," young Charles wrote to his father that November.

"She is always laying out the cards, to see if you will come back soon."

Still, when 1814 ended, she was stronger on her own than she had been when the year began. She even had a stronger sense of herself as an American. The War of 1812 had clarified her allegiance. Where before she had been cynical, more distant, now she spoke fervently of "our country." In that, she was like many Americans. Even from afar, John Quincy thought he could see that the war had brought together a fractured nation. He wrote to Louisa, "The sentiment is the same among us all — It is profound — anxious — and true to the honour and interest of our Country — It is a sentiment which is generally felt by the People of the United States, will rouse them to exertion."

She agreed. "Our situation is perilous in the extreme, but it is extreme distress alone which can ever discover to us the extent of our resources." It was also true of herself.

On December 27, John Quincy wrote to Louisa to announce that the treaty, finally, had been signed. The terms were not all he had wished for — it was *status quo ante bellum* — but still, it was peace. They would be headed next to London; he was the new minister plenipotentiary to Great Britain. First, though, as she had suggested he should, he would make a trip to Paris.

"I therefore now invite you, to break up altogether our establishment at St. Petersburg," he wrote to her, "to dispose of all the furniture which you do not incline to keep, to have all the rest packed up carefully, and left in the charge of Mr Harris to be sent next summer either to London or to Boston, and to come with Charles to me at Paris, where I shall be impatiently waiting for you."

"I am turned woman of business," Louisa declared to John Quincy. She had to sell the furniture, dispose of the house, and buy a carriage that could carry her across the continent. She needed supplies: food, drink, clothing, maps, and tools. As one who was so often sick, she needed medicines. If she consulted a guidebook for what to bring (John Quincy's library had several), she might have brought enough herbs and remedies for a small apothecary. One 1820 guidebook recommended: "Iceland moss — James's powder — sal volatile — aether — sulphuric acid — pure opium — liquid laudanum — paregoric elixir — ipecacuanha — emetic tartar — prepared calomel — diluted vitriolic acid — essential oil of lavender — spirit of lavender — sweet spirit of intro — antimoni-alwine — super-carbonated kali — court-plaster and lint."

Her largest expense was the carriage. She bought a berline, a large vehicle with four seats and glass windows, all balanced on an elaborate suspension of springs intended to smooth the rough ride. At first the carriage would travel on runners, like a sleigh; wheels — large for the rear axle, small for the front — were packed for when she reached melting roads. This was only the beginning. She needed to be able to sleep when they were forced to travel through the night. She procured a bed for Charles that could be spread on the carriage's floor, and blankets and pillows for herself. She needed servants, preferably ones who could handle weapons. She needed letters of credit, which she would exchange for cash on the road. She needed a great deal of money, because each post house exacted a toll, and her carriage, with its six horses and two postilions, was taxed at the highest rate. She sewed gold and silver into her skirts to hide her wealth from robbers on the road (and from her male servants). She bought a hooded sledge, called a *kibitka*, which would carry the servants as far as Riga. All of this was very expensive, so expensive that it "frightened me." Selling the furniture had brought her $1,693 — a good sum; she had negotiated well — but in the end, John Quincy's accounting reckoned that her trip, altogether, cost $1,984.99, or somewhere between twenty-five and thirty thousand dollars in today's value.

What she didn't sell, she packed up to send to Massachusetts, or to London to furnish their new home. There were tables, chairs, plates, clothes. There were gifts from their friends. Had John Quincy been with her, he might have insisted that she turn some of the treasures down. But he was not there, and she was not inclined to say no. According to family lore, an exquisite malachite and gold necklace, earrings, bracelet, and a brooch that she kept were given to her by the tsar. The jewelry remained in her descendants' possession, and it is hard to imagine where else the priceless jewelry could have come from.

No doubt because of the tsar's favoring of the Americans, the Russian minister of the interior (also the tsar's spymaster and prison warden) sent out orders that she should be treated well on the road "on pain of punishment." She also got passports — a Russian one for passage through the empire ("in pursuance of the edict of His Majesty, the Sovereign Emperor Alexander Pavlovic, Ruler of all the Russias, etc., etc., etc."), a Prussian one (*"im Namen seiner Majestät des Königs von Preussen"*), and one for France (*"au Nom du Roi"* — since Louis XVIII was restored to the throne after Napoleon was sent into exile). She had to chart her course, calculate travel times, locate post stations. There were many guidebooks, some in John Quincy's library, though in 1814 they were generally by and for men. It was almost unheard of for a woman to make this kind of journey alone.

The trip was nearly two thousand miles. Louisa would be on the road for forty days.

It was still winter, and though the solstice had passed and the sun hung just above the horizon for longer each day, the sky was still gloomy and gray and freezing. She wanted to move fast, however, because the frozen roads were to her advantage. Spring's thaw would make them treacherous. Louisa had three weeks to make all her preparations. She had no way of knowing if any decision she made was right, and experience had taught her to fear how John Quincy would respond. "My anxiety is unspeakable," she wrote to John Quincy. "If I do wrong it is unintentional," she wrote on another occasion. "Mon Ami I am so afraid of cold looks."

Before she left, she took leave of the tsarina, who had always been kind to her, and the empress dowager, who, in the end, had decided to like her. John Quincy had explicitly instructed her not to let them know that this farewell was for good, and so Louisa dutifully hinted that she would be back. But the tsarina saw the joy in Louisa's eyes and heard the thrill in her voice, and she laughed and said she'd never seen "a woman so alterd in her life for the better," and she wished Louisa the best for the rest of her life.

Louisa had not grown to love the society during her five years in St. Petersburg, where scandal masqueraded as civility, and the price of entry was a dress that broke the bank but the price of exclusion much worse. Her closest friend, her sister Kitty, was already gone. But there were a few others left, and they were dear to her. Annette Krehmer, the wife of the Adamses' banker, had been ready with advice from the moment Louisa had arrived in St. Petersburg, telling her what to buy, where to live. Some men found Mrs. Krehmer pushy and gauche, but Louisa had come to think that it was not a bad thing, in an expensive foreign city, to have a friend who would host large dinners in her elegant house in town, or arrange a country retreat during a time of great distress, or (having a young daughter) invite Charles and his friends to play. Annette had been the baby Louisa's godmother.

There was also a small group of expatriates and diplomats with whom Louisa was friendly, occasionally intimate. Some were already gone, their movements dictated by the constantly shifting alliances and unstable situations of their rulers. Madame Bezerra, wife of the Portuguese minister, had moved to Rio de Janeiro, though for a time they would keep in touch. ("Do you mix much in the gay world," Madame Bezerra would write to Louisa later. "If so you turn night into day.") Among those who remained was the Count Joseph de Maistre, the minister from

Sardinia, who, having not much diplomatic work to do, spent much of his time writing brilliant essays arguing against the Enlightenment or making conversation in a salon or parlor. With sweeping white hair, a bull's brow, and a noble, strong jaw, Maistre was, one Russian acquaintance wrote, "without contradiction, the outstanding personage of the time and place." The Sardinian minister first became friends with John Quincy, with whom he could discuss the excesses of the French Revolution or passages of Plutarch, but Louisa was delighted to find that he continued to visit her after her husband was gone. Together, they would swap morsels of gossip, crack jokes about the British, encourage each other's instincts for truancy at the suffocating palace parties, and laugh with their whole hearts.

Most important, there was the Countess María de Bodé y Kinnersley de Colombi. The Countess Colombi had come to Russia as a child, when her parents, an Englishwoman and a French baron, fled France in 1788 in order to save the baron's head. "She is so gay; so sensible; and so attractive it is impossible to know her without loving her," Louisa would write, and she would wear the turquoise ring the countess gave her for the rest of her life.

She would think of the Countess Colombi on her journey, and not only because she was her great friend. Something strange had happened when Louisa went to say goodbye to her. At Countess Colombi's, she encountered another visitor, a Countess Ekaterina Vladimirovna, the wife of Count Stepan Stepanovich Apraxin. She was very fat, very rich, a type of woman Louisa could too well recognize: an idle mischief maker. After the women finished their tea, Countess Apraxin called for a deck of cards and told Louisa to take a queen. Ekaterina studied the card, said that she could see Louisa's future in her choice, and, to Louisa's amusement, rattled off the predictable fortune: you are going on a long trip, you will be reunited with those you have not seen in a very long time, so on and so forth. But there was a twist. Halfway on her journey, Countess Apraxin said, Louisa would "be much alarmed by a great change in the political world, in consequence of some extraordinary movement of a great man which would produce utter consternation, and set all Europe into a fresh commotion." This event would disrupt Louisa's plans, and indeed make her journey "very difficult." Louisa laughed and assured her that there should be no trouble with her journey whatsoever, "as I was so insignificant and the arrangements for my journey so simple." But Louisa would have reason to remember what the woman had said. Despite her best intentions not to believe in superstitions, she would wonder if her fate had been foretold. Her imagination was warm. The world was so much stranger than reason would allow.

■ ■ ■ ■

PART FIVE:
NARRATIVE OF
A JOURNEY

From St. Petersburg to Paris, 1815

■ ■ ■ ■

1

Through the carriage's windows, the daylight was dim. Snow hushed and shrouded the late February afternoon. Louisa had timed her departure for this hour, five o'clock, on purpose, the time her friends would be sitting down to dinner. She wanted to avoid the familiar pain of saying goodbye.

She was joined for the long journey by a group of strangers. Traveling with her inside the carriage was a nurse for her son, a Madame Babet, an old woman who had fled France with the Countess Colombi thirty years before, and whom Louisa had hired only that day. The sled that would accompany the carriage, the *kibitka,* held two manservants. She could trust the one she called John Fulling, because he had worked for William Smith. She was uncertain about the other, a man identified as Baptiste. He had been a prisoner in Russia from Napoleon's army, and at the last second Louisa agreed to take him to France. Baptiste could use a gun and wield a knife, which meant in theory that he could provide some protection against bandits. But there was something about him that unnerved her, something that made her think she would need protection not by him but from him. There was, of course, also Charles, with his toy soldier's hat and toy sword, which he claimed to know how to use because Baptiste had drilled him. The postilions readied the horses. The carriage, mounted on runners, began to slide across the snow. The soft sound of harness bells carried through the air as the carriage crossed the canal, passed through the great triumphal arch, and left the magnificent city.

She would later say that she did not watch the city recede from view with regret, except to send a sigh to her daughter's grave. Instead, her thoughts had sped ahead to the end of her journey and to the man who was waiting for her there.

It was February 12, 1815 — as it happened, her fortieth birthday. "I could not celebrate my birthday in manner more delightful than in making the first step towards that meeting for which my Soul pants," she wrote to John Quincy just before she was about to depart, "and for which I have hitherto hardly dared to express my desire."

She traveled through the night, stopping only to change horses and pay the required tolls.

Her carriage moved steadily through the flat snow-covered countryside, passing here and there dark clumps of trees, scattered dwellings, and small Russian Orthodox churches, distinctive with their swollen domes. Long stretches of the road were empty except for the wolves, which darted in the snow unafraid. It was so cold that the wine she had brought froze in the bottles. The carriage veered toward the coast, close enough that she could hear the sibilant sea. In her later account of her journey and in her letters to John Quincy from the road, though, she did not indulge in descriptions of the landscape. There was not much to captivate her, since fields did not flower in wintertime, and she had seen enough of snow. Outside Riga, the frozen land began to thaw; the sled became useless, and the runners of the carriage had to be replaced by wheels that constantly stuck in the mud. When the snow returned outside the city, it became even harder to move; and the passengers had to ring a bell, the sound of which summoned anyone nearby to appear with a shovel and a pickaxe to dig the heavy berline out. At the time, there was nothing romantic to her about this mode of travel, driven, as she was, by "that restless anxiety for the future, which pervades all mankind."

For the most part, the trip was easy enough at the start. By now she knew to expect every manner of innkeeper, every quality of mattress; she was no longer a novice to surviving the lurches and bumps of a difficult road. And in fact, she was traveling in some style. Her large and expensive carriage and her impressive stack of official papers marked her as an important person, and so her arrival in town was often treated as an event. Officials were courteous, even deferential. Invitations from the local aristocrats to dinner or the theater would quickly follow. There were also often invitations to extend her stay, but these were invariably declined — to the surprise, sometimes, of personages who were unused to being denied. But impatience made her stubborn. She would not slow down.

When she reached Mitau, in Latvia, 375 miles southwest of St. Petersburg, she ran into a problem. She had stopped for a night at a cheerful, tidy public house, the best in town, for an excellent meal — the innkeeper, a French émigré named Jean Louis Morel, had once been Louis XVIII's chef — and to rest for a few hours before pressing on. After dinner, Morel entered the private dining room, said he wished to speak with her, and nervously looked for eavesdroppers as he closed the door. He told her that a "dreadful murder" had taken place upon the road, that it was much too dangerous to leave now, and that she must absolutely stay the night. Because she had heard this kind of bald ploy for business before, she coolly said that she would be safe, that her servants were armed, and that she was determined to continue onward. At this, Morel interrupted. Her servant Baptiste, he said, was known to him. He had been in town before, as one of Napoleon's soldiers. Morel said that he was "a desperate villain, of the very worst character; and that he did not consider my life safe with him." At the same time, Morel begged her not to dismiss Baptiste in Mitau, because he was afraid Baptiste would guess where she had heard of his past and would burn Morel's house down. Louisa was inclined to believe the innkeeper. She already suspected Baptiste of stealing her son's silver cup, the gift from the Westphalian minister, which had gone missing. But as she had no proof of any wrongdoing, and as Baptiste had behaved well, she had no grounds to end his service. So she said goodbye to Morel, climbed into the carriage, and the group traveled on.

A short time later, the carriage stopped and a postilion climbed down to tell her they had lost the road. In vain, they tried to find it, bumping over swampy land, through ditches and over hills, looking for any signs of a path. Midnight approached, and Morel's warnings rang in her ears. But she watched Baptiste closely, consulted with him frequently, and was impressed by his careful attention and steady hand. The dangers in the unmarked land — and even on well-maintained roads — were serious. Carriages broke apart, overturned, and bogged down regularly. Injuries and deaths were not unheard of. Finally, at midnight, Louisa consulted with the servants and decided that Baptiste should ride out and search for the road or for help in finding it. As he rode away, she wondered if he would abandon them, but he returned quickly with a Russian officer who lived nearby. Louisa described their situation to the officer "in the most execrable German," and they found the road and soon reached an inn. She felt stronger, more assured, and resolved "not to listen to any more bugbears" who might "weaken my understanding." She trusted herself.

Louisa would need confidence. Repeatedly on the voyage, she would have to disregard the stern warnings of men, men who told her to wait, to get help, to turn back. She would have to decide whether to order the carriage across a river's thinning ice. She would have to spend nights upright in the carriage or in dirty hovels. She would have to stand up to innkeepers who tried to take advantage of her sex and small size. She would remember ghost stories and gothic tales, and see long shadows all around her. She would have to pass through desolate scenes and evidence of brutal destruction, rape, and plunder. She would have to deal with suspicious guards and drunken soldiers. She would have to overcome her fears. And she did.

As she turned away from the coast and toward Prussia, she began to follow the path of French and Russian soldiers, moving over battlefields where Napoleon had fought and through towns terrorized by armies advancing and retreating. The ravages were still fresh: "houses half burnt, a very thin population; women unprotected, and that dreary look of forlorn desertion, which sheds its gloom around on all the objects, announcing devastation and despair." She saw too clearly, too painfully, what the great accounts of the battles left out: "the graphic delineations of war's unhallowed march — that speak in thrilling language to the heart, where the tongues of men are silent." More chilling, perhaps, than the half-burned houses was the way the survivors spoke of the soldiers. To her surprise, they praised the invader Napoleon and his forces. The Russian soldiers who had pursued the French back were more hated and feared, famous for raping — a reputation earned from atrocities both real and rumored. When "the Cossacks! The dire Cossacks!" were mentioned, Louisa saw the blood drain from women's faces.

She did not think, though, that she had to worry about such a fate herself. Europe was at peace. The leaders at the Congress at

Vienna had shipped Napoleon off to a small island in the Mediterranean, Elba, where he was made king of his own prison. She had the contacts to appeal to a king or two, if needed. She saw the ruins of war mostly through a glass carriage window. She was able to say, later, that the sights were "deeply interesting." And soon, she would be able to step out of the carriage, and when she did, she would smile.

The carriage's runners came off, the wheels on. The Russian ice was behind her. She was a thousand miles from St. Petersburg. On Saturday, March 4, after nineteen days on the road, Louisa crossed the river Spree in Berlin. As she remembered it, if not in the moment itself, memories of her life in the first years of her marriage flooded through her. "Youth seemed again to be decked with rosy smiles, and glad anticipations — and I wandered in the bright mazes of vivid recollections which every object called forth in fresher bloom," she wrote in "Narrative of a Journey."

"There I had felt at home," she said; "all the sweet sympathies of humanity had been re-awakened." With far Russia behind her, her heart "was thawed into life and animation."

2

She went straight to the Hotel de Russie, the same hotel where she had stayed when she had first arrived in Berlin in 1797. She could still look around and see much that was familiar: the palaces, the parks, the long avenue of lime trees. Here she had danced; there she had sung; around that corner had been her apartment. Her old friend Pauline Neale "flew" to greet her. Plans were quickly made, and soon she was with Princess Ferdinand, Princess Radziwill, "the Brulhs; the de Néales; the Golofkins; the Zeinerts; the De Bergs; the Hardenbergs; the Hadzfeldts; the Bishoffswerder, and many more." Everyone met her "with the most unaffected warmth." She felt among family, as if her old acquaintances were "long separated and beloved sisters."

But little else in Berlin was untouched by time. The palaces were half empty, absent of many of the country's leaders, who were in Vienna as part of the deliberations that would reshape the political and geographical balance of the continent, providing a framework that would hold, more or less intact, for the next hundred years. And some were dead. The Prussian army had been demolished by Napoleon in 1806; the city had been conquered; many of her friends had been forced to flee. Now, Louisa listened to the harrowing stories of how they had survived, and how some had not.

So the welcoming warmth with which Louisa was received by her friends in Berlin had a tempering melancholy beneath it. They lived with "no pretension of style among them," because so much had been taken from them. They were mellowed by hardship, more apt to find pleasure in small indulgences than satisfaction in ceremony. When she visited Princess Radziwill, she noticed how the princess had aged, how there was "a softer shade of character on her face." Princess Radziwill had lost her brother, her daughter, and her father; she had seen battlefields and cities on fire; she had been at Tilsit and witnessed the king and queen's humiliations, as they were forced to capitulate and beg for mercy. Napoleon's approach had been especially frightening for Pauline Neale, because Napoleon had a special desire to hurt her. After Louisa departed Berlin, Pauline had visited Paris, befriended Empress Josephine, and written a letter to her mother about

Napoleon's plans, which was intercepted. Princess Radziwill read aloud to Pauline what a newspaper reported Napoleon had said when he reached Berlin and found her gone. "Well, if I had caught her here," Bonaparte had told Count von Neale, "I should have had her hair cropped and sent her to Bicetre" — the lunatic asylum near Paris — "for her interference in having political opinions and expressing them publicly."

Berlin, then, was bathed in the stained light of Louisa's nostalgia, but also strange. There was a "perfect stillness" that unnerved her, a "foreign air" to the city, unsettling reminders of the degradation that had come with French control — first in the battles that had brought Prussia to its knees, then with the humiliation of being forced to supply and quarter Napoleon's army as it marched on Russia. Berlin's native attributes were less apparent, yet to revive in force; more people spoke French and wore French clothes than she remembered. There was less attention to protocol than there had been; there was more talk of resilience and freedom. The biggest change was the most alarming, a shadow cast over the entire population — affecting, Louisa thought, every inhabitant. It was the absence of the queen, killed by typhus in 1810. The queen's mere presence had "gladdened" the city, and without it, Louisa felt the chill of the gloom.

And so Louisa went out to the palace in Charlottenburg, where she had once spent happy summer days, and found her way to the marble mausoleum in a small grove by the gardens. It was built as a neoclassical temple, with Doric columns supporting a portico; on the pediment were inscribed the Greek letters alpha and omega. And there, she mourned the loss of her Queen of Queens.

She had hoped that a letter from John Quincy would be waiting for her to tell her which route to take out of Berlin. She waited and nothing came. She delayed her departure, uncertain what to do, certain that her husband would instruct her. Finally, with advice from others, she looked at the map herself and set her course. On Saturday morning, March 11, she set out and traveled southwest toward Potsdam and then Leipzig. She knew this land, these sandy roads; she had been here before. But as they continued west, she began to see something that unnerved her: small groups of disbanded soldiers, hungry and ragged, who were in no hurry to go home, and who made their living off the road. At another time in her life, Louisa might have fainted or fallen ill. Now, she made her small son lie flat upon the carriage floor, while she put on his military cap and held his toy sword so that the silhouette would show through the window. The two male servants rode on the roof; they were armed.

They drove toward Leipzig, which she would have preferred to bypass, and which, in "Narrative of a Journey," she would say she avoided, because the battlefield that she would have to cross there was famously grim. But she was either repressing the memory of the carnage or rewriting it, because in fact she posted a letter from the city.

She would have had good reasons for wanting to forget the place. The battle at Leipzig in October 1813 had produced more than a hundred thousand casualties — an average of thirty thousand a day. Tens of thousands of men were taken prisoner, all the farm animals killed for ten miles around, the houses in sixty villages destroyed. Even now, in 1815 — more than a year after the battle — the fields remained littered with random wreckage: straw, rags, harnesses, guns, carts, the decomposed bodies of animals and men. No one had cleared the land since the fight, except scavengers looking for scraps of leather or iron, something to melt down, stitch, sell, or eat.

She passed quickly through the devastation. The carriage entered the Thuringian Forest, the land of Goethe and *Sturm und Drang.* The forest was now as famous for its real horrors as its literary ones. She was on a path that Napoleon and his army had crossed not once but three times, looting, raping, and burning. She could calm herself by saying the path was now safe, Napoleon a prisoner in Elba, and the wars over. But one night, in a town "once probably strong, but now in ruins, miserably conditioned," an innkeeper told her of a rumor: Napoleon had escaped Elba and had landed on the southeastern coast of France. When she stopped at another post station, the rumor was repeated. And every time the carriage stopped for fresh horses, the news grew more detailed and wilder. It was said he had an army of a thousand men with him. Disbanded troops were answering his call. He was traveling north, toward her destination — toward Paris.

A mile outside of Hanau, on Thursday, March 16, Louisa passed ditches and "mounds like graves," and then came upon a plain "over which was scattered remnants of clothes; old boots in pieces; and an immense quantity of bones, laying in this ploughed field." This battlefield, perhaps seen in the light of Napoleon's return, affected her as other battlefields had not. She struggled not to faint. She did not have time to collapse, though. She had to keep going, because now there was no doubt about the truth of the rumors about Napoleon. The former emperor was back. On March 12, when Louisa reached Leipzig, Napoleon was in Lyons with thousands of troops. When she was in Hanau, he was nearing Auxerre, fewer than a hundred miles from Paris.

As Louisa advanced toward Frankfurt am Main — traveling faster and faster, the postilions pushing the horses — she saw evidence of soldiers mustering. Towns were busy with activity. She stopped in Frankfurt and visited her banker. Yet again she had hoped to find letters from John Quincy that would guide her, but yet again there were none. She was more dismayed by the silence now, because she was faced with a crisis. Her two male servants, John Fulling and Baptiste, came to her in Frankfurt and told her they were resigning, afraid that if they returned to France, they would be conscripted into Napoleon's army. She tried to bribe them to stay, but their fears were bigger than her inducements.

She asked her banker, Simon Moritz von Bethmann, to find her new servants. Bethmann was in a good position to help. *"Le roi de Frankfurt"* was among the richest men in Europe and the most well connected. The Prussian king Frederick William III had first laid eyes on Luise at a ball at Bethmann's; Tsar Alexander, while Bethmann's guest, had slept with Bethmann's wife. But when Louisa asked him for help hiring manservants, he shook his head. It was much too dangerous for a lady to be on the road now, he told her. He could arrange for her to stay in Frankfurt, he went on, and he would offer her his protection — an offer that was rarely refused, no doubt. But she was becoming accustomed to expressing her determination. "I insisted that it would be better for me to get into France as soon as possible," she told him, and added that if events were indeed so dangerous, she was sure her husband would ride out to meet her. She reasoned that the disorder around Paris might actually be an advantage. She could slip through before any barricades were set.

Bethmann was grave, but he could not stop her. He urged her, at least, to take a more circuitous path to Paris, in order to bypass the troops massing on the city's frontier. He promised to find a servant who might help protect her. In the end, the only male Bethmann could find who would agree to travel to Paris was a fourteen-year-old boy. So at four p.m. on Friday, March 17, the new group started — Louisa, Madame Babet, Charles, and the boy, whose name she never gave. He was such an unlikely protector that she had him ride inside of the carriage instead of on the roof, as the older men had done, because he was vulnerable and made the carriage seem more so. And probably, she wanted to talk to him, because she liked people's stories, and this boy had a good one. As a young aide to a Prussian officer during Napoleon's Russian campaign in 1812, he had seen the emperor up close. He talked of Napoleon's "sitting among his soldiers to warm himself! of his partaking of their soup, when they had any! His kindness to them in the midst of their misery &ce &ce." Yet the boy had seen the devastation that Napoleon's campaigns had caused. So "at the same time" as the boy spoke of Napoleon with reverence, "he expressed great hatred of the man, with all the petulance of boyish passion." She, who knew something about a conflicted heart, was fascinated "to watch the workings of this young mind, swayed equally by admiration and detestation."

As she moved through the post stations, changing horses and postilions, the number of troops on the roads increased. Their songs grew louder and their shouts more buoyant and aggressive. She crossed from Germany into France, and arrived at a hotel in Strasbourg, where the master of the house advised her that the situation was unsettled and "very *critical.*" To her relief, he was able to find her a manservant, named Dupin, whom she could trust. At Épernay, she stopped for "a capital dinner" and the best bottle of champagne she had ever tasted. She assumed that she could afford the break, having received assurances that the troops would not pass through the town until the next day.

But then, a mile and a half outside of town, she heard women hurling vicious curses at soldiers nearby. Then she heard the voices of the soldiers themselves, who had spotted the distinctive shape of the Russian carriage. "Tear them out of the carriage!" the soldiers cried. "Kill them!" It was the Imperial Guard, in their blue uniforms and feathered caps. Louis XVIII had fled, and Napoleon had reached the Tuileries, where among those to greet him was a man Louisa was well acquainted with, the former French ambassador to Russia, Armand de Caulaincourt. Napoleon's elite unit was now on its way to meet the former emperor in Paris.

Louisa's carriage was surrounded; soldiers held the horses and turned their guns against the drivers. After seeing her passport, a general cried out that she was an American. *"Vive les Américains!"* the men cried.

"Vive Napoléon!" she cried in return, waving her handkerchief.

"Vive les Américains! Ils sont nos amis!"

She rode slowly with the convoy; the general who had shouted to spare her rode by her side. As it happened, she was lucky. This general's name was Claude-Étienne Michel, and he had served Napoleon for many years. A day after meeting Louisa, when he reached Paris, he would be made a *comte d'empire,* and a few months later would play a role leading the assault upon the Duke of Wellington at Waterloo, where he would die. Now, he spoke to her through the window of her carriage and told her that her situation was very dangerous. The army was "totally undisciplined." She must provoke no one and show no fear. When the soldiers cried *Vive!* then she must cry *Vive!* in return. When they reached the next post house, they must spend the night and let the troops pass. She was lucky, he added, because of the quality of her French; she would not raise suspicions. She could pass for native. She listened to all of this calmly, though her heart beat wildly in her chest, while Charles, ice-white, sat frozen, and Madame Babet shook.

At the post house, the woman in charge refused to take the travelers in, because she knew she could not protect them. She relented only when Louisa promised to hide with Madame Babet and the child. Inside their chamber, once its windows were shuttered and door barred, Louisa's body finally collapsed, and she suffered a series of "faintings, head ache, and sickness." Charles was able to sleep, but Madame Babet was cracking. She had escaped the French Revolution only to return to France to find another about to begin. Clutching at her hands as fat tears rolled down her cheeks, she said she "was lost." "The Revolution was begun again," she insisted, "and this was only the beginning of its horrors." Outside the door, men were carousing and drunk. The innkeeper, a vivacious woman of forty or so, had the good sense to bring out the casks so that the soldiers would not trash the hotel in search of drink.

At nine the next morning, the place was quiet, and the locks turned and doors opened. The fourteen-year-old boy was waiting for them, a little worse for wear — prodded by bayonets, and his Prussian cap taken and burned — but not harmed. They piled back into the Russian carriage and continued.

The rumors were flying now. The army was at the gates to Paris. A battle was imminent. She was in danger. They did not know what to believe. But one rumor gave her confidence — a rumor about herself. Dupin had heard it whispered that the woman in the large, expensive carriage who was rushing toward Paris instead of away from it (as any sane woman would) must be one of Napoleon's sisters. When asked about it, Dupin smiled suggestively and shrugged, as if with meaning.

Emboldened, they passed through Meaux, where the landlady of the inn, with tears in her eyes, took her to see the graves of six girls, the victims of "savage war, with all its detestable concomitants" — which is to say, they'd been raped and killed. From there, and with this on her mind, Louisa entered the forests of Bondy, famous for tales of banditry, and when a man on a horse thundered after her, she imagined that she was being chased. She had to smile at herself when she discovered he only wanted to warn her of the carriage's loose wheel.

And then she was at the gates of Paris. She turned onto the Rue du Faubourg Saint-Martin. There was no civil war, only quiet. It was getting dark. At some point that evening, on Thursday, March 23, she said goodbye to the boy and to Dupin; Babet would leave the next day. Louisa drove down the Rue de Richelieu, to the Hotel du Nord. It was eleven o'clock at night when she arrived.

From the letters she had posted from the road, John Quincy was expecting her to come that evening. Her conviction that he would ride out to meet her if she was in danger had been hopeful at best. He had thought there might be a battle before Napoleon arrived in Paris, and he still worried for the region's peace. For the past few days, he had walked out among the crowds in Paris, past bonfires of the Bourbon king's handbills, watching the papers stamped with the fleur-de-lis curling as they burned. Louis XVIII had escaped to Lille, and Napoleon's fresh proclamations were already being pasted on the walls. But if he worried or wondered about his wife's safety on the road, he did not say so. They had been apart for eleven months.

That evening, John Quincy went to the Théâtre des Variétés, which was famous for the low-comedy farces that he loved. In his diary, he wrote that his wife and son walked into the hotel room soon after he returned. She would remember it differently. In her account, he was not waiting for her there at all. When she arrived, he was gone.

■ ■ ■ ■

PART SIX:
A LITTLE PARADISE

London and Ealing, 1815–1817

■ ■ ■ ■

1

Springtime in Paris, 1815. The trees flew the small flags of new leaves; fevered crowds filled the streets. On the grand boulevards, soldiers strutted and cursed the old king. Some who watched them muttered subversive jokes: "Why is bread dearer and meat cheaper since 20 March? Because the baker has left and the butcher has returned." But the critics kept their voices low. The streets rang with song. People gathered in the Tuileries below Napoleon's window hoping for a glimpse, a benediction. The mood was joyous. The gardens were packed. The theaters were full.

And many nights, Louisa and John Quincy were there too. The theater had been a lifelong passion for them both, something they always shared. They went to see tragedies, comedies, operas, ballets, low farces, and, once, to see Napoleon.

They heard a rumor that he would attend that night, April 21. The audience filled the Théâtre-Français past capacity. Everyone wanted to be in the place he was in, as if merely sharing air were a kind of contact. The orchestra, pushed by the crowd behind the scenes, played "La Victoria" and "La Marseillaise" over and over. Finally, during the play *Hector,* Napoleon entered his box. Louisa and John Quincy could not view him themselves — their box was on the same side as his — but they could not have missed the ripple of heads turning, the wave of emotion, the murmur swelling to a roar: *"Vive l'Empereur!"*

She had seen him before that night, clearly though at a distance. She, John Quincy, and Charles had been walking through the gardens at the Tuileries on a late afternoon in early April when they came upon a throng standing below Bonaparte's apartments. At that very moment Napoleon threw open the windows and stood for a time, showing himself, bathing in the late afternoon light and in the crowd's adoration. John Quincy had lifted Charles onto his shoulders for a better look. And there was Napoleon: the strong chin and long thin nose; the famous figure, now fat; the piercing deep-set eyes.

She had no reason to be frightened of him anymore. Civil war was not a threat in Paris. To her, Bonaparte had become an interesting attraction, the way the ancient marble statues at the museums were attractions. Later, the Adamses looked at Napoleon during mass at the chapel of the Tuileries. John Quincy noted the occasion in his diary in the same tone that he noted their trip to see the city's fortifications on the heights of Montmartre.

Their time in Paris was full of pleasure. It was "in many respects the most agreeable interlude of my life," John Quincy wrote. They went to the Louvre for the paintings and the awesome stillness. Louisa shopped for a new wardrobe: high-waisted taffeta dresses with elegant flounces; slippers as light as lacquered eggshells. She went to watch the review of soldiers in the square of the Place Carousel, the drills and peacocking. It wasn't all for show. France would soon be at war again, and she had seen enough wreckage to be sickened and saddened at the thought of the battles to come. When it came time for the Adamses to leave Paris, Louisa wrote to Abigail that she was filled with foreboding about the fate of France, and with the "utmost regret" at having to go.

She was not looking forward to returning to England, nearly twenty years after she left it. It would be, she told her mother-in-law, "a very disagreeable residence." The dislike between the United States and Britain after the War of 1812 was persistent. She felt it herself. Another posting would mean another meager minister's salary, too, and the certainty of great expenses; and several more years of late nights and parched mornings, of insincere smiles and insipid conversations with gouty old men. No doubt, too, her feelings were colored by her memories of the circumstances under which she had left London at twenty-two. She had been feeling the hot blast of shame after her family's flight. She had been pregnant and uncertain of what awaited her. Now she was forty years old and even more of an outsider in a place where she had never quite belonged.

Louisa, John Quincy, Charles, and Louisa's new French chambermaid, Lucy Houel, left the Hotel du Nord in Paris on May 16, passed through the city gates, and entered the countryside. Spring was turning to summer. That morning, John Quincy noticed street vendors selling small bunches of bright red cherries. The orchards showed pale blossoms. At dinner that first night on the road, Louisa tasted the season's first sweet green peas.

The journey to the coast was short, completed in "easy stages." She had made the trip before; she knew what to expect. It was a remarkably undemanding journey, especially compared with the arduous route she had followed only two months before. Yet, with John Quincy now in charge, it was all too much for her. When they reached Dover, Louisa insisted she could not continue on to London before resting. She was "excessively fatigued," John Quincy wrote in his diary, "and in the evening very unwell."

This is revealing of something essential about her character. In times of adversity, forced to rise to the occasion, she often thrived. She had crossed thousands of miles from St. Petersburg to Paris, fording half-frozen rivers and meeting with unruly soldiers. She had made difficult decisions quickly and well. She had taken care of her small and terrified son. She had traveled through the night, slept very little, dealt with deserting servants, crossed battlefields and ravaged villages, and faced the approach of a dictator. She had shown courage and self-command. She had not been overcome by fatigue. She had in fact completed the journey from St. Petersburg with such strength that her husband concluded the arduous trip had been crucial to her health. This same woman, once relieved from all responsibility and returned to the protection of her husband, after a much shorter and easier journey, was now helplessly tired and overwhelmed.

A surprise in London would revive her. Her two older sons, George and John, were waiting in the Adamses' hotel rooms on Harley Street, Cavendish Square. When Louisa wrote to Abigail three weeks later, she skipped over words, sped on by happiness: "You will my joy on arriving in London at finding my boys."

In the six years since she had seen them, they had changed. The eight-year-old George she had left in Quincy was now fourteen and nearly as tall as his father. He had the rough manners and the awkward bearing of a boy unused to the length of his limbs, but he also had a sensitive, delicate quality, often remarked upon, and dark velvet eyes. Books were his "meat and drink," his grandmother reported; he read indiscriminately. "Like the bee, he flies from sweet to sweet, always however collecting some honey which he brings home to his hive," Abigail had written the year before. "He delights his grandfather when he is at home by his readiness to find whatever book he wants in his library, and he will sit down like an old man to hold a conversation upon books for an hour together." He was special, though his grandparents openly worried he might be odd. "George is a treasure of diamonds," old John Adams wrote to John Quincy. "He has a genius equal to anything; but like all other genius requires the most delicate management to prevent it from running into eccentricities."

The younger boy was different. Twelve-year-old John was a foot shorter than George and, as John Quincy wrote, "as fat as a little seal." He swelled with confidence; his grandmother described him as "ardent, active zealous full of fire and spirit." He had no patience for reading. On the voyage from Boston, the sailors had taught him every knot and taken to calling him "Admiral," which he loved.

However transformed George and John seemed to their parents and Charles, their parents and brother must have been almost unrecognizable to them. Their father, once almost gaunt, had grown stout. Deep lines, permanent marks of worry, pinched his brow and cut from his nose toward his mouth. His round head was nearly completely bald; what little hair he had was close-cropped. Their mother, too, looked older, her long face more etched, her hair streaked with gray. And their little brother, who was a baby when they last saw him, was now a quiet child of nearly eight, poised beyond his years. While they grew up running through the woods of New England, Charles was a child of the imperial court. While they hardly knew their parents, he could interpret their father's inscrutable expressions. He could read their mother's mood with a glance.

John and George were accustomed to exploring mountains and stony hillsides, to slipping in and out of the houses of their large extended family. They had spent years under the benevolently neglectful tutelage of their grandmother and her sisters. Instead of their schoolwork, they had studied *Arabian Nights.* Now they found themselves in a small apartment on a crowded block in Cavendish

Square, with only the manicured parks to pass for wilderness, in a country with which they had just been at war, and which they had been raised to consider their enemy. They had crossed the Atlantic with one decent suit apiece. Louisa and John Quincy immediately hired tutors to instruct them in handwriting, mathematics, fencing, and dancing.

While John Quincy was busy addressing the issues unresolved at Ghent, Louisa looked for a place to live. It is almost inconceivable that she would have taken on this responsibility prior to John Quincy's leaving St. Petersburg, only three years before, but much had happened since then. Even the continent seemed to be entering a new order. On June 22, John Quincy received a note from the foreign minister, Lord Castlereagh, that the coalition army had destroyed Napoleon's forces at the Battle of Waterloo. Europe was at peace.

She found a house in Ealing, a small village seven miles outside of the city; the salary of an American minister, at least one who was allergic to debt, ruled out finding a decent establishment within London. The countryside held other appeals. Louisa and John Quincy hardly knew what to do with their sons in the city. The family had treated London like tourists, with trips to the theater, St. Paul's, the Tower of London; they went for walks and flew kites. But the two older boys, restless and bored, chafed at the city's fashionable avenues and cramped spaces, where the carts clattered over the cobblestones and the cries of voices began with the dustmen at dawn and ended with drunken revelers past midnight. Soon, John Quincy was complaining of the "hurly burly of confusion" his sons now brought into his life. "Their time is not fully employed and mine is so completely taken up that I have none left to attend to them," he wrote in his diary.

Louisa may have had her own unstated reasons for wanting to live at a distance from her old home on Tower Hill. There were painful memories there, the ghosts of friends and family. What remained reminded her of what had changed. She saw the Hewletts a few times, and her much-loved mentor from Berlin, Elizabeth Carysfort, and there were other visits with friendly familiar faces. Even those reunions, though, had something sad and haunting about them. "I have found but few of my old friends in this country and those few much changed," she told Abigail, "but after so long an absence and under such circumstances I could not expect to find it otherwise." With some sadness, she wrote that "the change which I perceive is most likely in myself."

Perhaps it was easier, too, to live a little at a distance from the British court and the rest of the diplomatic corps. She was accustomed to being welcomed by rulers and to finding in the court at least one or two intimate friends. But the Regency court was different. King George III, quite insane, was shut away; the prince regent, a self-styled king of frivolity, took no notice of her; and it was a year before Louisa had an opportunity to be presented to the queen. In the meantime, Louisa was more or less shut out of society. From the outside, no doubt, it was easier to see how opulent, giddy, and at times grotesque society was. The ladies she did meet struck her as harsh and arrogant.

Ealing, then, was an oasis. "It is a little Paradise," John Quincy wrote in his diary. Even the name given to the country house was fortuitous: "Little Boston House." Their new home stood at the entrance to the long private drive, known as "The Ride," that ran through the estate to Boston Manor, a massive seventeenth-century Jacobean pile; the Adamses' house was likely the original dowager house on the estate. (The earliest mention of the area, from the twelfth century, spelled Boston as Bordwadestone.) Smaller than the mansion but still spacious, Little Boston House had two-story bay windows flanking the front door, pleasant rooms, sheltering trees, and large gardens of fruit trees, shrubs, vegetables, and "flowers in profusion." Acres of woods and fields surrounded them. "The situation is beautiful, the house comfortable, and the distance from the great city supportable," Louisa wrote to Abigail, adding, "we enjoy every agreement that will render the country desirable, and within the compass of our means."

Rev. John Hewlett recommended that they send their sons to the Great Ealing School, only a mile from their house, and Louisa and John Quincy immediately enrolled Charles and John as boarders. John Quincy planned to educate George himself, devising a schedule that involved waking at six to read the Bible in Latin or French before turning to Gibbon or Cicero, but by fall George was begging to be allowed to join his brothers. By October, it was arranged for George to live at home and study with John Quincy at daybreak before walking the mile to school. Almost as soon as the family was reunited, it was divided again — as was typical in the place and time. But with a difference: all her sons were able to come home, and they often did.

At the end of October, John Quincy was trying to teach George and John how to fire a pistol when the gun, loaded with too much powder, backfired. His right hand was badly injured. With writing hard and painful, he spent all his time reading — only to contract an eye infection ten days later. The pain radiating through the left side of his face sickened him. "It seared me as if four hooks were tearing that side of my face into four quarters," he wrote. Various remedies were attempted: "physic, the foot bath, and the elder flower tea," but to no avail. He could not stand light; eventually he could not stand the sound of a human voice. The doctor came and applied six leeches to the skin around his eye, and Louisa and Lucy Houel, her chambermaid, kept the leech wounds bleeding for four or five hours, staying up with John Quincy as he lay feverish, "incessantly employed" in tending to the discharge from the weeping wounds, "not only of the lacrymal humor, but the purulent matter." Every half hour, Louisa or Lucy had to wash his eye with warm water. They took turns sweeping his eyelashes with a camel-hair paintbrush dipped in lard.

When he was well enough to resume working, Louisa read aloud to him, filed his letters, took dictation for his personal letters, wrote notes for his diary so that the record would remain unbroken. This was all a kind of experiment, John Quincy said, and he became satisfied that she could be trusted. She became his amanuensis not only for his private work but for his public business as well. "From this day," he wrote in his diary, "she will write for me long and often."

She was tireless, as she had to be. While she was nursing and working for her husband, their son John became so ill that he had to be kept home from school for nearly six weeks; she had to care for him, too. Then, at the end of December, all the boys were at home on holiday, and they looked to her to entertain them. "Mr. Adams's time is of too much importance to the public to admit of his attending them himself," Louisa wrote. Meanwhile, the rest of the house was in turmoil. When John Quincy, his health steadily improving, went into London one day, the servants came to Louisa with "mutual criminations" against one another; soon she found herself looking for a new cook, housemaid, and laundry maid to hire, capably dealing with the fallout. She had always complained that she was too untrained, too poor, too incompetent, and too ignored to be considered useful. At the age of forty, what changed? Partly, her new position reflected necessity and expediency. John Quincy needed a pair of eyes and hands, and he could command hers. At the same time, there had been a test, and she had passed. The most immediate and obvious change brought on by her newfound busyness and quiet confidence was in her health. Not even the bloated leeches were too much for her; only after the night dealing with the lachrymal humor and purulent matter was she faint the next day. At the moment her husband and son needed nursing, her body was stronger than it had ever been.

She was only doing what her role was supposed to require. A nineteenth-century American wife was expected to run the household, nurse the boys, and subsume herself to her husband. So she did not give herself much credit. While she tended to her husband's work, her own personal correspondence ceased, letters to her piling up unanswered. "Mr. Adams has written you a long letter today which I have assisted," she wrote to Abigail in late December, "and I think as long as I am occupied in this way you must cease to expect any letters from me and consider his as from us both." Nevertheless, without fanfare, she was performing a role she had always doubted she could do. Her sense of being "useful" did not diminish once John Quincy healed and much of the office work transferred to his new secretary, recently arrived from the United States. Her voice became more self-assured. Even her skeptical mother-in-law now found much to admire, and the two women grew more intimate. "Your letters are a treat from which I derive pleasure unalloyed," Abigail wrote to her in the summer of 1816.

If Louisa did keep a diary during those years, it has been lost. Her letters, though, suggest that she was generally as content as she could be. The family was together in one place, and even often together in one room. John Quincy's task as minister to Great Britain, whatever his initial apprehensions were, was remarkably easy; his most important job was simply not to disturb the peace existing between the two exhausted countries. Much of his time, in fact, was spent dealing with outlandish requests from Americans. "One would imagine that the American Legation at London was the Moon of Ariosto, or Milton's Paradise of Fools — the place where things lost upon Earth were to be found," he wrote to Abigail. They came to him asking to exchange their Revolutionary War paper money, or demanding old familial estates, or help with genealogy. But for the most part, the Adamses' focus was on one another, as a family. Their distance from London isolated them from high society to some extent, but they were somewhat isolated anyway. Instead of accepting (and reciprocating) every invitation, they spent their nights reading aloud *Guy Mannering* and *Waverley* by Sir Walter Scott or the latest novels by Maria Edgeworth.

Their oldest son, George, looking back ten years later, would remember his time in England as singularly happy. He found school "peculiarly pleasant," and the sights that London and the countryside offered "fanciful combinations and beautiful associations to the mind." Charles had a harder time fitting in. Used to the little cosmopolitan world of his school in the Russian court, and younger than all the other boys, he found it difficult to find his place at the Great Ealing School. The head, Rev. George Nicholas, an Oxford-educated classicist (spoken Latin was his specialty), was considered an excellent teacher, particularly admired for his strictness (his obituary called him "an almost unrivaled disciplinarian"). There was also the matter of being American, which was no small thing, considering that the other students sometimes sang "Rule, Britannia!" on the playground. The first time John Quincy visited Charles and John (George had not yet joined them), he found them "greatly discontented." But after their first few weeks, there were no more reports of unhappiness. George sometimes brought friends home to dinner, joined a small group known as "The Spy Club" (the future cardinal John Henry Newman, then a classmate, was another member), and helped start a literary magazine. John had a talent for mathematics but preferred playing to studying. "I approve of your eating and sleeping and living together; of your playing football, crickett; running, climbing, leaping, swimming, skating; and have no great objection to your play at marbles," his grandfather John Adams cheerfully grumbled after receiving one of John's enthusiastic accounts of his life at school. "These are good for your health: but what do you do for your mind?" John managed to get along well even with his would-be enemies. On the playground one day, one of the boys asked him whether he had ever been to Washington, a sly reference to the British burning the city. "No," retorted John (who had lived in Washington), "but I have been at *New Orleans*" — where the American army destroyed a British attacking force nearly twice its size.

Louisa watched her sons closely — because she finally could, after so many years apart, and because watching people is what she liked to do. She judged them with a blend of fascination, tenderness, and exacting expectations. Her observations about Charles were typical. "School seems to produce a strange effect on him," Louisa wrote to Abigail. "He is one of those observing, and imitative children, to whom everything becomes a matter of attention, and attraction. . . . He is not thought so highly of in the school as he merits, and does not improve as much as we had reason to expect." John Quincy, who had been so exacting from a distance, saw his sons in the flesh and changed his attitude. The messages in the long, stern, didactic letters that he had sent to George and John were, if not forgotten, then at least softened. "I comfort myself with the reflection that they are like other children, and prepare my mind for seeing them, if their lives are spared, get along in the world, like other men," he wrote to Abigail, though he could not help but add, "I certainly can *imagine* something more flattering than this."

They were happy, then. The walks through the gentle fields, the novels by the fire, the dinners with the neighbors, the local balls and country dances, the excursions to Windsor and to the theater in London, the evenings of Handel arias — it added up to something like the life that a young woman growing up on Tower Hill might have happily dreamed of. In September 1816, Louisa wrote to Abigail that her husband "never looked so well or so handsome as he does now."

Around that time, John Quincy wrote her a long poem.

And what are to the Lover's eye,
The beauties other damsels boast?
Trust me, they pass unheeded by;
Or raise a transient glance at most.
But thine are grappled to my soul;
They beat in every throbbing vein;
Warm with the tide of life they roll,
They tune my nerves, inspire my brain.

Like all of his verse, the poem was a little insipid and the humor awkward, but Louisa had a taste for the era's flowery style, and she laughed easily. She could recognize his affection in his lines. She responded with a poem for him, "On the Portrait of My Husband."

> The Painter's Art would vainly seize . . .
> That eye which speaks the soul,
> That brow which study gently knits,
> That soft attemper'd whole;
> That vast variety of Mind,
> Capacious, clear, and strong,
> Where brilliancy of wit refined.

At Little Boston House, nearly twenty years after they were married, Louisa and John Quincy appeared to have achieved the very domestic happiness that they both had always, frantically, insisted was their greatest desire. The startling thing is that once they had found it in Ealing, Louisa, not John Quincy, was the one who pushed to leave it behind.

2

London had a centripetal pull. "London is uncommonly gay this winter, but we do not partake of its pleasures in consequence of our residence in the country," Louisa wrote to Abigail. "We begin to find it very inconvenient." "We" is not quite accurate; her husband found not the distance of London but the very existence of London inconvenient. Once the season began, the invitations arrived in thick flurries, and even though they accepted only a small portion, it still brought them into the city three or four times a week. The balls and large "routs" began at eleven or midnight, the "fashionable hours," which meant that Louisa and John Quincy were falling into bed in Ealing just before dawn. While he groaned, she smiled. "I cannot conceive how it happens but this mode of life seems to agree perfectly well with me," Louisa wrote to Abigail, "for I never enjoyed such health, particularly since my marriage and I am only afraid of growing too fat." She could claim to prefer the quiet contentment of domestic life. But she could not hide the note of thrill in her voice when she wrote, "We are here plunged into the great world."

Once she was, though, the old sense of being excluded started to creep in. The seven miles to London came to stand for something bigger than a long drive. They did not get tickets to Almack's, the most selective subscription ball in London, even though tickets had been offered. They did not go to concerts and the theater as often as she liked. They stood at arm's length. It took nine months to receive a presentation to the queen, and when the day finally arrived, the woman who was supposed to present her, the foreign minister's wife Lady Castlereagh, arrived too late to do the job. The queen herself was gracious but automatic, performing the motions with an almost military routine. "She now stands still and receives the ladies, who simply pass through the room stopping immediately before her Majesty, who addresses a few words to them as they pass," Louisa described the scene to Abigail. "The room being very small the Ladies do not remain in it five minutes, and I think the present Drawing Rooms, might with great propriety be styled reviews, as the Ladies literally *file off* at the word of command."

It clearly rankled Louisa to be no more than a member of the march. After attending two parties at Carlton House, the prince regent's London mansion — a house so extravagant that Parliament was forced to bail the prince out of his debts and pay the bills — she sniffed that she was unimpressed. The octagonal room flanked by two staircases was *interesting,* she acknowledged to Abigail, and muslin draperies produced a "pretty effect," but the whole thing "did not strike me very much, after having witnessed the fetes in Russia upon the return of the Emperor which were infinitely more splendid and in a far better taste." Still, however much she tried to hold herself aloof, she saw it all with a kind of sad longing. She could mock the way British ladies waltzed, but she could not help finding them "more beautiful than I can describe." Their beauty "is so irresistible when I see them, I forget everything else."

It had been half a lifetime since she had been a child in London pretending that she was a duchess. Now finding herself in a crush of British duchesses, she was farther than ever from them. The courtiers had made room for her in Berlin and St. Petersburg, but in London, the rigid class system kept her pegged down a notch. When John Quincy called on the owners of Boston Manor, he found them "very much occupied," and they were "not at home" when Louisa left her visiting card. She had all the invitations she could want, but she was still among the thousands of "insignificants" that crowded the aristocratic scrambles and routs. No one bothered to introduce her to the prince regent. "I have been twice to Carlton House by invitation without even receiving a bow from its Master," she wrote. "I am so much of an old fashionist that I confess I feel very awkward under such circumstances and never know how to behave. I do not like to find myself in a house where I am not acknowledged as an acquaintance."

It probably did not help that at Carlton House, the crowd was straining and peering to catch sight of three beautiful American sisters, who arrived at the ball adorned with white ostrich feathers and diamonds. Louisa had known the Caton sisters in Washington, but in London they moved in aristocratic circles that were closed to her. The Catons' names were all over the London rags; they were celebrated for their uncommon beauty and great wealth. It was common gossip that the Duke of Wellington immediately fell in love with the eldest, Marianne, who was there with her husband. As if to make the contrast stark, when John Quincy met the Duke of Wellington for a second time a few weeks later, the duke struggled to remember who the American minister was. Afterward, John Quincy wrote in his diary that Wellington had "forgotten me. . . . This is one of the many incidents from which I can perceive how very small a space my person or my station occupy in the notice of these persons and at these places."

By October 1816, Louisa was hunting for a house in London. Ealing "really is too far from London either to be convenient for business or pleasure," Louisa wrote to Abigail, justifying herself against her husband's wishes to stay put. "The house in which we now live is so comfortable that I despair of finding one in London even at double the rent I pay for this, or half so convenient," he wrote in his diary. But she was persistent. She found a place on Gloucester Place, in Portman Square, but the lease fell through. The truth was that she was a social creature, enjoyed the parties, and imagined herself left out. Even after repeated nights of being almost ignored at large parties, she found herself enjoying the balls at least enough to describe them in vivid detail to Abigail. She wanted more.

More than the inconvenient distance to London may have motivated her house hunt. Ealing was not quite the paradise that John Quincy imagined it was. It was a normal English village in a time of economic crisis. Hundreds of thousands of men had been discharged from the British army and navy following the British defeat of the French at Waterloo, many of them without pensions. Every day, beggars came to the Adamses' door. The Corn Laws of 1815, passed to discourage imports of cheaper foreign grain, kept the price of grain artificially high, and thousands were starving. The *Morning Chronicle* reported that during one week in 1816, no trade at all had passed through the London custom house. After the victory at Waterloo, the country fell into a deep postwar recession. Even the ungodly rich were deeply in debt, living on credit, dancing at splendid parties throughout the night and fearing the dun and bailiff throughout the morning. Each person who asked for money or scraps arrived "with a different hideous tale of misery," John Quincy wrote in his diary. "The extremes of opulence and of want are more remarkable, and more constantly obvious, in this country than in any other that I ever saw" — an implausible observation, considering that he had lived in tsarist Russia. But in Russia the serfs were taken as a matter of course. Here, John Quincy was shocked to see a decently dressed man on the side of the street, dying from hunger. Even Louisa, who generally had an almost willful blindness to other people's poverty, was compelled to comment on the terrible plight of the country. "I am positively assured that the poorer classes of society do not taste meat once in several months and it is hardly possible to take five steps from your door without being surrounded with well dressed beggars who assure you they have not a bit of bread," Louisa told Abigail.

There may have been another reason that Louisa was slightly unsettled in Ealing, though it requires speculation. Her decision to start looking at houses in the city coincided with the end of a three-month stay with the Adamses in Ealing by a beautiful eighteen-year-old named Ellen Nicholas. She was the daughter of George Nicholas, the boys' headmaster. As neighbors, she and Louisa had become intimate, constant companions. It's not hard to imagine why. Ellen's mother had died in 1811, and in Ellen Louisa probably saw something of her sisters — and her deceased daughter. They played music together, laughed during church together, dedicated poetry to each other. When Louisa sat for her portrait, she wanted Ellen there, because Ellen put her at ease. But Ellen also had an enchanting effect on Louisa's husband.

He was bewitched by her — her youth and beauty, her sweet manners, her deep dimples when she smiled. Ellen sent John Quincy into "poetical paroxysms," he wrote in his diary. His tone became almost bewildered: "Something was become indispensable." He tried writing her a poem, ending it with a burlesque turn — the direction his humor usually went. But the paroxysms went on, and he continued to add verses in his head. These lines, "instead of the ludicrous character of the second, are too serious and even solemn written, as if from a youthful and ardent lover, and expressing sentiments which I neither do nor ought to feel for her," he wrote in his diary. "The love is all merely poetical, but has so much the appearance of reality that I scruple to show the lines now they are written." Some open flirtation between a man and young woman was permissible in their culture; the style of the time was gallant. Teasingly and seriously, it was acceptable for a man to acknowledge a woman's looks, openly and even to his wife. There is no reason to suspect that John Quincy ever behaved improperly toward Ellen; their relationship appears to have gone no farther than stargazing together in the garden. But the ingenue clearly responded to his attention. "How is the roseate tint of modest diffidence, mantling in my cheeks, at the idea of writing to so august . . . a seigneur," Ellen wrote to John Quincy the following summer, concluding, "Adieu, my kind friend, sometimes think of your little *'favorite.'* " Louisa may not have cared about the special attentions; her husband had never been shy about appreciating the beauty of other women. There is no question she was very fond of Ellen herself, whom she later described as "one of the loveliest girls I ever knew . . . accomplished, beautiful and amiable." But Louisa was a sensitive creature, and the contrast between the nature of the attention that John Quincy paid to her and to her young friend was stark. The poems that John Quincy wrote to his wife were tender and loving, but they also affectionately poked fun at her middle age and increasingly middling looks. Ellen, on the other hand, flustered him.

Whether or not Louisa was jealous of Ellen, she knew what jealousy felt like. She was wise about its effects on her own self-worth. "One of the greatest difficulties which we have to contend against in the course of a long life; *is,* what we term Amour propre!" she later wrote.

> Which is so exquisitely sensitive, that it is barely possible to praise one person without wounding his neighbor — for that still sly monitor conscience, however it may appear to slumber; always wakes to feeling when aroused by the flattering eulogy of qualities in others, which we know we do not possess ourselves; and the snarling propensity which wrestles within us on such occasions; acts pretty much as matrimonial squabblers do at the interference of another person; on whom the ire of both the belligerents falls with equal impetuosity, and they make up *their* difference, at the expense of the peace maker.

There was yet another reason that Louisa wanted to move to London, perhaps most important of all. She was open about it. She suggested that John Quincy needed to be in London to help his chances of becoming president.

That November, 1816, James Monroe was elected president. Even before then, rumors of his intention to appoint John Quincy secretary of state — "the best office," wrote John Quincy — had reached London. The position had been the stepping-stone to the presidency for the last three presidents. It was a natural fit: no American in government had more foreign policy experience than John Quincy. It also made sense on political grounds, after three straight Virginians in the role; many said it was time for a northern man. In his diary, John Quincy wrestled with his desire to believe the rumors. "I perceive no propriety in taking any step whatever to seek it," he wrote anxiously. His wife was not so circumspect. She argued that remaining in Ealing would keep him out of the public eye. The influential Americans who streamed through London were disinclined to make the long, expensive trip to the countryside. He needed to make his presence known.

"He laughs at me and says, I do not understand his interest," Louisa said to Abigail. "You my dear Madam must judge between us, understanding as you do every particular that the situation demands."

John Quincy waited for a letter from Monroe, anxious that it would come and anxious that it would not. Meanwhile, Ealing's spell was broken. Louisa's long run of unusually good health ended. She was yet again pregnant. Sick, she stayed shut in the house in Ealing for weeks at a time. The doctor was a frequent visitor; she was bled, given laudanum, and stuck with leeches. The weather mirrored her mood. London was particularly dreary that winter, the fog so thick that pedestrians carried candles in daytime. Nor did Little Boston House seem like such a refuge. The Adamses' idyllic garden was robbed twice in ten days; hungry thieves carried off their cauliflowers and new heads of lettuce, pulled up their plants, and broke the locks to the shed. In April, the Adamses moved to Craven Street, where the American delegation had its offices.

Before they left Little Boston House, John Quincy looked back one last time at the place, and the way of life, that he was leaving behind for good. "I have seldom, perhaps never in the course of my life resided more comfortably than at the house which we now quit, and which I shall probably never see again," he wrote in his diary that night.

In mid-April, the appointment from Monroe finally arrived, and John Quincy accepted.

"I find myself not altogether well," he wrote at the end of April, "and for some days past depressed more in spirits than in health. Every man knows the plague of his own heart. Mine is the impossibility of remaining where I am; and the treacherous prospect of the future. Let me hope."

Louisa was forty-two years old when she boarded the ship at Gravesend to return to the United States. Considering her age and history of unsuccessful pregnancies, she probably knew that she would not be able to make the long ocean crossing without losing the child and endangering her own life.

John Quincy stayed silent about her situation. In St. Petersburg, he had turned down the appointment to the Supreme Court by saying that he would not risk his pregnant wife's health for the sake of a public office. But now the stakes had changed; the secretary of state post was a job he actually wanted. He obscured the inconvenient truth of his wife's condition. To her brother, Thomas Johnson, he mentioned that she was suffering from pleurisy fever "among several other serious complaints." To a friend, he said that "the state of Mrs. Adams's health" might keep her in England when he left with his sons.

But she sailed. Aboard ship, on June 18, Louisa's sickness was so severe that she was given fifteen drops of laudanum — a mixture of opium and alcohol. The next day, the doctor administered twenty. For a week, her suffering was extreme. John Quincy described it in his diary with careful, unemotional distance, mentioning her seasickness "with other distressing symptoms." The next day, June 28, he wrote: "My wife had a quiet night's rest, and was easy all the morning until past noon when she was again seized with great violence. I was called to her from dinner; she thought herself dying. . . . She was in very severe pain at intervals until near sunset, when she found herself relieved, and the remainder of the evening was free from pain." That was that.

To Abigail, Louisa was blunt. She had endured, she wrote, "a bad miscarriage at sea."

Why did she risk the child by making the voyage? It is impossible to know for sure. She may not have wanted to stay in London alone, with an ocean between her and her family and few friends to rely on. Or she may have gone because John Quincy was presented with the greatest opportunity of his career, and his life was also hers. She wanted this for him; she understood, as she told Abigail, his interest. It was harder to admit, but it seems that she also wanted it for herself.

■ ■ ■ ■

PART SEVEN:
MY CAMPAIGNE

Washington and Philadelphia, 1817–1825

■ ■ ■ ■

1

The typical mix of lawyers, representatives, senators, military officers, federal bureaucrats, and diplomats — a mingling of neat lace ruffles, dusty bandanas, and splendid uniforms from France and Spain — crowded the rooms at the Adamses' house on a bitingly cold evening in February 1819. There was an impressive spread of refreshments (Mrs. Adams's parties rivaled anyone's for her almonds, cakes, sweetmeats, jellies) and, in one room, a cluster of musicians and an area cleared for a dance. But the guests there that evening saw something strange: there were conspicuously few ladies.

This was not happenstance — nor a reflection, any longer, of the makeup of the city's elite population. Washington, half built and then half burned by the British during the War of 1812, was still a sketch of a city in so many ways, but it had transformed since the Adamses had left it after John Quincy's resignation from the Senate in 1808. Where once there were groves of yellow poplars, now clusters of buildings cropped up; where there had been cattle, now there were people; where there had been mostly men, now there were also women. When the Adamses had lived in Washington at the turn of the century, senators and representatives generally left their wives in their hometowns, but by 1818, one congressman was writing that men who arrived without their wives were "like the odd half of a pair of scissors." The city had become a desirable destination when the members of Congress arrived for the annual session. More nations were sending diplomats and attachés to Washington; more federal officers — and office seekers — were flocking to Washington; as the country grew, more representatives swelled Congress. And as they did, the social sphere became an arena, where country dances only half distracted from the unspoken maneuvering, and where politesse was a proxy for politics.

In the Adamses' parlor, these forces met and clashed. During Louisa and John Quincy's absence from the city, the political and social landscape had shifted even more than the physical one, and not to the Adamses' advantage. Washington was predicated on the rejection of an aristocracy — but it still depended on a hierarchy. Perhaps even more so. The wife of the British ambassador was amazed and amused by how seriously precedence and etiquette rules were taken in Washington. "We minded our p's & q's far more than if we had been at one of the P[rince] R[egent]'s scrambles," she wrote to a friend.

While the Adamses had been away in Russia and England, a system of deference and reciprocity, ranking each person by post within the government, had hardened into accepted practice. It privileged Congress over the executive branch — and not only because the people were supposed to reign supreme over the president. In practice, during the early nineteenth century the president was chosen by a congressional caucus, and any hopeful would have to pay court to the kingmakers. The rules of etiquette had adapted accordingly. The administration's department heads — and their wives — were expected to make the first visit to every notable person, a formalized practice that then permitted more relaxed social relations. Mornings were spent in endless rounds of making and receiving "calls." The visits themselves were short and usually dull; the routine was repeated ad infinitum. Sometimes a caller would simply leave a small card engraved with his or her name. The person who made the first visit affirmed, implicitly, his or her inferior social position. As the secretary of state, John Quincy was informally considered the president's heir apparent, but it hardly helped his social status. He and his wife would find that they were expected to pay their respects first to hundreds of senators, congressmen, officers, and notable visitors.

Louisa and John Quincy refused. Innocently, perhaps, in the beginning — certainly, that was their defense. They would return any visit, they declared, but they did not imagine that they would have to make the first call. But there is little chance they were ignorant of the standard expectations for long. Eliza Monroe Hay, President Monroe's daughter, who often acted as his hostess, had announced that she would make no first calls, inviting criticism that had whistled through the city like a hot breeze. The Adamses, after their experiences in courts, were particularly attentive to local protocol. "Custom is the law," Louisa had observed in Russia. But custom, in this case, was against them: it put them in a subordinate position and at a disadvantage to the other Cabinet members, who had been in Washington long enough to have established most visiting relationships already.

So they ignored the rule — even after senators, who were strictest about visiting practices, visited John Quincy to spell out the situation; even after senators' wives started boycotting Louisa's parties. The fallout was quick and prolonged. The president's wife,

Elizabeth Monroe, summoned Louisa to the President's House to warn her of the widespread displeasure among Washington wives and to ask her to explain herself. (Elizabeth was not unsympathetic, being caught up in a controversy over visiting with the diplomatic corps herself.) One evening, sixty men and only two women had walked through her door.

That chilly night in February, the ratio was hardly more balanced. Harrison Gray Otis, a senator from Massachusetts — a rich man who'd hosted the Adamses many times in his Beacon Hill mansion, but who had fallen out with John Quincy over his desertion of the Federalists — looked around Mrs. Adams's tea party, quietly amused. There were "men without numbers," he wrote to his wife in Boston (with more than a note of self-satisfaction), "and but *few* ladies." Mrs. Adams, he added, "could not conceal from me her chagrin." She had looked at him with an extremely innocent expression. There had been a misunderstanding, she explained. The ladies must have been unaware that there would be dancing!

But Otis did not take her to be a fool. He knew that she must know what *everyone* knew, he told his wife: the ladies were engaged in a standoff with Louisa. John Quincy's refusal was less galling; after all, he was hardly known for his politesse. But the other women were taking "great offense." This was no small matter. In fact, there would be consequences for John Quincy's career. "Indeed I could hardly have imagined that a man's interests could be so dependent on his wife's manners."

Louisa knew that too.

Washington had changed, but so had Louisa. She was a different woman from the one who had sailed to St. Petersburg a decade before. She had spent her first stint in the United States as a visitor at her sister's residence in Georgetown and as a hothouse flower in her husband's home up north. But she was no longer a young woman content to see herself as helpless. Her parents were dead. She'd survived the loss of her daughter. She'd made herself indispensable to her husband when he had needed her; she had managed a dangerous journey with more fortitude than anyone had a right to expect. She had developed not only keen social instincts but a sense of authority. She was ready to build her own house and more.

Louisa and John Quincy moved into a rented house on the high ground at the foot of Capitol Hill. George, John, and Charles were once again left behind in Boston (George with a tutor, and John and Charles at Boston Latin School; all would in time enter Harvard), but this time, Louisa made no protest. Probably she was used to these decisions being made without her, certainly she knew about the high importance the Adams family placed on admission to Harvard, and perhaps she accepted the decision as the right course of action. The boys were older — though Charles was still only ten — and these separations were hardly the prolonged absences she had to endure in Russia; she saw them during summers in Quincy and usually over the Christmas school recess and in spring. Still, perhaps the distance was somewhat easier to bear, because she was preoccupied.

For all her insistence that she lived quietly, Louisa's days were overwhelmed with activity. Relatives and friends came to tour the federal office buildings, to attend the parties, and to watch the debates. They came to seek jobs — or husbands and wives. Dinners and balls, filled with young, restless, ambitious people, were so much a part of daily life that the British chargé d'affaires, Augustus Foster, called Washington "one of the most marrying places in the whole continent." Some of Louisa and John Quincy's guests stayed for weeks, and some for a few years at a time. Louisa's niece Mary Hellen, Nancy's daughter, orphaned when Walter Hellen died, moved in with the Adamses in 1817, when she was ten, and never left. The children of John Quincy's brother Thomas, who in Berlin had been so dear to Louisa but was now often drunk, were frequent long-term residents. Young friends and cousins from Philadelphia, Baltimore, Boston, and New York also visited, coming to Washington in search of a husband or a good time. The younger ones especially kept things interesting on F Street. At least one broke hearts and started a fight before she left. "Fanny Johnson went off this morning and left our young men in the depths of the *belle passion,* but relieved me by her departure of a load of care and anxiety," Louisa wrote after the twenty-two-year-old daughter of one of her Johnson cousins nearly provoked a physical fight among her suitors, including Louisa's own son. "She is a beautiful creature; but the most accomplished coquette I ever saw."

With reliable suddenness and severity, Louisa would fall sick and have to take to her bed. The erysipelas that she had contracted in Russia continued to plague her, and she was, as ever, prone to vague ailments and fits of fainting. But it may also be that some of those illnesses were simply a chance to collapse and recover, because she otherwise had little time to rest. There were trips to the Capitol, the Supreme Court, the Patent Office, the Navy Yards; there were dinners and teas; there were books to read and music to play; there were invitations to accept and decline and to issue. Louisa also taught school lessons to Mary Hellen — or tried, as Mary rebelled against Louisa's assignments, and Louisa despaired about Mary's uncultivated mind, which made her think of "those vast heaths in England." She was busy with charitable work, newly fashionable among Washington's elite women; she sat on the committee of the Washington Orphan Asylum. She maintained an extensive correspondence, socialized most nights, and copied John Quincy's personal letters. "Two such . . . industrious honeybees as John Quincy Adams and his wife were never connected together before," her father-in-law, John Adams, wrote in 1819.

The servants who helped the honeybees, of course, were rarely acknowledged, except when something went wrong. The household was run by her husband's valet, Michael Antoine Giusta, a former Napoleonic soldier who had served John Quincy since 1814, and her maid, Giusta's wife Ellen, who had come with the Adamses from England. Generally the "subalterns" beneath the Giustas, as John Quincy referred to them, were a source of persistent distress. The German girl the Adamses had indentured ran away, the German boy lasted only three years out of the six and a half years contracted (and only after "his own and his father's repeated solicitations" to John Quincy for a discharge), the chambermaid who had come over with them from

England left to teach at a boarding school. Louisa constantly complained about the quality of servants available for hire. Working for the Adamses was doubtless not easy. There may have been real tenderness between Louisa and her housekeepers or maids, but she presumed that the separation between them was natural, and she referred to servants with a tone of dismissive superiority.

So there was a hectic household and schedule to manage from the start. But there was also the matter of these visits — which was no small matter at all. Behind this petty issue lay a great one, one that was never far from her mind: advancing her husband's political career. This question of ambition was delicate, of course — for any woman, but especially for one like Louisa. She was an object of suspicion from the start. The old taints still pertained, perhaps had spread even deeper. She was British, or at least not fully American. She had spent years and years in European courts, where, it was rumored, courtiers were debauched and women presumed their own power. She was, furthermore, the wife of a man who was respected but not much liked. And it was true, there was something imperious about her, which the etiquette controversy immediately brought out. "I could not and would not be doomed to run after every stranger that thought proper to come to Washington," Louisa reported telling Elizabeth Monroe, the president's wife. The matter was "absurd."

And it *was* absurd, but it was also central and — ultimately — useful. President Monroe became involved. The Cabinet met to discuss the Adamses' visiting practices. But the matter would not die, and John Quincy and Louisa turned it to their advantage. John Quincy was asked to write an official memorandum. In it, he played the part of the simple republican, making it clear that he and his wife were acting in concert. They visited their friends and neighbors as private citizens, not as public figures, and they wanted to avoid making any invidious distinctions of rank among Americans. Their guiding principles, John Quincy added, were an abhorrence of hierarchies and a desire for a quiet private life. Later, revealingly, he would leak his memorandum to the newspapers. (A supporter of one of his rivals would use the leak as evidence that he had no friends.)

"The ettiquette question has become of so much importance as to be an object of State," Louisa wrote to her father-in-law, John Adams. She adopted the same line as her husband — that she was too humble, too unassuming, for all this nonsense — and, like him, protested too much. She had nothing to do with her husband's position in the government; she was only, she insisted, a "plain individual."

This was the kind of declaration that John Adams, who was always quick to declaim the old principles of republican virtue, liked to hear. *"Mais courage,"* John replied. He was not surprised. Everything Louisa and John Quincy did, he said, would be viewed as political. "Well done I say stand upon the defensive for your right and maintain it — your independence."

In her letter to John Adams, she spoke properly and smartly but also, it takes not more than a glance to see, disingenuously. She insisted that refusing to make the first visit was an act of humility, when in fact it made other women come to her, granting her the dominant social role. (As an article in the *Boston Courier* about her practice later put it, those making the first visit would "signify their desire to form an acquaintance" — not the other way around.) She insisted that she was a woman who loved only quiet time at home, when in fact she was embarking on a series of parties that would make her Washington's primary hostess. She insisted that the whole thing was silly, but with steely determination, she waited out the women who refused to come. For a plain individual without claims to any station, she was awfully stubborn. "Mr A & myself," Louisa wrote, "are determined not to give up the point."

Her commitment to returning visits underscores how seriously she took the practice. As it was, she spent her mornings in the carriage returning visits, traveling from door to door. In a loose but legible hand, she carefully logged each name in her narrow book, with lists of visits received on the left-hand page and visits returned on the right. It was miserable, exhausting work. She had to go nine miles one way, then three miles in the opposite direction; she sometimes returned twenty-five visits in a single day. She once spent two hours on the rutted roads, dropping by nine or ten boardinghouses in search of two women.

Her critics saw a woman who was trying to change the rules to her advantage — and in fact she was. Some ladies thought her "arrogant," one visitor noted. Her confidence wavered. "The other Secretarys ladies do just as they please, and nobody takes any notice," she wrote to Abigail. "Every hour adds to the conviction of my total inability to fill any station," she fretted. She could not imagine "being of any sort of consequence."

Her mother-in-law both encouraged and warned her. "I think you have a very circumspect and critical part to act," she wrote to Louisa. "Every step you take will be more critically scrutinized than in any situation you have ever before held. These baneful passions of envy and jealousy, are wide awake, and will follow you in every direction — you may trace from the chair of the speaker to members from all quarters of the union. With some you will find ready and willing supporters. But an heir apparent is always enveyed."

This was a very Adamsian way of looking at the political scene and the Adamses' place in it — watchful of conspiracy; sure of persecution; exceedingly proud. That does not mean that Abigail was wrong to call John Quincy "an heir apparent." Before Monroe had been in office a full year, the jockeying to succeed him was under way. Two candidates were clear from the start. One was Georgia's William Crawford, the secretary of the treasury, who had lost to Monroe in the Republican congressional nominating caucus. He had powerful insider support — and used his patronage at the Treasury to increase it. As secretary of state, John Quincy Adams was the other obvious candidate. Still, he was a Yankee, and a chilly one. Besides, as a Northern man, he had a distinct disadvantage: the three-fifths compromise in the Constitution inflated the voting power of the slaveholding states by increasing representation of the Southern states in the House and electoral college, counting slaves ("all other people") — who of course could not vote — as "three-fifths" of an inhabitant. Several men, most of them Southerners or Westerners, began to mount challenges to succeed Monroe, even though the next contested election would not be until 1824. (In 1820, Monroe was reelected more or less unopposed.)

Despite her anxieties, Louisa was becoming more confident in her relation to the Adamses. After her return from England, when John Quincy found himself too busy with his work at the State Department to send his usual lengthy letters to his parents, Louisa took over the job of writing to them. Her letters came in journal form, written first in a bound diary and then copied on loose pages that she would send to Quincy, occasionally with small changes. Those letters changed the elder Adamses' attitudes toward her. They also changed her.

Her relationship with Abigail had warmed since her first years in the United States. They had consoled each other for the deaths they had both mourned while she was in Russia, understanding each other's losses as few others could. In their letters, "Mrs. Adams" gave way to "my dear daughter" and "my dear mother." Louisa was never going to match the image of the frugal, enterprising New England woman that Abigail had wanted her son to marry, but they came to accept each other, and then appreciate each other. When Louisa returned to Quincy after eight years in Russia and England, the two women had a chance to lay bare past hurts and to forgive each other. Abigail told her "she was sorry she had not better understood my character," Louisa recalled, and Louisa recognized that she had "misconstrue[d] acts intended to be kind." Louisa never overcame her sense of inferiority toward the Adams matriarch, but at the end of Abigail's life, the two women came to respect each other. With Abigail, Louisa could discuss Unitarianism, or write freely about John Calhoun's cool response at the dinner table to Henry Clay's intemperate bluster about independence movements in South America, or describe a scene at a party, all with equal interest. Her journal's high quality surprised Abigail. It "makes me a sharer with you in your various occupations, brings me acquainted with characters, and places me at your fireside," Abigail told her. "One single letter conveys more information in this way, than I could obtain in a whole session of Congress."

Abigail died of typhoid fever at the end of 1818, just months before the dance party in February. Louisa's grief helped clarify for her what she had lost. Years later, while spending months reading Abigail's letters, Louisa would write a beautiful and self-revealing tribute — perhaps the best eulogy Abigail ever received: "We are struck by the vast and varied powers of her mind; the full benevolence of an excellent heart and the strength of her reasoning capacity. . . . We see her ever as the guiding planet around which all revolved, performing their separate duties only by the impulse of her magnetic power, which diffused a mild and glowing radiance over all who moved within the sphere of her fascinating attraction."

The death of Abigail struck Louisa as well as John Quincy. Abigail's powerful example had made its impact. But if anything, Louisa went further than Abigail in wanting to play a role in her husband's public life. She was not content to be an adviser. She sought a public presence that Abigail avoided, and she chafed when she ran up against its limits. With bitter sarcasm, she wrote that she was "being continually told that I cannot by the Constitution have any share in the public honours of my husband." She thought her husband should be president, and she thrived in the race, but by custom she had to deny it. Politics made her nervous; any misstep she made would be amplified by her husband's critics. Still, she came to crave the animation of the political scene. Abigail had always felt more comfortable in Quincy. Louisa immersed herself in the political scene of Washington. When Congress was not meeting, she wrote in her journal, she experienced "a sort of waking vacancy something between life and death."

John Quincy's work at the State Department was all-consuming. Not only was he in charge of charting the foreign policy for the government; his brief included everything from the census to pensions. Meanwhile, there were lingering issues with Great Britain left over by the Treaty of Ghent; France was eager to protect its interests as the United States negotiated trade and territorial disputes with Spain; anti-Spanish interests in the United States were advocating South American independence at the same time that the United States was looking to expand farther south and west. On top of that, the Senate directed John Quincy to reproduce a report on weights and measurements — a topic that triggered his obsessive impulses and inquiries into standardization, and which would occupy him for the next four years. Despite all the challenges — and by cleverly seizing the advantage produced by turbulence in the territories — he managed by the start of 1819 to negotiate a treaty with Spain, known as the Adams-Onís (or Transcontinental) Treaty, that granted the United States Florida and set the western boundary between Louisiana and Texas, climbing to the forty-first parallel and then west all the way to the Pacific. It was a monumental moment in American history.

Louisa complained about how work monopolized her husband. "Thank God we hear no more of Weights and Measures," she wrote when he was almost done. But she took a growing interest in politics — if not as much in policy. Her observations about statecraft in those days tended toward vague, cynical expressions about politicians' true motivations. She cared less about what men said than about how they said it. She could see, both in her parlor and in the Capitol, how easily men were influenced by personal appeals, by flattery, by small attentions, as much as — or more than — by appeals to reason. When Louisa went to watch the debates in Congress, she noticed the way Senator William Pinkney of Maryland had oiled his hair and perfumed his clothes. She observed how he preened before the throngs of ladies, pandered to his opponents, and basked in his own bad rhetoric as he argued for admitting Missouri as a state without restrictions on slavery. His speech was "copious, or at least he made it so; for there was neither figure, or trope spared, which art or nature could yield; and so heavy a tax was laid on poor common sense." When her husband gave one of the most brilliant speeches of his career on July 4, 1821, the speech that would help lay the foundations for the nonintervention doctrine that would guide American foreign policy for almost a hundred years, she responded to "his energy, his pointed expression, and the profoundness of his feelings." She watched people's faces. She saw the quick current of emotions running beneath the dry record of debates.

She knew there was a danger in appearing

to take too much of an interest in political debates. "The fear of being thought to interfere in the slightest degree in political affairs renders me careless to the proceedings of Congress and to the general measures of the administration," she wrote to John Adams in January 1819. But she was paying more attention to politics than she admitted, and though she could not openly acknowledge it, she was playing a role.

During her second year in Washington, she hosted weekly dinner parties for men only — that is, except for herself and whatever pretty young women happened to be staying or living with the Adamses at the time. Their female presence was crucial. When Louisa was too ill to attend these parties or dinners — because of her episodes of erysipelas or sharp headaches and fatigue — John Quincy was upset not to have her there. Louisa routinely denied being privy to any conversations about politics, but that was not true. At those dinners, frequented by senators and members of the House, not to mention the secretary of the navy or the vice president, the conversations turned on news. Her letters were filled with the reports.

Politics was still a dirty word — especially to John Quincy, raised under the strict influence of his father's views. Presidential hopefuls were not supposed to stump; they did not travel from town to town, promoting their platform and shaking strangers' hands; they admitted their ambitions only in private — and sometimes only obliquely. A woman, a wife, a hostess, could play an important subterfuge. She might help the pretense that no campaigning was happening, since politics were not permitted in mixed company. She could serve dinner with éclat, put people at ease, and spice the conversation with the wit that obscured the politics in political discussions.

That obfuscation that she provided was important; it was the ruse that Washington depended on. A candidate was not supposed to appeal directly to the people for their votes — not even to the stratum of white men that counted in those days as "the people." In some states, electors were still chosen by state legislatures. The House of Representatives, not the president, was considered the direct representative of the people. Presidential elections were intimate affairs and were intended by the nation's founders to be that way. The real power to pick a president in those days was understood to lie with the Republican congressional caucus. The Republicans were the only party in town; the Federalists had imploded by their active resistance to waging the War of 1812. Campaigning by a candidate — "electioneering," as newspapers deprecated it — was considered venal. "I should do absolutely nothing," John Quincy vowed, in pursuit of the presidency. The president was supposed to be a kind of tribune, a man who represented the people by upholding the Constitution, not by channeling their common spirit and voice — or even their votes. Until 1824, the popular vote was not even recorded, and in 1824, the first election for which there are some meaningful numbers, not all states tallied the individual numbers.

So politics happened undercover, in small conversations and coded letters and at the dinner table, sometimes with a glance or a nod. The men who wanted to succeed Monroe relied on their supporters. At a time when proto-political parties were called "intrigues" and "cabals," social meetings provided a convenient excuse. A supporter might drop a bit of gossip in the parlor and ask if he could call the following day. A candidate might say much by loudly saying little. He might have a dinner party with a few choice friends, pour a good glass of Madeira, and casually comment on his rivals. He might field visits and return them, paying special attention to newspaper editors, sympathetic congressmen, and their wives.

John Quincy was content not to be liked. The "preponderating motive for every electorial vote," he told a representative from all-important New York, must "be fitness for the place, rather than friendship for the man." It was a way of maintaining the fiction promulgated by his father's generation, that a republic's leaders must be disinterested, and the highest office would be awarded to the man whose record, not his smile, proved his talents. Let the cabals choose their man, he would say; let the demagogue warp the will of the people. To other politicians, John Quincy declared that he would not want the presidency if he had to ask for it. It had to be a reward for his long service, an acknowledgment of the superiority of his merit and not his charm. To himself (and to his wife), he admitted that he would not be able to get the presidency if he had to ask for it, because he was not very good at asking nicely.

While the other candidates were notable for their charisma and appealing manners, John Quincy's habitual aloofness seems to have gotten more pronounced when he reached Washington after the ten-year stint away. He had a reputation for receiving visitors in "a cold and mute way," wrote a traveler to Washington. He was "cold and reserved to excess," complained one member of Congress. His self-evaluation, typically, was the most damning of all. "I am a man of reserved, cold, austere, and forbidding manners; my political adversaries say, a gloomy misanthropist, and my personal enemies, an unsocial savage," John Quincy told his diary in June 1819, after receiving one particularly tiresome visitor with polite silence but obvious contempt. "With a knowledge of the actual defect in my character, I have not the pliability to reform it."

It was possible to turn the defect into a virtue, nonetheless. As his father, the old revolutionary, so much loved to put it, he could make it evidence of his "independence." That was only possible because of his wife. John Quincy was helped by being able to present another public face, one very different from his own. Louisa had learned a thing or two in Berlin, Boston, St. Petersburg, and London. She would do what John Quincy could not: if he could not be popular, then she could be. Had she truly kept herself distant, she never would have succeeded. But she was drawn to people, and people were drawn to her. Wrote one visitor, "She held us spell-bound." As useless as her upbringing and her experience as a diplomat's wife had seemed to her when she arrived in Quincy as a twenty-six-year-old, able to dance a polonaise but without a clue about how to milk a cow, they had prepared her perfectly for this moment. Louisa had always been sociable, however shy she sometimes felt. She brightened under the lamp of attention. And she was canny; she may have sensed that her initial defiance would make her more alluring.

And so, slowly at first but then increasingly, she began to succeed as a social presence in

Washington. She would come home to find a small, creamy calling card atop the tray: another senator's wife had conceded and called. Or she would happen to be in her parlor when another lady arrived, her face arranged in a bright smile. Of course, there were *never* any hard feelings, Louisa would suggest. She was only a plain individual, after all, seeking nothing but a simple life. Then she would extend an invitation to her next party — insisting that the invitation had always been waiting. Anyone, she liked to say, was welcome to come to her house. It took years, but by the end of 1822 she was triumphant: every single senator's wife had paid her a visit except for one, and that one's husband was "an inflexible enemy of Mr A." Louisa, of course, kept track.

She knew just how serious the business was — even if she was only permitted to treat it as a joke. Every morning, she reported to her father-in-law, John Quincy prepared a stack of calling cards for Louisa for the day. "You would laugh could you see Mr. A.," she wrote to John Adams. He performed the task "with as much formality as if he was drawing up some very important article, to negotiate in a Commercial Treaty — but thus it is; and he has been brought to it by absolute necessity."

Louisa once wrote to Abigail, "In this most scandal loving place, . . . I have made up my mind to go on my own way and set it at defiance." She went her own way to end up right where she wanted: at the center of Washington's social scene, working to promote her husband's chances for the presidency, waging her "campaigne."

2

It was her campaign for his presidency — and in some ways, the campaign really was hers more than it was his. Her entertainments made "our Congress less dependent on the foreign ministers for their amusement," Louisa wrote in her diary. The unspoken implication was that they made Congress more dependent on the secretary of state.

While Congress was in session in 1819–20, Louisa began holding her "tea parties" every Tuesday evening, in addition to occasional large balls. She began a diary before that session with her take on Shakespeare's famous lines:

All the world's a stage and all the Men
and women in it players &ce &ce.

She broke the line after "men" instead of after "stage," as Shakespeare had. Perhaps this was not merely happenstance. Women had a place on this stage, but where? It was said to be forbidden for men to discuss politics around women, but that was a rule rarely followed. In daily practice, the distinction between a woman's private self and her husband's public position quickly broke down. Louisa went where the government went: the floor of the Senate, the galleries of the House, the Supreme Court, the drawing rooms of the President's House. Margaret Bayard Smith, the author and doyenne, captured how Washington's political scene merged the house with the House:

> The women here are taking a station in society which is not known elsewhere. On every public occasion, a launch, an oration, an inauguration, in the court, and in the representative hall, as well as the drawing room, they are treated with marked distinction. . . . At the drawing room, at our parties . . . the ladies and gentlemen stand and walk about the rooms, in mingled groups, which certainly produces more ease, freedom, and equality than in those rooms where the ladies sit and wait for gentlemen to approach to converse.

Ease, freedom, and equality, of course, only went so far. The presence of women helped the men define themselves in opposition; they were what the women were not. Little gallantries helped build walls between the sexes, even as conversations broke them down. But it was a dynamic; the social and political worlds were interdependent.

John Quincy needed her parties to go well. "Mr. A. who is apt to take alarm, began to be uneasy and anxious," Louisa wrote after one. "The rooms were nearly full of Gentlemen, most of them Members 80 of whom attended, besides 13 Senators; when the young Ladies began to assemble so fast I could scarcely have time to make my salutations . . . all my guests were apparently satisfied, but what was best of all, Mr. A was so pleased with my success, that he joined in a Reel with the boys and myself." As usual, beneath the breezy tone was a keen and purposeful awareness. Louisa was not just concerned with whether her guests were enjoying themselves; she was counting the members of Congress.

Others, implicitly or not, began to make the connection too. Just before the start of Monroe's second term, Harrison Gray Otis wrote to his wife that Mrs. Adams was "advancing in public favor." He added, "I think too on the whole that John's chance for the Presidency brightens, but it is yet too early to begin our calculations."

Her weekly parties continued during the 1820–21 congressional session. Dozens and sometimes hundreds of guests would come to her house. "The fashionable world of Washington was all there," wrote a House member to his wife after one of Louisa's parties. She followed the grand style of entertaining established by Dolley Madison when she had been in the President's House, and by the diplomatic corps. But while the tradition was for a hostess to stand in one spot, where a servant would lead guests to greet her, and for the women to sit in chairs around the edge while men clustered in the center, Louisa went from room to room herself, seeming at ease, smiling, graceful, gracious, encouraging the guests to move fluidly about.

Young women from Philadelphia, Baltimore, and Boston who were in town for the social season might come to Louisa's parties, showcasing the new fashions — "if that can be called a dress which exposes the neck from the chin to the pit of the stomach before, and to the small of the back behind," wrote one shocked congressman after attending a ball at the French minister's home. Louisa rivaled the richest households for her spreads of cold meats, jellies, ice creams, oranges, and almonds. Roaming servants offered liqueurs, hot chocolate, champagne, and coffee. There were hired musicians or young women on hand to play Louisa's piano or golden harp. Sometimes she sang too.

When she was not denying her skill or claiming to desire only domesticity, she thought about the role she played and about how to play it well. "How much practice or what the French call usage du monde is required to receive company well," she wrote to John Adams. It took small, considered attentions — generous questions, guileless glances, and little flatteries — to put a guest at ease. Without them, she wrote, even "the greatest talents" — like those of her husband — "are obscured." She knew what she did was an art. She compared parties to kilns that hardened clay and set glaze, making something fragile into something durable. "By insensible degrees," she wrote, a good party warmed company "into brilliancy and solidity. This is one of those arts that every body feels, but few understand, and is altogether inexplicable."

It took work, this indescribable effortlessness. Louisa took the dresses she had bought in Paris in 1815 and recut them. (She remained tiny as she grew older; in 1822, she weighed only 102 pounds.) She bought needles, ribbons, and silk. She took tawny silk and trimmed it with black. She set off an empire waist with an iridescent silver sash. She ran ribbons through the eyelets of her satin slippers. She raided old worn-out dresses for their trimmings. Ornamental rope threaded around a skirt; tulle framed a neckline; glittering tinsel fringed the flounces along a hem. She was once so proud of the reconstruction of an old dress that she actually boasted of it to John Adams, who replied with a characteristic warning against extravagance. It took the help of servants, too, of course, though they went largely unacknowledged. There was the usual rotating cast, usually working for five dollars a month; a coachman; a woman to whom the washing was sent. For large parties, extra servants were sometimes hired. Another three maids might be on hand to cook and clean in the kitchen, and six extra servants to wait on the table.

She made do with what she had, drawing on her playful sense of style, but sometimes she sought more. Having shown she could manage by herself in Russia, she had become less shy about asking for money. These events were an investment. The lectures from John Quincy about thrift subsided. No longer needing to support an unsupportable St. Petersburg lifestyle, and with a $6,000 government salary and sound investments, including income from Boston properties, his finances were finally in decent shape. In April 1820, John Quincy bought Dolley and James Madison's old house at 244 F Street, a half-mile walk from the President's House. She complained about the purchase, then was annoyed when John Quincy insisted it was for her — but she quickly turned it to her purpose. Before the family moved from a rented place on Capitol Hill, Louisa hired a mason to build a large and expensive addition to the new house, and she "superintend[ed]" the construction herself. (In his diary, John Quincy grumbled that he had permitted it insofar as he had not stopped it.) The central feature was a room measuring twenty-eight by twenty-nine feet: a ballroom.

Both Louisa and John Quincy complained about the demands of their socializing, as they did more of it. Their roles were defined and obvious to see. Mr. Adams "moves silently about and seems to have but little conversation with anyone," noticed Representative Thomas Hubbard, but Mrs. Adams "receives company very elegantly." John Quincy could afford to be off-putting because she was welcoming; he could be awkward because she was graceful. While he would be criticized for acting aloof, she would come away from a dinner and ball saying she had "never laughed so much in my life." She could host the dinners and balls, and her husband would be almost a guest. He "had an extremely absent, preoccupied air," wrote one woman, but Louisa was "talkative and lively," and her parties "always pleasant and gay."

Not everyone admired Mrs. Adams. Her stubbornness during the visiting controversy had not endeared her to some. Those who saw her as too foreign — tainted by her years in Europe and her English birth — repeated a rumor that the British prince regent had asked Mr. and Mrs. Adams to stand in for him at the christening of the British minister's wife; Monroe even asked John Quincy if the story was true. (It was not.) Her parties made her even more of a target. Although Monroe had tried to put the nation on a "European footing" after the War of 1812 — even as soot and char still scarred the city after the British sacking, and as the white paint still dried on the reconstructed walls of the President's House — it remained popular to bemoan luxury and extravagance. Monroe's wife, Elizabeth, was criticized for being too aloof and aristocratic; women complained that she ignored them, and men studied the bright color of her cheeks for signs of makeup. Louisa felt sympathy and admiration for Elizabeth and nothing but scorn for those who accused her of being too courtly. Louisa was defensive for a reason. Western members referred to her "diplomatic tricks." She had to pretend to be less sophisticated than she was. "One of the greatest taxes I have to pay is that of concealing that I am a traveled lady," she wrote drily to her father-in-law.

"I find myself an object of continual suspicion and mistrust," she wrote to John, adding a little disingenuously, "though I never intrigued in my life but on the contrary have made many enemies in consequence of my proud independence."

She was not as sweet or conciliating as the last great hostess, Dolley Madison, who had been universally loved. Dolley herself took a shot at her when she wrote of Louisa's "keep-[ing] up the fashion for dissipation" — as if Dolley had not established the fashion herself. Louisa had set herself apart partly by breaking the accepted rules. Some chafed about having to pay their respects to her at her parties, after she had made such a point of refusing to do so first. And some suspected she liked the attention a little too much — that her smile was a little too beseeching to be real. "Mrs. Adams told somebody that Mrs. Munroe had been inclined to dejection of spirits and retirement, and that the ceremonials of her station were irksome to her. This is probably true," one senator wrote to his wife, and then pointedly added, "and so would they *not* be to Mrs. [Adams] herself."

She had to expect criticism. It was the price paid for being " 'esteemed the most brilliant lady at Washington by all odds,' " Abigail had written to her. "This is the report of a gentleman of New York who attended your ball."

But for the most part, her parties were admired, and so was their hostess.

"I am a very good diplomate," she wrote to John Adams. "You may laugh but it is so."

John Adams would laugh, but usually with delight. Six weeks after Abigail's death, in mid-December 1818, Louisa received a letter from John asking her to send him her journal, as she had done with his wife. His encouragement, like Abigail's, drew out her suppressed intelligence, the thoughts that she had kept huddled and hidden. She talked to him as she talked to no one else; he talked to her as he had once talked to Abigail.

She asked him questions about the differences between religious sects, wondering openly about her bias against Unitarians. "You will be surprized at my writing you on this subject," she wrote, "but I thoroughly despise a mean and narrow prejudice and am desirous of being convinced by reason of my error." She used her letters to him to map not only her activities but also her inner life — her confusion, frustration, triumphs, and ambivalence about her husband's presidential hopes. She could hardly talk to her husband about such things. "These are subjects which I never or very very rarely venture on with him," she confessed to John. Even if husband and wife had been able to be open emotionally with each other, John Quincy was too busy. He spent his time "pouring over his papers from morning till night," Louisa wrote, "and we do not often hear the sound of his voice." She needed a friend, someone who knew what was at stake and what were the risks, someone who knew her husband's character and her own. She needed the old president. She would often say that no one else — including her husband — understood her so well. At the end of his life, John Adams taught her and encouraged her, and she wrote to him like a flower opening toward the sun.

She sometimes wrote to John about books, and writing seems to have prompted her to read more. Soon, she was also writing her boys, away at grade school and then Harvard, about the books that passed through her hands — as if she were a student just as they were. She read constantly. Her diaries are strewn with quotations and allusions, and letters to her sons are filled with references to books. "I believe you have never read Johnson's Lives of the Poets . . . and the Life of Savage is as interesting as any novel," she wrote to her son John. She also told him to read Milton, Pope, Dryden, Gray — "not to say anything of Shakespeare, whose works like an everlasting spring pour forth new beauties on every perusal." To George, who, she worried, was developing intemperate habits, she recommended *The Autobiography of Benjamin Franklin,* which was rife with instruction in common sense and self-discipline. She read Voltaire and Molière in French. She read newspapers and literary journals — the *North American Review,* the *Edinburgh Review,* and *Blackwood's Magazine.* She was not afraid to say what she thought of them, though she would habitually apologize for having any opinions at all. "It is the consciousness of my own nothingness that causes the liberty," she wrote to her father-in-law.

She tended to read for moral instruction, as many of her contemporaries did (including her husband), and she preferred clarity to ambiguity. "The principal objection I have to W Scott's novels are that his heroes and heroines are almost always vicious and that he still paints them in so interesting a light that it is difficult even while you are aware of their great defects to restrain your admiration of their few good qualities," she wrote to Charles. *Humphry Clinker,* by Tobias Smollett, she could admire, but she disapproved of the author's own character. She cautioned her sons against novels, disapproving of their "mawkish sensibility." Yet she also had a strong preference for naturalness over artifice, and found herself bewitched even by books she might not have liked to approve of. One night, she became so engrossed in *Ivanhoe* that she forgot to get ready to go to dinner at the French minister's.

Her reading was as voracious as it was undisciplined. It included all kinds of texts, even political philosophy. In 1819, John Adams told her to read ancient and modern philosophy. In fact, she responded, she already had. Her reply was playful, apologetic, and winning. Political philosophy? Her mind was not "sufficiently strong, or capacious, to understand, or even to comprehend" it. "You certainly forgot when you recommended it, that you were addressing one of the weaker sex, to whom Stoicism would be both unamiable and unnatural, and who would be very liable in avoiding Scylla, to strike upon Charybdis — or to speak without metaphor, to rush into skepticism." But almost as if to prove herself wrong, she went on: "The systems of the Ancients have been quite out of my reach, excepting the Dialogues of Plato which Mr A. recommended to me last year, and which I read attentively. With the modern philosophers, I have become more intimate. . . . Locke has puzzled me, Berkley amused me, Reid astonished me, Hume disgusted me, and Tucker either diverted me or set me to sleep." In the end, she wrote, "I have never seen anything that could satisfy my mind, or that could compare with the direct and exquisitely simple doctrines of Christianity." She would go on reading in this manner for the rest of her life: Hogarth, Plutarch, Dryden, Samuel Johnson, Shakespeare, Dickens, travelogues, trashy fare, histories of the English Revolution. She would meditate upon genius. She would write of "instances of instability" that set ideas spreading like fires.

Motherhood was her excuse to study books. What she did, she would justify herself, she did for her sons. It was socially acceptable, even virtuous, for a mother to concern herself with her children's educations, though not her own. So when she translated Plato's *Apology* from the French, it was so that she and her boys could be "occupied in some measure in the same studies." When she asked Charles to teach her Latin, she excused the unfeminine behavior by claiming it might teach him humility to have such a poor student. She may have believed these things; certainly, she had no choice but to say them. Even John Adams, who did more than anyone to encourage her, expressed his "curiosity, astonishment, and excuse me when I say risibility" when he received her translation of Alcibiades.

She was by no means a feminist (a word that did not yet even exist), but she was curious about those who fought for women's rights, and perhaps even a little tempted toward radicalism. She read Mary Wollstonecraft, whose book *A Vindication of the Rights of Woman* had caused a sensation — and an extraordinary backlash in the United States when it had appeared more than twenty years before — and she admired it. She urged it on her son Charles. "I hope you benefited from your study of the rights of women," she told Charles, "which [in] spite of the prejudices existing against Miss Woolstoncroft [*sic*] are undeniable."

Her writing strengthened as she read and wrote more. She started to write all the time. "It is singular that I who have always had such a decided dislike to writing should all of a sudden have to launch out quite on a large scale," she told George. Her voice sharpened, becoming more particular and vivid. "Your style in writing is known to be that of the most animated conversation; but in this instance it seems to obliterate the ideas of time and distance and to bring me near to you," George responded to one thoughtful and honest letter, "not in the mood of mortified affection and extinguished expectation, but in that of gratified feeling arising from a sensible confidence imparted by a superior."

While her sons were in Boston, letters gave her a way to remain close, while their absence gave her mind the space to roam. She did worry about them. No doubt the lectures about smoking and eating vegetables she sent them could grow tiresome. She was anxious about Charles's confidence, especially after he entered Harvard at the young age of fourteen in 1821, and she worried about George's diligence and romantic sensibility as he approached and passed twenty years old. She would caution John, who was prone to finding trouble, against his quick temper — a characteristic, she was quick to say, she shared. But she also encouraged them, and she learned along with them. Through them, she entered into a more rigorous intellectual environment. As they grew, with her guidance, she grew along with them. The eldest, George, especially seems to have cherished her letters.

So did her father-in-law. He needed her as much as she needed him. Abigail's death had undone him. His best friend was gone. "The dear partner of my life for fifty four years and for many years more as a lover, now lyes in extremis, forbidden to speak or be spoken to," he wrote to Jefferson in 1818. Louisa was not Abigail, but she was a smart woman with whom he could exchange warm and wandering letters. Louisa brought out the best in John, as he did in her — the full force of his intellect, his humor, and his charm. "Your last three journals are three pearls," he wrote to her in 1819. "I have not been able to thank you for either untill now, they bear the form and impression of the age. They let me into the characters of statesmen, politicians, orators, poets, courtiers, convivialists, dancers, dandys and above all, of ladies, of whom I should know nothing, without your kind assistance. I am a little surprised at the depth of your speculations — upon oratory, phylosophy, and policy. But I need not be, when I recollect, who you are, where you have been, and who is your husband." Four years later, he wrote to her, "Your journal is a kind of necessary of life to me. I long for it the whole week."

"Write without fear and put down on your paper what you think, without thinking of what you must say," Louisa told her niece Mary Hellen, drawing firm lines beneath her words, "and your letters will be most acceptable." It was true of herself. More and more, the woman who had been afraid to write for so long had begun to write without fear. "What is the reason I am no longer afraid to write all that passes in my head or in my heart to use," she wrote to her husband when she was traveling without him. "Time was when my pen refused to mark the dictates of my fancy and I dreaded a censure where I claimed a friend." Back in Washington with their eldest son, George, he responded with the same language his father had used to describe what her letters meant to him. They had, he wrote, "become a sort of necessary of life to George and me."

These exchanges turned out to be a necessary of life for her as well. She was like John Adams in some ways. She was neurotic and proud, but she had some self-awareness. She could be caustic, but was also generous. She mocked others but also herself. She wrote wildly, freely — with ritual disclaimers about her poor intellect and lack of interest. Perhaps it was easier for her to write to John Adams, because she always had the sense, from the moment she had met him, that he cared for her and understood her. And perhaps he sensed in her a need to be acknowledged, and a fear of being overlooked. Perhaps he saw that in her because he saw it in himself — and in all men. Decades before, in his *Discourses on Davila*, John Adams had written that what really makes a poor man so poor is obscurity. He is a nobody: "*He is only not seen.* This total inattention to him is mortifying, painful, and cruel." There were times when Louisa felt that way. But in her journal letters, she stepped into the light, saw, and was seen.

3

There was one subject about which Louisa wrote to John Adams with particular delicacy — although the subject itself was anything but subtle. "Hear much of the Missouri question," she wrote to him in December 1819, at the start of the debate over whether Missouri would be admitted as a slave state. "Should like to know your opinion upon the right of Congress to stop the progress of slavery as this is a strongly disputed point — We shall hear much of this, this winter."

She was right about that. There was no avoiding the subject of slavery any longer, however much the members of Congress — and Louisa herself — might have wanted to avert their attention. For years, slavery had been a subject rarely broached inside the walls of the Capitol — a building dedicated to freedom and the rights of men but built by chattel labor. During those long years of silence, slavery had become only more entrenched in the Southern economy, and the slavocracy amassed wealth and power. Now, as the country expanded, the debate over slavery — would new land be slave or free? — was a wedge that was driving the country apart.

"The Missouri question . . . hangs like a cloud over my imagination," John replied to Louisa.

And it hung over hers. Louisa followed the debates with fascination and fear. She went to the Capitol to watch the arguments, read the newspapers, and struggled with her own assumptions — influenced by her London upbringing, her Southern father, her New England husband, her religion, her compassion, and her reflexive conventional racism. She used crude language to describe slaves. When their characters were called into question — usually through fearmongering by whites — she was always ready to assume the worst. She interacted with slaves all the time. In 1820, about 20 percent of Washington's population was made up of slaves. Slavery was everywhere.

Slaves served Louisa hot chocolate in Elizabeth Monroe's Drawing Rooms at the President's House. They delivered purchases from stores and drove hired hacks. They brought her groceries. They cleared her plate when she was done with dinner at the Calhouns'. Directly across from their F Street home lived their friends the Thorntons — slave owners.

A few doors away from the Adamses' house stood Lafayette Tavern, the hotel "most frequented" by slave traders. A few doors in the other direction stood Miller's Tavern, where, in 1815 — only a few years before — a slave had jumped from the third floor to avoid being sold into the killing fields of the Deep South. She broke her back and arms but survived, sentenced to be still a slave. Even antislavery congressmen often lived in boardinghouses that used slaves, and along with room and board, sometimes a "boy" was dedicated to each boarder for the length of his stay. "At day light my boy *Lewis* comes to my room and builds my fire puts a tin cup of water on, to heat and takes out my clothes to brush," wrote a New York congressman to his wife. (New York, of course, didn't abolish slavery until 1827.) Some of these "boys" (who could have been men of any age) may have been paid wages, but some were certainly slaves. "We were waited upon by a slave, appointed for the exclusive service of our party during our stay," wrote the antislavery advocate Harriet Martineau when she stayed at a Washington boardinghouse a decade later. There were pens where people were chained and held captive in view of government buildings. Almost everyone in Washington was complicit.

Not everyone who came to the city remained quiet about the evils of slavery, of course. After an educational reformer named Jesse Torrey saw a group of slaves chained together on the road near the Capitol, he wrote one of the first widely read and sensational antislavery tracts, *A Portraiture of Domestic Slavery in the United States*. It included accounts of free blacks who were kidnapped in Washington and sold to planters in Louisiana and South Carolina. Some congressmen — including slaveholders — declared their discomfort with slave pens so close to the Capitol. But their scruples were superficial. There was still no prominent advocate for ending slavery in Congress. Most white Americans at the time, slave owners and antislavery advocates alike, were racist.

There were a few who were starting to see the issue in light of the old Revolutionary ideals, who could see that the existence of slavery not only was something that the country would fight over, but that perhaps it was something it should fight over. John Quincy was one of those.

In this, he was braver than Louisa and becoming more so — though during the Missouri debates only to a point, and only privately. Years later, John Quincy would devote himself to arresting the spread of slavery and beginning the work toward emancipation. But not yet. As the two sides lurched toward a series of compromises, John Quincy began to reflect on slavery and the fate of the Union in his diary — repeatedly, passionately, and at length. At a Cabinet meeting, he expressed his qualified, reluctant support for the first Missouri compromise, brokered by Henry Clay, which admitted Missouri as a slave state and Maine as a free one, to preserve the balance of slave and nonslave states, and forbade slavery in the territories north of 36°30' north latitude.

In his diary, John Quincy raised a personal challenge. He called slavery "the great and foul stain upon the North American Union" and raised the question of its "total abolition." "A dissolution, at least temporary, of the Union, as now constituted, would be certainly necessary. . . . The Union then might be reorganized upon the fundamental principle of emancipation. This object is vast in its compass, awful in its prospects, sublime and beautiful in its issue. A life devoted to it would be nobly spent or sacrificed." He may have been echoing, faintly, a pair of widely circulated articles in the *Edinburgh Review* about Thomas Jefferson's *Notes on the State of Virginia*. "Every American who loves his country, should dedicate his whole life and every faculty of his soul, to efface this foul stain [of slavery] from its character," the reviewer wrote. But John Quincy was not merely aping someone else's opinion. He sometimes could have difficulty empathizing with the troubles of those in his immediate family, yet he was often the only one among them who stopped to consider the humanity of blacks. He saw how they were punished for crimes they did not commit and subject to injustice without recourse. He keenly felt the inhuman treatment of slaves, who were forbidden the most basic human rights — "from the bed, from the table, and from all the social comforts of domestic life."

Still, John Quincy was only beginning to connect the inheritance of Revolutionary ideals to the project of emancipation. For the moment, he had to consider politics, including his own future. He was "a servant of the whole Union," he told Senator Ninian Edwards of Illinois, for whom "there was neither East, West, North, or South to my duty or my feelings," whatever his views on the immorality of slavery. He remained aloof, not wanting to jeopardize the passage of his Transcontinental Treaty with Spain, already rabidly denounced by Henry Clay (not incidentally, a slaveholder) for setting the western boundary without including slaveholding Texas. Nor did he want to antagonize slaveholders who might support him in the 1824 election. He instructed Louisa to write a message to his talkative, frank, impolitic father, asking him to decline answering any questions on the subject from others, "as he does not think the time has arrived in which he can with propriety take a part in the business."

She was relieved at his cautious position. Really, she wanted to avoid the whole issue. At a party at the French minister's on the night of March 4, 1820, the day after the compromise bill granting Missouri statehood was passed by Congress, she found herself on the spot. "[T]here was an odd sort of crowing tone among some of the members of Congress which seemed to aim at my husband, and some queer questions were asked me concerning his opinion on the Missouri business which I could not understand," she wrote to the old president John Adams. "I have never pretended to understand the question in all its bearings as a political one; in a moral and religious point of view and even as a gross political inconsistency with all our boasted institutions, liberty, and so forth, it is so palpable a stain that the veryest dunce can see it and understand it. . . ." She excused herself, but she, no dunce, knew better.

Her discomfort may have been complicated by more personal reasons. The Johnson family — her family, the name she so fiercely protected — was a slaveholding family. Louisa's father had owned slaves. So did her sisters' husbands and, most likely, her brother in New Orleans. There may also have been at least one slave living in her own house. The 1820 census showed a female slave under the age of fourteen living in the Adams residence. In light of his antislavery views and his statement later that he never owned slaves, John Quincy almost certainly did not own the person himself; he may have rented her from her owners and paid her (and, likely, her owner) wages — a common practice in Washington at the time. Or she may have been owned by a member of the extended family who was living with them at the time.

The most likely possibility is that the slave belonged not directly to Louisa and John Quincy but to Louisa's young niece Mary, the daughter of her older sister Nancy. Mary's father, Walter, had been a slaveholder, and in 1816, the executor of Walter Hellen's will allotted Mary approximately $7,600 from stock and "cash, furniture and negroes." Mary may have brought a slave, a child, with her when she moved in with the Adamses. In the South, it was common for a wealthy white girl to be "given" a domestic slave about her age; it was thought to cultivate the slave's loyalty. Mary would later manumit a slave named Rachel Clark — but not until 1828, a decade after she moved in with Louisa and John Quincy. In 1834, Louisa's younger sister Adelaide, who married Walter Hellen after Nancy's death, freed a slave named Jane Clark, whom the Adamses called Jenny, and who "lived sometimes with us," John Quincy later wrote. Jane also had a son named Joseph, whom Adelaide sold, and who was taken by his new owner to Arkansas.

John Quincy later insisted that he did not tolerate having slavery in his family, but it seems that he did tolerate having slaves in his house — and, considering that he would consider Mary a kind of daughter, his claim was only technically true. He was like most whites living in Washington, making tortured distinctions between principle and practice. This would become harder; he would become braver — but not until later. Louisa was even less troubled by these compromises than he. She was opposed to slavery as an idea; she openly referred to it as an injustice. But she did not want to fight slavery herself. She wanted to close her eyes and have the debate disappear. She avoided using even the word "slavery." "It is really a pity that the Southern interest should have renewed a subject altogether so inimical to the peace and quiet of the country," she wrote to John Adams. "It is calculated to rouse a spirit which will prove more difficult to exorcise than all the ghosts who have been doomed to the Red Sea." Like many others, she would prefer the perpetuation of one of the worst atrocities in modern history for the sake of peace and quiet — peace for whites, that is, since there was no such thing as peace for those under the threat of the lash.

There may have been a psychic cost. The subject exhausted her to talk about; it also exhausted her to avoid it. As she wrote to John Adams that night after the French minister's party, the Missouri Compromise still on her mind, "Returned home very weary tired of myself and all the world."

4

Because March 4, 1821, Monroe's second inauguration day, fell on a Sunday, the swearing-in ceremony was pushed to Monday. Rain and snow further moved it from outdoors to inside the House chamber. Despite the grim weather, an immense crowd converged on the Capitol. Monroe had to struggle through the crush of people on his way to his chair on the platform. His black broadcloth suit was tugged at, his hat almost lost. People noticed the silver buckles at his knees and on his shoes. Already, he was out of style; he would be the last president to wear the clothing of the Revolutionary era. Monroe had taken part in the crossing of the Delaware River in 1776. By 1821, his "antiquated" clothing had become a legible symbol: one era was ending, another was coming. The next president would wear a suit with long pants.

There were strong signs of other changes. Monroe had been reelected almost unanimously. "Discord does not belong to our system," he once said. But the era of unity, such as it was, would be fleeting. Even then — even that very day — the fragility of the good feelings was apparent. The din of voices in the hall, the "disorder of loud talking and agitation in the Gallery," John Quincy noted, never wholly subsided, not even as the president took the oath and delivered his speech. The House galleries' attention was distracted by the members of the Cabinet, including John Quincy, who sat to Monroe's right. Speculation about who would take Monroe's place was rampant and noisy. The rivals for the next election were as much a part of the spectacle as the Marine Band.

That night, the Adamses went to the inaugural ball at Brown's Hotel. Louisa paid attention to Elizabeth Monroe moving amid the crowd, "more beautiful than I ever saw her." She thought of what the room would look like four years from that moment, and imagined herself in that place. Louisa could only hope, she wrote, that if fate gave her the role, she would perform it as well as Elizabeth Monroe.

As Louisa watched the incumbent, she could sense that people were also watching her. Heads were turning in her direction. "The eye of the public," she wrote, "is already on me."

Louisa watched Elizabeth Monroe with as much dread as admiration. She was a cautionary example, denigrated for being too haughty, too aristocratic, even too beautiful. There would be a price for success. "Can anyone see the miserable woman who now fills that seat and not shrink with fear and disgust from a situation so wretched?" Louisa wrote to her brother, Thomas, who was living in New Orleans. "To be slandered, vilified, and condemned . . . Oh defend me from such a situation."

That winter, 1821–22, was a hard one. Frequently sick — and believing she was pregnant — Louisa suspended her weekly parties. (She did hold one massive ball that winter; hundreds of curious denizens turned out to see the forty-seven-year-old hostess who was, as Louis McLane of Delaware put it, "as ladies who love their lords like to be." If she was in fact pregnant and not going through menopause, then at some point that winter she miscarried for the final time.)

She began to withdraw. She worried about her sons and worried more about their father's high expectations. George, now twenty years old, was sensitive. Her oldest son "magnifies his joys and sorrows," Louisa wrote, "until the real world in which he moves vanishes from his sight." He loved poetry and the natural world, and, like his mother, was liable to fall ill during times of stress. "His nature is kind and amiable, and his heart is excellent," Louisa wrote to her son John about his older brother. "Little oddities sometimes worry us but we should reflect on ourselves and remember that we are none of us exempt from peculiarities of which we are not aware." John Quincy was appalled to learn that George was ranked in the middle of his class when he graduated from Harvard that summer. John Quincy ordered him to Washington, where he might keep a watchful eye on his son, to work as his private secretary, and to study for the law.

The prospects of his two younger sons, John and Charles, upset John Quincy even more. He was so unhappy to learn that John's rank at Harvard sat even lower than his older brother's and that Charles, who had just turned fourteen years old, had performed badly on his entrance exams. He declared that both John and Charles would not be allowed to come to Washington for Harvard's Christmas break. "I could feel nothing but sorrow and shame in your presence," he wrote. Their mother, who delighted in their company, could not sway him. After her sons' — and her — last desperate plea, she wrote in her diary, "This day has blasted my hopes and I am absolutely refused the sight of my children — I must submit because I have no resources but it grieves me to the soul." In her characteristically melodramatic fashion, she guessed that she would probably die before she saw them again.

She was in fact ill, plagued by attacks of "my old friend" erysipelas, the painful bacterial infection she had contracted in St. Petersburg. Now her health went from bad to worse. It may have been, as she herself believed, related to her state of mind. Yet again, her husband was making decisions regarding their sons without her. She was reminded of what little standing she could claim for herself in her own family. For months at a time, she stopped writing her letters to John Adams. Without her parties, she felt her status as the city's doyenne slipping. Her "constellation," she wrote, was "in eclipse."

What drew her from the shadow, ironically enough, was illness. That June, 1822, Louisa took her chronically ill brother Thomas, who had returned to Washington from New Orleans, where he had been postmaster general, to Philadelphia. There, she sought the services of Dr. Philip Syng Physick, who recommended hemorrhoid surgery (the famous doctor's almost universal prescription). Louisa and Thomas settled into a hotel at 62 South Sixth Street, between Chestnut and Walnut streets and across from the State

House Gardens, run by a warmhearted spinster prone to malapropisms. Weeks turned into months, until Thomas was well enough for surgery and the heat had abated.

The health problems that plagued her brother (and — as ever — her) were significant and debilitating. But soon, she began to enjoy herself. The distance from Washington, the service for her brother, and the warmth of the attention from her friends and acquaintances in Philadelphia revived her. She was never so happy as when she visited the house of her closest friends, Elizabeth and Joseph Hopkinson, in Bordentown, New Jersey. On one trip, a group of young women, "as wild as unbroken colts," was also visiting. "Shouts and laughter resounded through the house," Louisa told John Quincy. There were fishing trips and long walks; visits with Napoleon's brother Joseph, who had escaped to the United States just before Napoleon's defeat at Waterloo and now had an estate nearby, and who tried to charm Louisa especially; and games of whist. On one rainy day Louisa pulled out a pack of cards and told the girls' fortunes. "This week has been one in which I have lived a year," she wrote to her husband. Play turned to politics; her "friends," including the Hopkinsons, had powerful political connections. Even in Bordentown, along with the gallivanting and card games, there was "familiar chat" on the piazza with Joseph —

pretense for discussions about politics. Back on Sixth Street in Philadelphia, Louisa had use of the parlor, and she turned it into a kind of political salon.

Her parlor in the little hotel became a kind of campaign headquarters. Nearly every day, men came to see her — not just any men, but some of the leading political figures in Philadelphia, men with a reach beyond Pennsylvania. Newspaper editors, generals, senators came to give her news, pass along messages, and discuss the race. They were electioneering.

Philadelphia was no longer the site of the nation's capital, but it was still the second-largest city in the Union, more populous than Boston, and five times more so than Washington. Its significance was reflected in its beauty, with its Palladian windows and pleasant squares, oil lamps that glowed at night, brick walks, shops stocked with elegant dresses and delicate shoes imported from Paris. Some of the shops kept Louisa's measurements on file. Politically, John Quincy was not the front-runner in Pennsylvania, but Philadelphia was still strategically important; the middle states were especially crucial for John Quincy's prospects. New England, John Quincy could safely assume, would be united behind him — though grudgingly, perhaps. ("He has few personal friends, and no very strong hold on their public feelings," wrote

New Hampshire senator Jeremiah Mason to Rufus King. ("A tremor in the popular pulse is often perceptible.") The South was already lost. The West, at this point in the race, was Henry Clay's territory. But the middle states were fiercely contested, with every man able to make a claim, and was home to newspapers with national reaches, both in circulation and through reprinting. It had a tradition of political engagement, the greatest tradition in the country. Its influence could be far-reaching.

Louisa's letters to John Quincy started to include roll calls of her visitors. *Major Jackson, Mr. Ewing, Mr. Cook, Mr. Sergeant, Mr. Ingersoll, Mr. Walsh . . .* It quickly became understood by all — including John Quincy — that his wife could send and deliver messages. She was not just a point of contact, though. She helped shape what was said. In her parlor, she would discuss resignations, appointments, the latest report from the Louisville newspapers. General Jacob Brown, commanding general of the U.S. Army, would come by to brief her on the state of support in Pennsylvania for Secretary of War John Calhoun, the tumultuous state of politics in New York, the prospects of a two-man race between Secretary of Treasury William Crawford and Adams. Invariably, she would close her letters reporting conversations to John Quincy with a demurral. Those selfabasements were so automatic that they couldn't have been entirely disingenuous; her insecurity and belief in a woman's subordinate place ran too deep. She cringed at her husband's praise of her political acumen. "I hate the word advice when you apply it as given from me to you," she wrote. But her ambivalence about her capacity didn't stop her or dampen her enthusiasm in Philadelphia. When she sat at her table and set her pen to paper, her accounts tumbled across the page, and her counsel was mixed in with them.

Her tone swung between operatic and cynical. "My courage will not fail me. . . . The object of competition is a noble one," she would write one day. Then another, she would joke about "a good receipt for a Presidential candidate": "Take a good deal of small talk; a very little light literature; just sufficient attention to dress to avoid the appellation of a dandy; an undesirable affectation of social affability; with as much suavity as will induce the fawners who surround him." She had heard rumors about the slovenliness of his dress. "I was asked if you really went to church without shoes or stockings. I replied that I had once heard you rode to your office with your head to your horse's tail, and that the one fact was as likely as the other."

But it wasn't all comic. There was a consistent thrust to her letters. She urged her husband to show his feelings, to let the public know that he was human. Her most eloquent appeal to him came while he was unmasking the duplicity of Jonathan Russell in a controversy over John Quincy's actions at Ghent in negotiating the treaty that ended the War of 1812. Russell, a representative from Massachusetts and a colleague at Ghent, had produced copies of correspondence that seemed to show that Adams, alone among the commissioners, had been willing to trade the right of New Englanders to fish off the Canadian coast for navigation rights on the Mississippi. The implication was that John Quincy was willing to sell out the West to protect eastern interests. But the documents were doctored. John Quincy easily showed that the copies did not match the originals, and in two articles published in the *National Intelligencer* that summer, he demolished Russell's integrity. At first, Louisa was elated. "Poor Jonathan! He has proved himself a flat fish, and seems to be killed as 'dead as a flounder.'" When John Quincy refused to stop hammering Russell, long after he had won his point, however, she tried to warn him against beating the dead fish.

The way she did it is instructive. She began by telling him that Robert Walsh, an influential Philadelphia newspaper editor who had printed both Russell's and the secretary of state's correspondence, was urging John Quincy to end his attack. She was only delivering someone else's message, she implied. Then she moved into her own language and advice.

> You are under a great error as it regards the interest of the late correspondence; the *personal* part of it has been the only part which has really occupied the publick mind, and it has placed you before the world in the character of a private individual, suffering under an unjust and ungenerous persecuted — in this light alone it is viewed and in this light it is powerfully *felt,* because every man can understand it and make the case his own. Persons long inured to public life accustomed to objects of great magnitude, *thinking* for a *world* and ever dwelling not on man individually but on the welfare of mankind at large, are apt to overlook the little *passions,* and the little every day *feelings* which contribute so largely to create the strong impulse of civil society.

With her instinct for the powerful force of personality, she could understand what her husband could or would not. Men were choosing their leaders from among men, whom they wanted to see as they saw themselves. They elected a representative of the people — not a list of accomplishments. "For this reason my best friend this controversy has placed you in a new light," Louisa wrote to John Quincy; "not as a negotiator of treaties alone, but as an *able* man."

He took the side of reason, intellect, facts, public duty. She argued for emotion, feelings, style, relationships. The era's stereotypes are impossible to ignore. Louisa considered herself a lady and wanted to be a lady. She preferred delicacy to strength, imagination to logic, modesty to confidence. She took her subjugation for granted, though it sometimes made her angry. "That sense of inferiority which by nature and by law we are compelled to feel, and to which we must submit, is worn by us with as much satisfaction as the badge of slavery generally," she wrote to John Quincy.

She was not, though, merely submissive. Writing from Philadelphia, humming with news and opinions, she converted what restricted her into a liberating force. Because she believed her emotions were legitimate, even if her thoughts were not, she said what she wanted and then excused what she said as the effusion of her feelings. She wrote daringly frank letters. Her words would not pause for a comma, for a break, for a breath; her thoughts and insights and observations would overtake one another in a great onrush, unruly and free. At the end, she would append a line that dismissed everything she'd said as nonsense, the meaningless ravings of a woman. She slipped into satire or hyperbole, or used metaphors to mock powerful men. On a blank page in the middle of her diary, following the entry for March 28, 1821, and preceding the entry for July 19, 1821, she had written a "Motto for 1820." It was a quote from Molière, *Le médecin malgré lui*, Act I, scene v: *"C'est une chose admirable que tous les grands / hommes onts toujour du caprice, quelque / petit grain de folie mélée à leur science"* — It is a wonderful thing that the great men always have something of caprice, some small grain of folly, mixed with their learning.

There was something of Molière in her, and it helped her to realize that there was something of a "woman's weakness" even in the greatest men. Men, like women, were driven by emotions. They wanted warmth and attention; they could feel frustrated and ignored. Their feelings were inconsistent. They were attuned to style, and sensitive to what could seem like small superfluities. Their powers of reason, however strong, were at the will of their hearts.

It was not that John Quincy entirely disagreed with her. He had grown up in an age that celebrated sensibility. He knew the power of pathos; he had watched emotional appeals move men to war or to tears. His parents had both been open about the depth of their feelings and the complicated motivations of men's behaviors. He was interested in psychology, too. His diary was full of observations about human nature. He understood vanity, including his own, all too well. But he struggled with empathy. His son Charles once said he hid his feelings behind an "iron mask." Louisa tried to get him to take it off.

Back and forth between Washington and Philadelphia their letters sped, keeping their conversation at a quick pace. The mail itself was one sign of how the political scene was changing. Gone were the days when men were isolated from one another — or their politicians. The webs were spun and expanded, the path of a daily mail tracing the shape of the net. The improvement in the mail system helped close the distance between husband and wife. The easy rhythm of their letters' arrivals kept their correspondence warm. He addressed her as "my dearest Louisa," "my dearest friend." She often spoke to him without address — or even salutation, picking up midthought. Her letters, written in journal form (as had become her habit), had the effect of inviting him into her daily life. Despite their distance — perhaps because of their distance — Louisa and John Quincy were very close that summer.

Their intimacy had another dimension. He

began to write to her about his work in a new way. He wrote as if taking part in an exchange, not as if delivering a report. "At every step I take I want a friendly adviser; and have had none but you," he wrote to her. He treated her as a partner, and she responded as one. "It is true that I talk or rather hear politics," she had written to John Quincy in 1822 from Philadelphia. "People seem to look upon me in this instance as part of yourself, and in the matrimonial light think *us one*."

Their union was intense, cooperative, and at times erotic. "With the dawn of morning I awaked and ejaculated a blessing to Heaven upon the semi-jubilee of our marriage — more than half of your life, and nearly half of mine, have we traveled hand in hand in our pilgrimage through this valley, not alone of tears," John Quincy wrote to her on July 26, their twenty-fifth wedding anniversary. "We have enjoyed together great and manifold blessings, and for many of them I have been indebted to you."

A few days later, Louisa received a desert flower, a night-blooming cereus. There could hardly have been a more fitting symbol for herself: resilient and yet fragile, "delicately elegant," blossoming in the dark. She wrote to John Quincy about it suggestively, describing the white globe of the bud and the small spiral of feathery yellowish green leaves that cupped it. "Like our sex," she told him, "it only displays its charms to advantage by candle light."

When the subject turned to politics, though, their tempers were sometimes provoked. Louisa wanted her husband to come to Philadelphia to meet with his supporters. He would not. She tried to put the idea on others; she wrote that she was only communicating advice, and said she only wanted to see him herself. But he could easily see her intent. She wanted him to encourage his "friends" — the networks of politicians, local leaders, newspaper editors, and power brokers who trumpeted a candidate's positions, defended him against opposition, and campaigned on his behalf. "Mr H[opkinson] Says you had better give up the point and come here," she wrote in late June. "Do pray leave Washington soon and come to your affectionate, LCA," she added in early July.

"I have told you before that I cannot come to Philadelphia," he responded sharply. He compared himself to Prometheus, chained to the rock of his work. "The spirit of martyrdom seems to come upon me, and I sometimes think it would be happy for me, if I could die at my post."

She was persistent and then spoke outright. It was a "critical time," she wrote, and the people were in his favor. He should "seize the happy occasion" to appear in person. His reticence and reclusiveness were self-defeating. Then she almost begged him. "Do for once gratify me I implore you; and if harm comes of it I promise never to advise again." His enemies presented his reserve in a bad light. "They must have a President that they dare speak to."

Just before she left Philadelphia, in October, he responded with a despairing, raw, and furious letter. "It is my situation that makes me a candidate, and you at least know that my present situation was neither of my own seeking nor of my choice." He should be president because he *deserved* to be president. "Of the Public History of Mr Monroe's Administration, all that will be worth telling to Posterity hitherto has been transacted through the Department of State," he claimed. There were treaties with Great Britain, Spain, France, and Russia. There was "the whole course of policy with regard to South America" — what would become known as the Monroe Doctrine. The secretary of state had made possible the purchase of Florida and the expansion of American territory straight to the Pacific. The extension of borders "has been obtained, I might confidently say, by me." What had his rivals done? He dismissed Crawford and Calhoun with undisguised contempt. "As to the Treasury or War Departments, what single incident has occurred in this Administration, which will tell with credit to future ages?"

What Crawford and Calhoun had done instead, he wrote, was slander him. "So much for the *Public* History of Mr. Monroe's Administration — Now for its Secret History." The administration's secret history was a litany of lies and intrigue. The Cabinet was filled with snakes, men more interested in poisoning one another than in the good of the country. He alone was virtuous. He had no allies, no one looking out for his interests. Did his friends think "a week's visit to Philadelphia" would change that? Adams wrote as if he were prey, not another viper, as if he could extricate himself from the administration, holding his list of achievements in his clean hands.

The truth was different. He wrote ferocious rebuttals to his critics' charges, usually in letters that somehow found their way into newspapers — or were printed at his own expense. He tried to discredit the other candidates or ship them out of the country altogether, proposing that Clay become minister to Colombia, or that Jackson be shipped off as a diplomat far away. These proposals were politely, pointedly, turned down. When his friend Joseph Hall — who had been a witness at his wedding in London and was now the editor of the *Portfolio* in Philadelphia — published an anonymous sketch of his life in 1819, John Quincy made no move to stop it. The sketch was expanded and republished in

1824 as a campaign biography, with traces of his own hand.

One man who knew him wrote that he "had an instinct for the jugular and carotid artery as unerring as that of any carnivorous animal." In his diary, where he spun the secret history, he called Crawford "a worm preying on the vitals of the Administration within its own body." Clay was "only half educated." Calhoun, he grudgingly respected. (He called Andrew Jackson, the man who would become his greatest threat, a hero — but Jackson was not a main candidate yet.) "There is hardly a passion in the human heart but that is arrayed against me . . . a single false step would ruin me," he wrote in his diary on July 11, 1822, his fifty-fifth birthday.

That was the story, the public history and the private one, that he told his wife. He mocked her pretended innocence. "You will tell me that I can't understand a joke, and that you only wanted me to come to you, to fetch you home."

5

On New Year's Day 1823, Louisa and John Quincy beat their way through stormy weather to a party at the President's House. She went with the future much on her mind. Weeks before, she had resumed her campaign, holding her tea parties now on alternate weeks. That evening, they hosted twenty men — governors, senators, representatives — for dinner at their house on F Street. Afterward, as rain tapped at the windows, she picked up her pen and opened her diary. She was pensive. "If the weather of today is ominous of the storms of the ensuing year we must not expect much quiet," she wrote. "Let it come I will not flinch be the end what it may."

A few days later, Louisa received a letter from Joseph Hopkinson. A powerful lawyer, former representative of Pennsylvania in Congress, and a recent member of the New Jersey House of Assembly, Hopkinson began by reminding her of her warm and happy visits to Bordentown, New Jersey. "Let me beg you to consider, for a moment, that you and I are sitting, with or without a bright moon as you please, on the Piazza looking into the garden," Hopkinson began. There, "one may say many things, which it would by no means be proper" for a man to say to a lady. The illicit romance was in fact an ongoing conversation about presidential politics; and the subject, their reciprocal desire, was the prospect of John Quincy's presidency.

John Quincy's conduct, Hopkinson went on, seemed "calculated to chill and depress" those who advocated his cause. He and others felt actively discouraged by the man they were trying to promote. "Now, my dear Madam, all this won't do. The Macbeth policy 'if chance will make me king, why chance may crown me,' will not answer where little is left to chance or merit, but kings are made by politicians and newspapers," he wrote, "and he who sits down waiting to be crowned either by chance or just right will go bare-headed all his life."

Louisa did what Hopkinson no doubt expected her to do: she handed the letter to her husband. John Quincy's own hand recorded the letter's receipt at the edge of the envelope, and John Quincy wrote Hopkinson a stern and righteous reply, disavowing any activity that would seem grasping. In her own response, Louisa echoed John Quincy's message. But she was not merely the messenger in this case. Hopkinson had meant for John Quincy to read the letter, but it was addressed to Louisa. If it were only for John Quincy, Hopkinson's allusion to Macbeth would seem odd. Macbeth, torn between his virtue and his ambition, resists acting to fulfill a prophecy until he succumbs to the lure of power. He has the king murdered, sends Scotland into chaos, and then is killed. When Hopkinson criticized the secretary of state's "Macbeth policy," John Quincy was able to make the easiest of rejoinders: look what terrible things happened to Macbeth once he took events into his own hands! But the allusion was richer, because the letter was to John Quincy's wife. If John Quincy was Macbeth, then Louisa was Lady Macbeth, who had pushed her husband to murder the king to gain the throne.

The letter was also an appeal to Louisa, then. If John Quincy was hesitant, then she could not be. If he would not act, then she should. Lady Macbeth had to show her husband what to do, to push him down the path. Hopkinson was not subtle here. He addressed Louisa as "the second lady of the republick, that 'shal't be first hereafter' " — an echo of the prophecy that three witches deliver to Macbeth at the start of the play: "All hail Macbeth, that shalt be king hereafter!" Hopkinson was a lawyer. He was clever. He knew John Quincy; he knew Louisa. His approach to John Quincy had been rejected. Now he appealed to Louisa's ambition instead.

She would have recognized the reference to Shakespeare's line, and she would not have missed its suggestion. She had read *Macbeth* and seen it performed on stage. Years later, she would meditate on the play at length and find its echoes in her own life. "Were we to look deeply and minutely into the secret histories of men; how constantly we should observe this same retributive justice," she would write in 1839. "It is one of the most remarkable facts; and it has caused me deeply to reflect upon its repeated and continued recurrence." Writing in 1839, Louisa may not have remembered her husband's use of the phrase "secret history" in 1822, but the echo was still there. Even before she read Hopkinson's letter during that tempestuous start to 1823, her mind was running along similar lines. She felt some temptation or threat that was strong enough for her, at the least, to feel the need to ward it off. "Let me be satisfied with my own conduct and I defy slander and the foul fiend," Louisa wrote on January 1, the very same day that Hopkinson was writing her.

Whether she would admit it or not, Louisa was electioneering. She met with men privately; she pushed her contacts to work on John Quincy's behalf. She went to Maryland as well as Philadelphia, again for her health but also with an eye toward her husband's presidential prospects. "As my connections in [Maryland] are of the most respectable and distinguished I am solicitous to secure them in his interest," she wrote with pride. "Maryland it is said will be his." Hurriedly, she continued: "For myself I have no ambition beyond my present situation." When she resumed her diary in November at the start of the congressional session, she began with a epigraph: "In a righteous cause I dare both good and ill —" When she copied the entries onto loose-leaf sheets to send as a letter to John Adams and her son George, she turned the line into a rhyming couplet and softened it: "In a righteous cause I dare both good and ill — / Obey Gods Laws, and act with virtue still." In her diary, though, the words remained in their stark original form.

More than two hundred years had passed since Shakespeare wrote, and yet the suspicion that a woman violated her sex by involving herself in affairs of state — that she "unsexed" herself, as Lady Macbeth did — was persistent and deep rooted. If anything, Louisa's situation was more perilous than it would have been even a short time before. Had Louisa lived where the Hopkinsons did, in Bordentown, fifteen years earlier, and had she had a little property to her name, she would have been able to vote. But New Jersey

452

rewrote its suffrage laws in 1807 to expand the vote for white men by abolishing the property requirement, while excluding women and blacks. Other states likewise wrote into their constitutions new explicit language forbidding women and often blacks from direct participation in politics. Before then, in many places gender restrictions on the franchise had been a matter of custom, not enshrined in law. The widespread celebration of American virtue and its connection to daily domestic life after the Revolution had encouraged women to think of themselves as integral members of the republic. Now, women were being written out of the laws.

"Kings are made by politicians and newspapers," Hopkinson had written, which was half true. The tradition whereby a small group of men picked the president from an even smaller group of men — mostly Virginia-bred secretaries of state — was coming to an end, and with it the power of the capital's social scene, where women might play an indirect part. The power of political insiders in Washington was waning. Networks of political supporters were becoming increasingly structured and institutionalized, and their centers were outside of Washington. The process was accelerated as new forms of communication and transportation arose, making it easier to speed information from one place to another, and as more men began to stake their claim in the federal government. Some of them were radicalized by a period of economic hardship known as the Panic of 1819, a downturn triggered by speculation in public lands with paper money and the postwar adjustments of Europe's economy. The popular resentment against banks and businesses joined up with resentment against Washington. Political parties were forming, and the players in them were men.

As the franchise expanded for white men, the roles allowed to white women were increasingly restricted. Politics were considered corrupt; the ideal American woman was pure. To keep "the fair sex" untainted, the two had to be kept apart.

A woman was always on display, even in Congress. When Louisa went to watch the debates, the expression on her face was scrutinized. Shopkeepers asked her to model their clothes. A New York businessman sent her a new kind of bonnet, explaining that her patronage might spur sales. She knew what people thought, and she knew she had to deny that she did. When she fell sick, she wrote that it was assumed that she suffered "in consequence of hopes and fears during this tremendous struggle for the Presidential election for which in fact I care very little."

The knocks on her door were incessant. Charles, who was home from Harvard for

Christmas, was nearly overwhelmed. "Visitors pouring in, in quantities which it is agreeable to Madame to refuse," he wrote in his diary in December 1823. (She often pretended to be "not at home," Charles noted — "a custom without which it would be impossible to move.")

It was tiresome, being always watched and judged. Yet it was worrisome when the public gaze wandered. By the beginning of 1824, there were five serious candidates for president — John Quincy, Henry Clay of Kentucky, John Calhoun of South Carolina, William Crawford of Georgia, and Andrew Jackson of Tennessee — and the efforts on behalf of each were freewheeling. Crawford, who had been unabashed about using his patronage powers at the Treasury to sweeten his appeal, was likely to be the choice of the congressional caucus. The rising star was Andrew Jackson.

Louisa had met Jackson in 1819, when he was in disgrace. That January, he had galloped to Washington from Tennessee because Congress was threatening to censure him. He had invaded Florida under the pretext of chasing Seminoles, executed two British subjects, massacred Native Americans, driven the Spanish from their land, generally disregarded his orders, and precipitated a crisis with Spain and possibly Spain's allies, especially Great Britain. These extralegal adventures burnished Old Hickory's fame in the rest of the country, but they were condemned in Washington. Those who saw him as a threat — to the country and to their own political prospects — tried to punish him. In the House, Clay harangued him for insubordination. In the Cabinet, John Calhoun and William Crawford called for his head. Only John Quincy, who recognized that his own attempts to secure Florida from Spain by treaty had just become much easier, defended him.

Louisa was sympathetic to Jackson. "Party intrigue is at this moment playing," she wrote later, after the Senate delivered a damning report of his conduct. "Old Hickory is the tool on this occasion." But his opponents had lit a fire they could not put out. Andrew Jackson would not be used. Inside Congress, he was condemned, but outside it, he was lionized. Pro-Jackson forces began to unite. The Hero, as he was called for his triumph at the Battle of New Orleans, attended one of Monroe's drawing rooms, and the crowd, eager to catch a glimpse, almost crushed him. Louisa had her first sight of the general there and immediately liked him. He was tall and rangy, with a roughhewn face and a shock of white hair. There was grace in his manners. It gratified her to see his critics catch their breath and widen their eyes at the sight of him. "I heard much astonishment expressed by some persons not friendly to him at his being so polite," she wrote to old John Adams, "as they expected to have seen him at least half *Savage*."

Jackson was a force that no one, not least himself, could control. As soon as he returned to Tennessee, he wrote to John Clark of Georgia and asked for "such facts relative to the character of Mr Wm H Crawford" that might involve "his private deportment" and show "depravity of heart" — what might be known in modern political parlance as opposition research. He hated Clay just as much, and Clay despised him with equal fervor. The movement to make Jackson president hadn't been serious at first. Those who put him forward generally supported Adams or Clay and believed that Jackson's name could be used for local political purposes. In 1822, the Tennessee legislature nominated him for president. In the summer of 1823, an anonymous pamphlet appeared extolling his virtue, arguing that he was the only man to rid Washington of corruption. That fall, the Tennessee state legislature elected him to the Senate. The other candidates weren't sure what to make of him. Never before had a serious candidate arrived in Washington so late in the game, with such a scanty record (outside of his military exploits). Never before had a candidate ridden a wave of such popular appeal — never before had the popular vote had such power.

He appealed to men who had never had the chance to vote, often men who had been terribly affected by the economic Panic of 1819. Those voters distrusted Washington. They were drawn to the outsider, the war hero Jackson.

The established candidates and their supporters eyed Jackson nervously and tried to be opportunistic. "Mr Frye told me that there was a combination among the friends of Mr C[rawfor]d should the Caucus fail to throw all their weight into Genl Jacksons scale to make him P[resident]," Louisa wrote in her diary in December. "Every day brings forth a new rumour not one of which can be believed or relied on." Jackson had already begun to sense the depth, breadth, and potential of his appeal among American men due to his outstanding military victories. A grassroots campaign, which he subtly encouraged, sprang up around him and quickly spread.

Things were changing, though haphazardly and in ways few could immediately see. The size of the franchise was expanding, as states were added to the Union and constitutions were amended to eliminate property requirements for voting. By 1824, electors in eighteen out of twenty-four states would be chosen directly by voters instead of by state legislatures. Likewise, what it meant to be a virtuous office holder was undergoing a transformation. The older values of disinterested service held less appeal for a second generation of Americans. Personalities mattered more. Some men were beginning to see that the road to Washington could start outside the capital, in the woods of New York or the hills of Tennessee.

For John Quincy, Jackson posed a particular problem — but also a possibility. John Quincy was the ultimate insider, the son of a president. He had nothing of Jackson's charisma or popular appeal. But Jackson was indebted to John Quincy for his repeated and robust defense during the Seminole Wars. In fact, the two men admired each other. They shared a desire to discredit the legitimacy of February's congressional caucus, which — largely due to the inexhaustible maneuvering of the New Yorker Martin Van Buren — was almost certain to select William Crawford. Months earlier, Crawford had fallen seriously ill, possibly suffering a stroke, and remained possibly incapacitated — which his supporters, who had much to gain by his election, did well to hide. Demonstrating the combined appeal of Jackson and Adams would lend credence to the notion that the choice of the caucus was the choice of cronies, not the people. John Quincy wrote in his diary, quite conveniently, that Jackson would make a very good choice for the vice presidency. It was "the place suited to him and him suited to the place."

But Jackson would need to be convinced of that. On December 20, 1823, John Quincy suggested to his wife that they have a ball on January 8 — the anniversary of the Battle of New Orleans. It would be in honor of Andrew Jackson. They would make a bid for his allegiance, and in doing so make his day their own.

Ladies climbed on top of chairs and tables to see Louisa and General Jackson as she led him through the room, having taken his arm. "Such a crowd you never witnessed," marveled Senator Elijah Mills, who rode with Jackson to the party. It took strenuous effort to achieve this little moment of grace. Louisa had turned the house, Charles complained, "topsy turvy" with preparations. She installed twelve pillars to keep the upper floor from falling in ("then what would become of all the Capulets aye and the Montagues too," Louisa sardonically joked), then disguised the supports with garlands and greenery. Doors were taken down and a pantry was removed. The family had to dine in her dressing room. Louisa threaded wreaths with roses and hung garlands from chandeliers. She hired the Marine Corps band. Five hundred invitations were handed out, then five hundred more. All the residents of F Street at the time — Johnson Hellen, John (the second), Mary Hellen, Thomas Adams's daughter Abby, and Charles — were recruited to deliver invitations, weave wreaths, purchase flowers, move furniture. Only the family dog, Booth, was spared. One suspects, though no Adams ever bothered to mention it, that the sizable staff of servants worked late night after night as the party approached. Louisa became so consumed by preparations that she nearly fainted, as she was prone to do.

Now, she did not need to turn her head to see that the party exceeded her hopes. "It really was a very brilliant party," a guest wrote to Dolley Madison afterward. The women were in their finest gowns, the men in dress attire: silk stockings, blue coats, white waistcoats, neckties, high chokers, and pumps. All the men, that is, except John Quincy, for whom careless dress had become a point of principle and pride. He had even been evicted from his study. Louisa had hoped to remove his bookcases for the party, but they were too heavy, and so she hid his precious books behind a mass of plants.

For days the newspapers had carried reports of the coming ball — "a great deal of nonsense" she called it in her diary with a touch of pride — and that morning the *National Republican* had even printed a poem for the occasion. Every stanza ended, "All are gone to Mrs. Adams'!"

See the tide of fashion flowing,
'Tis the noon of beauty's reign,
Webster, Hamiltons are going,
Eastern Floyd and Southern Hayne;
Western Thomas, gayly smiling,
Borland, nature's protege,
Young De Wolfe, all hearts beguiling,
Morgan, Benton, Brown and Lee;
Belles and matrons, maids and madams,
All are gone to Mrs. Adams'!

It was half past one in the morning by the time the last guests left. At the end of the night, "the tables exhibited a picture of devastation," groaned Charles. He had danced until he could barely stand. "I dragged myself to bed, complaining even of the trouble of undressing myself."

"It is the universal opinion that nothing has ever equalled this party here, either in brilliancy of preparation or elegance of the company," gushed Senator Mills to his wife. The party would become legendary; nearly half a century later, it was still talked about. That night, even John Quincy was more or less pleased. "It all went off in good order," he recorded in his diary, "and without accident." In her own diary, Louisa could not hide her true pleasure. She could claim to be triumphant.

Still, she had experienced enough to give even her happiness an ambivalent edge. There had been one mishap that night. Someone had jostled one of the suspended lamps, spilling oil down her back. "It was said that I was . . . anointed with the sacred oil," she wrote in her diary. "The only certain thing I knew was that my gown was spoilt."

6

Often, there were other things on her mind than presidential politics, and those subjects sometimes seemed more pressing. She worried about her sons, whom she had been forced to leave again when they returned to Washington. Frequent letters and visits made the separation less severe, but the boys missed their parents, and she missed them. "Children must not be wholly forgotten in the midst of public duties," old John Adams warned John Quincy.

The boys were closer to their mother than their father. When Charles came to Washington, he would spend his visits by the side of Louisa, whom he found "inexpressibly delightful." After entering Harvard at the age of fourteen, he struggled so much at first that his father considered sending him into the navy. Charles saw himself as passionate and romantic, hot-blooded and southern — like his mother, with her Maryland roots, and unlike his Puritan father. She fascinated him; he called her "the only fashionable woman I know." He liked "billiards, drinking parties, and riding," and snuck a copy of Molière's *La Comtesse d'Escarbagnas* into Latin class when he should have been reciting Tacitus. He felt crushed by his father's severe expectations, which his mother tried to deflect. "Remember that neither your father or myself expect wonders from a boy of your age and that we shall always be satisfied if you really exert yourself to the utmost of your ability," Louisa wrote anxiously to her youngest.

George and John, of course, had also struggled at Harvard, at least by their father's high standards. After graduating from Harvard, George came to Washington to study law with John Quincy, but he soon retreated back to Massachusetts. John Quincy told his son John he would not be permitted to come to Washington until he stood in the top ten in his class, and that he would greet him as "an affectionate and grateful child" when he equaled what had been John Quincy's own standing — which was second in the class. In 1823, just before graduating, John was expelled from Harvard, along with forty-two classmates, for his part in a class rebellion. John Quincy was so upset that he did not write to his son for a month. Louisa tried to close the breach. John's letter to his father explaining what had happened, she wrote to her son, was "manly and respectful," and a "very kind" letter was on its way from his father — only business got in the way. If he was given a second chance, though, she warned, "beware of *pride* and do not mistake it for honor."

"My children seem to have some very intemperate blood in them, and are certainly not very easy to govern," Louisa wrote. "John is somewhat like his mother a little hot headed and want of timely reflection will I fear often lead him to error." George was like his mother in other ways. When they rode together through the stony, wild countryside of Massachusetts, he would recite Byron to her, and they sent each other the poems they wrote — but she worried about him most of all. He was nervous, passionate, and sensitive, prone to "strong impulses not properly controlled." George had become engaged to his cousin Mary Hellen while living in Washington, despite his parents' misgivings. But when George went to Boston to study law, Mary's affections turned toward John. Charles, who had also fallen for Mary when they were young, bitterly wrote that John was "the victim of her arts." The house was roiled by the drama.

Louisa worried, too, about her sisters. Eliza died in 1818. Kitty's husband, William Smith, landed in debtor's prison. Harriet, who had moved out to Green Bay, Wisconsin, with her husband — after appealing to Louisa to help him get a patronage post — also wrote that she was in dire financial straits. (Adelaide, the youngest, lived in Washington, but the two sisters saw each other more rarely.) Caroline gave birth to twin boys and a daughter within two years, and all three children died; Louisa fed the dying infants barley water herself. She listened to her sisters' troubles and tried to help them, pushing the president, her husband, the secretary of war, anyone who might have access to patronage jobs. For their part, her sisters — especially Kitty Smith and Caroline Frye — were her closest and most consistent friends.

She needed her sisters, because she did not have many other close friends. Young women from Philadelphia or Boston who came to Washington for the balls and young men looked up to her, but these were more acolytes than equals. One in particular, Elizabeth Hopkinson (the daughter of Joseph), reminded her of her lost daughter. Louisa had her sons, her nephews and nieces, her cousins, her brother, a steady stream of visitors; she was always surrounded. But her connection to John Quincy and the perception that she played too visible a part in his campaign had its costs. The society figure Margaret Bayard Smith, for instance, might have been a friend under different circumstances. Margaret was an intelligent and perceptive writer. She harbored many ambivalent feelings about a woman's role in society — feelings that may have found an echo in Louisa's heart. When the two women first met, Margaret liked her. But Margaret was a Crawford supporter, and as the election drew near, the women stayed apart.

Even the success of Louisa's parties may have had a depressing effect. "I do not think she is in such good spirits this winter as usual," Charles wrote at the end of January 1824, three weeks after the Jackson Ball. "Not so fond of society, she has become less ambitious of keeping the lead, probably because all her rivals have fallen before her."

Louisa sat for two portraits around this time. In each, she seems almost a different woman. Charles Bird King painted her on a large canvas in rich and saturated colors, the figure almost life-size. Her expression is serene and clear, her gaze confident. She has some flesh, as a woman was supposed to, and she is dressed ornately, in a billowing white dress with a fashionably low neck and gossamer sleeves. A turban, like a large bird's nest, is perched on top of her auburn curls. In one hand she holds a large gold harp, and in the other a songbook, open to a piece by Thomas Moore: "Oh Say Not That Woman's Heart Can Be Bought" — a purposeful selection. The King portrait is romantic, commanding, and political.

Gilbert Stuart painted the other portrait. In

it, Louisa is small and thin. Her ornate bonnet, high lace collar, and scarlet shawl almost envelop her; there are deep shadows. The colors of her face are washed out, the lines soft. Her expression is kind but tired and sad. Louisa first saw the finished version at an exhibition at the Boston Athenaeum and thought it an accurate representation. It looked, she wrote, like a woman who has just felt "the first chill of death." She was half joking; there's something gentle, appealing, and intimate about the painting. But it is the portrait of an older woman, and it suggests some secret sorrows. Its tone is essentially private.

Both portraits — one political, one domestic; one lively, one exhausted; one powerful, one withdrawn — captured something essential about her. She was both women, however contradictory the images seemed. One visitor to Washington in the winter of 1824 remembered her as "very talkative and lively" and her parties "always pleasant and gay," but at home she was often unwell, and her family followed her mood. Despite her torrid activity, her health was terrible. "Nothing but opium affords relief at night," she wrote to her son John during the summer of 1823.

Her friends, she acknowledged, assumed that "the great struggle which is now making in the political world is in great part the cause of my indisposition." She had her doubts.

Finally, the election took place. When it was over, nothing was decided. Jackson easily won both the popular vote (with 42.5 percent) and a plurality of the electoral votes (99), but he had not won a majority of the electoral votes, as the Constitution required. Adams had won only 31.5 percent of the popular vote but had 84 electoral votes. (Had the Constitution's three-fifths compromise to count slaves not been in effect, these numbers would have looked different.) Under the Twelfth Amendment of the Constitution, the House of Representatives had the responsibility of picking the president from the top three finishers: Jackson, John Quincy, and William Crawford. Each candidate had a fresh chance, and each state — large or small, populous or uninhabited, Illinois or New York — had only one vote. States were not bound to vote for the candidate who had carried the state in the national election, and although state legislatures could send directions to their representatives on how to vote, those instructions could not be enforced. The scramble to curry favor among representatives was desperate. Boardinghouse messes hummed with activity. Visitors flew from house to house. "There is nothing done here but vissitting and *carding each other,*" Jackson wrote to his wife back in Tennessee. "You know how much

I was disgusted with those scenes when you and I were here, it has increased instead of diminishing."

John Quincy dropped his pose of disinterest and indifference to the election. He knew how this kind of politics worked, and with the game so close he was finally willing to play. No, he would not object to placing Federalists in plum jobs, he reassured one visitor. Yes, such a man might make a fine judge, he reassured another. He was available for meetings; he was at every dinner; he was at the theater, with his wife by his side.

"You must know society is now divided into separate batallions as it were," Margaret Bayard Smith wrote to her sister. "Mrs. Adams collected a large party and went one night [to the theater], Mrs. Calhoun another, so it was thought by our friends that Mrs. Crawford should go too, to show our strength." The Marquis de Lafayette, the old French general who had become a Revolutionary War hero, was in Washington that winter as part of his triumphal tour of the United States in commemoration of his service during the Revolution. His presence brought the candidates and congressmen into contact for dinners. They were civil on the surface, maneuvering beneath.

Louisa did her part, hosting her tea and dinner parties, going to the theater, fixing a bright smile and holding it even when Jackson appeared and cheers rose from the crowd. Even a Crawford supporter had to admit that "both the wine and the company were unusually good" at one of her dinners that December. "Mrs A. is most assiduous in her part of the campaign and she is by far the most successful," Delaware representative Louis McLane wrote to his wife. A month later, he added snidely, "I am half provoked, that you are not here, to play the politician with Mrs. Adams."

She waited, feeling unwell. If she kept a diary, it has not been found. She did not write many letters. "The times are such," she wrote to George at the end of November, "that it is hazard to note even the events of the hour."

At six o'clock on Sunday, January 9, 1825, Henry Clay stepped out of the frosty darkness into the Adamses' house on F Street. Perhaps Louisa was there to greet him, or perhaps not. "Harry of the West" did fascinate her. "There is something about Mr. Clay; that pleases me in spite of reason," she once wrote, speaking of both his good, open heart and "vicious habits" — his notorious gambling and philandering. When she saw him at a party, loose and jaunty, with his flashing eyes and curling mouth, she would engage with him, against her better judgment. The two of them did not speak so much as spar. "We meet but to war and each of us are ready with a jest on all occasions," she wrote after one encounter. She did not trust him — not at all. "Mr. Clay almost overpowered me with compliments," she observed suspiciously after one party. "Mr. Clay is playing a new game," she wrote after another. "I always mistrust these sudden changes and though I do not interfere in politics it is difficult for me to avoid knowing transactions which are talked of by every one and which places a man in the light of a decided enemy to my husband."

That January night, the decided enemy became the best friend. As a particularly capable Speaker of the House, Clay had wielded significant influence (and claimed probably more than he could actually offer). Denied the possibility of becoming president, he enjoyed the prospect of playing kingmaker. On January 12, at a dinner hosted by the members of the House of Representatives to celebrate the Marquis de Lafayette, Jackson and John Quincy were among the guests. Someone had the perversity to seat Jackson next to John Quincy with a vacant chair between them. Clay sauntered over and slid into the empty spot. "Well gentlemen," Clay said, "since you are both too near the chair, but neither can occupy it, I will slip in between you, and take it myself." Everyone laughed, except John Quincy.

So when Clay called on John Quincy that evening, he came aware of his power and purpose. It may be that some understanding passed between them — that in exchange for Clay's support, John Quincy would give him a plum post in the administration. Something seems to have happened of note, because John Quincy left half the page of his diary describing his meeting with Clay blank. His diary was, he told his oldest son, a "second conscience." In this case, it appears he wanted to hide something from himself. He never did say exactly what had passed between him and his old rival. Whatever it was, though, didn't matter. No laws were broken. Clay was never going to throw his support behind Jackson, whom he hated personally and considered a despotic threat to the republic. Clay's outlook, foreign and domestic — especially his ambition for an extensive system of internal improvements — was far more in line with John Quincy's agenda than Jackson's. Clay had already privately said that he would be supporting Adams before he arrived at F Street that Sunday night. The process played out as the Constitution mandated. But that meeting would come to haunt them. Jackson's supporters were crying foul even before the ballots in the House were counted. The appearance of collusion between John Quincy and Clay, the suggestion of backroom dealing, seemed to taint the election.

Did his wife know what really happened in

that meeting? No one defended John Quincy's integrity more fiercely than Louisa. Yet she knew that he would use men as means to his ends, that he would make compromises that he was unwilling to admit. She once wrote about a character she based on him that he saw other men as "the medium through which the great plans he formed for the welfare of his country were to be matured." He was not above making deals. John Quincy was pushing Maryland and Louisiana. He had Clay and Daniel Webster working on Stephen Van Rensselaer, who had the vote for New York and who sometimes played the fool but was shrewder than he looked. And he was in conversation with Daniel Pope Cook, who had the sole vote for Illinois and who would switch it from Jackson to Adams. As it happened, Cook was a frequent guest at the Adamses' house and a favorite of Louisa's — someone who responded to her charm. Cook also happened to be the nephew of Louisa's sister Eliza's husband.

Louisa held her last tea party on the evening of Tuesday, February 8, 1825 — the night before the House vote. Sixty-seven members of the House came to F Street, and "at least four hundred citizens and strangers," John Quincy noted in his diary. The next day the ballots were cast and counted. The family stayed at home, waiting for news. That afternoon, Alexander Everett came through the snow from the Capitol to the Adams house to tell John Quincy that he was the next president of the United States.

Exactly what Louisa said, thought, or did when she heard the news is unrecorded. She wrote no letters that survive; she kept no diary that day. "Your journal which has become a necessary of life to me has failed me for a long time," John Adams gently chided her at the end of March. In his own diary, John Quincy hardly mentioned her. "Congratulations from several of the officers of the Department of State ensued — from D. Brent, G. Ironside, W. Slade, and Josias W. King — Those of my wife, children, and family were cordial, and affecting, and I received an affectionate note from Mr. Rufus King of New York, written from the Senate chamber after the event."

That night, she accompanied him to the President's Drawing Room. Andrew Jackson was there, and Andrew Jackson was still the main attraction. From the start, there were signs of trouble, indications of the high price of success. The public's support — even in Washington — was clearly for the Old Hero. A few days later, she and John Quincy attended the theater. The applause that greeted them was smattering. But when the orchestra played "The Hunters of Kentucky" — a song celebrating Jackson's victory at the Battle of

New Orleans — the crowd cheered wildly and clapped in time with the song.

On Thursday, March 3, the night before John Quincy was inaugurated as president of the United States, Louisa was "seized with a violent fever," John Quincy wrote in his diary. The doctor was summoned and she was bled. She was ill all night, and before daybreak had "a long and alarming fainting fit." It seems that she was not in the audience at the Capitol the next morning to watch John Quincy take the oath of office. If she had been able to watch him speak, dressed in his plain black suit, or if she heard him practice his delivery the night before, perhaps while she lay ill in bed, she would have heard some quiet, perhaps unintended, acknowledgment of her own important role. "The harmony of the nation is promoted and the whole Union is knit together by the sentiments of mutual respect, the habits of social intercourse, and the ties of personal friendship formed between the representatives of its several parts . . . at this metropolis," John Quincy said. Those were the kinds of ties that were knit by his wife.

When the inauguration was over, John Quincy returned to F Street and the crowd followed him there. Louisa roused herself, fastened the hooks of her dress, and went downstairs. Her campaign was over. They had won — but what?

After dinner, while the rest of the family went to a celebratory ball, Louisa went to bed.

■ ■ ■ ■

PART EIGHT:
A BIRD IN A CAGE

Washington, 1825–1829

■ ■ ■ ■

1

One day in late April 1825, Louisa sat with blank paper in front of her. She had not written to her son Charles for weeks, not since his return to Boston after the inauguration more than a month before. "Even now I have no subject on which to occupy your attention," she wrote.

The "perpetual trouble" of the move to the President's House had consumed her. She disliked her new home, and that day she had put herself in a spot where she might dislike it even more. Instead of facing south, overlooking the gardens and the fields sloping toward the wind-shirred river, she looked north, out over the scrubby grass, the tall iron fence, and the locked gate. Instead of going to her own room, she sat in her son John's. It had been a stormy day and the wind was still violent. The loose glass panes made such a noise, she wrote to Charles, that her headache was "fit to split and I am obliged to close with a wish that you had seen our splendid misery."

She had been astonished to find that the Monroes had left the White House in disrepair. She wandered through the vacant rooms, aghast. The furniture, bought by James Monroe with public funds, was scuffed and threadbare. Walls were naked plaster. Finishing touches were unfinished. "I believe it would be difficult to find such unassortments of rags and rubbish even in an alms house," she told Charles. Vagrant drafts blew in and swirled around her. Twenty-five years after the President's House was first occupied, and a decade after the British had burned it, reconstruction was incomplete. Some parts were still closed off. "Like everything else in this desolate city," she wrote, it was "but a half-finished barn."

It galled her to think that the public perception of the President's House was so wrong. Closed doors had hidden the dereliction; in fact, the complaint was that the mansion was too magnificent. Louisa decided to have a public viewing, to let the people see the cracks in the walls, the bare fixtures, and derelict furniture — and to shame Congress into appropriating money for repairs. Instead, her open house was called unseemly. "Some people pretend I have done wrong," she wrote, "but as we are pretty much in the situation of the man and his ass in the fable" — the man who was criticized whether he rode

482

his ass or walked it — "I do not care at all who likes or dislikes."

The fable was apt; she was in an impossible position. She and John Quincy could be neither close to the people nor distant. Whatever she did, she would be criticized. Almost any stranger could call on President Adams, almost any morning — and almost every morning, strangers did. The president and his wife were not supposed to consider themselves superior, and yet they *were* socially superior, in a class by themselves. Admiration for the presidency was rivaled by distrust of authority. Everything they did was scrutinized; nothing could satisfy. There was little precedent to follow, no book to govern their behavior, and no one charged with codifying and insisting upon the rules. John Quincy, like President Monroe before him, at least could sometimes refer questions of protocol to his Cabinet. Louisa had no such body to advise her. So, when it came to etiquette, she followed her own course, as she had when she had been the wife of the secretary of state.

Only now, her independence was more defensive than calculating; her campaign was over. Dignity mattered to Louisa, and she wouldn't apologize for it. She always said that her great sin was pride. She did not call the President's House by its informal name, the White House, as others increasingly did; she was more likely to call it the "Palace." With the help of her nephew Johnson Hellen, who was among the extended Adams-Johnson clan living with Louisa and John Quincy for a time, she oversaw the arrangements and furnishing, and she had high standards. When her friend Joseph Hopkinson, who was in Philadelphia — where one could find the best of everything — offered to help, she sent long lists. She wanted tables, vases, consoles, and "one handsome sopha table." She needed a ground glass lamp and a gilded chain so that she could suspend it in the circular summer sitting room. She asked for alabaster ornaments and silk that might match the room's pale green walls. She requested a carriage light in color and "not too small." She needed a good French cook from Philadelphia for "25 dollars a month but that is the very utmost."

She tried to preserve some of the formality the Monroes had established. She followed Elizabeth Monroe's custom of holding Drawing Rooms every two weeks when Congress was in session. These were open to the public (or at least what passed for the public — not free blacks, servants, or slaves), and it was easy to get an invitation or to come without one. The parties were impressive. A staff of servants would wait on guests, carrying trays of ice cream, hot chocolate, champagne. The crowds would number among the hundreds or even thousands. The crush of people was oppressive. There were no dances, no recitals, and little of the joie de vivre that had characterized her Tuesday tea parties. Margaret Bayard Smith, who had once been so enthusiastic about the spirited, lovely Mrs. Adams, was not alone in objecting to her "silent, repulsive, haughty reserve" at the President's Drawing Rooms. Louisa herself seems not to have enjoyed these evenings much. Her job was to turn her head from one guest to the next. "Mrs. Adams I could scarcely see, the crowd around her was so great," recorded a visitor to one of her Drawing Rooms. It was tiresome, and perhaps it was harder to see the point of these parties than it had once been. Louisa could never acknowledge it, but there was no prize to work for anymore. Sometimes, she would come down for only an hour, excusing herself on account of illness.

She had been instrumental to her husband's election. It may have been difficult, then, to become merely ornamental. And it must have been hard to be criticized for being too visible, to be told to stay in the background. A pattern had already developed, and now it held. When exertion was called for, she was confident and capable. But when she was no longer needed, she no longer flourished. She could actually feel herself wilt.

"I am utterly weary of the thankless task of

wasting my life and strength for those who neither care whether I live or die provided their purpose is accomplished and I have arrived at that period of life when I believe women mostly meet with the same fate," she wrote to Charles. She had lost her sense of purpose. She was surrounded by people but felt alone. "*Isolation* is an evil," she added.

"There is something in this great unsocial house which depresses my spirits beyond expression," she wrote to George, "and makes it impossible for me to feel at home or to fancy that I have a house any where."

Summer brought heat, which grew worse as the weeks passed. It was too hot to move, too hot to think. Even John Quincy avoided his writing desk. His diary was reduced to shorthand scratches and scattered notes. His days were overwhelmed by drudgery. Petitioners and office seekers appeared at his door.

He had little goodwill to draw on in Congress. He had come into office with the support of a tiny majority of state delegations — including small states like Vermont and Rhode Island, which had as much weight in the House's presidential election as states like Virginia and Pennsylvania, but not when it came to getting his will done. A special session of the Senate called by Monroe just before his inauguration had rejected the treaty John Quincy had negotiated with Colombia to enforce the suppression of the international slave trade — as if to make a shot across the bow of the new president's ambitions. He was dealing with a contested treaty between the Creeks and the state of Georgia, a treaty that would be revealed as fraudulent. Andrew Jackson's 1828 campaign was already being launched in Tennessee. Jackson's supporters in Washington — soon including John Quincy's own vice president, John Calhoun — were also organizing and plotting. The cries of corruption and usurpation against the president continued unabated.

"We are all half dead with the heat," Louisa Catherine Adams wrote to a nephew in the summer of 1825. Inside the White House, the Adams family drifted "like floating logs upon a glassy stream."

The weather did not break as the weeks passed. Louisa tried to shake off her malaise. The Marquis de Lafayette was on his way to the White House, and she knew how much his visit meant to the nation. She had read the speeches delivered in his honor, the encomiums, the newspaper accounts, the florid poems. He was at the end of a thirteen-month triumphal tour of the United States in recognition of his service during the American Revolution, and everywhere he went, he was greeted with paroxysms of patriotism. The upswell of national spirit was unlike anything the country had yet seen. A crowd of eighty thousand had greeted his ship when he arrived in New York; another forty thousand people watched him lay the cornerstone of the Bunker Hill Monument. Fifty years had passed since the Battle of Bunker Hill. A new generation had come into power. The story that Americans told about themselves was passing from memory to myth.

Lafayette was an old friend; Louisa had visited his estate outside Paris ten years earlier, and John Quincy had first met him as a boy accompanying his father, John Adams, on missions to France during the Revolutionary War. At any other moment, Louisa wrote, she would have looked forward to his visit with pleasure. But in the intense heat, she groaned to think of the effort required to welcome him and his large retinue. Extra servants needed to be hired, excursions planned, and bedrooms cleared, with her sons, nephews, and servants doubling up to make extra room. Once Lafayette arrived, there would be formal dinner after formal dinner — fixed smiles, quick pleasantries, and heavy silk dresses trapping the humidity and heat. There would be toasts and speeches, fervent expressions of thanks and praise. She would have to take part in it, but without ever seeming to show her face too much. By the time he boarded the ship to sail back to France, she would add her own poem dedicated to Lafayette — written in French — to the pile of panegyrics. But she was self-conscious about seeming forward.

As she waited for Lafayette to arrive, her thoughts moved in eddies around the legacy of the Revolution, pooling in her own past. The stories that were being told and written down left her out. She heard the encomiums to the heroes of the Revolutionary War, saw the pantheon of American idols take shape. Her father had also played his part in the Revolution. Where was he? And so where was she? She had heard and read it said that she was not a real American, that she was British. As she had during her hardest times in Russia, she began to obsess over her father's failure, which she considered so unjust. She told herself that he had been an American hero; she told herself he was being neglected.

She was unhappy. She kept to her room. She thought how she had ended up where she was: the United States, Washington, the President's House, upstairs. She opened her diary and began to write her story down. She called it "Record of a Life."

2

Louisa was fifty-one years old when she began "Record of a Life" in 1825. Writing an autobiography was an unusual thing for her to do, a kind of claim for importance. She hedged at the start — even in the title. It was *a* life, as if it could have been anyone's. She justified her motivation as she often did when putting her pen to paper: she was a mother. "Someday or other," she wrote, "my children may be amused with it." At the very least, she added, a look back at her past "may have a good effect upon myself." But she was quick to add that she had no special talent, only a "Cacoëthes Scribendi" — a mania for writing — that sometimes gripped her. She had "no desire to appear any thing more than a mere commonplace personage with a good memory and just observation enough to discover the difference between a man of sense and a Fool, and to know that the latter often do the least mischief of the two." There was that characteristic turn: self-denigration followed by a sly, slightly bitter smile.

Though she would not have known it at the time, her memoir was part of a growing interest in life writing, as Romanticism's attention to the peculiar emotional experiences of individuals spurred a craze for memoirs. She was, in fact, a great reader of court memoirs, mostly of unhappy French queens and duchesses. But the result of her retrospection at this point was not a typical heroic narrative. It was a tragedy. It was a story of the corruption of innocence — a story modeled on the Fall.

Her history, her "Record of a Life," began thousands of miles away, in London. Her idol was not John Adams but Joshua Johnson, "noble in his sentiments; noble in his acts." She described him as a hero of the American Revolution, a man who personified patriotism: "Many were the Americans that he saved from imprisonment while residing in London at his own risk furnishing them with clothes money and passage on board vessels owned by him or his friends which convey'd them safe from danger either to their homes or to France," she wrote. He had exalted the name of George Washington to his children. He had taken a pair of tongs to place a pen used by Benedict Arnold into the fire. Joshua Johnson was, she was suggesting, as ardent a patriot as anyone — as any Adams.

As she indulged in a reverie, she retreated

from the prostrating heat and lassitude of the President's House into a buoyant, golden past. In her parents, she saw an idealized model for a marriage, as if out of a romantic novel. The father she described was not an indebted, anxious, charming but insecure merchant. Instead, he was strong and loving, and ostentatious in his affection for his wife. When Catherine was sick, he would roll papers around the handles of her knife and fork and heat them on the hearth. When she was weak, he would cut her food and feed her like a child. In the evening, he would ask his daughters, his three little graces, to perform an aria from Handel, and on a good day, they would roll up the carpets and he would join their dance. Louisa also described her mother in florid terms. She dwelled on Catherine's beauty, her tenderness, her vivid spirit. Her childhood, as she told it, was prelapsarian, like Eden. "All the scenes of my infancy come with such faint recollections," Louisa wrote, "they float upon my fancy like visions which never could have any reality yet like visions of delight in which all was joy and peace and love." Sometimes the kaleido-scopic dreamscape of her first memories snapped into focus, and her childhood past existed as if it were present. She could remember being a girl in Nantes and witness-ing a flood, seeing boats slip past the grand mansion, the roads turned to rivers. She could feel the cold stone floors on her knees as she kneeled in the cathedrals she had visited with the nuns at her convent school. She could trace the shape of a wrought-iron balustrade at Le Temple du Goût.

In the middle of her story, she burst into verse:

Oh halcyon days of bliss long past
Too good too happy long to last . . .
With blighted hopes to sorrow soon a prey
Wrecked on a foreign ruthless shore
They sunk subdued to rise no more.

She added, "Do not my children read this as romance for every word is true."

As in any story about the fall, there came the loss of innocence. As she told the story in "Record of a Life," the fall occurred at the time of her marriage.

Her marriage, as she saw it now, was the prologue to the disaster. She brooded over the misunderstandings and the misinterpretations between herself and John Quincy during their courtship. She had been unsure; he had been harsh; she had felt vulnerable; he had wavered. It was not love at first sight. It was hardly love. She barely tried to massage their relationship into something that might have lasted, as it had, for thirty years: "Without a particle of affection at the time I

493

suffer'd myself to be coaxed into an affection that lasted probably much longer than would have done love at first sight," she wrote in 1825.

The circumstances of her marriage had not been ideal; she had been hesitant, confused by John Quincy's mixed signals, and a little scared at the prospect of separating from her family. She had been under immense pressure. But to put it that way was not only exaggerated; it was not entirely true. She dwelled on the coaxing by others, and not her own desire; she said she suffered, when in fact she had also delighted in his tenderness and attention. He had courted her, promising her love and protection, and she had responded with promises of love and affection. He had been clear about his priorities. He had given her, even late in the game, a chance to withdraw from the engagement. She had made her own calculations when she did not. Some of them, surely, were practical and financial and due to the influences of her family. But at least part of her desire to marry him seems to have been something that comes through in her letters that were written at the time: she wanted to be in love, and in a very recognizable way, she was.

In the White House, though, feeling vulnerable and neglected, those initial feelings of vulnerability and neglect thirty years earlier became magnified; they darkened her view of three decades of a rich and complicated marriage. Feeling left out, she transferred her sense of exclusion to her father, her hero. As she told it now, her union had been battered by her father's bankruptcy and her family's flight. Recounting the old story, Louisa became almost hysterical. She had not spoken of her father's financial failure like this, with such raw pain, in more than a decade. She talked about Joshua Johnson's bankruptcy as the story of a good man wronged, betrayed by his partners, unjustly ruined. She laid it out in the high color of a sentimental novel. Her father was blameless, she insisted. *She* was blameless. Yet it appeared otherwise. She wrote as if it *still* appeared otherwise, as if everyone looked at her, even now, even as she sat in the White House, and saw a fraud. "Every appearance was against me; actions proceeding from the most innocent causes looked like deliberate plans to deceive; and I felt that all the honest pride of my soul was laid low for ever," she wrote. She had "forfeited all that could give me consequence in my husbands esteem or in my own mind." She had lost all her standing, and "the bitter knowledge of real life was acquired in almost all its varied forms of agony and mortification."

"From that hour," she declared, the melodrama reaching a high pitch, "all confidence was destroyed for ever in me and mine."

It bears repeating here that there is no evidence that John Quincy ever blamed her for her father's misfortunes or held a grudge. Certainly, whatever he had said to her in 1797 was long buried by 1825. The elder Adamses, too, had never held her father's fate against her. In fact, they had done everything they could to help the Johnsons. They had considered them as family. They had responded sympathetically, corresponded frequently, welcomed them into their house, and connected them with friends. John Adams had even taken a political risk to find a federal appointment for Joshua so that the Johnsons might have some income. But Louisa's version of the event had remained in her memory like a dormant virus. Her immunity now weakened by her loneliness in the White House, she felt herself attacked. She, of course, had been hurt by her father — she had been abandoned and left to deal with his mess — but she would never blame him. Perhaps it was natural that she would hunt for accusations from her husband and even from herself. Like a guilty conscience, her memory of her shame infected her thoughts. John Quincy could be incredibly self-involved. He could be bullying; he could be imperious; he could make her feel small. Yet he was also tender, at times passionate toward her, and stayed close to her when others would have put distance between them. Still, it was hard for her to see that now.

It did not matter that her childhood was never the paradise she claimed it to be — that a counternarrative ran through even her own idealized account, shifting and undermining her claims to perfect happiness, breaking through in revealing moments. She told anecdotes that revealed tension with her siblings, insecurities, and jealousies. Her portrait of her father was as terrifying as admiring: "His eye or the power of his eye was indescribable: its usual expression was sweetness and benevolence; but when roused to anger, or to suspicion; it had a dazzling fixed severity that was absolutely awful."

If "Record of a Life" was in fact for her sons, she made no attempt to soften the story for them — though no one would have expected her to; in 1825, parents were less concerned with shielding their children. Her language was brutal. Her determination to punish her husband, and herself, overwhelmed her at the end. She concluded that her marriage to him was regretted on both sides. She thought her father's flight must have made her appear corrupted in John Quincy's eyes: "It appeared impossible for him to view me in any other light than as a person who had known all these impediments and who determined for the sake of what is called a settlement to marry him at the expence of honour truth and happiness." Perhaps it's not a coincidence that she wrote this in 1825, as the cries of corruption against her husband and Henry Clay continued unabated. Appearances seemed so bad. The accusations were so loud.

Clearly, writing did not make her feel better, happier. It did not have a "good effect" on her. The tone when she broke off "Record" is more anguished than it was when it began. Then again, the pursuit of happiness was not her great aim. She was circling something else, something harder to name. She described herself as trapped. With no way out, she turned inward.

The Marquis de Lafayette arrived in Washington, nearing the end of his grand tour, on August 1. Outwardly, Louisa played the pleasing hostess. Privately, her thoughts ran dark. When she learned a niece, Eliza's daughter, had died, she was equanimous but morbid. "What is death, and why should we fear it?" she wrote to George, who had become her confidant. "Children almost always meet it without horror and without terror. . . . I know not why it is, but of late my thoughts are ever roving to something far beyond this sublunary sphere and at times they become utterly uncontroulable." She read of a young Irish girl who had been seduced by her employer and then killed herself on his marriage night. "I saw her remains borne to the grave without a friend perhaps without a pitying tear to mourn her dreadful fate," she wrote to George, "and my whole soul shuddered at the idea of his reveling in all the enjoyments of life while she was gone to give her last account with the dire crime of suicide upon her head." She wrote a lurid poem, "The Suicide," in the girl's honor.

Meanwhile, there were dinners, events, and excursions to attend to with Lafayette and his crowd. She was careful not to take part in the public ceremonies, since there had been, she told George, "a great sensitiveness" about her not remaining "in the background" in the past, about her being too visible during the election.

After Lafayette had left, Louisa and John Quincy went north to Quincy for their annual visit. John Adams was failing, mostly blind and toothless, his body looking melted like a snowman. John Quincy spent the autumn days at his desk, working on his first annual message, which he would deliver (in writing, as was the custom) to Congress in December. His plan was ambitious, with no concessions to the weakness of his support. "Liberty is power," he wrote, and man's purpose is to act. He called for a Department of the Interior, an astronomy observatory, a national system of roads and canals, byways for trade and transportation. He misestimated his own power, and his own liberty. Congress ignored his recommendations, except to mock them.

He was thwarted, and thwarted, and thwarted. His proposal to send envoys to the Panama Congress to form relationships with the new nearby republics was blocked and held up until the mission became useless. His opponents suggested that his push for infrastructure projects, which had broad support before he took office — three of the five major presidential candidates were enthusiastic proponents of internal improvements, as was President Monroe — were a sign of his plans for "usurpation" (though the same critics pushed individual projects that happened to be in their own constituents' backyards). By asserting federal powers, the administration, it was ominously threatened, was starting down a road that would end in the abolition of slavery. Democratic provocations and suffrage reform were expanding the franchise further. More people who had felt the pain of the Panic of 1819 were accruing power, and they were not inclined to let the government spend more money. The appearance of corruption in the appointment of Henry Clay as secretary of state continued to hang over the administration, hamstringing Clay's considerable political talents. By October 1825 — with John Quincy's presidency only seven months old — the Tennessee legislature nominated Andrew Jackson for the presidency

Louisa wanted comfort. She begged George and Charles in Boston to send her chocolate. She described her apathy, her dispiritedness. Always bad, her health grew worse. "Frequent and violent attacks of sickness" kept her in bed for days at a time. When she was well enough to rise, she felt no better. Lassitude and debility oppressed her. "Any exertion of thought," she wrote to George at the beginning of May, brought on "disagreeable sensations in my head and eyes."

A host of maladies attacked her with increased frequency and intensity. She had fevers, "fainting fits," bursts of pain in her chest, and nasty coughs that worried those around her. Often, more than one symptom would manifest at a time. She talked about her nerves as organs, and she described her imagination as feverish. She could not separate her mind from her body, her body from her mind. Her illnesses had always been integral to her sense of who she was. They were often the first thing others mentioned about her and the first thing she mentioned about herself. Other people were frequently, even constantly, sick, and other people, especially other women, had similar patterns of intense headaches, fevers, and unaccountable debility, but Louisa was singled out for her delicate health. It was true that she lived at a time when doctors did guesswork, diets were bad, hygiene was wretched, and remedies were often more toxic than the sickness they were meant to cure. Her body had been squeezed and deformed by the equipment of formal dresses, polluted by coal and wood smoke, stretched and wracked by at least a dozen pregnancies. Still, she herself recognized a psychological component to her poor health. She connected traumatic thoughts to physical breakdowns, and being sick to being cared for.

She wasn't merely seeking attention, not as a child and not in her fifties, but there is no doubt that when she was sick, she was noticed and treated more tenderly by her distracted husband and busy children than she was when she was well. Her sons would write her worried letters; Charles would race to Washington and sit by her bedside day after day; her husband would become anxious and even mention her in his diary, recording the status of her health along with great affairs of state. When she was ignored, her health would worsen. One night, for instance, in 1821, a headache caused her to stay in bed during one of her weekly tea parties, which went on without her while she remained in her room. No one bothered to see how she was. "The noise the sense of neglect and unkindness which this conduct indicated proved too much for me and I believe I was thrown into a state of delirium almost amounting to madness," she wrote in her diary afterward, her onrushing words as agitated as her mind, "and Mr Adams found me in this state when the company retired for several days I continued very ill."

She seems to have suffered more often, more suddenly, and more seriously when she felt lonely, stressed, useless, or excluded. It may have been, unconsciously, a way of striking back. Illness gave her body an outline in the world. It was, in a sense, a way of resistance. It stopped the day in its tracks.

3

On the morning of July 8, 1826, three letters arrived from Quincy, each saying that John Adams was on his deathbed. John Quincy packed immediately and headed north the next day, along with their son John, who was working as his secretary. Louisa stayed behind. An hour after John Quincy and John had left, Louisa received another letter, dated July 4, saying that John Adams had just died.

His death was not a surprise, but it was still a shock. In the White House, Louisa mourned. Her most cherished correspondent, the man she addressed as "father," was gone. John Adams had been her great friend and champion, and she had loved and appreciated him. "Every thing in his mind was rich, racy, and true," she would later say. Even in death, he seems to have inspired her. She wrote a poem in tribute to her old friend, which her brother-in-law Nathaniel Frye read aloud to a crowd at dinner without naming the author; the poem, to both her embarrassment and poorly concealed pleasure, was printed in the newspapers. John Adams's death also seems to have softened the harsh feelings toward John Quincy — and toward herself — that she had been expressing in letters and in "Record of a Life." They had shared their love for the wry, humane old man, and she was sensitive to the magnitude of her husband's loss. She found that she missed John Quincy after he had left. "Tell your father I feel sadly out of my element in this great palace without him," she wrote to George.

To John Quincy, John Adams's death was almost incomprehensible. His father had been his lodestar. When he reached Quincy, he clutched at what was left. His father's will, which made him executor, left the bulk of the estate to him: the mansion and 103 acres attached; his precious books and papers. But the costs of the terms were staggering. The will required that John Quincy pay $10,000 to Thomas for his share of the house, another $2,000 for two "rocky pastures," and half the value of the books and manuscripts. The proceeds of the rest of the estate were divided among John's descendants, some parts held in trusts to be paid out by John Quincy. The land was, in John Adams's view, his great legacy; it was the symbol of the place he had protected and fought for and loved. The only time old John's father, Deacon John Adams, had sold any acreage at all was to send John Adams to college. John Quincy decided not only to buy out Thomas for the house and land but also to buy all the land that had also belonged to John Adams, land that was slated to be sold to pay for the other descendants' legacies. He, then, was burdened with paying those legacies himself. "It will bring me heavily in debt," John Quincy acknowledged in a letter to Louisa soon after he arrived in Massachusetts, but "I cannot endure the thought of the sale of the place. Should I live through my term of service, my purpose is to come and close my days here, to be deposited with my father and mother."

Louisa's grief turned to disbelief when she saw John Adams's will. What it required from John Quincy astounded her. What had happened to his profound aversion to debt, which had been such a constant theme during their marriage? She begged her husband to reconsider his decision to buy out the others and keep the land, begged him not to go into debt for sentimental reasons, and begged him not to put himself in a position in which he would have to support Thomas, his wife, and their five children. John Quincy's younger brother had been her friend, but in the years since she had known him in Berlin, alcoholism had ruined his optimistic, gentle temper. "He is one of the most unpleasant characters in this world, in his present degradation,"

Charles had recently written about Thomas in his diary, "being a brute in his manners and a bully in his family." Thomas had come to depend on the largess of his father, and now he would depend on his brother: John Quincy would inherit his father's house, but for as long as the Adamses were in Washington, the arrangement was that Thomas and his family would live in it. They would be supported by trusts that John Quincy would have to finance. Louisa's relationship with Thomas and his wife, already strained, snapped.

She knew too well how debt could wreck a family. She did not even need to look at the fate of her own parents and siblings. The newspapers were full of reports that Thomas Jefferson — who, in a coincidence that some called providential, had died almost at the same moment as John Adams, fifty years to the day after the signing of the Declaration of Independence — had left huge debts behind. His daughter Martha Randolph was destitute, and the legislatures of Virginia and South Carolina had to raise money to support her. The thought that John Quincy was willing to risk his own children's inheritance and leave them in a similar position made her blanch. She was so angry that it took two days for her to answer John Quincy's letter about his decision to purchase all his father's property, and three attempts before she managed to write a response that was cool enough not to offend. As it was, her tone was still bitter and hot. She knew, she wrote, that he would not listen to her advice, wishes, or warnings, "that neither my opinions or feelings will . . . avail." But she had to speak out. "The trust is considering the situation of your brother and his family, and the relinquishment of Mr. Quincy, of so *essentially delicate a nature,* it is impossible, *utterly and decidedly impossible,* for you to do strict justice to them and to your own children," she wrote. It was "natural" that he wanted to own his father's house, but it could not be justified. She resented the fact that he thought it could be.

"For myself I care not a pin where I die," she added, furious and forlorn. "I have never had a home since I left my father's house, and it is a matter of perfect indifference if I never do."

A few days after arriving in Quincy, John Quincy wrote to Louisa to ask her to join him. Immediately afterward, he sent another letter recalling the first, saying there was too much for him to do. By the time she received it, though, she was already preparing to head north, and she refused to unpack — even if she was no longer wanted in Quincy. She left Washington at the end of July, with Charles, Thomas Adams's daughter Elizabeth, her maid Jane Winnull, and two other servants.

508

"I went very unwillingly, she went against the advice of all her friends," Charles wrote in his diary. "Her motive was unaccountable."

There was something perverse about her journey. It was as if she were determined to act out her sense of restlessness, her sense of not belonging anywhere. After the group reached New York City, instead of hugging the coast toward Boston, they veered up the Hudson River. There were Adamses in upstate New York, and popular watering spots, but she drifted without any fixed destination: West Point, Fishkill, Hudson, Ballston Springs, Albany, Saratoga, toward the frontier. The area was by no means wild. Given a map of the United States, any decent politician could have closed his eyes and put his finger on Albany's spot. The towns lining the Hudson were settled and getting richer; the Erie Canal had opened the year before. Still, it was a landscape of mountains, dark forests, and bald eagles. It was a place where the light was rich but veiled, where the light's source seemed not to come from the single sun but from elsewhere. The mode of travel alone made it an arduous journey. Overland, the carriage moved through rough terrain. They went from public stagecoach to public stagecoach, most of them crowded with strangers — or worse, prying "friends." On the river, the steamboats they rode could be lethal: between 1825 and 1830 alone, 273 people were killed by exploding boilers.

Inside the small, enclosed spaces of a coach or ship, pressure and tension among passengers only increased. Louisa could never let her guard down. She encountered fair-weather friends and old rivals from Washington heading toward the spas. The reunions were as ominous as they were disingenuously happy. Both Louisa and Charles noted how families formerly divided between the Jackson and Crawford camps (and opposed to Adams) were now socializing as a single group. They smiled and fawned over her. "You would suppose to see them that they were my most devoted friends," she wrote caustically to John Quincy.

Everyone was miserable. Charles was especially desperate to get back to Washington. "But my Mother was inflexible," he wrote in his diary. "She was fixed upon wandering about the country with no fixed purpose and with no intent."

Finally, he wrote in his diary, "I had prevailed upon my Mother to return home." He wrote too soon. When the party reached New York City, Charles continued south toward Washington, but Louisa turned toward Quincy.

"This morning my wife quite unexpectedly arrived here," John Quincy wrote in his diary on August 28. It's hard to imagine that he greeted her warmly; her arrival was not really

510

welcome. John Quincy was busy keeping pace with his official business while superintending the auction of his father's furniture, the execution of the will, and a massive survey and inventory of the land he was inheriting. The unacknowledged purpose of the survey was to reconnect himself to the land. He marked the progress of the trees he had climbed as a boy, slopes of the hillocks and boulders, the limits of pastures of wildflowers, the warp of the roots, sprawl of the shrubs. It was a way of grieving, no doubt, since the land was so intimately connected with his father, since his father had described it and redescribed it with unceasing fascination, and since his father had tended to it with his own hands. John Quincy heard the calls of the birds that his father had described with so much pleasure, the "long whoop of the nighthawk and the lofty clarion of all the game cocks in the neightbourhood. The robbins by dozens soon followed with their animating carrols. The woodpuckers, the larks, the bob olincotus, the goldfinches, the thrushes, the catbirds the Virginia nightingales, the blue birds, the springbirds, the swallows, the sparrows the yellow birds and the wrens." John Quincy was coming home as he never had before, after crisscrossing oceans and whole continents, after logging tens of thousands of miles in carriages, after achieving every possible success. As president, he had fulfilled his father's dream for him. Yet what he wanted most now was what the Adamses had always wanted: this patch of land in Massachusetts, set between the mountains and the bay, so close to the saltwater that a good breeze could carry the smell of it.

Louisa did not fit easily into his vision of the future — or the past. It is hard to imagine her hacking through brambles. To John Quincy's dismay, his two older sons turned out to be just as ill suited to the job. George, now twenty-five and living in Boston, working as a lawyer, and John, now twenty-three, who served as John Quincy's secretary in the White House, trudged after their father with dread. The young men were different in many ways. George was passionate and talented but undisciplined and highly sensitive; John was more calculating and more confident. But both had inherited their family's propensities for fathomless darkness. They had grown up largely without their parents, half raised by their grandparents. John Adams's death was hard on both of them, but on George especially, who had been there to witness it. They were totally unprepared for what their father was asking them to do.

"We have been out three days, two of them driven back by the rain, and the third surfeited by the heat," John Quincy wrote to Louisa shortly before she arrived. "George after one half-day found he had business in Boston, and I relieved him by sending him to you. John has discovered that he is of no use in the survey and takes a dispensation of attendance for the future. We march over tangled brakes and rattlesnakes, and have everything of heroic fatigue but the glory." He was half joking, but she did not find the situation funny when she arrived. George had broken down.

4

The health of George's body and mind, the eccentricity of his manners, and his erratic, passionate approach to life had worried Louisa and John Quincy for years. Neither knew quite what to do or how to help him. John Quincy was watchful, demanding, and stern with his sons. He saw them in his own image and expected them to mold themselves to him, as he had molded himself to the model of his father. From Russia, he had written his young children long pedagogical letters about how to be moral and great. They were expected to be industrious and irreproachable. When George struggled, John Quincy instructed him to keep a diary and to send him pages; he sent George pages of his own as examples. He told George to study a letter written by his grandfather John Adams at the age of twenty, hoping "to stimulate you to *perseverence* in the cause of virtue, by reminding you of the blood from which you came." The reminders were oppressive. As a freshman at Harvard, at the age of sixteen, George once described a dream in which the face of his father appeared behind the image of an attractive girl. "Remember, George," John Quincy's voice said in the dream, "who you are, what you are doing!"

Louisa was more forgiving and more overtly encouraging (although she also had a tendency to lecture). In a novella she later wrote, she described a character she based on George as a "poet and enthusiast" with the "imagination of a German sophist and a heart as simple as a child." To some extent, she saw herself in her oldest son. She was closer to him perhaps than she was to anyone else; she felt they understood each other — which made her worry. She cautioned him more than once against his romantic tendencies, his habit of "soaring into the regions of poetry and fiction while idolizing a shadow of your own creating." She knew of what she spoke. "You will smile my dear son and say my mother is a fine theoretical preacher, but miserable in practice it is too true."

In his response to that letter, George laid his character bare on the page. "If there be pain in 'a too sensitive mind' there is also pleasure," he wrote, gentle but grave. "It enjoys as richly its peculiar treasure as it suffers deeply its appointed sorrows; and I have always thought that imagination which was formed in early youth . . . a blessing rather than a curse; but life is supposed to begin to wane at twenty-five and the effervescence of youthful blood to be diminished from that time; this imagination must therefore be repressed and life regarded as it is. What mine may be it is impossible to tell; that I must form an artificial character or be forever nobody, is clear."

He was trying not to be "nobody." But he was failing, and he was haunted by his failure. "Dr. Huntt says he looks sick and worried," Louisa reported to John Quincy soon after John Adams's death. They did not know just how sick and worried he was. George, now twenty-five years old, was living in Boston. He had moved there to study law with Daniel Webster in 1823 and was admitted to the bar a year later. In August 1825, he had begun a diary, trying to take his father's instructions and admonitions to heart. He began with a "Table of Duty":

VI. Rise — analysis of Blackstone
VIII. Office — Journal
IX. Law
I. Various compositions
III. Literature till X.

What he loved was literature — but also cigars, friends, and women of whom his parents would not approve. He was in debt, which his parents did not know (but would soon find out). Following his father's habit, he began each diary entry with the time of his rising — which was never six in the morning. "Arose late this morning in consequence of retiring late last night. . . . Accustomed to smoke after breakfast I shall employ that time in reading Raithbys Letters on the Study of the Law," he wrote on day two. That diary lasted for all of three weeks.

On December 31, 1825, George started the diary again. "The necessity of a return to a more satisfactory path of life is so evident that I consider the coming year as a crisis in my life requiring vigilance severe and uncomplying over those vices the germ of which has been planted by past irresolution and has recently alarmed me by its gradual expansion," he wrote. "I close the year in melancholy feeling: its course cannot meet approval from a strict and scrutinizing conscience." This time his diary began with a look back to his childhood, at the years of being shuttled throughout New England while Louisa and John Quincy were in Russia. "Could my life have been passed with [my parents] its present results would have been probably very different but it was not to be; my Father's public employments imposed duties which compelled him to be often absent from his children and left him when with them little time for their instruction," he wrote. He looked back on his life with disappointment

— not unlike his mother.

He had so much promise. Everyone said it. He was handsome, with dark curling hair, full sideburns, a strong chin, and his mother's deep brown eyes. In 1825, only twenty-four years old, he had been asked by the town of Quincy to deliver the annual Fourth of July oration. That year, 1826, he was elected to the Massachusetts House of Representatives, expected to follow in the footsteps of his father. But his moods were volatile, and his emotions ran hot. He had become engaged to Mary Hellen against the family's wishes, and while he was living in Boston he had written her beautiful love letters, but only rarely. Her subsequent break from him and attachment to his brother John had affected him in ways that his family could only guess at. They tried to measure the difference between the equanimity of his conversation and the feverish glint in his eye. Louisa complained of his addiction to cigars but made no mention of his heavy drinking. There were other stresses, which his mother cautioned him against; she worried over the character of the company he kept and was desperate for him to marry a woman in his social class. She sensed he was looking for women outside of it. He hid so much.

He could not hide, though, how much his father unnerved him. The cumulation of his grandfather's death, his father's arrival, the public pressure upon him, and his private worries overwhelmed him. By early September he was sick, confined to his room in Boston. The immediate complaint was a toothache, but Louisa blamed John Quincy for their oldest son's trouble. George "was not treated with the kindness and consideration which his exertions merited," she wrote in a chaotic letter to Charles, "and laughed and sneered at because he was not able to bear the exposure to rain, and every species of bad weather as well as those who fortunately for them are more strongly constituted." Her scrawling handwriting was a mess upon the page, betraying her own agitated mind. George's dejected spirits, she said, "have impressed him with an idea that he is unfit for the society of the duties, for which other men are born." Charles knew she wasn't exaggerating, and he knew she was right about the effect of his father on his older brother. "George knows nothing of the character of my father," Charles had written in his diary in 1824, two years earlier. "He does not appreciate it and can not look upon him with any thing but fear. This is the true fault of his character, he is always afraid of men of a certain decided cast of character, he cannot associate their images with pleasure, he has an indescribable and involuntary awe of them."

When George fell ill, some sharp words

must have passed between Louisa and her husband, because she moved out of the big house in Quincy and into Hamilton's Hotel in Boston — perhaps to be closer to her son, but also, it seems, to avoid the paternal mansion. On September 13, she took George to Nantasket beach, on a long spit in Massachusetts Bay, for three days. John Quincy remained behind in Quincy. She and George, not yet fully recovered, returned to Quincy, but a day later, John Quincy walked in and found her packing to leave for Washington.

Accompanied by their son John, she made it only as far as Boston before abruptly sending John back to Quincy to give her husband a message. In that letter, she asked him to tell her where she should go. It may be possible to guess at the answer she wanted: she wanted him to tell her that he wanted her to come back; he wanted them to be together. Instead, John Quincy told John to tell Louisa "that I wished her to go wherever she thought it would most conduce to her health and comfort, and if she would let me know anything she wished me to do, I would do it."

She immediately became too ill to go anywhere at all.

The doctor who attended her in Boston went to Quincy the next day. "I enquired of him, what he thought of the state of my wife's health," John Quincy wrote in his diary the next day. "He said he believed there was disease in the right ovarum that it was ir-remediable and would occasionally be very troublesome; but he did not consider it as dangerous to life. . . . It was the occasion of great nervous irritability and excitement, but transient in its paroxisms. I took this opinion of him, because she herself thinks the disease mortal." While she thought she was dying, the doctor's diagnosis, more or less, was that she was a woman.

So she remained in a hotel in Boston, confined to her bed. John Quincy came to see her the following day. "She conversed with me on family subjects of painful inter-est," he wrote in his diary. He left her at the hotel, returning to Quincy — as she wished, he wrote in his diary, to take care of George. A week later, he returned to Boston and spent the morning by Louisa's bedside. He spoke openly with her about the future. "I told her my dispositions for the future, after my seclusion from public life," he wrote in his diary. His plans had "the approbation of my own heart, and upon which I must hope for aid and encouragement, which the world will not give." No doubt, he wanted her aid and encouragement. She was supposed to give it without his needing to ask. Everything in their history and culture suggested that as his wife, he had a right to her support. It angered her that his right was greater than hers.

By late October, Louisa and John Quincy were together back in Washington. (It was not unusual for the sitting president in those days to spend the summer and early fall months away from Washington.) Louisa's health was better, more or less, and she was a little chastened. "Let us mutually obliterate this summer from our memory," Louisa wrote to George, "or rather let it be stamped on our minds as a warning for the future, to lead to good. With energy of character, fixed principles, and faith in the mercy of divine Providence, there is nothing too difficult for the mind of man to achieve, and we are called upon to act, not to debate for the latter begets a habit of irresolution which leads to imbecility if not to ruin." George would have recognized her reference to Hamlet.

But there was no undoing anything, not by mother or son. There was no arresting the pattern that had begun. The following summer, events almost replayed themselves. In June 1827, a letter arrived from George saying that he had suffered "a succession of colds and rhumatisms" and had fallen and hurt his hip. Louisa burst into tears when she read it; by evening, she was packing for Boston. When she arrived, she found George weak, "miserably wan and pale and his debility is excessive. This is not imaginary," she wrote to John Quincy. The opium he was taking, as the doctor ordered, could not have helped.

A month later, with George doing better, John Quincy wrote to say that he was planning to head north for his annual summer vacation in Quincy. "Perhaps we will meet on the way," he said. She responded sharply in a letter written on their anniversary that made no mention of the occasion. Likewise, he did not acknowledge the anniversary in his diary.

She left Massachusetts before he arrived, overlapping with him for one night in New York, at the City Hotel near Trinity Church. It was not an intimate reunion. The group included not only Louisa but Thomas Adams's daughter Abby, her nephew Johnson Hellen, John Quincy's valet Anthony Giusta, their servants John Kirkland and Jane Winnull, and all three sons: George, Charles, and John. It was the first time the family had been all together in more than a year and a half, since John Quincy's inauguration in March 1825. Most of John Quincy's time in the city that evening and the next day was spent visiting with prominent New Yorkers. That afternoon, the family broke up again. With a sinking feeling, Charles saw how his parents barely interacted. "My mother does not appear either in good health or spirits," he wrote in his diary. "My own feelings inclined to great melancholy on seeing what I think to be the future prospects of our family. My father seemed excessively depressed."

With her son John, Louisa set out on yet another aimless trip around upstate New York spas. It was even more miserable than the previous summer's journey. Louisa found her son John to be peremptory, harsh, and calculating where his own interests were involved. "John is a tyrant who will have everything his own way and the eternal fighting every inch of ground upon every question so utterly destroys my health it induces me to be entirely passive and submissive," Louisa wrote to Mary back in Washington — adding that she was merely warning her, because John and Mary planned to wed. Her venting turned to a rant, an explosion of frustration and self-pity:

> However like the butterfly I appear to be wandering from place to place in search of pleasure, my thoughts turn only on that little home where sorrow and treachery are no more. . . . Like a bird in a cage struggle as I will there is an overbearing and preponderating influence which I cannot shake off in both my husband and my children that only make my exertions futile and destructive to my peace of mind and to my health. . . . Thus sickness passes for ill temper and suffering for unwillingness and I am deemed an encumbrance unless I am required for

any special purpose for a show or for some political maneuver. . . .

To her husband, now up in Quincy, she was curt: "As your time is very precious I do not expect or wish that you should waste it in writing to me. The boy can occasionally send me a line and save you the trouble."

5

Back in the White House, John Quincy would wake up without her, at a quarter past four in the morning or sometimes a quarter before. After rising, he took a long walk or a swim or a bath in the river, and after watching the sun rise from the long east window, he went out to the garden. There was a full-time gardener, but the president often tended the seedlings himself. He plucked leaves of balm and hyssop, mint, rue, sage, wormwood, and marjoram. He looked for signs of spring: the unfolding of fresh shoots on horse chestnut trees, the explosion of peach blossoms, the jonquils in bloom, the lamiums, the gloss of the holly leaves, the snowballs of petals on plum trees. He studied botany and kept track of his experiments: "Apples, apricots, ash, catalpa, wild and red cherry, chestnut, grape, white rock chestnut, and willow oak, palm, plum, peach, tamarind, orange, black, English, and shellbark walnut, all from the seed and growing in pots or in my nursery," he wrote to Charles. He planted oaks around the border and watched them anxiously. Some would not survive the first sharp frost, or the hailstorms that wrecked their tender leaves. His interest was first scientific, but he was not unaware of the anxious symbolism of his seedlings. He was concerned with his legacy. He should like to take for a motto, he told his son John, *"Alteri seculo."* It came from a line of Cicero: *Serit arbores quae alteri seculo prosint.* He plants trees to benefit another generation.

Louisa was there in the margins: painting a detailed botanical illustration of a white oak leaf that John Quincy had collected on a morning walk; watering the tamarinds; caring for silkworms, as he tried to encourage a domestic silk industry. There were moments of affection between them. At one point, she gave him the present of a seal, a picture of a rooster and the motto "WATCH." John Quincy had a gold ring made with the seal on it, and he always wore it. The bird was, he wrote to Charles, "the emblem of vigilance, of generous tenderness, of unconquerable courage." But the generous tenderness was hard for her to see sometimes, and in his work she was not even really a helpmeet, let alone a partner.

What they did share, even when most estranged, was their anxiety for their oldest son. John Quincy was as worried as she. For the first time, perhaps, since the death of his baby Louisa, his concern for his family rivaled his concern for the country. Traveling back from Quincy to Washington, about to face a hostile Congress, his thoughts were not on his work but on George. His oldest son's "self-distrust" was "painfully predominant, and my own anticipations at this crisis of my earthly destiny full of apprehension and of anguish," John Quincy wrote in his diary. "I commence my return to Washington with an aching heart. But why art thou cast down my soul? And why art thou disquieted within me? Hope thou in him."

Meanwhile, by the winter of 1827, it was clear that the ambitious program that President Adams had proposed for the country was stymied. He had no close allies in Congress that he could consistently rely on, which was largely his own fault. He was suspicious of those whom he might have relied on to carry out his program. He kept his distance from Webster, remained wary of Clay. His own vice president, Calhoun, was using his contacts and powers as Senate president to work against the president. The 1826 congressional elections had swept in a group determined to block him. "The Twentieth Congress," the historian Sean Wilentz has written, "organized itself into a virtual committee for the defeat of the president." John Quincy saw it too clearly. It was "a phenomenon entirely new," he wrote to Charles: "a majority of both houses of congress, composed of every factious opposition existing in the country, melted by a common disappointment into one mass, and invenomed by one spirit of bitter, unrelenting persecuting malice against me individually and against the administration, which they conspired to overthrow, assumed assuredly the control of the affairs of the nation." Their eyes were on the White House in 1828. Andrew Jackson's supporters had slush funds paying "bullies and assassins, to insult me, and everyone connected with me."

"Assassins" went too far (though an army surgeon, blaming the president for his court-martial for embezzlement, did show up at John Quincy's office to threaten him; John Quincy calmly sent him on his way). But there were real fights. One included his own son John, who, after a show of rudeness toward one of Jackson's supporters at one of Louisa's Drawing Rooms, was assaulted in the Capitol and provoked to duel. The two men were pulled apart; after a congressional investigation, the matter died away. But Louisa, who felt her son was defending her honor, never forgot the insults. Nor was John Quincy wrong about the slander spread by a coordinated network of opposition newspapers — funded by politicians and mailed with the use of congressional members' free postage.

He was called a gambler, an aristocrat, and a corrupt monarchist. Of course, his own (less organized) supporters did just the same, calling Jackson a demagogue, a despot, and a murderer. And for the first time in American history, the candidates' wives were drawn in. For this, Jackson's camp blamed Mrs. Adams. She provoked the feud, Jackson's supporters said. It's easy to see why.

In February 1827, Louisa apparently wrote a kind of campaign biography for the *Philadelphia Evening Post* that was reprinted widely. It was not about her husband; it was about herself. The essay was written anonymously, but there was little question about the identity of the author ("manifestly written by Mrs. Adams herself," said the *United States Telegraph*). The author's only goal, Louisa wrote, was to put an end to rumors that the president's wife was British. Her father, she declared, had acted daringly during the Revolution, risking his life to help his countrymen, making great sacrifices. As if unable to help herself, she described in high color his betrayal by his partners, his move to America, and his death as a broken man. The second half of the piece briefly and unwisely sketched her time in Berlin and St. Petersburg (calling attention to the flattering reception she'd been given by royal families) and then quickly recounted her journey to Paris.

It is a very strange text. It is extraordinary that she most likely wrote it at all. Never before had the wife of a candidate, much less the wife of a president, made a public statement about her own character. Never before had the wife of the president of the United States written something like that intended for print. Perhaps its existence can be explained simply; writing is what she did during those days in the White House to alleviate her boredom, provide an outlet for her anxieties, and give herself a sense of purpose. She may, naively, also have hoped that writing anonymously would protect her identity. The article did her no favors. It is clear that she wrote it to absolve herself of accusations that she was hampering John Quincy's campaign — and perhaps his life. And it was true, she was the target of some of the attacks against him. She was smeared as British, as aristocratic. After a rare visit to her Johnson relatives in Maryland, she wrote asking for anything in her uncle Thomas Johnson's papers that might help establish her American lineage. "The electioneering canvas calls forth questions which make this a question of high importance to me," she wrote.

But instead of helping, she indicted herself. Her article underscored her guilt over being a political liability to her husband, her sense that she was not an American, and her conviction that people thought she had "palmed" herself — her phrase — on John Quincy before her father had gone bankrupt. She put her situation in the worst possible light: "She lost the little property forever which she expected to bring to her husband, and became a beggar, with the appearance, of what was infinitely worse to her *proud spirit,* of having palmed herself upon a family under the most odious circumstances." The president is almost absent from the piece. The hero of the first half of the piece is her father, and the hero of the second half is herself. The piece culminates with her dangerous trip across Europe, which she did without her husband.

The tone of the document is almost a little deranged. Louisa was wound so tight that it seems she could not foresee the consequences of its publication — or, possibly, was less concerned with helping her husband's presidential chances than with presenting the Johnson family in a better light. Either way, it was misguided. Nothing like it would have been written by Rachel Jackson, the opposition press was quick to point out. As if to underscore the point, soon after, a pro-Adams paper called Jackson an adulterer and a bigamist, claiming that Rachel Jackson had been married but not divorced before living with Jackson. The Jackson forces read the two articles about the candidates' wives as a co-ordinated, malicious attack on Andrew Jackson's wife. Louisa's biography was written, said the leading opposition paper, the *United States Telegraph,* "to contrast her courtly education with that of Mrs. Jackson, and to demonstrate how much better qualified she was to discharge the duties of the drawing room than the unassuming, plain, old house-wife of the Tennessee Farmer." In retaliation, the *Telegraph* attacked Louisa, mocking her for trying to appear *"unambitious,"* and for claiming to have "retiring manners" and "republican virtues and connections." Day after day, it derided her attempt to appear as an *"unassuming"* woman "detesting politics." It called attention to her sympathetic reception by monarchs and scorned her "hair-breadth escape from St. Petersburg" (accomplished, it added, with taxpayer money).

Then Jackson's supporters struck back with an even more damaging attack. The *Telegraph* claimed to know the real *"truths"* about Louisa's background — "what is known to the boys in the streets of this City." The editorialist declared that he had no desire to print what everyone knew, information about Louisa's "mother's *family,"* which had vices that, "though found in the higher circles of Europe, are confined in this country to the most degraded and abandoned." In another editorial, the *Telegraph* was more explicit. The paper had no intention "to trace the *love* adventures of the Chief Magistrate, nor to disclose the manner, *nor the time,* at which *he,* his brother-in-law, and his father-in-law before him, led their *blushing* brides to the hymenial alter." It seems likely that someone in Jackson's camp heard that Joshua and Catherine had not been married before having children. It was, after all, not a secret in the Maryland branch of the Johnson family; he had been writing letters home protesting that he wasn't married at the time Nancy was born. There seems to have been salacious gossip about one of Louisa's sisters, too. (Perhaps it was another rumor that was contorted. Adelaide, who had married Nancy's widower, Walter Hellen, gave birth to a son long after Walter died. Whether out of charity or tacit responsibility, Harriet's husband, George Boyd, who was notorious for womanizing and had several children out of wedlock, registered the infant as his son.) The president was then impugned by the suggestion of premarital sex with Louisa. The insult was driven home.

Before the 1824 election, she had been integral to the campaign effort. But now she found that her attempt to help would cost her — and the cost was high. Duff Green, the *Telegraph*'s editor, was ecstatic at the Adams camp's response. "The effect here was like electricity," Green wrote to Jackson. "The whole Adams corps were thrown into consternation."

No doubt he was right. Whether or not Louisa knew that her parents had not been married before she was born, she was highly sensitive about her modesty and about her parents' reputation. It's possible that she never read the *Telegraph*'s attacks, but she had a habit of picking up rumors. She certainly heard something damaging; a year later, she wrote that had her parents not protected her, she might have become "a very vicious woman and deserving the obloquy cast upon my fair fame." It may help explain why she was already in an agitated state before she learned that George was ill a few days later. When she rushed to Boston, Charles told his fiancée, Abby, that he was especially worried for his mother for reasons independent of her health and George, reasons "which it is impossible at this time to mention in detail."

Jackson told Duff Green to leave Mrs. Adams — and women generally — out of his attacks. But of course in politics there is no stopping anything once started. A year later, Edward Everett gave a speech on the House floor refuting, while at the same time airing, charges that Louisa had presented her maid, Martha Godfrey, for the pleasure of the tsar.

It was the more frustrating, because it could seem to her that she was defending herself and her husband's presidency without her husband's help. Her sense of grievance became clear when her son John got into the scuffle in the Capitol with the lead editorial writer of the pro-Jackson *Telegraph* after the two had traded insults at one of her levees. Louisa was nearly undone by the incident, but she was also proud of her son for, as she saw it, defending her honor. The thin, sickly, doe-eyed woman was at heart a fighter.

She wanted to fight for the presidency, too, however miserable she was in the White House. She and John Quincy had their same old fight over "electioneering," after she encouraged him to meet with his supporters. "My journeys and my visits wherever they may be shall have no connection with the Presidency," he chided her. "I am sincerely sorry for it," she replied — with more iciness than sympathy. He was, she reminded him, not the only one who would be affected by his reelection; his supporters had something at stake too. Yet he refused to do much himself to help them or his own cause. He did not give speeches or encourage coordination, unlike Jackson, whose campaign was once again — and now more strongly — running on the strength of the candidate's magnetic personality. John Quincy's supporters were more inclined to disclaim their "personal predilections" for Adams, though they supported his general course. Daniel Webster's brother Ezekiel confessed that he supported Adams "from a cold sense of duty." He wrote to Daniel, "We do not entertain for him one personal kind feeling." John Quincy made it hard. Unlike Jackson, who for the most part followed the conventions of not campaigning too openly in public but welcomed any political operatives who came to see him in Tennessee, John Quincy refused to talk politics with hungry men who showed up at his door. A young Thurlow Weed — who would later become one of the greatest and most instrumental political advisers of the nineteenth century, and who had helped orchestrate John Quincy's 1824 win in New York — came to talk to John Quincy intending to work on behalf of the administration, only to be smoothly rebuffed. Later, Weed would bitterly write that President Adams, "with the great power he possessed," not only failed to recognize those who supported him but failed to make "a single influential friend."

He had trouble sleeping, only four or five hours "of not good repose," and was bothered by indigestion. His hand trembled, his pen wavered, his skin sagged, and his eyes watered. When he took his morning swims, he was shaking his fist at the incoming tide of time. Sometimes he wondered whether life had any point. For his whole life, John Quincy had struggled with dark moods, apathy, and sometimes severe depression. He never suffered so much, though, as he did when president of the United States. He labored under "uncontrolable dejection of spirits," he wrote in his diary at the end of July 1827, "insensibility to the almost unparalleled blessings with which I have been favoured; a sluggish carelessness of life, and in wish that it were terminated with a clinging to it as close as it ever was in the days of most animated hopes."

As his cares compounded, his depressed moods grew worse. John Quincy's doctor recommended a vacation, telling him "to doff the world aside and bid it pass; to cast off as much as possible all cares, public and private, and vegetate myself into a healthier condition." That ran counter to all of John Quincy's instincts. What he felt he needed was "a habit of useful industry." He had imagined difficulties, controversies, and what his father had liked to call stormy seas, to be sure, but not this drifting.

He looked forward to the day when he could exit the President's House, but he made no move to pull his name from the running. He distrusted Jackson's views and vision for the country, and it was humiliating to lose. Only one president had ever been expelled from the office after only one term; that man, of course, was John Quincy's own father.

It was difficult for him to see, with his

reflexive aversion to campaigning, that the new reality he couldn't accept in the election was the same reality that stymied his ambitious agenda. Politics were undergoing a fundamental realignment. Sectionalism deepened during a crisis regarding a fraudulent Native American treaty in Georgia, where the governor declared the federal government had no right to intervene. A fall in the price of cotton led to growing resistance to John Quincy's tariff reform efforts — and an explosion of anger toward the administration after the so-called Tariff of Abominations was passed in 1828. The solidarity among the slaveholding South that had begun to take shape during the Missouri debates was hardening. John Quincy's ambitious national economic program, Southerners especially felt, was only a prelude to the federal government's usurpation of states' rights. To some slaveholders, the implications were dire. If the federal government could exercise such power, who was to say it would not use it to interfere with slavery? Adams's own vice president, Calhoun, was working openly against the president. Outside of the obstructionist Congress, John Quincy's economic program had some support, but distrust of Washington was growing. Populist appeals gained traction. Farsighted politicians like Martin Van Buren built populist coalitions held together by little other than their dislike of the political elite — and John Quincy in particular. In the 1828 election, every state but Delaware and South Carolina would choose their electors by popular vote. It was a contest between visions of a country, one that appealed to betterment through national policy versus one that appealed to the virtue of common men. John Quincy held white-knuckled on to the idea that the election was a referendum on his economic program and not on the candidates' organizations or personalities. But the old ideal of disinterest-edness, the one John Quincy had inherited from his father's generation, was dead.

John Quincy was actually a cannier politi-cal animal than he allowed himself to be, which tore at him. He may have done noth-ing overt to promote his campaign, but he did nothing to stop it, either, and that became one more thing that oppressed him. It could be, though, that while he couldn't see the full scope of the transformation of American politics, he could see one aspect far too well: the increasing sectionalism of the country, undergirded by the awful existence of slavery. Disinterested or not, he faced an uphill battle: the three-fifths compromise put him, as a Northerner (and a Yankee at that) and as an antislavery figure, at a huge disadvantage. "I fell, and with me fell, I fear never to rise again the system of internal improvement by national means and national energies," he would write a decade later. In his place, as he came to see it, would be a series of presidents who would "rivet into perpetuity the clanking chain of the slave."

Perhaps the subject of slavery was more personal, perhaps it hit closer to home, than he ever dared admit to himself or anyone. At the Adamses' house on F Street, and later in John Quincy's White House, there may have been a slave or two, although he or she was probably not owned by John Quincy. "I abhorred slavery and did not suffer it in my family," John Quincy would tell an abolitionist in 1832, and John Quincy was not one to lie. But this distinction may have been semantic.

On February 23, 1828, John Quincy wrote in his diary, "Holzey, the black boy belonging to Johnson Hellen and who has been several years with us, died about five o'clock this afternoon. He has been sinking several months in a consumption." It is possible that "belonging" might have meant that he was Johnson's hired servant, but there is evidence to believe he was a slave. Johnson Hellen, who frequently lived with the Adamses, was a slaveholder; according to the 1830 census, he had two slaves. The day after, February 24, Holzey was buried. John Quincy marked the occasion with a quiet note of grief. In memoriam, he added lines from Horace about how death strikes all men equally: *"Pallida Mors aequo pulsat pede pauperum tabernas / Regumque turres. / Vitae summa brevis spem nos vetat inchoare longam."* Pale death beats with an impartial foot the inns of paupers and the towers of kings. The sum of brief life forbids us to begin a long hope.

The president's mourning, such as it was, occurred privately. So did his thoughts about slavery. He was known to oppose the institution, but he did nothing to help the antislavery cause as president. He even ignored letters on the subject. He may not have felt he could address it. He considered himself the tribune of the whole country, including the slaveholding South. He also needed the support of some slaveholding states and some slaveholders (Henry Clay, for one). Southerners and proslavery advocates already viewed him suspiciously, accusing him of claiming powers that would lead to the abolition of slavery. John Quincy was also remarkably good at compartmentalizing and rationalizing. He lived, after all, in Washington, where slaves were everywhere — in pens, in the shops, running errands on the Capitol floor, and working at places like Gadsby's Hotel, which hosted John Quincy's inauguration ball.

John Quincy, though, may have helped set free at least one slave while president, a slave who may have lived at least for a time in the White House. Two days after Holzey died, on February 25, 1828, Mary Catherine Hellen and John Adams were married. That same day, her wedding day, Mary filed papers liberating a slave named Rachel Clark. Rachel may have been the young girl who was listed as living in the Adams household on F Street in 1820. It's possible that Rachel did not live in the White House; perhaps she lived with one of Louisa's sisters (most likely Adelaide Hellen, whose slaves included Jenny and Joseph Clark). But it is also possible that when John Quincy later told an abolitionist that he "did not suffer" slavery in his family, he was thinking of Mary's emancipation of Rachel. Perhaps, though it can only be speculated, he made the manumission of Mary's slave a precondition for her marrying his son.

He never mentioned Rachel Clark's manumission in any extant diary or letter. Nor did anyone else, except the clerk who recorded it. In his diary, John Quincy recorded in great detail what else had happened that day of the wedding: his walk at daybreak, his sitting for a portrait, his visitors, his tasks, and the names of the twenty or so friends and family who gathered at the President's House to witness the marriage. "The servants of the family were likewise all present," John Quincy wrote in his diary. Whether "the servants" included Rachel Clark is not known.

John Quincy had strongly opposed John and Mary's marriage. But for whatever reason, John Quincy seems to have been particularly happy the day of their wedding. "May the blessings of God Almighty rest upon the Union!" he wrote in his diary. To the astonishment of all, he danced a reel.

Might Louisa have also pressured Mary to emancipate Rachel? Possibly. Louisa was opposed to slavery in the abstract. But her feelings were more anxious and conflicted than her husband's. Before she was an Adams, she was a Johnson, after all — and while she lived in the White House, she was obsessed with defending the Johnsons. The Johnsons owned slaves. Louisa did try to whitewash the extent of their connection to slavery. In "Record of a Life," she mentioned being horrified and uncomprehending at seeing how young Kitty Carroll of Maryland treated her slave, "as we had always been severely punished for improper conduct to Servants this matter produced many unpleasant scenes while [Kitty Carroll] staid between us young people." She recorded the names of prominent British abolitionists who were friends with her father. But the fact was, in 1800, after returning to Washington, Joshua Johnson owned four slaves. Unless they were sold to offset his financial troubles, Louisa would have seen them when she was reunited when her family in 1801. The 1820 and 1830 census records show that, like most Washington families, the families of Louisa's sisters mixed one or two slaves with hired white and black servants. So, it seems, did her nieces and nephews.

The day after John and Mary's wedding at the President's House, Louisa's sister Caroline and her husband Nathaniel Frye threw a party for the newlyweds. It is possible that at least one slave was on hand, greeting guests or carrying bowls of ice cream; the 1820 census shows that Nathaniel Frye owned a male slave between the ages of fourteen and twenty-five, and in 1830, Nathaniel owned a female slave between ten and twenty-three. Nathaniel himself was not originally a Southerner; he came from a prominent family in Maine. But in Washington, practices were local. Aside from a tiny but increasingly vocal abolitionist presence in Washington, few had the courage or inclination to publicly protest slavery. It touched everyone, and to varying degrees almost everyone, not only Southerners but Northerners, Easterners, and Westerners, the Jacksons and the Adamses, lived with it.

6

Even more than her husband, Louisa withdrew in the White House, often pleading sickness and confining herself to her bedroom. For stretches of time, she was almost alienated from John Quincy. "You know how little he communicates with me on any subject at any time and now we only meet at table," she wrote to Charles. She, who had played such a central role in John Quincy's election, was now living in the White House, as close to the center of power as a woman could be. But she felt herself an exile.

For company, she had music: Mozart, Handel, Vincenzo Pucitta, Thomas Campbell. Sometimes she copied out their scores herself, onto page after page of blank stanzas. She had her sisters and her sons, though worrying about them could bring her pain. And she had her journals, their pages blank, their marble covers stamped with her name. She had, too, her sadness. She sometimes tended its flames as if they could keep her warm.

Her self-pity could be outrageous; she lashed out almost with rage against her sense of isolation. She begged Charles to send her something to translate from French, "as I cannot bear the loneliness of my life and you know that my mind is easily absorbed by any pursuit to which it devotes itself." She wrote prolifically and began to experiment with forms. She wrote farces and poetry, which she would send to George. She sometimes set her poems at sea.

> Thou art gone thou art gone away love
> Across the briny sea
> Sure, long thou wilt not stay love
> And I away from thee? . . .
> In the blooming month of May love
> Thy bark shall homeward turn
> My throbbing heart will pray love
> To speed thy blest return
> The winds shall swiftly waft thee love
> To me and to thy home
> And thou no more wilt leave me love
> Across the seas to roam.

She was more social than she claimed to be; her letters are full of references to parties, dinners, and levees. But when she drew on them for her writing, she had the critical distance of an observer. She wrote a work of fiction called "The Metropolitan Kaleido-scope / or / Winter Varieties," featuring Lady

Sharply and her husband, Lord Sharply, a man of "high station" in Parliament. The Sharplys' guests, whom she depicted as British courtiers, were easily recognized public figures — drawn dazzlingly with texture, colors, and firm lines.

She sketched a parade of politicians, generals, dandies, ambassadors, and wives. She captured the mighty aspect of Lord Leadall (Daniel Webster), whose dark brow and dark eyes communicated something stormy and brooding, "something vast and powerful; of thought even to madness," but whose mouth could twitch into a smile like the sun cutting through the clouds. Andrew Jackson and his wife, Rachel, arrived as "Lord and Lady Playfair." She captured what made them so appealing to so many — and so appalling to others. "Her Ladyship was an unaffected unpolished friendly woman. . . . Her mind was strong and untutored," Louisa wrote. "His Lordship was one of those gifted children of nature that as Shakespeare says were *born great.* He was rude and rugged in feature; art had done little to fashion him into order, loose in his morals, above the shackels of fixed principles, daring in his projects, with a deep and profound knowledge of mankind acquired by an enlarged experience and acquaintance with human nature in all its moods and tenses; he was a perfect master of their passions, tho' he took little trouble to control his own. His mind was of the strongest and boldest cast; full of energy, enterprise, and activity, he scorned personal danger." Life itself was his school, she wrote, and "man was the *book* from which he drew all his knowledge, all his views." Louisa's portrait of Martin Van Buren, or "Lord Vandyke Maneuvre," is as revealing as any account of his political cunning. "His Lordship was one of those singular beings who gain a prodigious and unaccountable influence with mankind, without apparently possessing any of those great or shining qualities which we naturally *look* for," she wrote. Lady Sharply recognized — rightly — that he was positioning himself to join forces with Lord Playfair (Jackson). Yet it was "impossible" for even an enemy to speak to Lord Maneuvre without liking him. "He possessed that greatest and perhaps most subtle of all arts, that, of so naturally addressing himself to the capacity, the taste, and the style of those with whom he talked, that they forgot that he was a *Star.*"

Much went unobserved in her sketch, as was polite. She left out the servants. Off the page, in the real White House, she counted sixteen of them: a steward, a housekeeper, a butler, housemaids, cooks, coachman, scullion, two "boys" who carried wood and waited on the table, a porter who answered the door and lit the fires. The servants lived in the west end of the attic and in the basement, off a vaulted passage, in little rooms with walls washed white or yellow. The floor of the basement's long hallway, where Washington, Jefferson, Madison, and Monroe had kept their slaves, was slick and covered with sand or sawdust grit. The kitchen was a furnace; its fire never went out. The servants began flowing through the house before dawn, knocking on doors to rouse the sleeping, carrying basins of fresh water, ready to light the morning fires. They brushed out the day's clothes, cleaned the night's messes. They cooked and carried dinner, trays, plates. A system of bells would summon them to respond to some request. They rode on the outside of the carriage, in snow and in rain, over dangerous roads, brought inside the vehicle only when injured in an accident. They were half invisible, noticed only when there was a problem.

Some of the servants were black, members of Washington's sizable free black population — though their freedom was limited at best. In 1827, Washington's corporation passed laws requiring free blacks to register with the mayor and get a permit to live and work within the city. There was a citywide ten p.m. curfew for blacks, and a permit was required for free blacks to assemble. They were routinely fingered as suspects in crimes, even when there was no evidence. They were regarded with suspicion and degraded daily. In this, Louisa was no better than most. Her set of instructions for her servants made her prejudices plain. "The coloured females to apply to Housekeeper for permission to go out and to be sent away if they are not at home at ten o'clock at night," she wrote. This was in accord with the local law — but then she added "or for imprudence or disrespect to any of the White people in the family." (If there were in fact any slaves, of course, in the White House, they went unacknowledged altogether.)

She had that blindness. But she was clear-eyed in other ways, as sharp as the name she gave herself in "The Metropolitan Kaleidoscope." In her fiction, she described herself as Lady Sharply, capturing her character only by contradictions. "She was the oddest compound of strong affections and cold dislikes; of discretion and caprice; of pride and gentleness; of playfulness and hauteur; that I ever met with — irritable one moment, laughing the next, there was nothing tangible in her character on which you could rest, to censure or approve."

She also described Lord Sharply, and in doing so, perhaps captured John Quincy better than he has ever been described, then or since.

Lord Sharply was a man of extraordinary talents. . . . His natural disposition was ardent and impetuous, but a perpetual watchfulness over these natural defects, had taught him to master them completely, and it was only those who were the most constantly with him, who were aware that occasions could arise in which the internal volcano would sometimes produce an eruption that was short but violent in its explosion. A fond father, a negligent and half indulgent husband, and utterly indifferent to almost all the other branches of his family, he often appeared to forget or not to know, that others had found obstacles in their path which he had never dreamt of, and deemed things must be so, without considering how or why they were so. He was full of good qualities but ambition had ever been the first object of his soul to attain that object no sacrifice would have been deemed too great.

This was incisive. But it wasn't quite fair. She rejected sympathy; she refused to see, too, how high the stakes were, and how terrible his powerlessness was. She was angry with him. During those years in the White House, he may have been only a half-indulgent husband, but it's safe to say that she was only a half-indulgent wife.

As the 1828 campaign moved toward its conclusion, Louisa watched, at once wanting to win and wanting release from her miserable situation. Her mood swung back and forth as the year progressed. One day she could be cheerful, and the next listless and depressed. In September, with the election entering its final pitch, she suffered a "severe attack," "inflammation of the head pressing on the brain, and also on the heart." Charles rushed to Washington from Boston and, though he was relieved to find the expression in her eyes as tender and intelligent as ever, she was so weak that she could not sit up. She "was recovered by being most purposely bled, by being almost rolled in mustard and cayenne and by blisters," Charles wrote to his fiancée, Abby Brooks, who came from a wealthy Boston family. While in Washington, Charles also noticed that his father was making preparations to leave the capital, two months before any votes were counted.

The president's loss seemed a foregone conclusion. When the ballots were finally counted, no one was surprised. Jackson had won 68 percent of the electoral vote and 56 percent of the popular tally. More than a million men voted — about four times as many as in 1824.

John Quincy was, at times, morose and morbid. His life had been oriented toward one ambition, and now it was gone. When the first day of 1829 dawned overcast, John Quincy saw omens. When he began the morning's writing, his lamp had gone out, *"self-extinguished."* But he could not totally hide his relief. Nor could his wife. "Although we have lost our main mast and have come in a wreck we are all well in very good spirits and that your father grows so fat he could no longer wear your pantaloons," Louisa cheerfully reported a week after the election.

She began the year with a sleepless night, sick and in pain. But she began to emerge from her long darkness. Life continued, as life does. On December 2, John and Mary had a daughter, and Louisa and John Quincy became grandparents. Louisa's mood was elated. She was once again her husband's greatest champion and advocate. "Your father is well and growing very fat. It is impossible to behave with more real dignity than he does amidst trials which are sufficient to shake the nerves of a Pallas," she wrote in December.

At one of their last Drawing Rooms, in late December, they were so cheerful that the guests could not believe it. "Mr. and Mrs. Adams have gone a little too far in this *assumed* gaiety," Margaret Bayard Smith wrote, noting their "social, gay, frank and cordial manners. What a change." The doors to the East Room, never before used, were thrown open. A band was hired and there was, for the first time during one of Louisa's White

House Drawing Rooms, dancing. The ladies of the Cabinet showed up "in new dresses just arrived from Paris." Margaret, for one, was suspicious. "Every thing in fact was done to conceal the natural feelings excited by disappointment and to assume the appearance not only of indifference, but of satisfaction."

But it was not affectation. The weather that winter was unusually freezing and wet, but they were finally able to tell themselves that spring would come.

■ ■ ■ ■

PART NINE:
BEGINNING THE
WORLD ANEW

Washington and Quincy, 1829–1836

■ ■ ■ ■

1

Winter was stubborn. Storms came in quick succession, and wet snow still covered the ground in mid-March. For weeks, thin traces of ice lay in the shade. But by the end of March 1829, Louisa could write to Charles, who was up in Boston, that it was "almost summer," describing the chirrups of hidden frogs and the reviving hum of insects. By the beginning of April, the fields were patched with color, fresh with the green scent of new grass. Spring blossoms broke from dead branches. Cascades of white flowers tumbled from the horse chestnuts. Strong shoots pushed out of the mud, and yellow forsythia erupted like laughter. Louisa shook off the cold that had numbed her. "Like a grasshopper," she had once written of herself, "I sing my hour according to the degree of heat."

At the beginning of March, she and John Quincy, along with John and Mary, their daughter Mary Louisa (whom they called Louisa), and a few servants had moved into a mansion on Meridian Hill, located on the original centerline of the District of Columbia. The very stone that marked the longitude stood on the house's land. Louisa could have walked due south from its central door to the iron gate of the White House. From the crest of the hill she could look south and see the White House's boxy shape a mile and a half away. But that was the last place she wanted to go. She had no desire to get any closer.

She heard stories of how a crowd of people overwhelmed the reception at the President's House after Andrew Jackson's inauguration. Office seekers, shopkeepers, farmers, senators, and children had pushed past one another into the parlors. Men had climbed in and out of the reception through open windows. With mud and slush clinging to their boots, they stood atop the damask chairs, the very chairs she had so carefully chosen. The drapes were torn, and when the waiters appeared with tubs of spiked orange punch, the surge of the crowd had knocked over her cut glass — now the new president's cut glass — and the glass had shattered on the floor. She had heard, too, that Jackson was removing federal appointees and replacing them with supporters of his campaign. "Rumor has again set forth her hundred tongues and each tongue announces a dismissal," Louisa wrote to George. Jackson had even fired her servants and brought in his slaves. Only the Giustas, who had come with the Adamses from Europe, remained, and they were permitted to keep their jobs only on the condition that they not speak to their former employers. "We are in a state of banishment," Louisa wrote. The Adamses were being blamed for the death of Andrew Jackson's wife, Rachel; Jackson's supporters said that she had died from the strain of the slander against her. Louisa, though, mourned the woman's death. "I learnt the pangs the malignity of slander can inflict not to pity one so severely oppressed," she wrote to Charles.

She kept all of this in the distance, though still in view. She made no visits to anyone in the city. Though the Adamses had once socialized with friends and opponents alike, no one from the new administration, except for Martin Van Buren, now secretary of state, came to visit them. Meridian Hill seemed a kind of exile — which Louisa liked. It was like Little Boston had been in Ealing, a kind of oasis — a place to be a family once more. Though the house was only rented, she wrote that the family was "forming a home of real domestic comfort." It had been a long time since she worried about "good housewifery," she admitted, years since she superintended the meals, the laundry, and the small trials of daily life. There was a time — she could remember it too well — when her incompetence caused her husband annoyance and

561

herself great pain. Now, though, "we laugh at my blunders," she said, and the laughter was cheerful. She was delighted with the place and confident enough to call herself its mistress. The house was large and tasteful, with separate wings for John's family and her own, connected by large sliding doors that separated two elegant parlors on the south side. There were "very pretty" bed chambers, a long gallery, good closets, and a large room in a garret, where she had placed "the offensive billiard table" that John Quincy had bought for the White House, which the opposition press had pointed to as evidence that the president was gambling and abusing public funds after John, as secretary, had mislabeled the account. She could joke about that now. Spread out over the estate were cellars, stables, a dairy, an icehouse, servants' chambers, a laundry, a washhouse, a kitchen garden, flower beds, a nursery for new trees. Yellowwood trees lined a long graceful drive to the estate. There was a farmhouse and woods, and more than a hundred acres of land. John Quincy's study overlooked a little flower garden and the plant nursery.

"The ex-President I think enjoys himself in his little study . . . infinitely more than I ever remember him to have done since I have been married," Louisa wrote to Charles.

Since leaving the glare of the President's House, her husband had grown brighter and bigger in her eyes. "Your father leaves them all far behind and displays that real yet true dignity that seeks no occasions for ostentatious display but commands the respect of all who approach him," she wrote. "Conscious rectitude is a shield which no arms are powerful enough to destroy." Charles reminded her that she had been furious with him, despairing about his plans for Quincy. She half pretended not to know what her son was talking about. "I have totally forgotten," she responded, adding, "Your father is as kind as possible and appears desirous of doing everything in his power to make me comfortable."

Her granddaughter, Mary Louisa, was often in her arms. She was amazed at the change that marriage and fatherhood had produced in her son John. "He is active steadily industrious and much more cheerful than for years," Louisa told Charles. As for herself, she knew that she was also in a new state. She was rarely sick anymore. "I am always busy about nothing and have no time to think of my health which certainly is no worse if it does not improve." She knew that eventually she and John Quincy would have to head north to the Old House, but she did not dwell on when. John Quincy began to talk about buying Meridian Hill. She did not, it seems, object.

She wrote to George, "You have no conception how happily we live here."

■ ■ ■ ■

A letter arrived from Charles in the first week of April. It was about George. George was not doing well, Charles said. He had withdrawn from his friends; he was languishing; he needed some sort of excitement, some spur for his career and his spirits. This came as no surprise to Louisa. She had been feeling distant from her oldest son for a year. Their correspondence had fallen off. They were like "floating icebergs," she wrote. She had already tried to thaw the freeze, but she recognized it would take time. She couldn't say whether the fault was hers or his, but it no longer mattered. "One of the pleasures most earnestly anticipated by me is the renewed and affectionate intercourse of my sons," she had written to him on April 1. Her concern for him was an unceasing current in her mind — sometimes fast, sometimes slow. She had always had great hopes for her firstborn, but most of all she just wanted George to be well.

"With all his nonsense he is a glorious creature," she told her son John the year before, "and should he fail to get over the singular waywardness of his nature he will still be all I wish and desire."

On April 8, after receiving Charles's letter, she wrote to George again and urged him to come to Washington. In her letter, she was gentle and kind. She gave no hint that she had been prompted by Charles, no echo of Charles's concern. She simply said that she and John Quincy would need his help in moving to Massachusetts, and before that time came, they wanted him with them in Washington. She offered many inducements. "[O]ur little ménage goes on so quietly and modestly and I think I never saw your father so mild and so pleasant and take such a general interest in what is going on among us as he does now," she wrote. If he came, he could save money on rent. He could have a comfortable room. He would have freedom. "Your father will probably keep a horse and gig and you will always command the use of it," she wrote. After she signed her name, she added, "If you come you will see our pretty baby."

George agreed immediately, and Louisa was relieved. She was seriously worried, but she imagined that at Meridian Hill he might find, as she had found, some hope for the future. "It is probable," she wrote to Charles, that George will "begin a new life when with us."

She expected him to reach the house on Saturday, May 2. But at around one o'clock that same afternoon, Louisa's brother-in-law Nathaniel Frye appeared at the door instead. He asked whether John Quincy had received any letters. That morning Nathaniel had read an announcement in the *Baltimore American* that somewhere between Providence and New York, before sunrise on Thursday morning, George Adams had gone overboard the steamboat the *Benjamin Franklin*. About half an hour later John Quincy's cousin Judge William Cranch arrived with three letters confirming the death.

John Quincy was the one who told Louisa. Her condition, he wrote in his diary afterward, "is not to be described." The doctor was summoned to see her, "but there was no medicine for this wound."

Over the next few days, John Quincy read the newspaper accounts of the death and spoke with another passenger. He pieced together a story of what had happened, a story that he could accept, a story about his son's death that would let him live on. "I see the causes of it distinctly," John Quincy wrote in his diary. George was seasick. The jostling of the boat "had produced a fever with a rushing of blood to the brain." He had asked the captain to be put on shore so that he might be bled. George was cheerful with other passengers. He gave a missionary a little money. But he was under a great strain, John Quincy wrote in his diary, and his mind snapped. George's fellow passenger told John Quincy that George imagined that the other passengers were laughing at him. He imagined that the birds were speaking to him. He imagined that the steamboat engine was speaking to him, saying "Let it be, let it be, let it be, let it be." In the middle of the night, George again asked the captain to put him ashore, saying that the other passengers were conspiring against him. Not long afterward, his hat was found on deck, and then his coat.

His corpse would be found a month later. John Quincy went to meet the body. "His watch and small pocketbook were still in their places, and his name yet legible within his boots," he wrote to Louisa.

John Quincy's diary returned continually to his concern for his wife. "Human suffering can go but one degree beyond what she endures," he wrote. He prayed for mercy. He prayed to God that she would not see herself as Job. "Let her not say, My God! My God! why hast thou forsaken me?" She was, somehow, able to rise from her bed and leave the bedroom. He was amazed by her resilience, which he thought stronger than his own. But at night the fevers would come. When she tried to come down to dinner, she fainted. She begged John Quincy not to listen to anything she said during those days, fearful that her words were deranged by her grief. For a second time, she had lost her child, and yet again she thought she might be driven mad. She was also afraid that she would blame her husband for their son's death. Afterward, she wrote a short and strange statement in her diary in which she said, "The idea struck me after I became more composed; that as human nature is ever prone to think ill; that I might perhaps be thought to have some secret uneasiness that I was fearful of exposing." She wrote it to deny it. She wanted, she said, "to declare that I had no terror of conscience or of guilt, but only the apprehension of expressing some *regrets*, that might have increased the anguish of us all." There is no better evidence, of course, that she really did have some secret uneasiness — about suicide, about the stigma, about her husband's culpability, about her own — than this sad statement.

To Charles, she wrote of John Quincy's consoling devotion. "To me he is a ministering angel always at my side and lavishing on the most soothing tenderness. To me! alas how unworthy."

Husband and wife prayed together. Always religious, Louisa had become increasingly so during her time in the President's House, and though her religion was idiosyncratic, it always tended toward the High Church ceremony of her youth — the colors of her Catholic nursery school, the Anglican services she had attended as a child. Now, at her request, John Quincy, though a Unitarian himself, read aloud the Episcopalian service for the dead.

On May 21, John Quincy picked up the *National Journal* and saw a poem by George Washington Adams, reprinted from the *New Bedford Mercury.*

> There is a little spark at sea
> Which grows 'mid darkness brilliantly,
> But when the moon looks clear and bright,
> Emits a pale and feeble light,
> And when the tempest shakes the wave
> It glimmers o'er the seaman's grave.
>
> Such friendship's beaming light appears
> Through the long line of coming years
> In sorrow's cloud it shines afar,
> A feeble but a constant star
> And like that little spark at sea
> Burns brightest in adversity.

Louisa copied it into her album, alongside some of the poems that she had written and sent to George. *Thou art gone thou art gone away love / Across the briny sea. . . .* Despite the commonness of the romantic tropes, it would be hard to blame her if she read it as a message to herself sent from a distant place.

What story she constructed for herself about his death is unknown. She abhorred suicide. "I think suicide is the most contemptible crime a human being can commit," she had once written to her nephew, in unsympathetic horror, when he had confessed to thoughts of taking his own life. "The memory of a man who thus dies, is a constant reproach in this world; and what has he to hope in the next?" But this was her son, and she never could curse him.

She worried that she had provoked his death by persuading him to come to Washington when he was unwell: "My heart tells me that perhaps I urged your unfortunate brother beyond his strength to exertion foreign to his nature," she wrote to Charles. "If so may God Almighty forgive the mistaken zeal of an offending mortal." She would blame her husband's ambition, and she would blame herself too. When he was a child and needed her, she had been in Washington, then in Russia, gone.

Louisa remained alone with Mary, her granddaughter, and the servants at Meridian Hill while John Quincy and John were in Massachusetts, tying up George's affairs. Bereft, she confessed to Charles, "Every bleeding vein in my beating heart tells me that I am not mistress of myself."

And yet the world began to draw her back in. She started to report snippets of news: "Mr. Walsh it is said is to purchase the *National Intelligencer* and to reside here." Trouble was brewing between the New Yorker Van Buren and the South Carolinian Calhoun, who had remained vice president for Jackson;

"Carolina is up in arms." She kept the ex-president abreast of appointments and removals, and of who had Jackson's ear. It was better to keep her mind on the world than on herself. She considered herself weak, but she was always stronger when she faced adversity.

Her focus turned to the Columbia Mill, which John Quincy had rashly and disastrously purchased in 1824 from her cousin George Johnson. Now John was taking over the mill, in its sorry state, and running it on behalf of his father. She went to visit the mill herself, at the foot of a hill by Rock Creek. She examined the grist and flour, discussed the business with the new manager, and watched the great wheels turn. She followed the cost of corn and the price of meal, and she worried when it rained, because the rain swelled the creek and flooded the mill. The sky was inexhaustible. She had never seen such rain.

She missed her husband. "As soon as ever you wish me to come on only write me and I will set off immediately after the arrival of John as I cannot leave Mary alone," she wrote to John Quincy in mid-June. "I cannot much longer bear my absence from you," she wrote three weeks later. Another pull was drawing her toward Massachusetts. Charles was to marry Abby Brooks in September, and he begged her to be there. "Should you be absent from my wedding," he wrote, "it would lose half it's pleasure."

She had wanted to accompany her husband north from the start, but she had been dissuaded. John Quincy had his reasons for wanting to keep her from Quincy for some time. There was, for starters, the matter of the Old House, as broken as its owner. The shambling house was in a "helpless, shattered, antiquated state," Charles told Louisa. Thomas Adams, who would soon die from the effects of alcoholism, had not kept it in good repair. Water had breached the mansard roof and ceilings; mold stains spread across the walls. Sooty drafts raced through the rooms from the massive fireplaces. The floors were uncarpeted; there was hardly a bed to sleep in. Scraggly saplings stood wretched in the seedling nursery, strangled by vines. John Quincy set about repairs. "It seems like beginning the world anew," he wrote to his wife.

He probably also wanted to keep her away from George's affairs. He paid George's debts, totaling about a thousand dollars. Whether he knew where some of George's money had gone is unclear. There was a child. The infant's mother, Eliza Dolph, had been a chambermaid at Dr. Thomas Welsh's, where George had boarded. After the baby was born in December 1828, George had asked the doctor who had delivered it to find the baby and its mother a place to live. The doctor had persuaded Miles Farmer to take them in. The problem was that George had continued to see Eliza and the child, and people started to wonder why the president's son was such a frequent visitor to an ex-chambermaid and her illegitimate child. George had paid Farmer off, but now the supply of money was gone, and Farmer was threatening to blackmail Charles. Later Farmer would press the doctor who had delivered the baby for payment, and there would be a trial. Charles was determined to keep the existence of Eliza and the child from John Quincy. Louisa, it seems, was never told.

Whatever John Quincy did or didn't know, however, there was now no trace of the judgmental nature he had once been so quick to show. "My father looks pretty well," Charles wrote in his diary when he saw him, "but he has a manner which I never before saw in him of quiet sadness, in itself really affecting."

Louisa finally set out for Quincy, with John, Mary, the baby, and several servants in the middle of August. Charles met them in New York, at the City Hotel, in order to accompany them the rest of the way. He was sobered when he saw his mother. Though he knew her to be "fond of show and ornament," she wore a black dress of "utmost plainness." She looked worn and ill. She had not combed her hair.

He dreaded telling her that he had arrived from Providence aboard the *Benjamin Franklin,* the ship that George had gone overboard from, and that the *Benjamin Franklin* was to carry them back to Providence in two days. She was "affected" when she learned. By the following evening, it was "so evident" to Charles that she would not be able to board the ship that he did not even mention their departure the next day. Mary tore into his hotel room that night, just after the clock had struck midnight, and shook him awake, telling him that his mother had been struck terribly ill. He found everyone — Mary, John, the servants — trying to help her. The attack was "violent"; she was crying of a coldness in her breast. "It will be useless to detail the two hours which passed," Charles wrote in his diary afterward. "Suffering was dreadfully stamped on them in my memory forever. I had never seen anything like this before, and it affected me to the soul."

She was somewhat better the next day, though she still flinched at every sound. Charles reluctantly urged her to return to Washington. From his tone in his diary, it seems he half hoped she would say no. But John's baby was ill, teething, and she was in no state to board the steamboat. The next day Charles reached Quincy alone. He found John Quincy waiting for Louisa. "My father came out with a smiling face to meet disappointment," Charles wrote, "deep and severe."

Back in Washington, the sky was gray and everything soaked. The rain continued unabated. "Nothing looks as it used to," Louisa wrote to John Quincy. Meridian Hill was sold that summer, and so Louisa found herself once more packing and unpacking, this time in John and Mary's new house on Sixteenth and I Streets — just two blocks north of the President's House.

She could not ignore the stories emerging from the Jackson administration even if she tried. At her tea table, she could hear the servants gossip about the latest controversy between the president and his Cabinet involving the secretary of war's wife. Once again, there were warring camps of women, and Louisa commented in her wry manner on the power play between Calhoun and Van Buren behind it. She was, she declared, sick of Washington.

In May 1830, Louisa, John Quincy, Mary (pregnant again), and Mary Louisa left the capital for Quincy. It took a week to reach New York by carriage and stage, moving inland to avoid the boats for as long as they could. In New York they boarded the steamship *Providence*. The sky was overcast and the sea steely. That night, as the boat rocked in the swells rounding Long Island, she became extremely seasick. At sunrise, the thick fog dissipated, and the *Benjamin Franklin,* the boat that George had been lost from, came steaming into view. By the time the *Providence* reached Rhode Island, Louisa had fainted. Soon after she arrived in Quincy, she was seized by a chill and fever, and was in "agonies of pain." The doctor was called; she was bled. The diagnosis was erysipelas; and so the pattern continued.

When she recovered, though, she began to seem well. Charles, who lived with his new wife in Boston but frequently visited Quincy, thought her changed for the better. He had sensed that being in Washington oppressed her; now she seemed "more cheerful than I have known her for years." She had some independence. She listened to the sound of her granddaughter's laughter in the hallway. That summer, another granddaughter, Georgeanna Frances (Fanny for short), was born.

She had never taken to Quincy, but now it was, as Charles wrote in his diary, "a house of her own." She went out riding. The air was hot with the scent of pine trees, hay, saltwater, and horses, and from the hills she could see the bright blue bay. The house was filled with the furniture they had brought from Russia and England in 1817. She could look around and see her Sèvres porcelain, her sketches from Silesia, her leather-bound books the size of a hand. In a small alcove in the corner, she had her own desk: a secretary built of rich, polished mahogany inlaid with lighter wood. A small bookshelf with glazed cabinet drawers was perched above a writing surface, lined with green felt, which slid open like a drawer.

When she sat at her desk and looked out the window, she could see a newly planted yellowwood tree among the perennials in the garden, its tiny teardrop flowers trembling when it blossomed. The tree stood out from the oaks and walnuts and fruit trees on the property. It was not native to Massachusetts. Future generations of the Adams family would say that the tree was planted for her, and for George. According to one version of the story, she planted it herself.

2

She started a new life, calm and quiet. A trip to the milliner in Weymouth, an afternoon of gathering elderberries, the christening of her granddaughter Fanny. The fall's first night fires, cool mornings, and the sunshine's warmth at noon. She was fifty-five years old now, in 1830, and the next stage of her life was beginning. John Quincy and Louisa planned to return to Washington at the end of fall to live with John and Mary and their grandchildren over the winter, but their trip south would be only temporary. The old mansion that John Quincy had inherited was still in bad need of repairs, with faulty chimneys and a roof that leaked when it rained. Nor was Louisa up for the snow and harsh cold of a New England winter. But she accepted, with relief, that Quincy was now her home.

She may have read the small anonymous notice that ran in the *Boston Courier* on September 6, 1830, nominating John Quincy Adams for Congress from the Plymouth district. If she did, she may have taken it to be a hoax; the *Courier* was known to be unfriendly to John Quincy, and he was obviously out of public life, spending his mornings counting walnut seeds and planting apples, cherries, and plum stones in his nursery. She also may have seen Joseph Richardson, the incumbent member from Plymouth, come up the drive to her house on Saturday, September 18, to ask the ex-president whether he would serve if elected. She probably did not, however, hear what the men discussed in his white-painted wood-paneled study, or see that John Quincy offered no promises but gave the proposal a wink and a nod. After all, he did not want to admit that a coordinated movement was under way. If the people wanted to send him back to Washington — as he desperately desired them to do — then he thought their votes should be "spontaneous." It appears he did not tell Louisa anything. He probably knew what his wife would say.

Still, she could not have remained in the dark for long. The stream of prominent visitors to the house was small but persistent, and the local newspapers started to announce their support. By Friday, September 24, at the latest, she knew what was going on. And she was furious.

She wanted nothing to do with this election. She did not even want to go to Washington if he won — not even for the winter as they had previously planned. (His term would not begin until the following winter, 1831.) "Many circumstances are arising here which may induce me to remain in Quincy through the winter," she wrote to John. She was done with political life. That resolution, she wrote, "I fully and conscientiously believe ought to have been taken long ago."

The election took place November 1. On November 6, the evening newspaper reported the final returns: John Quincy Adams 1,817 votes; Arad Thompson 373; William Baylies 279. "I am a member-elect of the Twenty-Second Congress," John Quincy wrote that night in his diary. The next day, he opened his diary again and this time expressed his private feelings of relief and joy. He had taken the loss of the presidential election to be a repudiation of his entire life's work, a judgment against his merit. "No one knows, and few conceive the agony of mind that I have suffered," he wrote, since the moment that "circumstances" had made him a candidate for president fifteen years earlier. "They were feelings to be suppressed, and they were suppressed." Then, to have had his son die — that was the worst tragedy of all, "far heavier than any political disappointment or disaster can possibly be." He had felt, he wrote, "deserted by mankind." This election was redemption. To those who said the office was beneath a president, he said no call from his countrymen was too small and no service too humble. To himself, he admitted that it was the people's approbation that he craved. He had not been forgotten; he was needed.

But he was alone in his feelings. "No election or appointment conferred upon me ever gave me so much pleasure," he confided to himself. "I say this to record my sentiments; but no stranger intermeddleth with my joys, and the dearest of my friends have no sympathy with my sensations."

His wife made no effort to hide her unhappiness. When her sons, alarmed by her refusal to come to Washington, urged her to reconsider, she lashed out. What was being asked of her was not fair. She appealed to her rights. A republican marriage was taken to be egalitarian, modeled on friendship and reciprocity. But Louisa took it further. Didn't a wife, after all, have *rights* — even if those rights were not acknowledged, not protected, and not invoked? "In the marriage compact there are as in every other two parties, each of which have rights strictly defined by law and by the usages of society. In that compact the parties agree before the face of heaven to promote as far as in their power the welfare and happiness of each other," she wrote. "The woman being the weaker of the two is expected and does nine times out of ten make great sacrifices for her husband" — but enough was enough. What did she have to show for her sacrifices? Poor health? Comfort? "The grave of my lost child?" She railed against "the grasping ambition which is an insatiable passion swallowing and consuming all in its ever devouring maw."

Her rage, though, was impotent. In the end, she gave in. She would come south, she wrote to John, because of money. John Quincy's finances were under stress. It would be expensive to keep Louisa in Quincy over the winter. The house was derelict, and it would cost too much to make it comfortable for her to live in over the winter. The chimneys were faulty, the windows leaked, and the mansard roof needed replacing. After buying his father's land, John Quincy was land rich but in debt. His $25,000 presidential salary — which had also had to support the expenses of living and entertaining in the White House — was gone. He was helping to support not only his children but his extended family. The Columbia Mill, which he had bought in haste before the 1824 election, saddled him with tens of thousands of dollars in debt. In 1832, he calculated that he owed $42,000. She knew the details well enough. "He does not know where to turn at this moment for a dollar," she would later tell John. In Washington, they would be able to live at John and Mary's house, at 1601 I Street, along with their granddaughters Mary Louisa and Fanny, and so save rent.

"I have no right to encumber the family with expenses because I brought poverty into it," she wrote, her pen a knife nicking the never-healed wound her father's bankruptcy had left. She slashed at her husband as well. "To pretend that I make this sacrifice willingly would be ridiculous and false."

She reached Washington just before Christmas and found the place cold and drenched. "The city is more gloomy than you can imagine," she wrote to Charles, with more than a hint of satisfaction in her voice. "Rain! Rain! Rain!" Water streamed down the walls and the ground sank beneath feet. When the rain finally stopped, the temperature dropped and the river froze.

At first, Louisa was as miserable as the weather. "All the troubles I foresaw are breaking around us," she wrote to Charles in early January. On New Year's Day, between three and four hundred people had come to the house to pay their respects, leaving her "utterly exhausted." Andrew Jackson's lieutenants Martin Van Buren and Edward Livingston had come to visit as if they were old friends, but she avoided them. Had she spoken to them, "my feelings might have got the better of my judgment." She saw herself doing wrong at every turn: insulting Thomas Jefferson's daughter Martha Randolph; offending Mary and her sisters; antagonizing John Quincy. Less than a quarter of a mile south, in the White House, her nemesis, Andrew Jackson, now seemed to run the country as if he were a king in a farce. "I only mention it to show you how correct I was in my gloomy forebodings."

Her thoughts often slipped into deep, well-worn grooves of despondency. Her self-reprobations were constant, her tone self-pitying. She was a burden, she claimed; she was "the cause of disunion" in the family. She was sick of the craven habits and selfish ambitions of politicians. Democracy, she wrote, turned governance to politics and politics into perpetual campaigns. "In an elective government where the fame is never allowed to expire: but, like the vestal are, is forever renewed and kept alive by the most combustible materials: even the hearts of the most honest must at last be kindled into rage; by the constant unshrinking malevolence of party spirit; and the judgment obscured by the rankling and ever accumulating thorns, that like the venemous bites of paltry muske-toes wound by the perpetual itteration of the sting, until the whole mass of the blood is enflamed and corrupted," she wrote, her di-ary becoming a screed. Sometimes, she talked about George.

Her mood, though, was always up and down, and as the weeks passed it was more often improved. By the end of January she was waving off her complaints as "a silly feeling of pique." The political machinations exhausted her, but they also exhilarated her, as they had when John Quincy was secretary of state — perhaps even more so now that she had less at stake. She tunneled her way out of her depressions with the sharp spade of her sardonic humor, making hilarious what might have been intolerable. As a congressman's wife, with no ambition to speak of (or deny), and with some — however short — distance from the President's House, she had more freedom. As an observer, she had no one to please but herself and her correspondents. "My experience has taught me; that Shakespeare thoroughly read mankind when he blended the ridiculous among the most distressing of his tragic scenes," she once wrote to a friend. "In my career such have I found human nature." Her voice flashed with laughter, and she gained a reputation for her skewering wit. She was a master at *lusus politica,* as Benjamin Waterhouse, one of the cofounders of Harvard Medical School, described her jokes about Washington.

Her sharp edge was sharper, though, because her anger was undiminished. If anything, her fury at Jackson and his supporters had intensified after George's death. Like something wounded, she took wild swipes at the administration. Jackson was a lion, or half horse and half alligator; his administration was one of foxes and grubs. After Martin Van Buren was elected president, she heard that his grandmother's name, Goes, was pronounced "goose" by the Dutch, and she quipped:

For the King of the Beasts we find no
    further use
And the choice of the Nation now falls on a
    — Goose —

As usual, she disclaimed any interest in or knowledge of what was happening in government. "Of politics I can write but little," she would write to Charles or his wife, Abby, before launching into news. "We have no news," she would say, and then go on to report all the news: "Mr. Webster took tea here last evening. You will have heard that Justice Baldwin has gone crazy. It is announced that Mr. Buchanan is to be recalled from St. Petersburg and to take his place. Mr. Smith the Register is to be P.M. in N.Y. in the place of Governor, and it is whispered that Noah is to come here to edit the official." She was like her husband in some way. "Your father is in high spirits dabbling as usual in public affairs while *fancying he has nothing* to do with them," she wrote to her son John.

She set herself up as a truth teller, a kind of Greek chorus in a tragedy — someone who would step back and comment upon the action, who would say what others would not. She tracked everything — bills, appointments, scandals; who was in, who was out. "*Swartout* is *here,* and it is rumoured has *frightened* the P. into the recent measures," she would write. "Amons holds his head as high as ever, but rumour says he *totters.*" Her pen flew across the page, speeding through news and gossip, updates about the Panic of 1837, the Seminole War in Florida, or presidential elections. "We are so inundated with *newspapers* from every corner of the country, that I expect like Dr. Valpy's hero to go off some day in a blazing idea. It is true there is a good deal of fire in some of them but many contain only bitter ashes that make the reader sick. I wish some means could be taken to put a stop to this paper currency or we shall surely *stop payment*!!!"

Politics, she finally admitted to Charles, were her "bread meat and desert."

But family was her real sustenance. To her surprise, living with John and Mary was a good arrangement. Parenthood had changed the two of them, she thought — made Mary softer, John more generous, and both more tender and attentive. Her grandchildren astonished her. "Louisa is a lovely child with an intellect that almost frightens me," the girl's grandmother wrote, "wild" but also "everything that can be wished. As to Fanny she is one of those gifted things that seem to have been formed in an existence prior to her birth."

Within a year, Charles and Abby were having children of their own; they named their first, a daughter, Louisa Catherine Adams. "When I venture to anticipate what the rising generation are to produce," Louisa wrote to Abby, watching her grandchildren grow, "I am lost in ecstasy of wonder, and entirely deny Solomon's assertion that there is nothing new under the sun."

The biblical allusion was not unusual. More and more often, her lines would curve into the familiar phrases or parables of Scripture, sometimes spiraling tighter and tighter, until the train of her thought was diverted altogether. Louisa had always had a strong religious impulse, ever since her childhood in Nantes, when she'd fallen to her knees on the stone floor to worship the wretched figure of Jesus on the cross. During her time in the President's House and especially after George's death, her religiosity had become more reflexive. Almost anything — any little provocation, stray comment, or beautiful sight — could trigger her reflections. More and more often, as she grew older, her letters ended in homilies. She would say: only in Christ could she find comfort, only in God forgiveness. Her words would veer toward the formulaic. In contrast to the originality of her own language, her prayers sounded genuine but rote. This was not a bad thing to her. She wanted the strength of inherited tradition, the sense of submitting what she could not understand to the wisdom of something she could never know. Sounding new was not her aim.

No one blinked when she spoke of God and the superiority of Christianity to all other philosophies and modes of faith. Her fervor, after all, was no hotter than that of many at the time, and not as intense as that of some. An evangelical spirit was sweeping through the country. Men — and some women — were riding from town to town preaching salvation, and calling for people to receive the spirit and to be born again. Revivals crowded town greens; denominations fissured; sects built new communities. Not far from Quincy, people — some of whom she knew — were talking about the inherent goodness of men instead of their natural depravity, about the divine spark in nature, and about the purity of the individual uncorrupted by the corrosions of conventions. It was in this far-flung and fertile religious climate, the Second Great Awakening, that she turned and turned again toward Christianity.

That atmosphere affected her, but only indirectly, as the weather does. She kept a careful distance. Twice, she went to see the Shakers in New York, and was at once fascinated, admiring, and repelled. She read about Unitarianism and Swedenborgianism, which appalled her; if doctrines undermining the divinity of Christ were adopted, she trembled to think where the subversion would end. Transcendentalism perplexed her; she thought it left "nothing but shadows behind a mass of ideal and imaginative confusion." But she was hardly a traditionalist herself. She often skipped church and had no special love for ministers of any kind. Her faith had always been idiosyncratic, out of line with almost everyone around her. Raised an Anglican, and with early exposure to the Catholic Church in Nantes, she was inclined toward the aesthetic pleasures of Episcopalianism, the way the forms and language spoke to the heart. In 1837, her confirmation in Rock Creek Church, near the graves of her mother and her sister Nancy, gave her more of a "melancholy satisfaction" than an actual commitment to the Episcopal Church. Living abroad, she had attended whatever service was nearby, if any at all, and her confirmation did not change her flexibility. God was too much of a mystery for men to assume their own answers were true. She was, she wrote, "*bigoted* to no creed."

She was sure, though, that she did not like Puritanism, which she thought too cold and stony, or transcendentalism, which was complacent and naive. Once, on a trip by herself north, she found herself seated with a "very *pretty* transcendental companion," eighteen years old, just graduated from college and about to study in Heidelberg. He "hopes shortly to compete with his great friend Carlysle; his protoype Emerson . . . he is to supersede Kant etc. etc., to correct the errors which have crept in to our religious faith, and to produce a revelation far exceeding any yet discovered by the Christian World," she wrote, bemused. "We are to be entirely independent of everything but the *divinity within ourselves.*" He was, she continued, pointedly, "a Virginia aristocrat and a slave holder; and thinks *our sex* very well calculated to write pretty familiar letters; and to live in modest seclusion, taking care of their husbands and children and superintending their servants." One can easily picture her cocked head and bemused smile.

But there was poignancy, too, in her portrait. His simplicity, sensitivity, and sweetness she found "really attractive and winning: and it recalled to my mind too forcibly the past, where I had so often witnessed the same ambitious yearnings, hoping *so much,* only to be blasted by death and disappointment." Her mind, it seems, was turning to another young man with a poetic soul — to her son, whom she had loved and lost. Her traveling companion "seems to me to be one of those beautiful visionaries, whose vitality is to be extinguished in the too great brightness of its own blaze, which while it illumines the mind, consumes the body which contains it, and leaves no trace behind."

She had watched her children die and mourned the loss of those who had not been born; she had been blasted by death and disappointment. She had seen too much corruption to believe in the perfectibility of man, and she knew too much of her own darkness to believe in the untrammeled divinity within herself. She had experienced worldly success through her husband's career, and had played a real and unmistakable part in it, but that had not brought her real and lasting happiness. She often felt lonely. Her body was forever breaking down. Sicknesses scared her — even though she declared herself, often with a maudlin flourish, ready for death. She was never ready for the deaths of those around her, and terror at the idea consumed her. In 1832, when Louisa was in Quincy, a cholera outbreak killed thousands along the East Coast and gripped the population in terror. In her letters, she returned to the threat of cholera again and again. Other serious ailments threatened the family: scarlet fever, influenza, undiagnosable maladies. John could "scarcely crawl." Mary was losing weight. "Their suffering is *real*," Louisa wrote to John Quincy, "ours only imaginary."

When Louisa was anxious or sad, her religious beliefs became a lens that she turned on herself. She used religion like a magnifying glass, not only to study her own sins but as a tool to start a fire. She would catch a ray of truth and use herself as tinder, as if her soul were like withered grass. It might burn, but from the scorched earth would come new growth.

3

She had outbursts of shame. They came
unprompted, at any time. But they had
special intensity in the summer of 1834.
Instead of returning to Quincy for the summer with her husband, she had stayed behind
in Washington to take care of her brother,
Thomas, who was sick, and her son John,
who was also unwell. The stress of the situation seems to have affected her and provoked,
with a vengeance, her self-doubt. When John
Quincy wrote to praise her kindness to those
around her, she turned against herself, and
her response streamed out in a rush of
uninterrupted anguish and regret for her
"rash acts uncharitable constructions mistakes never properly elucidated and false
impressions." She lamented "the most unhappy effects" that her mistakes had upon
herself. Her temper, she wrote, was "wildly
irascible and rendered by mortification disappointment and misfortune I fear vindictive."
John Quincy was gentle in his response.

"There is nothing vindictive — nothing unkind — nothing ungenerous in your natural disposition — nor after all that you have suffered in the world or by the world, or even by those whom you loved, and from whom you had the right to expect love in return, after all there is nothing but full and overflowing kindness and affection in your nature now," he wrote. His grammar was contorted, as hers had been in her lament, but the thought was clear. Everyone surrounding her knew the goodness of her heart, he wrote — most of all himself.

But she replied that she did not deserve his kindness, and she could not accept it. Only the grace of God could offer comfort, and only by his standards could she be judged. "Truth therefore must be severe: and the leniency that hoodwinks it, is decidedly vicious." With a wrenched, wrenching tone of submission, she asked for John Quincy's forgiveness for subjecting his temper to so many trials.

Her severity was extreme, but so was the situation she then faced. If she felt the hand of God pressing against her, plunging her down, it is no wonder. Her second son, John, was dying, and she was watching it happen in front of her.

John was only twenty-nine years old when his body began to shut down. For several years, his illnesses — periods of blindness and weakness, symptoms that his parents, at least, flinched from describing — were hard for doctors to diagnose, but one thing was not a mystery. He was an alcoholic. "I do not know whether vices are hereditary in families," Charles wrote in his diary the following summer, 1833, while John was visiting Quincy, "but it would almost seem so from the number of examples which one meets with. The Smith blood" — his grandmother Abigail's family — "seems to have had the scourge of intemperance dreadfully applied to it."

Living with him, Louisa and John Quincy saw his decline too clearly. Their alarm turned to panic as his health grew worse. John, Louisa wrote to Charles in 1833, was "seldom able to get out of his bed until twelve o'clock and then shuffles about the house wrapt up in his wadded coat." She and John Quincy tried to help, tried to bolster him as they never had before. They were clearly scared and desperate. Louisa praised his talents and urged him to try writing fiction, perhaps hoping that he would find the outlet in writing that she had found for herself. John Quincy's hectoring about John's management of the Columbia Mill ceased, even though the mill faltered. Instead, he and Louisa praised John's effort and diligence.

In July 1834, it became clear that their encouragement was not enough. John was giving up and letting go. Louisa asked John Quincy to help her persuade John to leave Washington altogether. "The convenience resulting from the residence of our children in this place for political purposes has blinded us to the truth of its difficulties in so far as it regards any possibility of promoting their personal interests," she wrote to John Quincy. Her reference to their residence "for political purposes" was as accusatory as it was desperate, of course, and even then she could not resist a jab about the sacrifices the family had made for John Quincy's ambitions. "In no way as you know have I ever been consulted or have I ever participated in the settlement of my children" — a pointed reminder of those many years of separation, against her will, long ago — "but it is impossible for me any longer to remain a silent spectator when I think timely and judicious exertion might save them from years of misery."

John Quincy listened. He urged John to leave the District and move to Quincy. "I say it with a heart full of affection and of anxiety," he wrote on July 23. Three days later, he coaxed his son again. "Nothing could be more easy. . . . Come and stay here the remainder of this unparalleled summer, recruit your health, recruit your spirits, and take time to consider what you shall determine upon for your future prospects. . . . Washington is no place for enterprize. Here so long as I live and have a house over my head, it shall be yours and your children's."

Faced with few alternatives, John started to make arrangements to move. But the plans moved slowly, because John's body, mind, and will were failing. Louisa left for Quincy without him on July 31, bringing her young granddaughter Mary Louisa with her. She brought the child reluctantly; she was having premonitions of her own death. But her conviction that her son would die first was stronger, and she begged John to hurry his departure from Washington, hoping that it might save him. "I shall be perfectly miserable until I hear that you have left the city as the health of yourself your wife and Fanny's make it essential and the season leaves no time for deliberation," she wrote from Philadelphia. If he needed money, she added, then he should sell her silver breadbasket and waiter and take the money for himself. "Do not hesitate to take this step as they are my own and if they can prove serviceable they will yield me more pleasure and more solid wealth than they ever have since I have owned them."

To his wife, Mary, she wrote, "Language cannot express the affection I bear him."

It was too late. On Monday, October 6, a letter arrived from Caroline saying that both Mary and John were very sick. Twelve days later, on Saturday afternoon, October 18,

Charles received a letter from Mary's brother Walter saying that John's situation was critical. Charles rode out to Quincy immediately, arriving just after dinner, and gave the letter to his father.

"Then came the most trying part of it, the disclosure to my Mother," Charles wrote in his diary afterward. Her suffering, John Quincy recorded, was "agonizing" to watch. She had been ill herself since the beginning of September and was still unable to walk across the room. Still, she insisted that she would go to Washington, changing her mind only when the doctor arrived to convince her that the trip would kill her.

John Quincy left the next morning, traveling by a succession of steamboats — including the *Benjamin Franklin,* the boat from which his George was lost — and stages and railway. The trip that had once taken weeks of fast travel now took, though at a punishing pace, three days. Even that was not fast enough. He arrived at his son's house on October 22 at ten at night. John was already unconscious. John Quincy bent down and kissed his son's smooth, warm brow.

He found Mary upstairs, "emaciated." When she saw him, she began to cry. "I promised her," he wrote, "that I would be a father to her and her children."

Around two in the morning, John Quincy went to sleep. At half past four, he woke up and went to John's room. Caroline's husband Nathaniel Frye was there, closing John's eyes. John was thirty-one years old.

"My dearest, best beloved friend," John Quincy wrote to Louisa later that day. "Your message to our dear departed child, was faithfully retained by me, to be delivered in all its tenderness and affection, so far as a father's lips can speak the words of a mother's heart." He had not been able to give it to John in time, but had John been able to speak, "he would repeat to you the same message in almost your words."

By the time his letter reached her, she knew what it would say. On October 26, Kitty and William Smith had appeared at the house in Quincy. Charles greeted them. They came from New York, where they had received a letter from Thomas Johnson saying that John was dead. They had traveled to Quincy straightaway.

Charles went upstairs to his mother's room. When she asked who had come to the door, he told her that it was Kitty. He did not need to say anything else; she knew why her sister had come. "She lay in a state of almost stupor for some time," he wrote in his diary, "followed by a violent and indefinite emotion."

A year later, on Sunday, November 6, 1835, she began another diary. On the first page of the book, she wrote:

Mélanges d'une
Délassée

It means: Miscellaneous writings of one who is refreshed. It seems possible that she may have meant to write *Mélanges d'une / Délaissée* — miscellaneous writings of one who is forsaken.

She began the diary in despair and anger. She opened with a question: "Is it not singular that I can scarcely ever make an observation upon any subject without clashing with the opinions or the prejudices of some one or other?" At church that morning, Mary and Caroline had been appalled when she refused to approach the altar to take communion. They were horrified by her explanation: "I said that I felt afraid to present myself at the Lords table; as there was still a livid spot in my heart." In that moment, the proxy target of her anger was Andrew Jackson. She was furious with him; she could not forgive him for how his campaign had insulted her and her family, especially John.

"The spirit of forgiveness is angelic," she wrote, "and I would fain feel as my loved Son did, when four or five months before he died he said, in that tender tone of melancholy enthusiasm. 'Mother I am at peace with all mankind; I know not the living being that I would harm.' " She was not at peace with all men. John Quincy wrestled with his Christian faith after John's death, but quietly. Christian resignation, he wrote, was "my duty, but is not always in my power." Louisa, though, felt herself to be in a full state of rebellion — against herself, against others, and so against God.

This diary, unlike most of the ones that she had written before, was not meant for the eyes of others. It was private. It was not a record of her days but of her mind, her confusion, her doubts, her convictions, her desires, her prayers, her hopelessness. Over that long winter and spring, she wrote searchingly about the nature of free will, predestination, and the frailties of human nature. She asked questions and proposed answers. What was the relationship between reason, will, and conscience? "As I understand reason the so much boasted triumph of man is the medium by which will is actuated and conscience the means by which *will* is govern'd." The next day, a revision: "I should say conscience dictates — Reason regulates — and impulse is the action of human instinct — always true to human nature but often in contradiction to conscience and reason combined."

At the start of the diary especially, she wrote as a penitent, sometimes in language borrowed from the psalms. The appeal of those verses to her is obvious, in their expressions of pain, guilt, stain, darkness, light, cleansing, mercy, and redemption. They offered her a way through her pain, an inward path to salvation. By this exercise, she could weave her personal crisis into a larger but still intensely private pattern of confession and redemption. They connected pain of the body with pain of the soul. They helped her say, with the weight of ages but in a lone thin voice, "My God my god have mercy on me." They gave her a language to describe her "stains of despair"; they gave her words to send up "the cry of my desolation." She borrowed from the psalms. There was a story there, a story about a king who finds himself divided not only from God but from his family. Echoing the psalms allowed her to praise God even when she was anguished. They allowed for the otherness of God and the loneliness of a woman. If she could submit, she might then be able to transcend. Her prayers let her acknowledge her faith despite her doubt: "Forsake me not in the hour of my distress, and if this is religion teach me not to despise it."

It took something heroic not only to survive but to see the worth in her life, and to make something of it. She endured months, as she had endured years, of suffering, sometimes mixed with boredom. She punished herself often, especially for the deaths of her children. "O my racked conscience," she wrote in her diary, "night and day I reproach myself for my passiveness and never shall I cease to regret the past for I was a — Mother." The following June, 1836, she opened her diary again. John Quincy was still chained to his desk in the House, once even through the night. The weather was hot and oppressive. She might have given way to her grief, or dwelled on her powerlessness or her children's deaths or her father's bankruptcy. She might have felt wretched and looked for solace only in God.

But she did something else — something extraordinary. Instead of thinking of how she had failed, she thought of something she had accomplished, something of which she could be proud. She began thinking about her journey from St. Petersburg to Paris. As she saw it now, it was not only a good story. It was something that had meaning — and something from which she could *make* meaning, something from which she could illuminate, for herself and others, something of her fortitude, her inventiveness, her curiosity — something of her personality, and indeed her very self. And in that, she might find a larger meaning, a lesson that could apply to all women.

It occurred to her that it might help for other women to hear it, because women as a rule heard so little that encouraged them to be brave and strong. They were discouraged from exerting their existence. Women were shadows in the histories of men. She knew that well. While her husband debated the admission of the new states Michigan and Arkansas, while he thundered in defense of fundamental freedoms, disregarding cries of "Order! Order!" she stayed inside, fell ill, claimed to be quiet. Since her children had been grown, she had been told that boredom was her lot. Louisa had been constrained by conventions and buried by tragedy. Many people were crushed by much less than what she had to bear. Many accepted their fate in silence. It took courage, then, to underscore her existence — to say that she was "one, *who was.*"

"Narrative of a Journey from Russia to France" begins at five o'clock in the evening on the 12th of February, the moment that she departed St. Petersburg, and ends the moment she arrived in her husband's hotel room in Paris. She had made no notes during the journey itself; she had only her memory and perhaps the letters she had sent to John Quincy, which he had saved, to rely upon. She disavowed her capacity for — and interest in — research, but she must have used a map; her geography was, for the most part, surprisingly good. She put a great deal of effort into it. She worked on the text, writing a second draft on unbound pages, for at least a year and a half.

This was not a private remembrance. It was

written to be read "at some future day" —
written for those who knew her, but perhaps
also for those who did not. In the American
tradition of autobiography, she meant to
encourage emulation. It was the story about
the making of a self — and in particular, a
female self. She wanted to show that women
were stronger and braver than they were said
to be. She thought her story might "show that
many undertakings which appear very difficult and arduous to my sex, are by no means
so trying as imagination forever depicts them
— And that energy and discretion, follow the
necessity of their exertion, to protect the
fancied weakness of feminine imbecility."

She wrote about Baptiste, innkeepers,
haggard soldiers she had passed on the road,
frightened faces of the women she met, cries
of *Vive Napoléon!* She remembered the practical difficulties she had overcome: the moment the carriage wheel had come loose, the
problem of procuring servants, the dangerous decision to ford a half-frozen river. She
wrote about her growing confidence, which
rippled out of her descriptions and into her
voice. Her story was energetic and clear and
a little romantic, which was understandable,
because there was romance in what she had
been through.

Her story was her own. No other woman in
America had experienced anything like it. But
she made its lessons universal. It was a story

about women and what women could achieve. She was, as ever, ambivalent; it was her weakness, she claimed, that encouraged her to have faith that she would be protected. Yet she also did not deny her strength. She wrote: "Under all circumstances, we must never desert ourselves."

■ ■ ■ ■

PART TEN:
IN MY OWN NAME

Washington and Quincy, 1836–1852

■ ■ ■ ■

There was more behind Louisa's impulse to write "Narrative of a Journey" than resilience. Tragedy was not her only school. She had begun to think about women's rights and responsibilities more broadly, prodded by what she saw in public, not only private, life. She was forced into thought at times, and there were days when she would say it was all too much. She would close her door, stay in her room. But even there, her thoughts dogged her. How could she account for herself and her life? What rights and responsibilities did people have — women, Americans, politicians, slaves? Louisa was about to turn sixty-two — at a time when the life expectancy of an American white woman was around forty — but she was still growing. She was asking questions that the nation's leaders were strenuously trying to avoid — or most of them were. John Quincy was the great exception.

Louisa had not planned on being at the

Capitol on February 6, 1837, when John Quincy took part in an extraordinary scene. She was only there trying to "spin out the time." An afternoon of returning visits with her niece Elizabeth Adams had gone long; it had grown late, until it was nearly time for the House of Representatives to adjourn. Elizabeth proposed that they visit the Rotunda, which had been completed in time for Lafayette's visit to the city, so that Louisa could see Colonel Trumbull's new paintings. They would wait in the library until John Quincy was ready for a ride home.

Had Louisa mentioned to John Quincy that she would be at the Capitol that day, he might have told her not to come. It was Monday, a petition day, time set aside for the House to hear what the people wanted from their representatives. The petitions could concern anything at all; they were commonly called "prayers." That particular Monday was Massachusetts' turn in the roll call. Everyone in the House knew what kind of prayers the old representative from Massachusetts would deliver. Everyone knew that a fight was coming — John Quincy most of all, because John Quincy was the one who planned on provoking it.

For more than a year, Congress had been engaged in a battle over the right of the people to petition the House for the abolition of the slave trade and of slavery in the District of Columbia, and other issues that touched on the South's "peculiar institution" — though calls for immediate abolition of slavery altogether were still rare. Since the "Missouri question" had inflamed Congress more than fifteen years earlier, the fight over the expansion of slavery had been ever present but largely sublimated, fought in proxy battles over federal powers and the right of states to nullify laws. But the previous winter, the issue had surfaced and would not be suppressed — largely because one man, John Quincy, now refused to stay silent. He was relentless. He tried to submit the pleas, one after another. They came from Dorchester, from South Weymouth, from Plymouth and Salem. Their signatures numbered in the hundreds, sometimes thousands. They called for forbidding slavery in the territories, for repealing the gag rule, for ending the internal slave trade. Antislavery petitioners (many of them women), driven by a confluence of religious zeal and a culture of uplift, and able to mobilize because of vastly improved communications and transportation, were flooding the offices of sympathetic congressmen with letters. Some rolls had a few signatures, some had thousands. No one introduced more of these petitions than Louisa's husband.

Southern "hotspurs" hated and feared John Quincy. Behind him they saw a phantom army of abolitionist "fanatics," and behind the abolitionists they saw the specter of their own slaves ready to rise up violently against them. The Southerners were terrified of insurrections, terrified that any encouragement from Congress might spark a slave rebellion. They kept stoking memories of revolts like the one in Southampton County, Virginia, in 1831, led by Nat Turner, in which some sixty whites were murdered. The Northern congressmen, by contrast, were nervous, disordered, and ineffective. Most of them were sympathetic to slave owners, keenly aware of the political and practical difficulties of emancipation, and racist. Abolition was a dirty word in much of the North, too.

John Quincy was not an abolitionist. He saw a civil war coming and thought his job was to forestall it. But the abolitionists looked to him to carry their message, if not yet to endorse it. He stood up. That spring of 1836, Congress passed a "gag rule" ordering that any petition regarding slavery would be immediately tabled without discussion. Nothing could have strengthened John Quincy's resolve more. He stood up again. When his name was called for the vote on the gag rule, he did not say yea or nay but instead cried out, "I hold the resolution to be a direct violation of the constitution of the United States, the rules of this House, and the rights of my constituents." Since then, he had constantly tested the resolution, and that February 6, he planned his biggest challenge yet.

When they arrived at the Capitol, Louisa and Elizabeth summoned a member of the House to show them into the Rotunda. As Louisa waited to see the famous scenes painted by Colonel John Trumbull — the signing of the Declaration of Independence, the surrenders of General Burgoyne and Lord Cornwallis, George Washington resigning his commission — perhaps her mind was on the painter. After all, Colonel Trumbull had played a great role in her life. He had tried to teach her to paint, had introduced her to her husband in London, and had told her that he wished he were younger, for he would have pursued her himself. Whatever she was thinking in that moment, though, was forgotten when she saw George Lay, a young congressman from New York, approaching. He looked distressed. He told the women that "the House was in a state of *prodigious excitement;* Mr. Adams being the principal actor." He was not sure they should go inside. The women went to the library instead and were looking at "some choice views of the Rhine" when Lay reappeared. The scene in the House had calmed, and John Quincy was speaking. Louisa and Elizabeth went into the House chamber to watch him.

They made their way to the gallery, behind

the oval of the members' mahogany desks that ringed the Speaker's chair. John Quincy, sixty-nine years old, was just sitting down.

He had shrunk a little since the last time she had seen him in that cavernous space, when he was secretary of state. His great, round, bald head had sunk toward his small but mighty chest; white sideburns framed the sharp lineaments of his face. But he had a way of appearing bigger and more immovable than he was. His opponents usually described the small man in gigantic terms, so great was their fury against him alone.

That morning he had introduced a petition from "nine ladies of Fredericksburg" calling for the prohibition of the slave trade in the federal city. The petition was of course tabled under the gag rule, but a member from Virginia saw the women's names on the document and announced that he recognized one, a "free mulatto woman of the worst fame and reputation." And how, John Quincy asked slyly and suggestively, did the good congressman know of this woman's bad reputation? He followed that by approaching the Speaker's chair to ask about the status of another petition, one purported to be sent by slaves. The House erupted. "Expel him!" members cried. "Expel him! He ought to be expelled!" Quickly, Southern members drew up resolutions to censure him. The member from Massachusetts — the former president of the

United States — had "committed an outrage on the rights and feelings of a large portion of the people of this Union, a flagrant contempt on the dignity of this House; and by extending a privilege only belonging to freemen, directly incites the slave population to insurrection; and that the said member be forthwith called to the bar of the House, and censured by the Speaker," their proposed resolution declared. A congressman from Georgia shouted that the petition from slaves should be carried out of the Capitol and burned.

Representatives from antislavery states, meanwhile, sat silently. A few members sympathetic to John Quincy may have tried to reach the floor, but the Speaker, future president of the United States James K. Polk, an ardent slaveholder, made sure not to see their approach.

Three days later, John Quincy would hold the floor for the full day to defend himself. This was the way the representative body of Congress conducted debates, he thundered — by silencing them! This was the contempt with which the champions of slavery held the rights of people from another state — not to mention the first right of a democracy! Sarcasm gleamed in his words. He was almost playful as he tugged the rug from under his opponents' feet. They had been too quick to dismiss the petition from slaves without reading it. In fact, he revealed, the slaves were petitioning *not* to abolish slavery. Did the slave owners disagree?

At this trick, the enraged congressmen exploded again. At their desks, they furiously revised their resolutions: John Quincy had "committed a gross contempt of the House." He had "trifled with the House." He should "receive the censure of the House."

John Quincy did not agree with the many petitioners who came to him saying that it was the right moment for abolition, he continued, or even to end the slave trade in the District; his argument was not to end slavery. His defense was only of the right to petition, which he held up as sacred. It was the foundational right not only of the people of the United States but of humanity. "Petition is supplication — it is entreaty — it is prayer! . . . And, so far from refusing to present a petition because it might come from those low in the estimation of the world, it would be an additional incentive, if such an incentive were wanting," he told the House.

The fury had not died when Abijah Mann of New York, a free state, stepped in to defend John Quincy — or at least as much as anyone would defend him that night. It was true, Mann said, that the representative from Massachusetts was putting on a "deplorable spectacle." But perhaps they should excuse him, because he was old, and perhaps a little senile. "The high noontide of that life has long since passed with him," Mann said, "and its wane is no doubt upon him, before he is either aware or sensible of it." Surely some allowance, "by the aid of liberal charity," Mann suggested, should stay the vote that would censure him.

John Quincy was indeed old, the oldest member of the House. His eyes watered, and his lungs strained for breath, and his hands trembled; he was known to fall asleep at his desk. But he was also known for enduring marathon sessions — seventeen hours, twenty-eight hours — with only a few crackers in his pocket or a thumb of stale bread. Mann's belittling speech could not touch him. People talked about him now as a force of nature: a lion, an elephant. One who watched him withstand the attacks by the proslavery faction said it was like seeing "the sting of so many musquitoes upon the hide of a rhinoceros." Ralph Waldo Emerson put it best. "When they talk about his old age and venerableness and nearness to the grave, he knows better," Emerson wrote. "He is like one of those old cardinals, who, as quick as he is chosen Pope, throws away his crutches and his crookedness, and is as straight as a boy. He is an old roué, who cannot live on slops, but must have sulpheric acid in his tea."

His wife was different. A ripple had passed through the chamber when the members noticed that the small old woman, dressed in mourning, was present. Heads swiveled to see Mrs. Adams and gauge her reaction. "I found myself," she wrote, "in the brunt of the fight."

The feeling of a fight, at least, was real: she fought within herself. On the one hand, Louisa opposed slavery; on the other hand, she dreaded turning against her family. Opposing Southerners meant opposing the Johnsons, the name she had clung to and defended for so long. "Although I can fairly justify your fathers opinion, and fully discriminate the justice of his cause; still I deplore the necessity which brings him in contact so often and so painfully with the public," she wrote to Charles. "You know that I can have no southern feeling on the subject, other than sympathy with my connections."

For more than a year she had struggled with her divided loyalties: her husband and her abstract sense of the injustice of slavery on one side; her sisters and relatives, her prejudices against blacks, and her fear of violence on the other. "Every friend is turned into an enemy; and now the prospect terminates with the fear of losing the love, the friendship and the society of my own nearest and dearest connections," she wrote when John Quincy first spoke out publicly against slavery. Her sisters' husbands were slaveholders, and her brother had a morbidly paranoid "fear of blacks." Her niece Mary may have set Rachel Clark free in 1828 — and Rachel may have been on good enough terms with the family to continue working for the Adamses as a domestic servant, as it appears she did — but Mary remained openly proslavery.

Louisa wasn't afraid to let the Johnson side of her family know that she disagreed with them. "John Randolph's exit was attended with one good act at least the emancipation of his slaves," she had written to Mary after Randolph died. "You will not approve of this act nevertheless it is a good and an honourable one which will give more real fame to his memory than all the éclat his talents ever produced." In her diary, though, Louisa was more conflicted and anguished. Her compassion was limited. As she had during the Missouri debates, she wanted politicians to remain silent on the subject, even at the cost of perpetuating an injustice. "The awful question of slavery is before the publick and the question is of so fearfully exciting a nature it keeps me in a state of perpetual alarm — God has said blessed are the peace makers! then why should we to promote the ends of a few factious politicians endanger the lives of thousands? or occasion panics and alarms almost worse than death?"

She could imagine the real battles too clearly — the scenes of wreckage, the rubble, the blood. She knew what war looked like; she had driven across battlefields herself. In fact, while writing her "Narrative of a Journey," she had just been thinking of those weeks of passing through an exhausted, war-torn Europe on her way from St. Petersburg to Paris. There were border wars already taking place in the United States, in Florida and Texas, wars that disturbed her. She connected them to the desire of slaveholders to expand and strengthen their hold, deploring "the injustice and oppression so wantonly shown; not only to the poor miserable Indians, who fight in a *just cause* to protect their *families,* their *property* and their *rights,*" she wrote, but also the injustice and maltreatment shown to the soldiers. She had nephews fighting on the borders, and she was mad with worry. When one of them died, she considered the loss of his life to be theft. "Our frontiers," she wrote, "will weep tears of blood."

Slavery would only end in war, and before that war, she imagined bloodshed of another kind. She shared the widespread fear that slaves would rebel and unleash a wave of violence against whites, murdering them in their beds. For this imagined threat, abolitionists came in for nearly as much blame in her mind as militant slavocracy. If the moment had come for "the calamity which sooner or later must end the strife," she did not want her husband to be the agent, "the scourge through which this great event is to be atchieved." Like all but a small number of white Americans, she was too blind and prejudiced to see that slavery itself was predicated on and perpetuated by violence and brutality. She could not see that there was already a kind of civil war under way. Americans were fighting Americans — sometimes even their own relatives, though the white paternity of many slaves was never acknowledged. That unacknowledged civil war was waged on fields and inside houses throughout the South and West, fought against bodies and minds, with nooses and lashes — only the violence was almost all on one side.

Unlike most white Americans in the 1830s, though, she tried to face and understand her fears. In the weeks after witnessing the ferocious scene in the House, she repeatedly wrote about slavery in her diary. "Stray thoughts," she wrote the following Sunday — her sixty-second birthday. "It is often said that Scripture encourages and authorizes slavery!" But, she wrote, referencing Moses, Cain, Jacob, Ishmael, and Jesus's ministry, "the basis on which the principles of Christianity are founded, militate so strongly against the system of slavery, that it was utterly unnecessary" for Jesus to have preached against it. And then she would backpedal, repeating the racist cant of the day. "Death is the end destined to all; and even in our day we are forced to realize the sad truth; that there are races of men still existing on the earth, whom we can in no way civilise." Progress, she wrote, was a matter better left to God.

Her racism was not unusual, but it ran deep. She made crude claims about the pernicious tendencies of blacks. When she heard of a crime, she was quick to spread reports that a black person was suspected, even where there was no evidence. She treated blacks with suspicion and contempt. Her reaction to the plight of a woman in Washington named Dorcas Allen is illustrative. After having lived as free, Allen was about to be sold at auction — likely to work the deadly cotton or sugar fields of the Deep South — and committed infanticide rather than let her children also be sold. Louisa was sympathetic at first; she saw Dorcas primarily as a mother. She supported John Quincy's efforts to help untangle the complicated chain of ownership that finally allowed Allen's husband, a free black, to raise the funds to buy her (John Quincy himself gave fifty dollars). But when Allen called on Louisa, wearing her finest clothing — no doubt meaning a show of respect — Louisa was appalled and had her sent away. She had expected Allen to be wearing mourning attire, to look pitiful and grieving for her children, and had a bigoted response when Allen did not.

Even as John Quincy was leading the anti-slavery movement in the House, speaking out in ever more forceful terms, the Adamses remained, as ever, complicit in the District's complex economy of slavery. They followed a common practice in hiring a slave named Julia from her owner as an occasional servant. Even if part — or all — of the wages went to Julia herself, allowing her to save money with the hope of buying her freedom, the fact remained that Julia was a slave, subject to the whims of her owners. Louisa liked Julia, but her sympathy had short limits. When Julia, "an excellent servant," was about to be sold by her owner to "a brute, a Virginia slave holder," Louisa wrote that she wished she "could raise the sum wanted to release her from her bondage. . . . If I could be put into a way of raising a subscription for this purpose; I should be *very* happy." But Louisa was quick to add that she would *only* give a little money. "I could not appear in the business in *any way,* but by contributing."

As he had for years, Louisa's husband had more courage than she. He reached the pinnacle of his career, the presidency of the United States, only to find himself in the valley of his own despair. But instead of staying there, he found the higher challenge. Others fought to preserve the Union for the sake of its preservation. He fought to fulfill the promises that it had made. It took a rare imagination. It required traveling beyond, and sometimes against, the boundaries of Washington's polite society. (And even in this, his moral vision was limited. Though his antislavery credentials were beyond dispute, he believed that sexual relations between whites and blacks was, as he wrote in an essay about Shakespeare's *Othello,* "unnatural.") It may be that he came to oppose slavery rationally, through his reading and thinking, as historians usually assume. Or it may be that he came to it more emotionally, and more personally. In January 1843, after John Quincy had established himself as an antislavery crusader, Adelaide Hellen's former slave Jane Clark — by then, Jane Davis — appealed to John Quincy for help after her son, Joseph, whom Adelaide had owned and sold to a man who took him to Arkansas, was wrongfully resold after being promised his freedom. "Can I not possibly do something for this man?" John Quincy wrote in his diary after learning of the crime. The note of anguish in John Quincy's voice is clear; there may also be a note of regret. Jane Clark, Rachel Clark, and perhaps Joseph himself had lived with him for years. But he had not done anything when Adelaide sold Joseph in the first place, and so divided the Clark family. He had not done anything, and now it seemed he could do nothing. He had not worked to end slavery as president, and now there was a slaveholder, John Tyler, in the White House, willing to go to war to fight for Texas, wanting to go to war to expand the slave land. He could do something, at least, to counter that.

If Louisa learned of the Clark family's plight, she did not mention it in the few extant letters she wrote from that time. She sometimes did empathize with slaves — especially with women. But she was afraid of slave revolts, and also of the violence that defenders of slavery were willing to use. She felt threatened. She thought those who were organizing a grassroots network for the immediate abolition of slavery were irresponsible. She thought that the evangelical Christians who channeled their tremendous energy toward inflaming moral outrage against slavery were reckless. She considered her husband's stand — even as tentative as it was at first — dangerous to his country and to his family. As a moral question, she had once said, slavery was a clear evil. As a political and practical one, it made her shudder. "I am absolutely sick of politicks and would give anything almost for peace," she wrote Charles in February 1843.

John Quincy's position *was* dangerous. There were real threats against his life. He was isolated as the congressman to whom the abolitionists consistently turned, even if they were frustrated that he did not fight for more.

The scholar William Lee Miller tried to count the antislavery petitions submitted by the Twenty-fifth Congress, 1838–39, still in the archives of the House. John Quincy Adams submitted 693. The next, William Slade of Vermont, submitted 450. After that, the falloff was severe and instructive. Joshua Giddings presented 42, and eleven others had 15 or more. Even Charles, who would soon enter Massachusetts politics on an explicitly antislavery platform, thought his father was making a long series of big mistakes by insisting on pushing the issue. Louisa was furious with her husband for exposing himself (and her) to contempt and attacks, and feared for his safety, although she was fiercely proud of him.

At times, she saw a greater and nobler role for herself. Like her husband, it came late in her life. But she had a more conflicted sense of it than he did. She was not, on this subject, a heroine. But her struggle was a start.

2

At times, she was galvanized. The fight over the right to petition — however conflicted it made her feel — gave Louisa a goal and a grievance. A few weeks after witnessing her husband challenge Congress — a sight she had initially described with dismay — she was in a jesting, daring mood. Recalling the scene now exhilarated her. She now made herself out as a soldier. "The platoons came so swift and thick while I was present," she wrote at the end of February. "Instead of damping my spirit they seemed to produce a contrary effect, and inspired a degree of ardor to my hotspur head, fully equal in force and energy to their own." She delighted in her scorn for John Quincy's adversaries. "If you have ever seen a puppy in fits it will give you some idea of the *foaming violence* of the scene," she wrote. The proslavery faction "at last . . . sneaked away under the lash, which they had so well merited to receive."

It was lucky, she added, for the Southerners that she was not allowed to take part in the debate. Had she had "the *privilege of speech,* the ne plus ultra of woman's right," she continued, she would have "overmastered them by dint of *words,* notwithstanding the miserable deficiency of *ideas* which they so handsomely displayed."

The ne plus ultra of woman's right! It was a radical thing to say. Louisa put it playfully — but in a way that suggested something serious underneath. How to address the evils of slavery tore at her, but she connected it — as a small number of people, especially women, did — to the injustice of women's exclusion from politics. A woman's rights were supposed to be nonpolitical; they concerned her duties to her family and her family's duties to her. Even female reformers in the 1830s were not sure what to make of the interjection of female voices into the men's debates in Congress. Harriet Beecher Stowe, who would go on to write the seminal antislavery sentimental novel *Uncle Tom's Cabin,* criticized women who signed petitions. A woman, Stowe wrote, "takes a subordinate station" in civil and political decisions. Her interests were "entrusted to the other sex." She was emphatic and plain. "IN ALL CASES," Stowe wrote, petitions to Congress "fall entirely without the sphere of female duty."

Despite her battle cry about free speech and women's rights, Louisa did not quite know what to think of the petitions from women flooding her husband's office. She watched John Quincy disappear behind the tall stacks on his desk. He rose at three in the morning to file petitions before eating stewed peaches with a little warm milk and heading to the House. The petitions were a nuisance, and she was resentful that her husband fielded the lion's share of them — from all over the country, not just from his own constituents. "O these hosts of petitions!!! They will kill your father! and those milk and water *Members*!!! Would it not be possible to get a law passed in the Massachusetts Legislature compelling the members of each district to present the petitions of their own constituents," she wrote to Charles. "Start petitions to them on this subject and relieve us from this *oppression.*"

She tried her own lobbying, too. "My proposition did not take with the Massachusetts Members because they neither like the trouble nor the responsibility, and they like a two-sided game better," she wrote. "Women and Quakers are pretty helpers in such a cause. If this persecution lasts much longer who knows but what I may join the *Grimkies* and lecture too!"

That was another joke — but a loaded one. Sarah and Angelina Grimké, sisters born in

South Carolina, had become leading abolitionists. Their tour of New England, in which they vividly described the evils of slavery, had made them famous. In February 1838, Angelina testified on behalf of the abolitionists before the Massachusetts legislature, making her the first woman in history to address an American legislative body. She and Sarah Grimké were also among the first to demand political rights for women. "Men and women were CREATED EQUAL; they are both moral and accountable beings, and whatever is *right* for man to do is *right* for women," Sarah wrote in an article, "On the Province of Women," part of a series that the Grimkés published as a pamphlet called *The Equality of Sexes and the Condition of Women.*

These were incendiary ideas. Even the newspaper that published "On the Province of Women" tried to distance itself from the content of the essays. Angelina was widely known as "Devilina." Postmasters burned the Grimkés' pamphlets.

But when Louisa read "On the Province of Women" in the winter of 1837–38, she was impressed. It was saturated in the language of Scripture, language that spoke to Louisa. It addressed issues that were already on her mind. Louisa had been writing "Narrative of a Journey," meditating on the capabilities of women. That summer in Quincy, she had also read Abigail Adams's letters, and was "struck," she wrote, "by the vast and varied powers of her mind; the full benevolence of an excellent heart and the strength of her reasoning." She added, "I cannot refrain from wishing that they were published." To read them, she wrote — using words that anticipated the Grimkés' — might help "many a timid female whose rays too feebly shine, not for want of merit but for want of confidence."

She wrote to Charles, "I cannot believe that there is any inferiority in the sexes, as far as mind and intellect are concerned."

"On the Province of Women" impressed Louisa so much, in fact, that she wrote Sarah Grimké a letter.

"Although I have not the happiness of a personal acquaintance with you," Louisa wrote, "the pleasure which I derived from the perusal of your two letters on the Province of Women, induces me to address you." Grimké responded, and a correspondence between them began — an exchange rooted in ideas. Equal rights for women was a familiar, if embattled, arena for the Grimkés. For Louisa, the exchange was more extraordinary. She took a risk in pursuing it. But there was something about Grimké's seriousness that may have awakened the memories of the strong-willed educated women to whom Louisa had been drawn throughout her life — a lineage that included her teacher Miss Young,

Elizabeth Carysfort, and others. She sometimes felt timid in their presence, not sure if she was up to understanding, but she admired them, and she longed to be engaged.

The idea that Louisa proposed to Grimké reflected the prejudices of her time and her own sense of conflict. She tried to reconcile her instinct for equality with her acceptance of what was said to be a woman's place. Adam and Eve, she wrote, were "equal in mind" and in God's eyes, but Adam had excused Eve from labor due to her superior "exquisite" beauty. Grimké responded with an argument for "simple equality" between the sexes and turned the subject to slavery, trying to persuade Louisa to join her cause by appealing to the especially grim plight of enslaved women. When Louisa responded by talking about her distrust of blacks and her fears of freed slaves as a mass of uneducated, unrooted, propertyless people, Grimké challenged her, encouraging her to question her assumptions. "Please inform me whether thy opinion of them is founded on actual and extensive knowledge or whether it is the result of hearsay evidence," Grimké wrote.

Louisa admitted to Grimké that she despaired about the quality of her education and doubted the strength of her intellect. Her mind was too undisciplined, too weak. She had suffered in her domestic life, which drove her to distract herself with trifles. She wrote freely. Her anguish poured onto the page.

Grimké replied sympathetically. "How often we thus find woman suffering all her life from the defects of that system of education which has been adopted and which can hardly fail to nurture in us a desire for trifling pursuits," Grimké wrote. "We have aimed to be the idol of man's worship rather than the companion of his heart. . . . With a mind like thine my sister I feel persuaded that had not the trammels of education fettered thee thy pursuits would have been far different."

So many women felt so small, so alone. Louisa would not have needed to look farther than her own family. "Every day I feel how little I am calculated to take a share in conversation and shrink into consciousness of my insignificance," her sister Caroline wrote to her in 1845. The walls that Louisa ran up against, in herself and in her culture, were so high. Even in Grimké's avowal of sisterhood, there was something frustrating. Louisa was making a plea to be heard in her own right. But Sarah Grimké was not writing only to Louisa; she was writing in order to reach John Quincy. She saw Louisa as a means to access. One can hardly blame Grimké; the abolitionist was committed to her agenda, and writing to Louisa was a way of getting the attention of the most faithful antislavery member of the House. Still, Grimké's letters, as patient and admirable as they were, can be painful to read. Grimké was constantly looking over Louisa's shoulder to find John Quincy. "Please present my regards and respects to thy husband. Will he please inquire whether a letter I addressed to William Slade reached him . . ." Grimke would write. "Please tell him . . ." "If thy husband had the time and would write to me stating his views . . ." "Tell him as an American, a woman I am his debtor. . . ."

Even Grimké's response to Louisa's letter about her insecurities about her education, a letter that Louisa had clearly written in trust, was not to Louisa alone. In fact, Grimké addressed the envelope to John Quincy Adams, not to Louisa, and John Quincy was the one who opened it. "As it was directed to me, and as I expected it would be more edifying to me than to you, I took the liberty to read it," John Quincy told Louisa when he passed it along. *More edifying to me than to you* — his words were blithe and cutting. "There was with it a small volume of her sister's letters to Catherine E. Beecher; but as I believe you have it already, I shall leave this one here; but I have written the initials of your name and the date upon it to identify the property."

What property, though, was really Louisa's? Even that small act of identifying what was hers was only a fiction. The legal doctrine of coverture meant that her rights were subsumed under her husband's. Her property

was his. She could not take complete ownership even over a letter from a fellow woman.
It was directed to her husband, and she had
to receive it from her husband's hand.

There was no groundswell of support for
women's rights in the late 1830s, no burgeon-
ing movement. If anything, women's roles
were becoming more restrictive. But the
moralistic slant of the times — the fervor of
religious revivalism, the politics of betterment
— brought women into contact with politics
in a new way. The contest played out in the
question of petitions, which women often
spearheaded. That summer, 1838, while
debating the annexation of Texas, Benjamin
Howard of Maryland rose in the House and
expressed his "regret" that women were playing such a large role in expressing their
prayers to the government. "These females,"
he said, "could have a sufficient field for the
exercise of their influence in the discharge of
their duties to their fathers, their husbands,
or their children, cheering the domestic
circle, and shedding over it the mild radiance
of the social virtues, instead of rushing into
the fierce struggles of political life." It was, he
added, a "departure from their proper
sphere."

It stood to John Quincy, as ever, to defend
the right of anyone to petition Congress. He
did it in stirring, capacious terms. Where, he

asked, was it written that women had no access to anything out of the "domestic circle"? Not in the Old Testament, where one might read about the heroics of Miriam, Esther, Judith. Not in history, with the examples of Queen Elizabeth or Isabella of Castile. Not in American history, either. He picked up a history textbook written by a Southerner and read aloud a passage about the role the women of South Carolina had played in the Revolution. "Politics, sir! Rushing into the vortex of politics! Glorying in being called Rebel ladies!"

He agreed that it was a woman's "duty" to attend to her "sphere," and he admired women who did. But why should she not be allowed to expand it? "Why does it follow that women are fitted for nothing but the cares of domestic life? For bearing children, and cooking the food of a family? Devoting all their time to the domestic circle — to promoting the immediate personal comfort of their husbands, brothers, and sons?"

John Quincy is now remembered for that speech and those good sentiments. That was not, however, the only thing he said on the matter.

When a woman from Hingham wrote to thank him for defending the right of women to petition, he pointedly said he was doing it to honor his memory of his *mother* — and really, only his mother. "My intercourse with the sex, since that time has not left me ignorant of the imperfections in which they participate as a portion of the human race nor of the frailties incidental to their physical and intellectual nature," he wrote. "My attachment to them is not enthusiastic, nor have I ever been remarkably exemplary in the observance of those delicate attentions."

In early September, on a late summer day, Louisa went with John Quincy to a picnic that the women of Quincy were giving in his honor. He made a short speech there "on the right of women to petition, and on the propriety of their taking a part in public affairs," John Quincy wrote in his diary afterward. He damned the idea with his praise.

There was not the least danger of their obtruding their wishes upon any of the ordinary subjects of legislation, banks, currency, exchange, sub-treasuries, internal improvement, tariffs, manufactures, public lands, revenues and expenditures, all which so profoundly agitate the men of the country; the women, so far from intermeddling with them, could scarcely be prevailed upon to bestow a thought upon them; and, knowing that, it was scarcely consistent with civility so much as to name them in their presence. I now alluded to them only to discard them. But, for objects of kindness, of benevolence, of compassion, women, so far from being debarred by any rule of delicacy from exercising the right of petition or remonstrance, are, by the law of their nature, fitted above all others for that exercise.

What must it have been like for his wife to hear these words? As he spoke, Louisa sat beneath an evergreen arch in the park, shaded from the warm sun by the leafy lime trees. What did she think of what she heard? Did she nod in agreement — or did her thoughts turn to her sister Kitty, who, that spring, "was full of the Sub Treasury; and rattled off *finance,* as I rattle nonsense; until I actually stared at the extent of her knowledge"? Did she remember the letters she had written to her husband the previous year, when she was in Washington and he in Quincy, in which she'd given regular updates on the run on the banks during the Panic of 1837, reporting minutely the flurry of activity at the Treasury as it tried to keep enough cash on hand? "I am told by good *authority* after three anxious Cabinet meetings and it is generally *asserted* and that very loudly that if the bank can get on until the first of the month it will not then be able to meet in payments for government and that the Treasury will stop," she added. Did she recall the discussion at the dinner table about Mr. Lawrence's "fine speech" on the "tariff question" in the House? Banks, currency, subtreasuries, tariffs —

these were not her areas of expertise, to be sure. She was the first to say so. But to suggest, even rhetorically, that she had never bestowed a thought on these subjects — it was as if John Quincy had said that his own wife's letters did not exist.

She defended herself. In 1841, as Southern members fought to tighten the gag rule and her husband fought to end it, Louisa would write a short statement, "On the Right to Petition." The ideas she expressed were in line with what her husband had said about the right of women to petition Congress. What was different was that she took the initiative — and claimed the right — to say it herself, instead of letting her husband simply speak for her. She sent her statement to Charles. "You will think that I am turned a crazy polititian and I believe I am my dear Charles," she wrote, "but as no eye sees what I write; and no one knows that I have written this, I only send it to you that you may understand my feeling which is that all may petition although all petitions cannot be granted."

Her thoughts about gender, as they had been for decades, remained fraught as she tried to work through them. In her view, the genders were equal but separate. Implicitly, she recognized the fluidity and fragility of the differences — but feared the idea. She suggested that even adopting, for only a few hours, the outward trappings of a man might taint a woman, that to put on a pair of pants "unconsciously injures the manners" of a lady. When Charles's spirited, athletic, tomboyish daughter Louisa was to act in a school play, for instance, her grandmother wrote and begged her parents not to let her take a male part. "The masculine stride, the bold look" were not merely unbecoming, Louisa wrote: they might "destroy the timid and blushing graces of a girl of sixteen on her entrance into a world, where feminine elegance has assumed a positive and fixed standard."

Essays like one in a popular magazine of the time, the *Portfolio,* made the warning plain: "A woman always loses by attempting to be a man." The social pressure to embody a strict model of femininity was enormous and growing more intense as the century progressed. "Warlike women, learned women, and women who are politicians, equally abandon the circle which nature and institutions have traced round their sex; they convert themselves into men," read an essay in *Boston Magazine.*

Nothing less than the social order seemed to rest on the maintenance of this well-defined "circle." Those who lived outside its bounds, like the French writer and intellectual Germaine de Staël, "could not be fitted for the common relations of society,"

Louisa wrote. De Staël's extraordinary talents made it impossible for her to "bear the shackles and restraints which man for his own comfort necessarily imposes, and would soar above that social and moral compact, which forms the strong basis of family union, peace, and happiness." However strange it sounds now, Louisa believed that "shackles and restraints" were necessary for those common goods.

Where did that leave women? At times her view was dark. There were men, Louisa wrote, who made marriage a "badge of slavery." In 1839, she would use the phrase "*chains* of wedlock" in a negative, nervous tone. She was writing about a divorce suit in Connecticut; a minister had struck his pregnant wife. Connecticut courts had one of the most equitable traditions for granting divorce — and yet the woman still lost her case. "I do not by any means wish to favour my sex!" she wrote, "but when we reason fairly we must be aware that the world adjudges all the weakness and the frailties of temper, as on our side — We know that the power the property and the law are all on the other, as well as publick opinion; which created by man is, always in favour of himself. . . . In the full and almost unlimited possession of power [men] rarely tie up their own hands!!!"

Louisa did not want to be radical. She did not want to stand against public opinion. She wanted to reflect the consensus. She wanted to fit in. Her own logic agonized her. "I and all the Ladies cry out against my doctrines on this point! they say forbear, and be silent!!"

She was conflicted, then — but her respect for strong women was unshakable, no matter how hard she tried to deny it. In her writings, she sketched portraits of women in quick, broad strokes, with all the chiaroscuro that she used to paint herself. Women who had strongly "masculine" characteristics, including some of the most formative figures from her life, fascinated her. Elizabeth Hewlett had been eccentric, with a strong mind and stronger passions, but also another mother figure. Her favorite teacher at school, Miss Young, had grown up studying Greek and Latin and dressed like a boy. Lady Carysfort had been masculine and forbidding, but also a second mother. Louisa was drawn to them and yet insisted that she was not like them.

It wasn't only that Louisa shared the common assumption that "masculine" was a derogatory way of describing a lady. In the late eighteenth and early nineteenth centuries, a woman's strength was said to be coupled with — in fact dependent on — her weakness. Intellect, appearance, and gender were inextricable in Louisa's world. Women with "masculine manners" had "ugly and coarse" styles and were intimidating. Yet in the same breath, she might describe them as "remarkable" and "pleasant and amusing." She would say that she wasn't up to the level of conversation of strong-minded women, but when she wrote of meeting the bluestocking Hannah Adams, after her arrival in the United States, she described with pride sending Hannah into a reverie of "poetic fervor" while speaking of Rousseau. "I really felt proud to have had the power to draw out a mind of such strength and such purity," Louisa wrote.

How should a woman think, speak, feel, behave? Louisa was of two minds, and she never could sort out which one was her own. "There is generally a want of feminine grace and sweetness, in these showy, strong minded women; which produce fear in us lesser lights: and this has always been my first impression on becoming acquainted with them," she later reflected, "yet they always appear to me to be *what God intended woman to be,* before she was cowed by her master *man.*"

For Louisa to make something of herself, then — to assert herself, to try to understand how to be, to insist that she, too, had rights, had a story — was brave. The struggle for women to claim rights and defend their abilities had barely begun. At the end of 1838, a few months after John Quincy's speech in the park, the correspondence between Louisa and Sarah Grimké ended. So, for the most part, did the Grimké sisters' agitation for women's rights, at least for the moment. Pressure from within the abolitionist movement cut it off; it was considered a distraction from a more important cause. The Seneca Falls Convention, the first women's rights convention in the United States, was still ten years in the future.

How hard it was for her is reflected in the periods of silence she sometimes went through — or in her destroying what she wrote. For months after the abrupt ending of her correspondence with Sarah Grimké, Louisa stopped writing altogether. She was depressed and scared. Assassination threats against John Quincy continued to arrive. "Some Gentlemen in this section are ready and anxious to pay a large premium for the head of J.Q. Adams," wrote one man. "If you don't you will when least expected, be shot down in the street, or your damned guts will be cut out in the dark," wrote another. "I shall be in Washington next March and shall shoot you. *Remember!!!*" "On the first day of May next I promise to cut your throat from dart to ear."

When she did pick up her pen, she repeatedly tried to persuade John Quincy to stop his antislavery activities, however "just" his cause. Her warnings and fears had no effect. When he took on the case of thirty-six

Africans from the Mende tribe who had been kidnapped into slavery and rebelled aboard the ship *Amistad,* she tried to talk him out of it, believing it would bring the family more distress. Charles agreed. After John Quincy successfully argued the case before the Supreme Court, he rebuked his son. "The agony of soul that I suffered from the day when I pledged my faith, to argue the cause of the Africans, before the Supreme Court, till that when I heard Judge Story deliver the opinion and decree of the Court, was chiefly occasioned by the reprobation of my own family, both of my opinions and my conduct, and their terror at the calamities which they anticipated they would bring upon *them,*" John Quincy wrote. But his ancestor, Saer de Quincy, had been one of the men who signed the Magna Carta, the Charter of Liberties, six hundred years before; John Quincy had seen the signature on the document in the British Museum himself. There was more to life than personal comfort, he told his son. Freedom was worth fighting for.

He must have said something along the same lines about Saer de Quincy to Louisa, because that month she signed a letter *"Louisa Catherine De Quincy Adams."* It was a joke, but perhaps it hid a sting. Who, after all, was she, with her terror at calamities, set against the great Saer de Quincy, with his petition against the king?

She kept to her room, returning no visits. On New Year's Day, 1840, 240 visitors came to pay their respects to the ex-president and his wife, but Louisa stayed upstairs. She left the house only three times that winter. Her granddaughter Fanny, Mary's daughter, died in November, only nine years old. When Mary Louisa fell sick soon after, Louisa was desperate with worry. Her granddaughter's life, she wrote, was almost a part of her own.

She had no one to talk to, she wrote, because she was "imbued . . . with strange and singular opinions." Time passed slowly and heavily. Her correspondence, at least that which survives, trailed off, and she wrote only occasionally in her diary — her thoughts dwelling on religion, Plutarch, Shakespeare. She partly absolved Lady Macbeth from Macbeth's crimes; it was *his* ambition and guilty conscience that motivated his actions and warped his mind, before he had even seen his wife. Her husband had once used the phrase "secret history" in a letter to her to describe the backstabbing and double-dealings of the Monroe administration. She used the phrase now. "Were we to look deeply and minutely into the secret histories of men; how constantly we should observe this same retributive justice — It is one of the most remarkable facts; and it has caused me deeply to reflect upon its repeated and continued recurrence."

Even as she struggled with her sense that her family had sacrificed so much for her husband's ambitions, she defended him. She worried about him, too, and not only because of the threats against his life; he was becoming more frail. In May he tripped in the House and dislocated his shoulder. The way he handled himself made her see too clearly her own lack of grace. She resented him and admired him at the same time. Not for the first time, she described him as Socrates and herself as Socrates's nagging wife. John Quincy tolerated her "with the patience of Socrates; but . . . like Socrates glides smoothly on in the course which he has laid out for himself enjoying the turmoil," she wrote to Charles. When she thought about "all his fine qualities, his easy temper, his quiet home habits, and his indefatigable powers of application," she added, she was "ashamed" by her cravings for "some social comforts; some soothing influence to fill up the lagging hours." She turned, as she did in times of sadness, to her memories.

On July 1, 1840, at the age of sixty-five, she started her most ambitious project. Begun as a letter to Charles, it grew to seventy pages and two drafts. She called it "The Adventures of a Nobody."

It was, in part, a record of pain, starting with the events that she described as disillusionment: the coincidence of her marriage, her father's failure, and her first miscarriage, all within a few months. But it was also an extraordinary account of a long, complicated, and deeply felt life — a life, indeed, of adventures.

She wrote about catching sight of Queen Luise, like seeing the first flower of spring, and about the shivers that Pauline Neale's Polish and Bohemian ghost stories had sent rippling down her spine. She described her anguish on seeing her father when she returned to Washington, a broken man. She wrote about reaching Quincy for the first time, how utterly strange it had been — stranger than stepping onto Noah's ark. She wrote about meeting Aaron Burr, eating canvasback ducks at Thomas Jefferson's dining table, and burning cakes in the little saltbox cottage on Penn's Hill. And, with the knowledge of all that had happened since, she wrote of being taken by surprise, forced to leave her two older sons when she, John Quincy, and Charles had left for Russia — the two sons who would die before her. She wrote about Russia, the tsar and the ice and the sad splendor. The story ended in September 1815, with the death of her daughter. The last line was, "My Child gone to heaven." Possibly, she could not bring herself to go on.

Many historians and biographers who study

John Quincy have read "Adventures" and taken her self-pity at face value. "Sickly and delicate, [Louisa] lacked the mental toughness, the resourcefulness, the strict standards of thrift, and the zest for life that made her mother-in-law, Abigail Adams, the measure of womanly excellence in New England," wrote one of John Quincy's biographers. Another described Louisa with clichés about Victorian womanhood: "Louisa Adams accompanied [John Quincy] in his subsequent diplomatic wanderings, was the tender and affectionate mother of their three sons, faithful companion of all his later political adventures and vicissitudes. To her the Adams family owes its continuance in direct descent from the Presidents; it also inherited from her a gentle mother's kindness — and fortitude — if character can be inherited."

Louisa's voice in "The Adventures of a Nobody," though, is not the voice of a woman who was sickly and delicate, nor very gentle. It is vivid and propulsive. Her story cannot be completely trusted, of course. (She appears to have used old diaries and John Quincy's diary as an aid for facts.) She was writing about events long past, and her view was colored by her feelings as she wrote. She said so herself. "Thus you find," she once wrote a friend, telling a story about Berlin, "that I am the Heroine of History (or the present, remembering the history of the past only as a 'tale that is told')." Still, "The Adventures of a Nobody" is a rich historical text. It offers glimpses into Berlin and St. Petersburg during the Napoleonic Wars and into New England and Washington during the early republic. It reveals undercurrents of anxiety about the massive transformations taking place. It features memorable portraits of some of the most significant personalities and politicians of her day. It is also, more important, the story of something more peculiar: the adventures of someone who called herself a *nobody*. In an obvious sense, that "nobody" is self-effacing. She was describing herself as inconsequential, almost nonexistent. But there is also another way to read that word. "The Adventures of a Nobody" describes the extraordinary experiences of a woman whose body constantly kept her aware of her frailty and limitations. Her body miscarried, fainted, fell. It kept her down. The words on the page, though, needed no body. She left for us a voice.

3

In 1844, Louisa sent her daughter-in-law Abby, Charles's wife, a washbasin that had been in the Johnson family for generations. The basin looked like nothing special, she cautioned Abby. It was cracked. It was ordinary. It was the kind of thing often ignored and unvalued. But perhaps it was a mistake to think of it that way. After all, she wrote, it had a hidden history.

"Among the many and constant changes which have befallen my family in the last fifty years; it is truly wonderful that a thing so brittle should have nearly out lived a third generation of human beings; who have 'struted their little brief hour' to give place to the *fashionable fame* of a *wash basin*," Louisa wrote to Abby. "Could it speak of times past, what mysteries it might disclose; what sorrows and what happiness it might reveal." She was writing as a woman to a woman, and in any woman's life, there were things kept hidden. "But as every day furnishes its quota;

we must rejoice that these silent witnesses can tell no tales of the past; which they must have seen so frequently washed away; while they have probably assisted to embellish many a face, and to dry many a tear which has graced the cheek of a suffering maiden whose grief was (perhaps) not even suspected. Yet [it] may have added beauty to many a beaming smile sweetly reflected in the transparent waters which it contained."

Unlike the washbasin, which could never whisper what it saw, she was a participant and interpreter of history — on the most intimate and epic scale. She witnessed a world in transformation and a country inventing itself, and she played a role in that invention. But her inner life was just as important and loomed just as large. She traced the narrative of her secret history sometimes when alone. Her journal and her letters were, to the end of her life, a place where she could dwell in her memory and study her thoughts. But there were things she alluded to that she never made explicit, and doubtless there were things she left out. Sometimes she would find herself lost in memory's labyrinth. She had seen so much in her life — tremendous success, inconsolable pain.

It amazed her to think sometimes of how much she had experienced, how far she had come. When Charles told her that he had been nominated for president on the Free Soil ticket, she had to laugh. "*I little I* stood alone in this great nation, as the daughter of a *President* the *wife* of a President, and the *mother* of a *nominated* President," Louisa told John Quincy and Mary. With typical pride and self-deprecation, she joked about it with a smile and a shrug. She was at once proud, and yet knew how fleeting the fame was. "And after all what is it? The worms will feed as well and no better than if I had died Miss Johnson."

Her eyes and voice had sharpened in her final years, even as her body continued to let her down. With little to lose personally, she could be witty and scathing, taking delight in a good story or even a turn of phrase. Politics was theater, and she no longer had the burden of being a player. She remained transfixed by the "mixture of meanness and extravagance; of vacillating folly and perplexed talent; of ludicrous incident and profound disappointment. . . . A treasury without a dollar; a Cabinet without authority; a vane to guide us," as she once wrote. Her tone, though, was softer than it had been — more amused than depressed. "Nothing my dear Charles but the pencil of a Hogarth can do justice to the scenes passing here before our eyes every day . . . in the great metropolis of this anything but Union." But despite all the caustic things she had to say, she encouraged her son. She had "strong faith" in his principles, she told him, and she trusted him to pursue his own goals and form his own views. She was mellowing toward John Quincy, too. She was proud of her husband. In her complicated way, of course, she had always been proud of him, but now it was easier for her to say it. She was no longer so quick to compare her powerlessness with his power, nor to resent him for it. "The only thing that distresses me is that he expends much of the strength of his great mind upon the butterfly race," she wrote to Charles. Men flew around him "as the moth round the candle and consume themselves if he would let them alone."

At the same time, she found some satisfaction that those butterflies now clustered near him. It was easier for her to be comfortable with his antislavery stand partly because she had spent years thinking through her own position, but partly because it wasn't so lonely anymore. A generation of men who had been inspired by him was coming into power. (And, in fact, some younger women were beginning to take their own influential antislavery stand.) After John Quincy survived another desperate attempt to muzzle him after Congress tightened the gag rule and pushed another resolution to censure him, he became a legendary figure. Even his fiercest opponents had come to respect his stubbornness and rectitude.

Every New Year's Day, all of Washington descended on Louisa and John Quincy's house to pay their respects — abolitionists and Southern congressmen, men of "every political creed." He was considered by nearly all as a great man, and by some as a hero. And she was, in a different way, seen as a monument.

She liked to joke that she was a relic. There was a grimness to her humor sometimes, and it was understandable. The greatest equalizing force, death, was all around her: the death of her grandson, Charles's son Arthur; the deaths of nephews; the deaths of old friends. There were reminders everywhere, of course, of the deaths of her children. She continued to claim that her own death was imminent — even though she had long since proven herself to be one of those women who looks breakable but endures and endures.

In 1843, Louisa's brother, Thomas, died following a long decline after a stroke. In his will, he left her $10,000. Just how rare — and legal — this was is unclear. (Abigail Adams, for one, had drawn up a will.) Few records concerning the legitimacy of married women's property exist. It is difficult for legal historians to know how often married women controlled their own assets. Coverture laws generally diverted the possession of a wife's property to her husband. Louisa, though, left no doubt that this money was hers and hers alone. One of the first things she did after receiving it was draft her own will. She had, she wrote at the top, "in my own right . . . the possession in my own name of a Legacy of Ten Thousand Dollars." Before a statute was passed in 1842, a woman in Massachusetts was not allowed to draft a will; even afterward, writing a will required the permission of the husband. But whether by coincidence or design, John Quincy Adams was not one of the witnesses of her will.

When she needed cash, she had access to it herself. It brought her pleasure to be able to buy Charles a carriage and to discuss her accounts with him. The money was liberating. She had always felt poor. The loss of her dowry had, she had so repeatedly written, deprived her of her "standing" in her marriage. It had been the source of so much regret. There was a measure of redemption, then, when she wrote: *In my own right . . . in my own name.*

By that time, she spent most of her days quietly, a figure at once distant and admired. The family referred to her as "the Madam." In his memoir, *The Education of Henry Adams,* Louisa's grandson Henry wrote about visiting the Madam in Quincy during summers when he was a child. He would find her by her mahogany writing desk, looking out the window at the flowers and yellowwood tree inside the garden's box walk. She was, Henry wrote, elegant and different, a "vision of silver gray." She fascinated the child, and she would continue to fascinate him for his whole life. Some sympathy flashed between the old woman and young boy. "He might even then have felt some vague instinctive suspicion that he was to inherit from her the seeds of the primal sin," Henry wrote in *The Education,* "the fall from grace, the curse of Abel, that he was not of pure New England stock, but half exotic." By the time he wrote his memoir, he had read her memoirs, diaries, and letters. Henry thought, in fact, of publishing them; he copied and edited some two hundred pages before abandoning the project.

He would go on to become the great historian of the early nineteenth century instead, writing the magisterial nine-volume *History of the United States During the Administrations of Thomas Jefferson and James Madison* — a history, not incidentally, in which his great-grandfather John Adams, and his grandfather John Quincy, played a great part. Louisa is absent in his account of men's deeds. But when Henry wrote fiction and his own history, *The Education* — the story of a life, an exploration of thoughts, feelings, and perceptions — he looked to Louisa. Henry saw in her what he needed, a genealogy for his own vague sense of not belonging. But he also saw in her what was there: "some of those doubts and self-questionings, those hesitations, those rebellions against law and discipline, which marked more than one of her descendants."

On July 11, 1847, John Quincy turned eighty. Two weeks later, at the old house in Quincy, he and Louisa celebrated their fiftieth wedding anniversary. He gave her a bracelet. Inside the medallion, she put snippets of hair from Charles, his wife Abby, and her grandson Arthur, who had recently died.

Their old quarrels faded into half-stubborn, half-indulgent routines. She would brew tea for him every day in her large old silver tea service, a wedding present; he would drink only hot water. He refused to wear anything but an old brown coat, "which I cannot get off his back long enough to get the buttons covered," she complained. He would cover caterpillars with her fancy tumblers in order to watch them turn into butterflies, only to forget them on the closet shelf. She tolerated this "with fortitude," their grandson Henry would remember, "but she made protest when he carried off her best cut-glass bowls to plant with acorns or peachstones that he might see the roots grow, but which she said, he commonly forgot like the caterpillars."

Both of them had at times privately regretted their marriage. There had been periods in which they had hardly spoken to each other, months and years in which they had lived more or less apart. Even late in his life, John Quincy could not forget that he had loved someone else first and had fallen for that woman more intensely. In 1838, he was walking through Mount Auburn Cemetery when he came across the headstone of Maria Sargent, the daughter of Mary Frazier, the young woman he had loved before meeting Louisa, and his mind turned again toward Mary. She had been, he wrote in his diary afterward, "to me the most beautiful and the most beloved of her sex." He had done his duty in ending the relationship, but nearly half a century later, he still felt the pain. "Dearly! — how dearly did the sacrifice of her cost me, voluntary as it was."

If Louisa ever desired to be with any particular person but her husband, she did not leave any evidence.

She had felt that he had not understood her, been sympathetic toward her, taken her feelings, needs, wishes, and capacities into account. And she was right. In Louisa's retrospective accounts of her first years of marriage, "Record of a Life" and "The Adventures of a Nobody," her protracted illnesses, her insecurities, and John Quincy's slights stand out: he left her at events to fend for herself, he made their relative poverty pointedly clear, his anxiety for her health made her feel guilty, and she was not the woman he wanted her to be. "Happy indeed would it have been for Mr. Adams if he had broken his engagement, and not harassed himself with a wife altogether so unsuited to his own peculiar character, and still more peculiar prospects," she wrote self-pityingly in 1840. But this was unfair. There had also been moments of real tenderness, companionship, support, and joy. They had needed and depended on each other, sometimes in ways they could not admit to each other. They had loved each other over many years.

Together, they had endured many things that could have shattered them both. Of the four children to whom Louisa had given birth — and the ones whom she had lost before bearing — only one would outlive Louisa and John Quincy. It is impossible to say whether they would have done better apart than they did together. But together, they did survive, and together they grew.

The previous November, 1846, after their annual journey to Quincy, Louisa had returned to Washington with Mary and her granddaughter ahead of John Quincy, traveling south before the New England winter set in. Soon after she arrived, she learned that John Quincy had collapsed on a walk. Immediately she turned around and rushed north. Traveling unattended, by steamboat and railroad, she made the trip in thirty-six hours. When she had arrived in the United States thirty-five years before, that journey had taken three weeks.

She found John Quincy looking better than she had hoped but far from well. He had suffered a stroke, temporarily losing use of his right arm and his right leg below the knee. There was a gash on his head. When he regained a little feeling in his leg, he unwisely rose from his bed and tried to walk; Charles's wife, Abby, found him on the floor.

Louisa sat with him, reading French verses aloud and watching him sleep. He slept like a child. "His complexion looks uncommonly clear pure and fine," she wrote to Mary, "and although his face sharper and thinner he is handsomer than ever."

As the weeks passed and the new year began, he slowly grew stronger. By January, he was talking of returning to Washington, and by the beginning of February, the doctor proclaimed him well enough to make the trip. He planned on going to his desk at the House of Representatives as soon as he reached the city. "He is already full of fire and fury threatening sense / But signifying nothing . . . As he cannot be heard across a room at present," Louisa wrote. They arrived in Washington on February 12, her seventy-second birthday. The next morning, he did go to the

House. All the members rose to honor him when he walked in.

John Quincy knew that he would not have long to live. When he had finally recovered enough use in his hand to pick up his pen, in March, he opened his diary and, in faint, shaky letters, wrote that from now on, he was writing "posthumous memoir."

Louisa also knew better than to hope that he would fully recover from the stroke. She knew better, too, than to imagine that he would give up the work that might hasten his death. Retirement would mean "risking a total extinction of life," she had written, "or perhaps of those powers even more valuable than life, for the want of a suitable sphere of action." At the thought of his death, she was stricken. "Never, never has it entered my imagination that he could leave me in this world alone and widowed," she wrote to Mary, "and the very thought seems to paralyze my soul."

The Adams house on F Street, where John Quincy, Louisa, and their extended family had returned a decade earlier, was not quiet the following winter, 1848. Their granddaughter Mary Louisa was twenty years old and fully a part of Washington's social life. Nieces, nephews, and guests regularly passed through the house. Young men and women were drawn to Louisa, as they had always been. "Few, were as talented accomplished and witty as Mrs. Adams," wrote Mary Cutts, Dolley Madison's niece, who had become Louisa's frequent companion. "A keen sense of the ridiculous tempered by extreme goodness of heart, would make her pause abruptly in uttering a sally of wit or brilliant repartee, which might give pain, but the merry twinkle of her eye was infectious, even were the cause unknown."

Louisa had lost what little weight she could spare. Every day, she wore plain black dresses and little lace caps that framed her delicate face. She looked frail, but her voice remained strong. She even resumed her practice of writing a daily diary letter to Charles, launching from her typical disclaimers into the latest political news: what was happening in Albany, who was set for vice president, and the maneuvering between James Polk, Zachary Taylor, and Winfield Scott. Threaded through the news were descriptions of the dandy who had come to her party wearing a lace-edged cravat, the color of the roses pinned in a young beauty's hair, and any visitor who amused her. Unsuspecting men who met her at a party and saw her as a fragile relic were sometimes startled to hear her banter with them.

John Quincy, though, was struggling. His mind suffered as much as his body. The pain was worse, she thought, because shortly after the new year, he had become unable to write. Writing "was the occupation of his life," she wrote to Abby and Charles. Now his active mind had no release.

When he was unwell she would urge him to stay home from the House of Representatives and rest. He would reply that if he did, he would die.

On February 21, Louisa received a message that John Quincy had collapsed on the floor of the House. She had the impression that he had only fainted.

When she arrived at the Capitol, attended by her young friend Mary Cutts, she found him close to death. He had fallen shortly after voting against a proposal to suspend rules so that Congress might consider resolutions for thanks and awards for "gallantry" in the Mexico campaigns — a war, of course, which was bound up in the expansion of slavery, and which he opposed. He had been carried to the area in front of the Speaker and placed on a sofa, then carried into the Rotunda, then the east portico, and then, finally, into the Speaker's room. He called for Henry Clay.

By the time Louisa arrived, he was mostly incoherent. He did not recognize his wife.

The room was full of men, most of whom she did not know. They stood between her and him. The following day, while he lay in a coma, his breath shallow, the family was allowed to spend a few hours with him in the Speaker's room. Then the members and attendants returned, and it was once again crowded. The following day, February 23, he appeared to be fading.

It was decided that the women should not be present. "I was *forced* to leave him," she bitterly wrote her sister Harriet in Wisconsin. But she was surrounded by strangers, "without even the privilege of indulging the feelings; which all hold sacred at such moments. My senses almost gave way and it seemed as if I had become callus to suffering while my heart seemed breaking." She acquiesced and left. Most of the Massachusetts delegation, along with attendants and officers of the House, were in the room when he was pronounced dead. It was a public death for a public man.

Louisa was at home, where she had been sent. She was bereft, she wrote to Harriet, that she had not had the chance to receive his last look and to close his eyes.

She was not well enough to attend the funeral, but from her room she would have heard the guns that went off to bid John Quincy Adams farewell. The cannons began their salute at daybreak that Saturday morning, and there was gunfire until noon, minute by minute. The funeral procession marched close to her house, down Pennsylvania Avenue. His body was taken to the crypt in the congressional burying ground. A week later, his coffin was taken by train, in a black-draped car, to Quincy. Flags flew at half-mast along the route. Strangers lined the train's path.

Louisa spent the next months quietly, in the company of her family. She wrote that she was broken by grief. A year later, on March 18, 1849, she wrote her last diary entry. "I am left a helpless widow to mourn his loss which nothing on this dreary earth can supply — *Les Soupirs étouffe le Chagrin! Les larmes soulage le coer!!!*" Sighs smother grief! Tears soothe the heart!!!

Three weeks later, she had a stroke.

She would live for another three years, regaining enough of her strength to hobble across the room without assistance and — for her, more pressingly — enough strength to write. Her handwriting was loose and labored but legible. On New Year's Day, 1852, she was well enough to receive about forty guests in her room upstairs at F Street. President Millard Fillmore came, along with General Winfield Scott and his aides, Charles Sumner, and several other members of Congress. "She was delighted, and the fatigue of the day did her no harm," her grandson wrote to Charles's wife, Abby.

But she looked "as if a breath would kill her," Abby thought when she saw her mother-in-law in February. Louisa had contracted influenza, which she could not shake. She lay in bed for eleven weeks. The side affected by her stroke began to swell. By May, she was unable to sleep except when given opiates. "She is constantly in an alternate excited or low state and very nervous," her niece Elizabeth Adams wrote to Charles.

On Friday, May 14, she was so restless that she demanded to be taken from bed and allowed to sit. Mary tried to dissuade her — her legs were badly swollen — but finally she yelled, "For *God's* sake take me out of this bed or *I will* get out." She was able to sit for three minutes before asking to be put back in bed, and became so distressed that more opiate was called for.

On May 15, Charles left Quincy for Washington, anxiously hoping to reach the city in time to say goodbye to his mother. His train pulled into Washington at half past six the next morning, May 16, under a clear sun. No one was waiting for him at the station. When he reached the door at F Street, he found a small black ribbon attached to the bell.

Louisa's funeral was held two days later. Both houses of Congress adjourned as a mark of respect. "This is a thing unexampled in our history thus far," Charles wrote in his diary. Charles planned on having only pallbearers who had meant something to his mother during her life, but after more reflection, he added a few others, including the president of the Senate and the Speaker of the House. His mother had lived a public as well as a private life.

A westerly breeze brightened the light of the sun that morning, and the grass and the leaves were a fresh spring green. A huge number of citizens, "official and unofficial," came to the church, reported the *National Intelligencer.* Rev. Smith Pyne read the Episcopal service, as Louisa had wanted. The coffin was covered in black velvet and lined with silver lace. Afterward, according to the *Intelligencer,* "the body was followed to the grave by one of the longest funeral processions ever witnessed in this city."

Charles was later told that the president of the United States, the heads of the departments, and the naval and army officers were all there. He noticed almost no one at the burial. He was overcome, he wrote afterward, with loneliness.

He was the only child who outlived her. He was the only child who was never taken from her. There was no one, he had said more than once, to whom he was closer. "I never questioned her kindness or her love," he wrote in his diary after the funeral, "and her going leaves a blank which nothing can replace."

That December, her body was reinterred in

Quincy. Charles did for his parents what John Quincy had done for his own: he had their bodies placed in a crypt in the United First Parish Church, which was built with granite from the Adamses' own quarry. Louisa was not a member of that church and had never quite felt at home there, but she was the one who made the choice to be buried next to her husband. "My mother's religious feeling was always much greater than her attachment to any forms," Charles reflected a week after her death. His father's beliefs, too, "conformed exactly to no church."

The crypt still sits below the square church. It is plain and small, with rough-hewn stone walls, and nearly filled by the massive sarcophagi of John, Abigail, John Quincy, and Louisa Catherine Adams.

The sarcophagi are plain and granite; they sit side by side. They are identical, except for the names etched deep in the stone.

ACKNOWLEDGMENTS

The thousands of letters, diaries, poems, plays, account books, memoranda, wills, and other family artifacts housed at the Massachusetts Historical Society comprise as rich a resource as a biographer could dream of. For the past half century, the MHS and the Adams Papers Editorial Project have made a remarkable commitment to making those materials accessible. I am grateful to Judith Graham, Beth Luey, Sara Martin, Jim Taylor, Sara Sikes, Mary Claffey, and the other editors and staff for their generosity, assistance, thoughtful suggestions on the manuscript, and own scholarship, which mine builds upon.

I am also grateful to the staffs and archivists at the Library of Congress, the Historical Society of Pennsylvania, the New-York Historical Society, the Maryland State Archives, the Historical Society of Washington, the Wisconsin Historical Society, Butler Library at Columbia University, Universitätsbibliothek at Freie Universität, the National Archives at Kew, the Cumbria Archive Centre Carlisle, the American Antiquarian Society, the Morgan Library, the Huntington Library, the New York Public Library, Schlesinger Library at Harvard University, Houghton Library at Harvard University, Manuscripts and Archives at Yale, the Boston Athanaeum, the Merton Historical Society, Bodleian Library at Oxford, and Carl A. Kroch Library at Cornell University.

The Adamses wrote (and wrote, and wrote), but they left behind more than words. At the Adams National Historical Park, Kelly Cobble, Caroline Keinath, Patty Smith, and Karen Yourell showed me buildings, paintings, furniture, jewelry, and the slant of November light in Quincy. At the Smithsonian, Sara Murphy let me turn over the pages of Louisa's songbook and produced a pale petite dress and a small pair of silk slippers. Rev. Dave Johnson led me into the crypt at the United First Parish Church in Quincy, where Louisa's body rests.

Catherine Allgor, James Traub, Ed Papenfuse, and Joan Challinor shared and discussed with me their work on Louisa and John Quincy Adams. Michael O'Brien's reconstruction of Louisa's journey across Europe, *Mrs. Adams in Winter,* and Margery Heffron's incomplete but graceful biography, *Louisa Catherine,* were valuable resources.

This book was written with the support of a fellowship from the New America Foundation. It also benefited, in indescribable but indisputable ways, from the now-extinct sports and pop-culture site Grantland.

In London, Kristina Bedford helped me reconstruct Louisa's genealogy and untangle Joshua Johnson's complex affairs. At the Massachusetts Historical Society, Jim Connolly and Amanda Norton verified transcriptions. Jessica Gallagher deciphered difficult handwriting and chased down details in the earliest stages. Louisa Hall, Jamie Johnston, and Jesse Ruddock transcribed letters, checked facts, read drafts, and helped me see what the project could be.

Sarah Chalfant, at the Wylie Agency, believed in this project from the start, made it possible, and then helped make it better. I am also grateful to Matthew Boyd, Darren Haggar, William Heyward, Brooke Parsons, Caitlin O'Shaughnessy, Casey Rasch, Claire Vaccaro, and the rest of the team at Penguin Press — and especially to Ann Godoff, my masterful editor. Less formally, a few friends and my family were excellent editors and advisers, giving me faith in the book when I most needed it. I am grateful to them most of all.

NOTES

Introduction

"Have a beautiful plan" Louisa Catherine Adams (hereafter LCA), "Diary," in *Diary and Autobiographical Writings of Louisa Catherine Adams,* ed. Judith S. Graham et al. (Cambridge, MA: Belknap Press of Harvard University Press, 2013), 2:680–88 (hereafter DLCA); Charles Francis Adams (hereafter CFA), *Diary of Charles Francis Adams,* online edition, in *Founding Families: Digital Editions of the Papers of the Winthrops and the Adamses,* Boston: Massachusetts Historical Society, http://www.masshist.org/apde2/, 2015, 1: January 5, 6, 8, 1824 (hereafter DCFA); Richmond *Enquirer,* January 13, 1824; New York *Spectator,* January 16, 1824; New York *Statesman,* January 16, 1824.

Louisa and John Quincy were "Diary," DLCA 2:444. I have taken the liberty of silently correcting capitalizations for ease of

677

reading. Spelling and syntax, unless unclear, are for the most part left as they appear in the original.

The United States were turning John Quincy Adams (hereafter JQA) to LCA, June 2, 1796, microfilm edition of the Adams family papers, Massachusetts Historical Society (hereafter AFP); *The Diaries of John Quincy Adams: A Digital Collection,* Boston: Massachusetts Historical Society, 2005, http://www.masshist.org/jqadiaries, February 3, 1819 (hereafter DJQA). The Adams family correspondence through April 1798 has been published. For letters between July 1795 and April 1798, see *Adams Family Correspondence,* Vol. 11, edited by Margaret A. Hogan et al. (Cambridge, MA: Belknap Press of Harvard University Press, 2013), and *Adams Family Correspondence,* Vol. 12, edited by Sara Martin et al. (Cambridge, MA: Belknap Press of Harvard University Press, 2015). The United States is now considered singular, but before the Civil War the noun was plural. Benjamin Zinner, "Life in These, Uh, This United States," http://itre.cis.upenn.edu/myl/languagelog/archives/002663.html (accessed May 1, 2015).

This book follows LCA to Abigail Brooks Adams, November 27, 1840, AFP.

"But she did something" LCA to JQA,

May 14, 1845, AFP.

"In the entire span" L. H. Butterfield, "Tending a Dragon-Killer: Notes for the Biographer of Mrs. John Quincy Adams," *Proceedings of the American Philosophical Society* 118, no. 2 (1974): 165–78.

Part One: Fraught with Bliss

1

The first time "Record of a Life," DLCA 1:37, 19, 21.

More than a month For the gloves, see Nancy Johnson to John Trumbull, undated, John Trumbull Papers (MS 506), Manuscripts and Archives, Yale University Library.

There were frequent Regarding the possibility that Joshua took advantage of his position, it is also possible that Jefferson paid for Joshua's "political intelligence" out of a secret slush fund. (Margery M. Heffron, *Louisa Catherine: The Other Mrs. Adams,* ed. David L. Michelmore [New Haven, CT: Yale University Press, 2014], 32–33.)

Louisa barely noticed JQA to LCA, June 2, 1796, AFP; DJQA, December 26, 1795.

She was almost "Record of a Life," DLCA 1:4; Heffron, *Louisa Catherine,* 15–16; Joan Challinor, "Louisa Catherine Johnson Adams: The Price of Ambition," Ph.D. dissertation, American University, 1982, 43–44.

She remembered her "Record of a Life," DLCA 1:4; Jon Meacham, *Thomas Jefferson: The Art of Power* (New York: Random House, 2012), 181.

The school was only LCA to Abigail Brooks Adams, March 2, 1834, AFP; "Record of a Life," DLCA 1:4.

the Johnsons returned "Record of a Life," DLCA 1:7. There was a famous bluestocking named Elizabeth Carter, but she is not the same as the Elizabeth Carter who ran the school. This Elizabeth Carter ran the girls' boarding school until 1798. Dr. Tony Scott, vice chairman, Merton Historical Society, e-mail to author, November 21, 2012. Around 1787, Mrs. Carter's school was relocated to Mitcham, where it occupied Baron House for ten years. See E. N. Montague, *Lower Mitcham* (Merton, UK: Merton Historical Society, 2003), 100–1.

What happened next "Record of a Life," DLCA 1:6–9, 19; LCA to Abigail Brooks Adams, March 2, 1834, AFP.

John Hewlett, Louisa wrote "Record of a Life," DLCA 1:19; George Clement Boase and Colin Matthew, "Hewlett, John (1762–1844), biblical scholar," *Oxford Dictionary of National Biography,* ed. H. C. G. Matthew and Brian Harrison (Oxford, UK: Oxford

University Press, 2004), online ed.; Mary Wollstonecraft to Eliza Bishop, September 23, 1786, in *The Collected Letters of Mary Wollstonecraft*, ed. Janet M. Todd (New York: Columbia University Press, 2003), 79; Mary Wollstonecraft, *Thoughts on the Education of Daughters: With Reflections on Female Conduct, in the More Important Duties of Life* (New York: Cambridge University Press, 2014).

So Louisa began "Record of a Life," DLCA 1:11–12, 17; LCA to [illegible], April 9, 1849, Everett-Peabody Papers, Massachusetts Historical Society.

Louisa was pulled "Record of a Life," DLCA 1:17; Kirsten Olsen, *Daily Life in 18th-Century England* (Westport, CT: Greenwood Publishing, 1999), 34. For more on the pervasive suspicion of educated women, see Lawrence Stone, *The Family, Sex and Marriage in England 1500–1800* (London: Weidenfeld and Nicolson, 1977), 356–58.

Louisa romanticized her childhood "Adventures of a Nobody," DLCA 1:64; "Record of a Life," DLCA 1:57.

She had to be careful "Record of a Life," DLCA 1:22, 35–37.

Joshua planned "to get" Joshua Johnson (hereafter JJ) to Thomas Johnson, February 17, 1786, Joshua Johnson Letterbook, Peter

Force Collection, Library of Congress (hereafter LC).

2

Joshua would have "Record of a Life," DLCA 1:37, 17, 33.

The American men Ibid., 33, 29, 23, 36.

One night at the Johnsons' "Record of a Life," DLCA 1:40–41.

What did John Quincy Andrew Oliver, *Portraits of John Quincy Adams and His Wife* (Cambridge, MA: Harvard University Press, 1970), 45–46; for another portrait, see also ibid., 25; "Record of a Life," DLCA 1:32.

Louisa would always "Record of a Life," DLCA 1:17, 26, 7; "Adventures of a Nobody," DLCA 1:76.

So there was something LCA to Abigail Brooks Adams, March 2, 1834, AFP; "Record of a Life," DLCA 1:33, 37.

At the end of January DJQA, January 27, 1796; "Record of a Life," DLCA 1:41.

Louisa might have DJQA, February 21, 1796.

Despite how close "Record of a Life," DLCA 1:11.

It was, in fact Ibid., 11, 40. For Colonel Trumbull, see JQA to Louisa Catherine Johnson (hereafter LCJ), December 5, 1796, AFP.

He was alternately direct Thomas Boylston Adams (hereafter TBA) to JQA, April 17, 1796, AFP.

"At present without" JQA to Abigail Adams (hereafter AA), February 20, 1796, AFP.

In his diary, though DJQA, February 1, 11, 1796.

He was silent DJQA, February 29, 1796; March 1, 1796. The Latin is by Horace. Alison Weisgall Robertson helped with the translation.

Passions were pernicious JQA to John Adams (hereafter JA), December 29, 1795, in *Writings of John Quincy Adams,* ed. Worthington Chauncey Ford (New York: Macmillan Company, 1913), 470.

His career was drifting Samuel Flagg Bemis, *John Quincy Adams and the Foundations of American Foreign Policy* (New York: W. W. Norton, 1949), 68–69.

He could have JQA to JA, December 29, 1795, in *Writings of John Quincy Adams,* 470; Bemis, *John Quincy Adams and the Foundations of American Foreign Policy,* 77–79.

For nearly two years Ibid.

He was used Heffron, *Louisa Catherine,* 47; AA to Martha Washington, June 20, 1794, AFP. There are dozens of biographies of

JQA. Bemis's *John Quincy Adams and the Foundations of American Foreign Policy* and *John Quincy Adams and the Union* (New York: Knopf, 1956) remain among the best. For the full scope of the life, see also Fred Kaplan, *John Quincy Adams: American Visionary* (New York: Harper, 2014); Paul Nagel, *John Quincy Adams: A Public Life, a Private Life* (New York: Oxford University Press, 1997); Marie B. Hecht, *John Quincy Adams: A Personal History of an Independent Man* (New York: Macmillan, 1972).

It might have been easier JQA to JA, December 29, 1795, in *Writings of John Quincy Adams,* 470.

He went to galleries DJQA, November 28, 1795.

He carried his loneliness JQA to AA, November 24, 1795, AFP; DJQA, November 12, 1795.

He had been in love JQA to AA, November 24, 7, 1795, AFP; DJQA, November 12, 1795.

Marriage had been Kaplan, *John Quincy Adams,* 131; JQA to TBA, November 2, 1795, JQA to AA, November 7, 1795, AFP.

His parents' goal JQA to JA, December 29, 1795, in *Writings of John Quincy Adams,* 470; Phyllis Lee Levin, *Abigail Adams* (New York: Thomas Dunne, 2001), 129; JQA to JA, December 29, 1795, in *Writings of John*

Quincy Adams, 470; Edith B. Gelles, *Portia: The World of Abigail Adams* (Bloomington: Indiana University Press, 1992), 138.

John Quincy had tried *Memoirs of John Quincy Adams: Comprising Portions of His Diary from 1795 to 1848,* ed. Charles Francis Adams (Philadelphia: J. B. Lippincott, 1874), 1:7–8.

When he was only eleven Heffron, *Louisa Catherine,* 49–50; JQA, "William Vans Murray," in *Letters of William Vans Murray to John Quincy Adams, 1797–1803,* ed. Worthington Chauncey Ford, reprinted from the Annual Report of the American Historical Association for 1912, 347–48.

"I see you sitting" JQA to LCJ, June 2, 1796, AFP.

"Wherefore must this" DJQA, March 19, 1796.

"Solitude is the only" DJQA, February 20, 1796.

A maelstrom of emotions JQA to AA, July 25, 1796, AFP.

What Louisa could see was "Record of a Life," DLCA 1:41–42; DJQA, May 10, 1796.

John Quincy wrote about the situation DJQA, February 29, March 2, 1796; Challinor, "Price of Ambition," 154.

If his real desire DJQA, April 1, 13, 1796.

Joshua Johnson had arrived Edward S. Delaplaine, *The Life of Thomas Johnson* (New York: Frederick H. Hitchcock, Grafton Press, 1927), 13–15; Edward Papenfuse, *In Pursuit of Profit: The Annapolis Merchant in the Era of the American Revolution, 1763–1805* (Baltimore: Johns Hopkins University Press, 1975), 53; Jacob M. Price, "Introduction," *Joshua Johnson's Letterbook 1771–1774: Letters from a Merchant in London to His Partners in Maryland,* ed. Jacob M. Price (London: London Record Society, 1979), British History Online, http://www.british-history.ac.uk/london-record-soc/vol15/vii-xxviii (accessed May 10, 2015).

Early success made JJ to the firm, June 4, 1771, JJ to John Davidson, July 22, 1771, in Price, *Letterbook.*

When he arrived JJ to the firm, April 26, 1773, in Price, *Letterbook.*

Business was volatile Price, "Introduction," *Letterbook;* Jacob M. Price, "Joshua Johnson in London, 1771–1775: Credit and Commercial Organization in the British Chesapeake Trade," in *Statesmen, Scholars, and Merchants: Essays in Eighteenth-Century History Presented to Dame Lucy Sutherland,* ed. Anne Whiteman, J. S. Bromley, and P. G. M. Dickson (Oxford, UK: Clarendon Press,

1973), 155–59.

In 1773, he moved JJ to the firm, November 6, 1771, November 29, 1773, in Price, *Letterbook*.

Joshua and Catherine Price, "Introduction," *Letterbook*.

The first reference Heffron, *Louisa Catherine*, 14.

After that, and without Joan Challinor, "The Mis-Education of Catherine Johnson," *Massachusetts Historical Society Proceedings* 98 (1986): 24; JJ to Matthew Ridley, July 21, 1786, Letterbook, Peter Force Collection, LC.

Since he kept For Martin Newth as a shoemaker, see *Gazetteer and London Daily Advertiser*, August 11, 1756; London *Public Advertiser*, October 23, 1776; *Morning Chronicle and London Advertiser*, November 7, 1776; and Old Bailey Proceedings Online, January 1730, trial of Richard Smith, www.oldbaileyonline.org, version 7.2, accessed May 7, 2015. Land tax records locate Martin Newth in Portsoken in 1769, around the corner from Tower Hill, and in Stepney between 1773 and 1781 (London, England, Land Tax Records, 1692–1932), London Metropolitan Archives, database online accessed through Ancestry.com. "Record of a Life," DLCA 1:7.

So why did "Record of a Life," DLCA 1:20.

It is possible Ibid., 3.

She invested it Recuperating from their daughter Harriet's birth in 1781, Catherine dictated a letter to Joshua ("Mrs. Johnson's indisposition will prevent her from doing it herself"): "Inclosed we forward you an invoice . . . amounting to £502 which Mrs. Johnson [asks] you will please to receive & dispose of on her account, for bills or hard money *only* & remit the net proceeds immediately in good bills of exchange on Europe." Other parcels, he added, would follow. (Heffron, *Louisa Catherine*, 17.)

It is, of course Stone, *The Family, Sex and Marriage in England 1500–1800,* 609; E. A. Wrigley and R. S. Schofield, *Population History of England, 1541–1871* (New York: Cambridge University Press, 1989), 254, 266; Sarah M. S. Pearsall, *Atlantic Families: Lives and Letters in the Later Eighteenth Century* (Oxford, UK: Oxford University Press, 2008), 48. Stone's evolutionary approach and handling of evidence has come under some criticism. For a sharp take, see Alan Macfarlane, *History and Theory, Studies in the Philosophy of History,* 18 (1979), 103–26.

The ruse worked *Hanson's Laws of Maryland 1763–1784,* 203:383, Archives of Maryland Online, http://aomol.msa.maryland.gov/

000001/000203/html/ (accessed May 10, 2015).

And he seemed JJ to Matthew Ridley, January 6, 1773, JJ to Ridley, November 3, 1773, and JJ to Denton Jacques, March 18, 1773, in Joshua Johnson Letterbook, 1771–74, Hall of Records, Maryland State Archives.

It would have been Nancy Ridley to Matthew Ridley, October 20, 1778, Ridley Papers II, Massachusetts Historical Society.

Joshua Johnson and Catherine Newth Challinor, "The Mis-Education of Catherine Johnson," 24; Joshua Johnson and Catherine Newth, August 22, 1785, Saint Anne Soho, Westminster, Church of England Parish Registers, 1538–1812, London: London Metropolitan Archives, database online accessed through Ancestry.com.

Catherine had her own Frances Huttson to Matthew Ridley, August 6, 1783, Ridley Letters II; William Cranch to AA, May 8, 1798, AA to JQA, May 15, 1800, AFP.

How much JJ to John Jay, September 9, 1785, Joshua Johnson Letterbook, Peter Force Collection, LC.

"All families are not" LCA to Abigail Brooks Adams, March 2, 1834, AFP.

Louisa's descendants in fact Henry Adams to Charles Francis Adams Jr., July 12, 1900, Fourth Generation Adams Papers, Massachusetts Historical Society; Michael

O'Brien, *Mrs. Adams in Winter: A Journey in the Last Days of Napoleon* (New York: Farrar, Straus and Giroux, 2010), 76.

But Catherine Newth's Catherine Newth baptismal record, May 25, 1749, St. Thomas the Apostle, Church of England Parish Registers, 1538–1812, London: London Metropolitan Archives, database online accessed through Ancestry.com. Martin Newth and Mary Young, February 13, 1728, St. Andrew Holborn, England Parish Registers, 1538–1812, London: London Metropolitan Archives, database online accessed through Ancestry.com. Examples of birth and burial records of children of Martin and Mary Newth include William Newth baptism, July 30, 1730, St. Botolph Aldersgate; William Newth burial, February 12, 1731; Mary Newth baptism, November 12, 1731, St. Botolph Aldersgate; Martin Newth baptism, February 19, 1737, St. Stephen, Coleman St.; John Newth baptism, December 23, 1739, St. Stephen, Coleman St.; Anne Newth baptism, July 2, 1742, St. Stephen, Coleman St.; Anne Newth burial, April 4, 1747, St. Thomas the Apostle, England Parish Registers, 1538–1812, London: London Metropolitan Archives, database online accessed through Ancestry.com.

Whatever Louisa discovered "Record of a Life," DLCA 1:19.

In his diary DJQA, April 13, 15, 16, 18, 1796.

She admitted to him O'Brien, *Mrs. Adams in Winter,* 215.

Faced with an engagement "Record of a Life," DLCA 1:38.

Louisa was devastated Ibid., 43.

She did try, once Ibid., 42–43.

They said goodbye JQA to JA, June 6, 1796, in *Writings of John Quincy Adams* 1:490; JQA to AA, June 30, 1796, AFP; DJQA, May 27, 1796.

So he went "Record of a Life," DLCA 1:43.

5

Their betrothal was LCJ to JQA, July 4, 1796, AFP.

His first letter JQA to LCJ, June 2, 1796, AFP.

Her memory did "Record of a Life," DLCA 1:44; LCJ to JQA, July 4, 1796, AFP.

It had been six years LCJ to JQA, December 30, 1796, February 17, 1797, AFP.

She was determined "Record of a Life," DLCA 1:46.

There was no way JQA to LCJ, July 9, 1796, LCJ to JQA, July 25, 1796, AFP.

The news shook him JQA to LCJ, August 13, October 12, 1796, AFP.

"If possible teach" LCJ to JQA, December 6, 1796, AFP.

She tried to convince LCJ to JQA, September 30, December 30, 1796, AFP.

Meanwhile, John Quincy's parents JQA to AA, November 17, 1795, AA to JQA, August 10, May 20, 1796, AFP.

John Quincy still blamed JQA to AA, August 16, 1796, AFP.

The elder Adamses Joseph J. Ellis, *Passionate Sage: The Character and Legacy of John Adams* (New York: W. W. Norton, 1993), 72–75; AA to JQA, August 10, 1796, AFP.

"A young lady" JA to JQA, August 7, 1796, AFP.

6

Louisa grew desperate LCJ to JQA, November 29, 1796, JQA to JJ, January 9, 1797, JQA to LCJ, January 10, 1797, AFP.

John Quincy did not Price explores the volatility of JJ's first venture into the London market in "Joshua Johnson in London," 152–80.

Joshua had dark eyes William Cranch to AA, May 8, 1798, AFP; Papenfuse, *In Pursuit of Profit,* 202–29.

His latest problem JJ to John Trumbull, November 18, December 13, 1796, May 6, May 12, 1797, Trumbull Papers, MS 506, Manuscripts and Archives, Yale University Library.

John Quincy had some hint JJ to JQA, November 29, 1796, AFP.

Whatever the truth JQA to LCJ, January 10, 31, 1797, AFP.

She recoiled from LCJ to JQA, January 31, 1797, AFP.

They engaged in JQA to LCJ, February 12, January 31, 10, 1797, AFP.

She found his LCJ to JQA, January 1, 1797, AFP.

They were at cross-purposes JQA to LCJ, May 31, 1797, AFP. At the time, spouses generally addressed each other formally. See, for instance, JA on the subject in JA to Charles Adams, December 31, 1795, AFP. I am grateful to Amanda Norton for pointing out the letter.

"I am so miserably" LCJ to JQA, December 30, 1796, AFP.

"I will freely confess" JQA to LCJ, February 20, 1797, AFP.

They were pushed LCJ to JQA, February 17, 1797, AFP.

On April 13, 1797 JQA to LCJ, April 13, 1797, AFP.

He gave Louisa JQA to LCJ, May 12, 1797, AFP.

That she would be JQA to LCJ, February 7, 1797, AFP.

7

John Quincy arrived DJQA, July 13, 1797; "Record of a Life," DLCA 1:47–48.

In fact, the wedding JQA to JA, July 22,

1797, AFP.

Late mornings followed DJQA, October 15, 1797.

Louisa was happy "Record of a Life," DLCA 1:50.

The celebrations for Ibid.; DJQA, October 15, 1797.

Unknown to Louisa "Record of a Life," DLCA 1:52; DJQA, August 25, September 8, 1797.

The story she "Record of a Life," DLCA 1:50–52.

She had small *Taylor et al. v. Johnson et al.,* May 14, 1805, *Prerogative Court of Canterbury: Wills and Other Probate Records,* Kew, Surrey, England: PRO Publications; *Taylor v. Maitland,* bill and answer, 1806, C 13/71/37, the National Archives, Kew, England; JJ to Matthew Ridley, February 14, 1787, Joshua Johnson Letterbook, Peter Force Collection, LC.

The thought did cross DJQA, October 9, 1797.

John Quincy loathed Edmund S. Morgan, "Slavery and Freedom: The American Paradox," in *The Confederate Experience Reader,* ed. John Derrick Fowler (New York: Routledge, 2007), 15–16; JQA to Charles Adams, August 1, 1797, Letterbook 9, AFP; David McCullough, *John Adams* (New York: Simon and Schuster, 2001),

548. The status of debt relief in the United States was a critical topic at the turn of the nineteenth century. See Bruce H. Mann, *Republic of Debtors: Bankruptcy in the Age of American Independence* (Cambridge, MA: Harvard University Press, 2002).

To Louisa's humiliation Frederick Delius to JQA, September 29, 1797, AFP; "Record of a Life," DLCA 1:52.

John Quincy passed JQA to JJ, October 11, 1797, AFP; "Record of a Life," DLCA 1:52; JQA to JJ, October 11, 1797, JQA to Frederick Delius, September 10, 1797, Delius to JQA, January 18, 1797, AFP.

Years later, recounting "Record of a Life," DLCA 1:52.

There is little evidence "Record of a Life," DLCA 1:51–53.

Louisa saw her character LCA to CFA, July 30, 1828, AFP.

The memory of her "Adventures," DLCA 1:77.

Part Two: Life Was New

1

They arrived at Gravesend DJQA, October 18, 19, 21, 1797; JQA to JA, December 10, 1797, AFP.

She was sick "Record of a Life," DLCA 1:53; JQA to AA, December 28, 1797, JQA to JA, December 10, 1797, AFP.

From Hamburg they traveled "Record of a Life," DLCA 1:54; "Adventures," DLCA 1:67, 71.

A lieutenant stopped DJQA, November 7, 1797.

The tired travelers DJQA, July 25, 1781.

What Louisa thought Alexandra Richie, *Faust's Metropolis: A History of Berlin* (New York: Carroll & Graf Publishers, 1998), 75; "Record of a Life," DLCA 1:55.

It was a good place DJQA, November 12, 1797; "Record of a Life," DLCA 1:55.

At least her husband DJQA, November 12–December 1, 1797; JQA to AA, February 5, 1798, AFP.

But as he returned, "Record of a Life," DLCA 1:56.

She was not locked "Adventures," DLCA 1:67.

Finally, Miss Dorville, Ibid., 71; O'Brien, *Mrs. Adams in Winter,* 145–46; *The Correspondence of Priscilla, Countess of Westmorland,* ed. Lady Rose Weigall (New York, 1909), 104; Princess Louise Radziwill, *Forty-five Years of My Life (1770 to 1815),* trans. A. R. Allinson (New York: McBride, Nast & Co., 1912), 431.

"a face like a horse" "Record of a Life," DLCA 1:57.

So arrangements were "Record of a Life," DLCA 1:57–59; O'Brien, *Mrs. Adams in*

Winter, 147–49.

The queen, though "Record of a Life," DLCA 1:57; Christopher Clark, *Iron Kingdom: The Rise and Downfall of Prussia, 1600–1947* (Cambridge, MA: Harvard University Press, 2006), 319–21.

It was not out Michael O'Brien makes this point well in *Mrs. Adams in Winter,* 121.

After her presentation "Record of a Life," DLCA 1:59; "Adventures," DLCA 1:74.

2

John Quincy was determined *Writings of John Quincy Adams,* 1:158.

Here is where Bemis, *John Quincy Adams and the Foundations of American Foreign Policy,* 78.

The American Revolution DJQA, February 23, 1795; Bernard Bailyn, *The Ideological Origins of the American Revolution* (Cambridge, MA: Belknap, 1992), 135–36; Catherine Allgor, *Parlor Politics: In Which the Ladies of Washington Help Build a City and a Government* (Charlottesville: University Press of Virginia, 2000), 21–22.

John Quincy did not "Adventures," DLCA 1:108, 74.

It was not easy "Adventures," DLCA 1:78–82, 91–92; AA to Mary Smith Cranch, June 13, 1798, quoting LCA to Catherine Johnson (here after CJ), AFP; O'Brien, *Mrs. Ad-*

ams in Winter, 148–50.

Louisa also spent countless hours AA to Mary Smith Cranch, June 13, 1798, quoting LCA to CJ, AFP; "Adventures of a Nobody," DLCA 1:79, 95; "Record of a Life," DLCA 1:60.

Her husband was interested "Adventures," DLCA 1:82, 146, 86, 111–12, 150, 32. For Kant, see, for instance, JQA to AA, June 11, 1798, and JQA to JA, January 3, 1798, AFP. At the time, facts — and history — were considered men's pursuits, while emotions — and novels — were feminine. For an insightful discussion, see Lepore, *Book of Ages,* 237–42.

The reading was LCA to TBA, October 6, 1798, AFP.

Louisa and John Quincy celebrated DJQA, July 31, 26, 1798.

Still, there were LCA to Nancy Hellen, July 8, 1799, LCA to AA, June 12, 1798, AFP.

When the rare letters "Adventures," DLCA 1:113; LCA to Nancy Hellen, September 11, 1798, AFP.

And there was "Adventures of a Nobody," DLCA 1:82, 79; TBA, January 25, 1798, *Berlin and the Prussian Court in 1798: Journal of Thomas Boylston Adams, Secretary to the United States Legation at Berlin,* ed. Victor Hugo Paltsis (New York: New York Public Library, 1915) (hereafter DTBA); "Adventures," DLCA 1:79.

Her success at court JQA to AA, March 16, 1799, AFP.

The conflict arose "Adventures," DLCA 1:101, 103–4, 131; DJQA, February 13, 1799.

3

At the start DJQA, February 16, 1798, March 21, 1798, July 14, 1798.

The exact number "Adventures," DLCA 1:113; DJQA, December 30, 1800.

Her body baffled "Adventures," DLCA 1:149.

It wasn't only DJQA, December 4, 1799.

When it came DJQA, April 27, July 17, 1798, December 31, 1799, February 28, 1800.

After yet another JQA to TBA, August 2, 1800, Letterbook 10, AFP. JQA's account of the trip through Silesia, written to TBA, was published in the United States in 1801 and in London in 1804. John Quincy Adams, *Letters on Silesia, Written During a Tour Through that Country, in the Years 1800, 1801* (London: J. Budd, 1804).

He was tender "Adventures," DLCA 1:162.

He heard the news JQA to TBA, February 7, 1800, AFP; DJQA, February 5, 1801; JQA to AA, March 10, 1801, AFP.

There were signs "Adventures," DLCA 1:143–44.

Six years later JQA to LCA, February 16, 1807, AFP.

Queen Luise was "Adventures," DLCA 1:140, 138; JQA to TBA, March 28, 1801, Letterbook 10, AFP.

She and John Quincy "Adventures," DLCA 1:144, 152.

In mid-April, Louisa "Adventures," DLCA 1:154–56; JQA to AA, April 14, 29, 1801, AFP; DJQA, April 29, 1801.

Part Three: My Head and My Heart

1

The *America* floated "Adventures," DLCA 1:157–58. In "Record of a Life," Louisa places the revelation of John Quincy's love for Mary Frazier earlier. ("Record of a Life," DLCA 1:61).

But the city of Philadelphia McCullough, *John Adams,* 75–84; DJQA, September 11, 1801.

She was not alone "Record of a Life," DLCA 1:158; LCA to JQA, September 16, 1801, AFP.

They crossed the limits AA to JQA, September 13, 1801, AFP.

Did Louisa know Papenfuse, *In Pursuit of Profit,* 229–30; Catherine Johnson to LCA, April 26, 1798, AFP.

When Louisa arrived "Adventures," DLCA 1:158.

The morning after "Record of a Life," DLCA 1:158, LCA to JQA, September 16, 22, October 2, 4, 1801, AFP.

He responded to her JQA to LCA, October 8, 1801, TBA to AA, September 20, 1801, AFP.

Louisa was in no DJQA, October 30, 1801.

They had only DJQA, November 3, 1801; "Adventures," DLCA 1:176; JQA to AA, November 16, 1801, AFP; "Adventures," DLCA 1:160; DJQA, November 14, 24, 1801.

Before that day JQA to AA, November 16, 1801, AFP.

He thought the group "Adventures," DLCA 1:160; DJQA, November 14, 24, 1801.

2

"Quincy! What shall I" "Adventures," DLCA 1:162–65.

The shock she felt Caroline Keinath, *Adams National Historical Park* (Lawrenceburg, IN: The Creative Company, 2008), 10–30; "Adventures," DLCA 1:164–65; Ellis, *Passionate Sage,* 22–24.

No doubt Abigail AA to JQA, May 20, 1796, AA to TBA, July 5, December 27, 1801, AFP.

But this, as unfair McCullough, *John Adams,* 468; JA to AA, October 12, 1799, AA to JQA, January 29, 1801, AFP.

So there was a chasm "Adventures," DLCA 1:162.

Everything seemed to go Ibid., 165.

She heard the way AA to Elizabeth Smith Shaw Peabody, June 5, 1809, Shaw Family Papens, LC.

For the most part Catherine Johnson to LCA, April 26, 1798, AFP. For the attitudes and expectations of republican women in the late eighteenth century, see Gelles, *Portia;* Rosemarie Zagarri, "Morals, Manners, and the Republican Mother," *American Quarterly* 44 (1992): 192–216; Mary Beth Norton, *Liberty's Daughters: The Revolutionary Experience of American Women, 1750–1800* (Boston: Little, Brown, 1980); Jan Lewis, "Republican Wife: Virtue and Seduction in the Early Republic," *William and Mary Quarterly* 44 (1978): 689–721; Linda Kerber, *Women of the Republic: Intellect and Ideology in Revolutionary America* (Chapel Hill: University of North Carolina Press, 1980). For Abigail as an intelligent and canny financial manager as well as a farmeress, see Woody Holton, *Abigail Adams* (New York: Free Press, 2009).

Louisa tried, but "Adventures," DLCA 1:167; AA to LCA, March 8, 1802, AFP.

The atmosphere around JQA to TBA, January 9, 1802, AFP; "Adventures," DLCA 1:174, 187.

Despite their sad "Adventures," DLCA 1:165, 183; DJQA, January 7, 1803; "Adventures," DLCA 1:247.

As Louisa spent more DJQA, January 28, 1802; JQA to TBA, January 2, 1803, AFP.

"Of course with so much" "Adventures," DLCA 1:171; DJQA, November 3, 1803; Bemis, *John Quincy Adams and the Foundations of American Foreign Policy,* 112–14.

When Louisa heard AA to TBA, June 20–26, 1803, AFP; "Adventures," DLCA 1:188–89.

3

They drove through "Adventures," DLCA 1:192–95.

Now, because they Samuel Allyne Otis to JQA, October 20, 1803, AFP; Bemis, *John Quincy Adams and the Foundations of American Foreign Policy,* 119.

He planned on keeping "Adventures," DLCA 1:196; LCA to CFA, February 10, 1837, AFP. Joshua Johnson had four slaves living in his household in 1800. (1800 U.S. Census, "Joshua Johnson," Washington Ward 2, District of Columbia, accessed through Ancestry.com.)

So life was different LCA to AA, February

11, 1804, AFP.

She went to Congress "Adventures," DLCA 1:215, 204–6; Catherine Allgor, *A Perfect Union: Dolley Madison and the Creation of the American Nation* (New York: Henry Holt, 2006), 176.

She may have felt "Adventures," DLCA 1:204–5; Meacham, *Thomas Jefferson,* 398. This was one more example of the politics being played out through the battles of politesse. Jefferson had a political motivation — forced to accept Britain's paternalistic treatment and flagrant disrespect of its former colony because the United States could not afford a war, Jefferson was using the Merrys to send a message to Britain in a way that would not provoke a full rupture. He used the social sphere to rattle his baguettes. He had abstract ideas about republican equality and he wanted to try them out. In the name of simplicity, he asserted a "pell-mell" philosophy. There would be no special treatment or deference to rank, no pomp.

Louisa was in Catherine Allgor, *Parlor Politics: In Which the Ladies of Washington Help Build a City and a Government* (Charlottesville: University of Virginia Press, 2000), 115. Allgor's work is particularly trenchant in her exploration of women's largely unacknowledged role in Washington's early political culture.

Louisa claimed to "Adventures," DLCA 1:185; LCA to JQA, February 15, 1807, JQA to LCA, November 28, 1806, AFP.

It was hard Fredrika J. Teute, "Roman Matron on the Banks of Tiber Creek: Margaret Bayard Smith and the Politicization of Spheres in the Nation's Capital," in *A Republic for the Ages: The United States Capitol and the Political Culture of the Early Republic,* ed. Donald R. Kennon (Charlottesville: Published for the United States Capitol Historical Society by the University Press of Virginia, 1999).

Quincy was not LCA to JQA, April 9, 17, 1804, AFP.

"Our separation" JQA to LCA, April 9, 1804, LCA to JQA, April 17, May 12, 1804, AFP.

He was the one DJQA, August summary 1804, December 4, 1803; JQA to LCA, May 20, 1804, AFP.

But her anger LCA to JQA, May 6, 20, 1804, AFP.

Her sisters, her mother LCA to JQA, May 29, June 6, 1804, AFP.

She had her arias LCA to JQA, May 29, June 6, June 26, May 13, 1804, AFP.

He responded caustically JQA to LCA, May 25, 1804, LCA to JQA, May 13, August 12, 1804, AFP.

"It grieves me to see" LCA to AA, November 27, 1804, AFP.

4

In the summer "Adventures," DLCA 1:225–26.

It would have been DJQA, May monthly summary; AA to Eliza Susan Quincy, March 24, 1806, AFP.

An offer from Harvard LCA to JQA, July 20, 1806, AFP.

So they tried AA to LCA, January 19, 1806, LCA to AA, May 18, 1806, AFP; "Adventures," DLCA 1:232; LCA to AA, May 11, 1806, AFP.

The following summer Ibid., LCA to JQA, May 5, 1806, JQA to LCA, May 18, 1806, LCA to JQA, May 25, 1806, AFP; "Adventures," DLCA 1:236.

The tragedy, for a while DJQA, June 30, 1806; LCA to JQA, July 6, 1806, AFP.

It was never "Adventures," DLCA 1:238, 244; DJQA, August monthly summary, 1806.

The following winter AA to JQA, January 16, 1807, LCA to JQA, November 25, 1806, AFP.

"The last paragraph" JQA to LCA, December 8, 1806, February 6, 1807, LCA to JQA, February 20, 1807, AFP.

As it happens Heffron, *Louisa Catherine,* 190; LCA to AA, December 6, 1805, AFP;

"Adventures," DLCA 1:187. O'Brien makes the point about Louisa's view of parental love well in *Mrs. Adams in Winter,* 230–32.

When she reached "Adventures," DLCA 1:269; Bemis, *John Quincy Adams and the Foundations of American Foreign Policy,* 140–49.

So the embargo JQA to JA, December 27, 1807, AFP. For JQA's tendency toward nonconformity, see also Robert R. Thompson, "John Quincy Adams, Apostate: From 'Outrageous Federalist' to 'Republican Exile,' 1801–1809," *Journal of the Early Republic* 11 (Summer 1991): 161–83.

His wife was LCA to AA, January 24, 1808, AFP.

When they reached Bemis, *John Quincy Adams and the Foundations of American Foreign Policy,* 147–49; "Adventures," DLCA 1:274.

Louisa and John Quincy fought LCA to JQA, January 28, 1809, JQA to LCA, February 8, February 21, 1809, LCA to JQA, February 21, 1809, AFP.

On February 26 JQA to LCA, February 26, 1809, AFP; DJQA, March 6, 1809.

But the following day JQA to LCA, March 9, 1809, AFP.

But the children "Adventures," DLCA 1:283; O'Brien, *Mrs. Adams in Winter,* 233;

AA to Elizabeth Smith Shaw Peabody, July 18, 1809, Shaw Family Papers, LC.

Just before they "Adventures," DLCA 1:284–85; Oliver, *Portraits of John Quincy Adams and His Wife,* 49.

Part Four: The Gilded Darkness

1

The voyage took O'Brien, *Mrs. Adams in Winter,* 11; JQA to TBA, August 7, 1809, AFP; DJQA, August 12, 1809; "Adventures," DLCA 1:285; "Adventures," DLCA 1:290.

They sailed into "Adventures," DLCA 1:291; DJQA, October 23, 1809.

The travelers found "Adventures," DLCA 1:293; Nagel, *John Quincy Adams,* 193.

When the cold stone "Adventures," DLCA 1:319; O'Brien, *Mrs. Adams in Winter,* 27–29, 29–30; Heffron, *Louisa Catherine,* 211.

Among American government O'Brien, *Mrs. Adams in Winter,* 27; JQA to AA, February 8, 1810, AFP.

Louisa and Kitty "Adventures," DLCA 1:297, 304–5, 315; LCA to AA, May 13, 1810, AFP.

The constant talk LCA to AA, January 7, July 9, 1810, AFP.

On Sunday, November "Adventures," DLCA 1:297–98; O'Brien, *Mrs. Adams in*

Winter, 16–17, 20–21, 37–38.

2

The tsar paid Alfred W. Crosby Jr., *America, Russia, Hemp, and Napoleon: American Trade with Russia and the Baltic, 1783–1812* (Columbus: Ohio State University Press, 1965), 14–15, 28, 150–52, 225; Bemis, *John Quincy Adams and the Foundations of American Foreign Policy,* 161, 169; Crosby, *American Trade with Russia,* 276–79.

Most of the daily David Mayers, *The Ambassadors and America's Soviet Policy* (New York: Oxford University Press, 1995), 17–19; deposition of Christian Rodde, December 4/16, 1814, in Nina Bashinka et al., eds., *The United States and Russia: The Beginning of Relations 1765–1815* (Washington, DC: Government Printing Office, 1980), 1098.

Alexander, after all, For one evocative exploration of the effects of the godlike status of the tsar by a foreigner, see Astolphe de Custine, *Letters from Russia,* ed. Anka Muhlstein (New York: NYRB Classics, 2002).

The other job JQA to AA, February 8, 1810, AFP; Bashkina, *United States and Russia,* 666.

An English lord W. H. Lyttleton to Sir Charles Bagot, January 22, 1827, in Josceline Bagot, ed., *George Canning and His Friends* (New York: E. P. Dutton, 1909), 2:362.

So it helped Catherine Allgor, " 'A Republican in a Monarchy': Louisa Catherine Adams in Russia," *Diplomatic History* 21 (Winter 1997): 37; DJQA, November 4, 1809. Allgor's article adroitly assesses Louisa's role as a partner in John Quincy's diplomatic work and places her in St. Petersburg's social and political context.

She saw little "Adventures," DLCA 1:304, 306–10, 300; Cornelie de Wassenaer, *A Visit to St. Petersburg, 1824–1825* (Norwich, UK: Michael Russell Publishing Ltd, 1994), 50; "Adventures," DLCA 1:336–37. For a vivid description of the waltzing machines, see de Wassenaer, *A Visit to St. Petersburg, 1824–1825*, 45.

Not long afterward DJQA, November 5, 1811.

The tsar wanted "Adventures," DLCA 1:316, 318, 326; DJQA, January 9, 1810.

The French ambassador "Adventures," DLCA 1:302.

By May 1811 Ibid.; "Adventures," DLCA 1:344.

There was so much JQA to AA, October 2, 1811, AFP; James Madison to JQA, October 16, 1810, AA to JQA, March 4, 1811, JA to JQA, March 4, 1811, AFP.

But John Quincy declined DJQA, May 22, 1811; "Adventures," DLCA 1:348, 351; JQA to AA, September 10, October 24, 1811, AFP.

Winter drove the Adamses DJQA, March 19, 1812; William Steuben Smith to TBA, June 10, 1812, AFP; "Adventures," DLCA 1:353.

At the end of March JQA to AA, March 30, 1812, AFP.

All of this touched LCA to GWA, June 14, 1812, AFP.

Then that child DJQA, September 7–15, 1812; O'Brien, *Mrs. Adams in Winter*, 248–52; "Diary," DLCA 1:358.

3

On September 15 JQA to AA, September 21, 1812, JQA to JA, October 4, 1812, AFP.

His grief stayed JQA to JA, August 10, 1813, JQA to AA, June 30, 1814, AFP.

He watched her DJQA, September 30, 1812; Benjamin Rush, *Medical Inquiries and Observations, Upon the Diseases of the Mind* (Philadelphia: Kimber and Richardson, 1812); "Diary," DLCA 1:373, 357.

In her diary "Diary," DLCA 1:359–60, 367.

To an extent Sarah Nehama, *In Death Lamented: The Tradition of Anglo-American Mourning Jewelry* (Charlottesville: University of Virginia Press, 2012); LCA to AA,

September 2, 1813, Autograph File, A, Houghton Library, Harvard University.

"I am condemned" "Diary," DLCA 1:358; JQA to LCA, July 22, 1814, LCA to JQA, November 22, 1814, AFP.

There were tensions DJQA, July 26, 1811, January 15, 1813.

The other duties JQA to AA, December 31, 1812, AFP; "Diary," DLCA 1:360–61, 366, 369.

"We must live almost" Bemis, *John Quincy Adams and the Foundations of American Foreign Policy,* 186–87; LCA to AA, September 2, 1813, Autograph File, A, Houghton Library, Harvard University; JQA to AA, December 31, 1812, AFP; "Diary," DLCA 1:370.

4

The British rejected Bradford Perkins, *Castlereagh and Adams: England and the United States, 1812–1813* (Berkeley and Los Angeles: University of California Press, 1964), 65.

It seems that he was JQA to LCA, June 12–19, 1814, LCA to JQA, July 19, September 4, May 20, 1814, AFP.

For months she had felt JQA to LCA, December 29, 1806, AFP.

So one of his first Ibid., LCA to JQA, December 21, 1806, JQA to LCA, May 3,

1814, LCA to JQA, May 19, 1814, AFP.

His will was only JQA to LCA, July 15, 1814, AFP; O'Brien, *Mrs. Adams in Winter,* 35–37; LCA to JQA, December 15, June 13, 1814, JQA to LCA, December 16, 1814, AFP. For news, see, for instance, JQA to LCA, July 15, 19, September 2, 1814, AFP.

Admiring Louisa's own LCA to JQA, September 10, August 25, October 23, August 15, 1814, AFP.

She liked the independence LCA to JQA, July 8, August 5, 7, 1814, AFP.

Charles began to appear "Diary," DLCA 1:303–4.

On some days LCA to JQA, August 7, November 22, 1814, AFP; "Narrative," DLCA 1:391; LCA to JQA, January 6, 1814, AFP.

"Mama is a great Amateur of Cards" CFA to JQA, November 18, 1814, AFP.

Still, when 1814 JQA to LCA, October 14, 1814, LCA to JQA, October 23, 1814, AFP.

"I therefore now" JQA to LCA, December 27, 1814, AFP.

"I am turned" LCA to JQA, January 31, 1815, AFP; Mariana Starke, *Information and Directions for Travellers on the Continent,* 5th ed. (Paris: A. and W. Galignani, 1826), 325, quoted in O'Brien, *Mrs. Adams in Winter,* 56–59. For the preparations for Louisa's trip, I am indebted to O'Brien's work.

What she didn't sell Caroline Keinath, discussion with author, November 27, 2012.

No doubt because of O'Brien, *Mrs. Adams in Winter,* 3–4; passports, LCA to JQA, February 7, 1, 1815, AFP. Showing political savvy, Louisa would get a second French passport in Berlin from the French ambassador to Prussia, whose name was better known. (O'Brien, *Mrs. Adams in Winter,* 269. I'm grateful to Beth Luey for calling attention to the significance of the second passport.)

Before she left LCA to JQA, March 5, 1815, AFP; Mme. Bezerra to LCA, July 2, 1816, AFP; Joseph de Maistre, *St. Petersburg Dialogues, or, Conversations on the Temporal Governance of Providence,* ed. and trans. Richard A. Lebrun (Montreal, Canada: McGill-Queen's University Press, 1993), iv.

Most important, there was "Diary," DLCA 1:342.

She would think "Narrative," DLCA 1:387–88.

Part Five: Narrative of a Journey

1

Through the carriage's windows "Narrative," DLCA 1:376–77, 391–92; LCA to JQA, February 12, 1815, AFP. For this account of Louisa's journey, I rely heavily on the extensive and deep research of Michael O'Brien, who impressively reconstructed Louisa's trip from St. Petersburg to Paris in *Mrs. Adams in Winter*.

She traveled through "Narrative," DLCA 1:378, 397. For a rich account of another journey through the Russian winter, see Custine, *Letters from Russia*.

When she reached "Narrative," DLCA 1:379–82; O'Brien, *Mrs. Adams in Winter*, 218 99–100, 104–7.

As she turned "Narrative," DLCA 1:384, 386–87, 391.

2

She went straight "Narrative," DLCA 1:388–90.

But little else Ibid.; Radziwill, *Forty-five Years of My Life*, 231–376, 254–56; O'Brien, *Mrs. Adams in Winter*, 159–63; Clark, *Iron Kingdom*, 357–59.

She had hoped "Narrative," DLCA 1:392; O'Brien, *Mrs. Adams in Winter*, 186, 184; Clark, *Iron Kingdom*, 373–74.

She passed quickly Alan Schom, *One Hundred Days: Napoleon's Road to Waterloo* (New York: Atheneum, 1992), 27–29; "Narrative," DLCA 1:394.

As Louisa advanced "Narrative," DLCA 1:396.

As she moved through Ibid., 398–402; O'Brien, *Mrs. Adams in Winter,* 281–82.

At the post house "Narrative," DLCA 1:402–5.

That evening, John Quincy Ibid.; DJQA, March 20, 23, 1815.

Part Six: A Little Paradise

1

Springtime in Paris Alistair Horne, *The Age of Napoleon* (New York: Random House, 2006), 178; DJQA, April 21, 23, 1815; Louis Antoine Fauvelet de Bourrienne, *Memoirs of Napoleon Bonaparte* (New York: Charles Scribner & Sons, 1889), 4:152.

Their time in Paris JQA to AA, March 4, 1816, LCA to AA, June 12, July 8, 1815, AFP.

She was not looking forward LCA to AA, June 12, 1815, AFP; DJQA, May 16, 17, 25, 1815.

A surprise in London LCA to AA, June 12, 1815, AA to JQA, March 8, 1815, JA to JQA, March 4, 1811, AFP.

The younger boy JQA to AA, March 25, 1816, Diary of George Washington Adams (hereafter DGWA), December 31, 1825, AFP; DJQA, June monthly summary, 1815.

While John Quincy DJQA, July 21, 28, 29, May monthly summary, 1815.

Louisa may have LCA to AA, July 8, December 23, 1815, AFP. For Ealing, see *An American President in Ealing: The John Quincy Adams Diaries, 1815–1817* (Ealing, UK: Little Ealing History Group, 2014); Jonathan Oates, "A Tale of Two Ealings," Ealing Local History Centre, unpublished paper provided to author.

Perhaps it was easier LCA to AA, April 8, 1816, July 8, 1815, AFP.

Ealing, then, was an oasis DJQA, June monthly summary, 1816; LCA to AA, August 6, 1815, AFP.

Rev. John Hewlett recommended DJQA, August 5, October 4, 1815. For the Great Ealing School, Jonathan Oates, "The Great Ealing School: Myth and Reality," Ealing Local History Centre, unpublished paper provided to author.

At the end of October DJQA, October 13–14, 23, 25–29, November 14, 23, 1815.

She was tireless LCA to AA, November 27, December 23, 1815, AFP.

She was only LCA to AA, December 23, 1815, AA to LCA, August 8, 1815, AFP.

Much of his time JQA to AA, March 25, 1816, AFP.

Their oldest son DGWA, December 31, 1825; "Obituary — Clergy deceased," *The Gentleman's Magazine Historical Chronicle* 100 (January to June 1830): 186; DJQA,

August 10, 1815; *Letters and Correspondence of John Henry Newman During His Life
in the English Church* (London: Longmans,
Green & Co, 1891), 19–20; JA to John Adams II (hereafter JA2), July 31, 1816, JQA
to AA, March 25, 1816, AFP.

Louisa watched her sons LCA to AA, January 25, 1816, JQA to AA, June 6, 1816,
LCA to AA, September 11, 1816, AFP.

"And what are to" JQA, poem, 1816; LCA,
"On the Portrait of My Husband," 1816,
AFP.

2

London had a LCA to AA, June 7, July 4,
1816, AFP.

Once she was LCA to AA [n.d.], April 8,
July 4, 1816, AFP; Heffron, *Louisa Catherine,* 286.

It probably did not For the Caton sisters,
see Jehanne Wake, *Sisters of Fortune: America's Caton Sisters Home and Abroad* (New
York: Simon and Schuster, 2012). DJQA,
August 8, 1816; LCA to AA, November 11,
1816, AFP.

By October 1816 LCA to AA, July 4, 1816,
AFP.

More than the inconvenient DJQA, November 8, 1816; LCA to AA, June 12,
1815, AFP.

There may have been DJQA, October 12, 1816.

Some open flirtation "Gallant" was a noun, adjective, and verb. "I offered my arm and services to our friend Mrs. Storrs," an American member of the House could write to his wife, "and became her particular Gallant for the evening, attending her wherever she inclined to go, and in thus coursing round the room I had a more intimate serving of the many beauties which adorned each respected group." (Thomas H. Hubbard to Phebe Guernsey Hubbard, January 7, 1819, Thomas H. Hubbard Papers, LC.)

There is no reason Ellen Nicholas to JQA, August 4, 1817, LCA to JA, December 25, 1818, AFP.

Whether or not Louisa "Diary," DLCA 2:731.

That November, 1816 DJQA, December 24, 1816, February 4, 7, 21, April 7, 14, 28, 1817; LCA to AA, November 11, 1816, AFP.

John Quincy stayed JQA to TBA, February 28, 1817, LCA to AA, August 14, 1817, AFP; Heffron, *Louisa Catherine,* 295.

Part Seven: My Campaigne

1

The typical mix Harrison Gray Otis to Sally Foster Otis, February 19, 1819, Harrison Gray Otis Papers, Massachusetts Historical Society; Allgor, *Parlor Politics,* 110. For an incisive analysis of the so-called etiquette war, see Allgor, *Parlor Politics,* 149–83. For Washington society in general, see Constance McLaughlin Green, *Washington: Village and Capital, 1800–1878* (Princeton, NJ: Princeton University Press, 1962), 81–82; James Sterling Young, *The Washington Community 1800–1828* (New York: Columbia University Press, 1966), 214–18, 223–28.

In the Adamses' parlor Wake, *Sisters of Fortune,* 87.

Louisa and John Quincy "Adventures," DLCA 1:315.

So they ignored LCA to AA, January 23, 1818, LCA to JA, December 10, 1818, AFP; Allgor, *Parlor Politics,* 165.

That chilly night Harrison Gray Otis to Sally Foster Otis, February 7, 1819, Harrison Gray Otis Papers, Massachusetts Historical Society.

For all her insistence Heffron, *Louisa Catherine,* 299; "Diary," DLCA 2:543–45, 549; DJQA, January 13–15, 24, 1821.

With reliable suddenness LCA to GWA,

April 29, 1821, AFP. For the growing importance of charity work among elite women in the era, see Lori D. Ginzberg, *Women and the Work of Benevolence: Morality, Politics, and Class in the Nineteenth-Century United States* (New Haven, CT: Yale University Press, 1990). JA to LCA, May 25, 1819, AFP.

The servants who helped DJQA, November 28, May 3, and January 10, 1818; LCA to AA, January 1, 1818, AFP. For trouble with servants, see, for instance, JQA to LCA, July 24, 1827, AFP; LCA to AA, January 1, 1818, AFP; DJQA, February 2, 1818. In her attitude toward servants, she was not alone. "It appears that Mr. Adams has some affection for this old servant," wrote one European visitor who watched John Quincy and Antoine Giusta together and spoke to the valet, "but he is said never to confide in, and to be without exception and according to American custom stern and cold to his servants." Christian F. Feest, "Lukas Vischer in Washington: A Swiss View of the District of Columbia in 1825," *Records of the Columbia Historical Society, Washington, D.C.,* 49 (1973/1974): 105.

So there was a hectic LCA to AA, January 23, 1818, AFP; DJQA, December 23, 27, 1819; JQA to Daniel D. Tompkins, December 29, 1819, AFP; Green, *Washington,* 81;

Allgor, *Parlor Politics,* 120–23; *The Papers of Henry Clay: Presidential Candidate, 1821–1824,* ed. James F. Hopkins and Mary W. M. Hargreaves (Lexington: University of Kentucky Press, 1961), 3:200.

"The ettiquette question" "Diary," DLCA 2:447; JA to LCA, January 13, 1820, AFP; *Boston Courier,* January 6, 1825, quoted in *Connecticut Herald,* January 18, 1825; LCA to AA, January 27, 1818, AFP.

Her commitment to Margaret Hall, *The Aristocratic Journey,* ed. Una Pope-Hennessy (New York: G. P. Putnam's Sons, 1931), 168.

Her critics saw Ibid.; Feest, "Lukas Vischer in Washington," 105; LCA to AA, February 16, 1818, AA to LCA, January 3, 1818, AFP.

Her relationship with Abigail "Diary," DLCA 2:713; AA to LCA, January 3, 1818, AFP.

Abigail died of typhoid "Diary," DLCA 2:713, 669.

John Quincy's work Kaplan, *John Quincy Adams,* 330–38; Bemis, *John Quincy Adams and the Union,* 108; "Diary," DLCA 2:540.

Louisa complained about "Diary," DLCA 2:459; LCA to JA2, July 5, 1821, AFP.

She knew there was LCA to JA, January 7, 1819, AFP.

During her second year For dinner parties, see, for instance, "Diary," DLCA 2:430.

That obfuscation that Daniel Walker Howe, *What Hath God Wrought: The Transformation of America, 1815–1848* (New York: Oxford University Press, 2007), 206–8; DJQA, March 18, 1818; Lynn Hudson Parsons, *John Quincy Adams* (Lanham, MD: Rowman and Littlefield, 2001), 166.

John Quincy was content JQA to James Tallmadge, March 12, 1824, Adams Family Letters, 1673–1954, Mss. boxes A, American Antiquarian Society, Worcester, MA.

While the other candidates Feest, *Lukas Vischer in Washington,* 101; Louis McLane to Catherine McLane, December 19, 1817, Louis McLane Correspondence, Manuscript Division, LC; DJQA, June 4, 1819.

It was possible "Mrs. Adams," *The Huntress,* June 2, 1849; "Diary," DLCA 2:640, 448.

Louisa once wrote LCA to AA, January 11, 1818, AFP; "Diary," DLCA 2:444.

2

It was her campaign "Diary," DLCA 2:444, 440; Margaret Bayard Smith to Jane B. Kirkpatrick, March 13, 1814, *First Forty Years of Washington Society,* ed. Gaillard Hunt (New York: Charles Scribner's Sons), 96–97. For discussions of women in Washington and their indirect participation in politics, see Allgor, *Parlor Politics;* Allgor, *A Perfect Union,* 152–53; Fredrika J. Teute, "Roman Matron on the Banks of Tiber Creek: Margaret Bayard Smith and the Politicization of Spheres in the Nation's Capital," in *A Republic for the Ages;* Jan Lewis, "Politics and the Ambivalence of the Private Sphere: Women in Early Washington, D.C.," in *A Republic for the Ages.*

John Quincy needed "Diary," DLCA 2:457; Harrison Gray Otis to Sally Foster Otis, January 1, 1821, Harrison Gray Otis Papers, Massachusetts Historical Society.

Her weekly parties John W. Taylor to Jane Taylor, December 10, 1822, John W. Taylor Letters, 1859–1863, New-York Historical Society. The setup of Louisa's parties may have been something she picked up in Europe. Mary Bagot, the wife of the British minister, was struck by the practice at Mrs. Madison's levees of men clustering in the center in the middle of rooms while women hugged the walls. David Hosford and Mary Bagot, "Exile in Yankeeland: The Journal of Mary Bagot, 1816–1819," *Records of the Columbia Historical Society, Washington, D.C.* 51 (1984), 35.

Young women from Philadelphia, Thomas H. Hubbard to Guernsey Phebe Hubbard, December 25, 1817, Thomas H. Hubbard Papers, LC; LCA to JA, December 22, 1818, AFP.

It took work "Diary," DLCA 2:654; LCA to JQA, September 9, 1819, AFP; LCA dress, First Ladies Collection, Div. of Political History, Smithsonian Institution, United States National Museum.

She made do LCA to JA2, August 8, 1820; "Diary," DLCA 2:517; DJQA, June 8, 16, September 14, November 14, 1820.

Both Louisa and John Quincy "Diary," DLCA 2:418; Recollections of the wife of an aide to General Jacob Brown, Moore family papers, 1751–1939, Kroch Library Rare & Manuscript Collections, Cornell University.

Not everyone admired Harrison Gray Otis to Sophia Gray, November 18, 1818, Harrison Gray Otis Papers, Massachusetts Historical Society; Allgor, *Parlor Politics,* 106; LCA to JA, January 8, 1819, AFP; "Diary," DLCA 2:556; LCA to JA, January 8, 1819, AFP.

She was not as sweet Dolley Payne Madison to Sarah Coles Stevenson, ca. February 1820, in David B. Mattern and Holly C. Shulman, eds., *The Selected Letters of Dolley Payne Madison* (Charlottesville: University of Virginia Press, 2003), 239, quoted in O'Brien, *Mrs. Adams in Winter,* 121; Harrison Gray Otis to Sophia Gray, November 18, 1818, Harrison Gray Otis Papers, Massachusetts Historical Society.

She had to expect AA to LCA, March 17, 1818, AFP.

She asked him questions LCA to JA, November 5, 1821, AFP; "Diary," DLCA 2:486; LCA to AA, January 13, 1818, AFP.

She sometimes wrote LCA to JA2, April 10, 1819, LCA to GWA, May 11, 1818, AFP; "Diary," DLCA 2:433

She tended to read LCA to CFA, April 4, 1818, LCA to JA2, December 22, 1818, LCA to CFA, April 6, 1818, AFP; "Diary," DLCA 2:481.

Her reading was JA to LCA, April 8, 1819, LCA to JA2, April 10, 1819, LCA to CFA, June 6, 1836, AFP.

Motherhood was her excuse LCA to GWA, May 16, 1819, JA to LCA, June 11, 1819, AFP.

She was by no means LCA to CFA, August 30, 1822, AFP.

Her writing strengthened LCA to GWA, November 13, 1817, GWA to LCA, May 6, 1825, AFP.

So did her father-in-law Quoted in Ellis, *Passionate Sage,* 198; JA to LCA, April 2, 1819, January 14, 1823, AFP.

"Write without fear" LCA to Mary Hellen, September 3, 1819, LCA to JQA, August 8, 1822, JQA to LCA, August 12, 1822, AFP.

These exchanges turned For the connection to Davila, I am indebted to Robert F.

Sayre, "Autobiography and the Making of America," *Iowa Review* 9 (Spring 1978): 6–7.

3

There was one subject "Diary," DLCA 2:444; JA to LCA, December 23, 1819, AFP. For a provocative and convincing revisionist history of the Missouri Compromise, see Robert Pierce Forbes, *The Missouri Compromise and Its Aftermath: Slavery and the Meaning of America* (Chapel Hill: University of North Carolina Press, 2007).

Slaves served Louisa Alison Mann, "Slavery Exacts an Impossible Price: John Quincy Adams and the Dorcas Allen Case, Washington, D.C." (Ph.D. diss., University of New Hampshire, 2010), 117–19; Thomas H. Hubbard to Guernsey Phebe Hubbard, December 11, 1821, Thomas H. Hubbard Papers, LC; Harriet Martineau, *Retrospect of Western Travel: Volume 1* (Carlisle, MA: Applewood Books, 1838), 144. For slavery in Washington, see: William C. Allen, Henry Chase, and Robert J. Kapsch, "Building Liberty's Capital," *American Visions* 10:1 (February–March 1995): 8–15; Walter Johnson, *Soul by Soul: Life Inside the Antebellum Slave Market* (Cambridge, MA: Harvard University Press, 1999), 7; Don E. Fehrenbacher,

"The Missouri Controversy and the Sources of Southern Sectionalism," in *The Confederate Experience Reader,* ed. John D. Fowler (New York: Routledge, 2007), 60, 67. For my discussion of the Adamses' relationships to slaves and slavery throughout this book, I am especially indebted to Mann's research.

New York, of course A gradual emancipation law was passed in 1799. In 1817, New York freed slaves born before 1799 — but not until 1827.

Not everyone who came Jesse Torrey, *A Portraiture of Domestic Slavery in the United States* (Philadelphia: John Bioren, 1817); John Davis, "Eastman Johnson's Negro Life at the South and Urban Slavery in Washington, D.C.," *The Art Bulletin* 80:1 (March 1998): 71. See also Paul Finkelman, "Slavery in the Shadow of Liberty: The Problem of Slavery in Congress and the Nation's Capital," in *In the Shadow of Freedom: The Politics of Slavery in the National Capital,* ed. Paul Finkelman and Donald R. Kennon (Athens: Ohio University Press, 2011).

In this, he was braver *Memoir of John Quincy Adams,* 5:210. For the Missouri Compromise, see Fehrenbacher, "The Missouri Controversy and the Sources of Southern Sectionalism"; Robert Pierce Forbes, *The Missouri Compromise and Its*

Aftermath: Slavery and the Meaning of America (Chapel Hill: University of North Carolina Press, 2007); William W. Freehling, *Prelude to Civil War: The Nullification Controversy in South Carolina, 1816–1836* (Oxford, UK: Oxford University Press, 1965).

In his diary *Edinburgh Review* 30 (June 1818): 146; *Edinburgh Review* 31 (December 1818): 148; Forbes, *The Missouri Compromise and Its Aftermath: Slavery and the Meaning of America,* 34–35.

But John Quincy DJQA, February 24, 1820; *Edinburgh Review* 30 (June 1818): 146; *Edinburgh Review* 31 (December 1818): 148; *Memoirs of John Quincy Adams,* 5:210; Forbes, *The Missouri Compromise and Its Aftermath: Slavery and the Meaning of America,* 34–35.

Still, John Quincy *Memoirs of John Quincy Adams,* 5:54; LCA to JQA, January 26, 1820, AFP.

She was relieved "Diary," DLCA 2:481–82.

Her discomfort may 1820 U.S. Census, "John Quincy Adams," Washington Ward 3, District of Columbia, accessed through Ancestry.com; Mann, "Slavery Exacts an Impossible Price," 120.

The most likely "Diary," DLCA 2:664; Wake, *Sisters of Fortune,* 27; Dorothy S.

Provine, ed., *District of Columbia Free Negro Registers, 1821–1861* (Bowie, MD: Heritage Books, 1996), 92; Mann, "Slavery Exacts an Impossible Price," 111–12; DJQA, January 24, 1843.

John Quincy later insisted "Diary," DLCA 2:530, 482.

4

Because March 4, 1821 DJQA, March 5, 1821.

There were strong signs Howe, *What Hath God Wrought,* 92–93; Noble E. Cunningham, Jr., *The Presidency of James Monroe* (Lawrence: University Press of Kansas, 1996), 112–13.

That night the Adamses "Diary," DLCA 2:571.

Louisa watched Elizabeth LCA to Thomas Johnson, August 17, 1818, AFP; Louis McLane to Catherine McLane, January 8, 1822, Louis McLane Correspondence, Manuscript Division, LC.

She began to withdraw "Diary," DLCA 2:595; LCA to JA2, June 19, 1821, AFP.

The prospects of JQA to JA2, December 16, 1821, AFP; "Diary," DLCA 2:618.

She was in fact "Diary," DLCA 2:615–16.

What drew her LCA to JQA, June 25, 1822, AFP.

The health problems LCA to JQA, September 16, 19, 1822, Joseph Hopkinson to LCA, January 1, 1803, AFP.

Philadelphia was no longer *Memoir, Autobiography, and Correspondence of Jeremiah Mason* (Kansas City, MO: Lawyers International Publishing Co., 1917), 281.

Louisa's letters to John Quincy LCA to JQA, August 7, 1822, AFP. For political news and reports of visits from politicians, see, for instance, LCA to JQA, August 6, 7, 8, 9, 10, 1822, AFP.

Her tone swung LCA to JQA, September 9, August 18, 1822, AFP.

But it wasn't all comic LCA to JQA, July 8, August 7, 1822, AFP.

He took the side LCA to JQA, August 8, 1822, AFP; "Diary," DLCA 2:581.

It was not "Introduction," *Diary of Charles Francis Adams,* ed. Aida DiPace Donald and David Donald (Cambridge, MA: Belknap Press, 1964), 1:xxxi. (Hereafter, DCFA.) For an incisive look at the role of sensibility in the "social regeneration" during the American Revolution, see Sarah Knott, *Sensibility and the American Revolution* (Chapel Hill: University of North Carolina Press, 2009).

Back and forth JQA to LCA, September 6, 1822, LCA to JQA, August 31, 1822, AFP.

Their union was JQA to LCA, July 26, 1822, LCA to JQA, August 3, 1822, AFP.

When the subject LCA to JQA, July 8, 1822, AFP.

"I have told you" JQA to LCA, July 10, 1822, LCA to JQA, July 31, October 2, 1822, AFP.

Just before she JQA to LCA, October 7, 1822, AFP.

The truth was different Bemis, *John Quincy Adams and the Union,* 19.

One man who knew DJQA, March 3, 9, 1821, July 11, 1822.

That was the story JQA to LCA, October 7, 1822, AFP.

5

On New Year's Day LCA to JA, January 1, 1823, AFP.

A few days later Joseph Hopkinson to LCA, January 1, 1823, AFP.

She would have "Diary," DLCA 2:438, 747, 641.

Whether she would Ibid., 664, 669, 670n2.

More than two hundred years Rosemarie Zagarri, *Revolutionary Backlash: Women and Politics in the Early American Republic* (Philadelphia: University of Pennsylvania Press, 2007), 30–34, 154, 6.

"Kings are made" For two sweeping, divergent but complementary accounts of the vast transformations of the social, economic, and political landscape, see Howe,

What Hath God Wrought, and Wilentz, *The Rise of American Democracy.*

A woman was always "Diary," DLCA 2:464, 525, 669.

The knocks on DCFA 1: December 26, 1823.

It was tiresome "Diary," DLCA 2:665, 430; Bemis, *John Quincy Adams and the Foundations of American Foreign Policy,* 313–16; "Diary," DLCA 2:411.

Jackson was a force Robert Vincent Remini, *Andrew Jackson and the Course of American Empire, 1767–1821* (New York: Harper & Row, 1977), 378; "Diary," DLCA 2:678.

Things were changing Lynn Hudson Parsons, *Birth of Modern Politics: Andrew Jackson, John Quincy Adams, and the Election of 1828* (New York: Oxford University Press, 2009), 45; Wilentz, *Rise of American Democracy,* 242, 246; DJQA, March 27, 1824. For the maneuvering of Jackson's entry into the race, see Charles Grier Sellers Jr., "Jackson Men with Feet of Clay," *American Historical Review* 62 (1957): 357–61.

Ladies climbed on top "Letters of Hon. Elijah H. Mills," *Proceedings of the Massachusetts Historical Society* 29 (1881–1882): 40; DCFA 1: January 5, 6, 8, 1824; "Diary," DLCA 2:680–88; LCA to GWA, January 1, 1824, AFP.

Now, she did not need *Memoirs and Letters*

of Dolley Madison: Wife of James Madison (New York: Houghton Mifflin, 1886), 169; DCFA 1: January 8, 1824; "Poetry," *Metropolitan,* January 13, 1824 (reprinted widely from the *Washington Republican,* January 8, 1824).

It was half past DCFA 1: January 8, 1824; "Letters of Hon. Elijah H. Mills," 40; DJQA, January 6, 8, 1824; "Diary," DLCA 2:688.

6

Often, there were JA to JQA, May 20, 1818, AFP; DCFA 1: September 23, 8, May 10, 1824; LCA to JA2, May 6, 1822, LCA to CFA, May 6, 1822, AFP.

George and John Quoted in Nagel, *John Quincy Adams,* 279; LCA to JA2, May 11, 1823, AFP.

"My children seem" "Diary," DLCA 2:519; LCA to GWA, February 12, 1824, AFP; DCFA 1: September 6, 1824.

Louisa worried, too Nathaniel Frye to Duncan Stewart, April 23, 1827, Herbert Battles Tanner Family Papers, 1790–1972, Wisconsin Historical Society, Library-Archives Division; "Diary," DLCA 2:494; LCA to AA, February 10, 1818, AFP.

Even the success DCFA 1: January 31, 1824.

Louisa sat for two Oliver, *Portraits of John*

Quincy Adams and His Wife, 81–87, 102–6.

Her friends, she acknowledged Recollections of the wife of an aide to General Jacob Brown, Moore family papers, 1751–1939, Kroch Library Rare & Manuscript Collections, Cornell University; LCA to JA2, July 18, 1823, LCA to GWA, November 28, 1824, AFP.

Finally, the election Howe, *What Hath God Wrought,* 208; Parsons, *Birth of Modern Politics,* 83.

John Quincy dropped Smith, *First Forty Years of Washington Society,* 170; Louis McLane to Catherine McLane, December 24, 1824, January 29, 1825, Louis McLane Correspondence, Manuscript Division, LC; LCA to GWA, December 14, 1824, AFP.

At six o'clock "Diary," DLCA 2:488, 657–58.

That January night Louis McLane to Catherine McLane, January 13, 1825, Louis McLane Correspondence, Manuscript Division, LC; DJQA, January 9, 1825; JQA to GWA, November 28, 1827, AFP. There has been a massive amount written about the meeting between JQA and Henry Clay, including James F. Hopkins, "Election of 1824," *History of Presidential Elections, 1789–1968,* ed. Arthur M. Schlesinger Jr. and Fred L. Israel (New York: Chelsea House, 1971), 349–409; David S. Heidler and Jeanne T. Heidler, *Henry Clay: The Essential American* (New York: Random House, 2010), 179–80; Robert V. Remini, *Henry Clay: Statesman for the Union* (New York: W. W. Norton 1987), 251–72; Howe, *What Hath God Wrought,* 247–48.

Did his wife know LCA, "Metropolitan Kaleidoscope," AFP; DJQA, February 8, 1825.

Exactly what Louisa said JA to LCA, March 30, 1825, AFP; DJQA, February 9, 1825; Louis McLane to Catherine McLane, February 12, 1825, Louis McLane Correspondence, Manuscript Division, LC; Heidler and Heidler, *Henry Clay,* 185.

On Thursday, March 3 DJQA, March 4, 1825; "Inaugural Address of John Quincy Adams," March 4, 1825, in the Avalon Project: Documents in Law, History and Diplomacy, Yale Law School, http://avalon .law.yale.edu/19th_century/qadams.asp, accessed May 10, 2015; *Independent Chronicle & Boston Patriot,* March 12, 1825.

Part Eight: A Bird in a Cage

1

One day in late LCA to CFA, April 20, 1825, AFP; William Seale, *The President's House,* Volume I (Washington, DC: White House Historical Association, 2008), 156–59.

The fable was apt James Sterling Young, *The Washington Community, 1800–1828* (New York and London: Columbia University Press, 1966), 216.

Only now, her independence LCA to Joseph Hopkinson, April 21, 25, and May 1, 1825, Hopkinson Family Papers (Collection 1978), the Historical Society of Pennsylvania; Smith, *The First Forty Years of Washington Society,* 248; Mrs. Basil Hall, *The Aristocratic Journey: Being the Outspoken Letters of Mrs. Basil Hall Written During a Fourteen Months' Soujourn in America, 1827–1828* (New York: G. P. Putnam's Sons, 1931), 169.

"I am utterly weary" LCA to CFA, July 25, 1828, LCA to GWA, November 6, 1825, AFP. I have resisted pathologizing or diagnosing her psychological state using modern lenses. Others have not. For a short argument that she suffered "severely from mental disease, characterized as dysthymia, chronic depression, and even hysteria," see Ludwig M. Deppisch, *The Health of the First Ladies: Medical Histories from Martha Washington to Michelle Obama* (Jefferson, NC: McFarland & Co., 2015).

He had little goodwill Young, *Washington Community,* 188–95; Howe, *What Hath God Wrought,* 251–60; Kaplan, *John Quincy Adams,* 401–12; LCA to Thomas Hellen, June

19, 1825, AFP.

The weather did Howe, *What Hath God Wrought.* Though it focuses on an earlier period, for a study connecting the rise of nationalism in the early republic and celebrations, see David Waldstreicher, *In the Midst of Perpetual Fetes: The Making of American Nationalism, 1776–1820* (Chapel Hill: University of North Carolina Press, 1997).

Lafayette was an old friend LCA to GWA, September 11, 1825, AFP.

2

Louisa was fifty-one "Record of a Life," DLCA 1:2. In the past twenty-five years, academics have paid far closer attention to women and autobiography in the early republic, sometimes through different theoretical lenses. See Lepore, *Book of Ages,* 328–29n2. For an early survey, see Estelle C. Jelinek, *The Tradition of Women's Autobiography from Antiquity to the Present* (Boston: Twayne, 1986), 57–88.

Her history, her "Record of a Life," DLCA 1:21–23.

Her marriage, as she saw it, Ibid., 41, 51.

It did not matter Ibid., 8, 61.

The Marquis de Lafayette LCA to GWA, August 8, September 4, 1825, AFP.

Meanwhile, there were LCA to GWA,

August 22, 1825, AFP; Howe, *What Hath God Wrought,* 251–60.

Louisa wanted comfort LCA to GWA, May 1, 1825, AFP.

A host of maladies For a psychological connection with illness, particularly migraines, see Megan Marshall, *The Peabody Sisters: Three Women Who Ignited American Romanticism* (New York: First Mariner Books, 2006), 190, 196, 220, 228, 261, 513, among others, and Oliver Sacks, *Migraine: Understanding a Common Disorder, Expanded and Updated* (Berkeley and Los Angeles: University of California Press, 1985), 178–80, 206–9.

She wasn't merely "Diary," DLCA 2:542. The neurologist and author Oliver Sacks has written about the "dramatic role in the emotional economy of the individual" that migraines can serve. While the symptoms are undeniably real, "rooted in physiological reactions," Sacks wrote in *Migraine,* they can be "summoned to serve an endless variety of emotional needs." Sacks, *Migraine,* 207.

3.

On the morning LCA to JQA, July 10, 1826, AFP; DJQA, July 8, 1826.

His death was LCA to GWA, July 14, 1826, AFP.

To John Quincy JQA to LCA, July 14, 1826, AFP; Bemis, *John Quincy Adams and the Union,* 11–12.

Louisa's grief turned LCA to JQA, July 18, 1826, AFP; DCFA 1: May 31, 1824.

She knew too well LCA to JQA, July 18, 1826, AFP.

A few days after DJQA to LCA, July 14, 1826; DCFA 2: July 25, 1826.

There was something Howe, *What Hath God Wrought,* 214; LCA to JQA, August 21, 1826, AFP; DCFA 2: August 9, 1826.

Everyone was miserable DCFA 2: August 14–23, 1826.

"This morning my wife" DJQA, August 28, 1826; JA to GWA, JA2, and CFA, April 4, 1815, AFP.

"We have been" JQA to LCA, August 26, 1826, AFP.

4

The health of George's body JQA to GWA, November 12, 1827, AFP; Bemis, *John Quincy Adams and the Union,* 116.

Louisa was more forgiving LCA, "Metropolitan Kaleidoscope"; LCA to GWA, May 1, 1825, GWA to LCA, May 6, 1825, AFP.

He was trying LCA to JQA, August 11, 1826, AFP; DGWA, August 1 and 2, 1825, AFP.

On December 31, 1825 DGWA, December

31, 1826, AFP.

He could not hide LCA to CFA, September 9, 1826, AFP; DCFA 1: September 6, 1824.

When George fell DJQA, September 20, 21, 27, 1826.

By late October LCA to GWA, October 29, 1826, AFP; DJQA, June 28 and 29, 1827; LCA to JA2, July 16, 1827, AFP.

A month later JQA to LCA, July 24, 1827, AFP; DFCA 2: August 3, 1827.

With her son John LCA to Mary Hellen, August 19, 1827, LCA to JQA, September 22, 1827, AFP.

5

Back in the White House Seale, *The President's House,* 168–69; JQA to CFA, May 28, 1828, AFP; Mona Rose McKindley, "With a Heart of Oak: John Quincy Adams, Scientific Farmer and Landscape Gardener" (Master's Thesis, Harvard University, 2013), 26–50; Kaplan, *John Quincy Adams,* 415.

What they did share DJQA, October 7, 1826.

Meanwhile, by the winter Wilentz, *The Rise of American Democracy,* 294; JQA to CFA, May 28, 1828, AFP.

"Assassins" went too far For the controversy with JA2, see Samuel Flagg Bemis, "The Scuffle in the Rotunda: A Footnote to the Presidency of John Quincy Adams and to the History of Dueling," *Proceedings of the Massachusetts Historical Society* 71 (October 1953–May 1957): 156–66; "Concerning an Altercation with John Adams, 1828," Russell Jarvis Papers, Houghton Library, Harvard University. For the attacks on JQA, see, for instance, editorial from the *United States Telegraph,* May 4, 1827, reprinted in Arthur M. Schlesinger Jr., Fred L. Israel, and William P. Hansen, eds., *History of American Presidential Elections 1789–1968* (New York: Chelsea House, 1985), 449–51.

In February 1827 "Biographical Sketch of Mrs. Adams," Natchez, Mississippi, *Ariel,* April 13, 1827, reprinted from the *Philadelphia Evening Post; United States Telegraph,* June 16, 1827.

It is a very strange LCA to John Grahame, July 28, 1828, printed in Thomas John Chew Williams and Folger McKinsey, *History of Frederick County, Maryland* (Baltimore: Genealogical Publishing Company, 1797), 112–13; "Biographical Sketch of Mrs. Adams."

The tone of the document *United States Telegraph,* June 16, 1826.

Then Jackson's supporters *United States Telegraph,* June 18, 20, 1826; Heffron, *Louisa Catherine,* 338.

Before the 1824 election *The Papers of Andrew Jackson: 1825–1828,* ed. Harold D. Moser and J. Clint Clifft (Knoxville: University of Tennessee Press, 2002), 355.

No doubt he was LCA to JQA, July 10, 1828, CFA to Abigail Brooks, June 30, 1827, AFP; Bemis, *John Quincy Adams and the Union,* 147.

She wanted to fight Fletcher Webster, ed., *The Private Correspondence of Daniel Webster* (Boston: Little, Brown & Co., 1857), 1:469; Parsons, *The Birth of Modern Politics,* 116; Thurlow Weed, *Life of Thurlow Weed Including his Autobiography and a Memoir* (Boston: Houghton, Mifflin, & Company, 1884), 1:181.

He had trouble sleeping DJQA, July 31, 1827.

It was difficult Wilentz, *The Rise of American Democracy,* 262–63, 299–300; Howe, *What Hath God Wrought,* 250, 276–81.

John Quincy was actually Quoted in Freehling, *Road to Disunion,* 342, and Bemis, *John Quincy Adams and the Union,* 151.

Perhaps the subject DJQA, January 10, 1832. I am grateful to James Traub for pointing out this line to me; 1830 U.S. Census, "Johnson Hellen," Washington Ward 2, District of Columbia, accessed through Ancestry.com; DJQA, February 23 and 24, 1828 (Alison Weisgall Robertson helped with the translation); Mann, "Slavery Exacts an Impossible Price," 131.

John Quincy, though Provine, *Free Negro Registers,* Vol. II, 92.

He never mentioned DJQA, February 25, 1828.

Might Louisa have "Record of a Life," DLCA 1:25, 19; 1800 U.S. Census, "Joshua Johnson," Washington, District of Columbia, accessed through Ancestry.com; 1820 and 1830 U.S. Census, "Nathaniel Frye," Washington Ward 1, District of Columbia, accessed through Ancestry.com.

6

Even more than her husband LCA to CFA, July 16, 1828, AFP; Louisa Catherine Adams, Collection of vocal music in MS, Adams-Clement Collection, Division of Political History, Smithsonian Institution, United States National Museum; LCA to George Washington Adams, June 29, 1828, AFP.

She was more social LCA, "The Metropolitan Kaleidoscope / or / Winter Varieties," AFP.

Much went unobserved William Seale and Adele Logan Alexander, "Upstairs and Downstairs," *American Visions* (February 1995): 16; Seale, *The President's House,* 194–95; quoted in Mann, "Slavery Exacts an Impossible Price," 127.

She had that blindness LCA, "The Metropolitan Kaleidoscope," AFP.

As the 1828 campaign CFA to Abigail Brooks, September 18, 1828, AFP; Wilentz, *The Rise of American Democracy,* 309.

John Quincy was DJQA, January 1, 1829; LCA to CFA, November 15, December 25, 1828, AFP.

At one of their last Smith, *First Forty Years of Washington Society,* 248–49.

Part Nine: Beginning the World Anew

1

Winter was stubborn LCA to CFA, March 29, 1829, AFP; LCA to Elizabeth Hopkinson, June 15, 1823, Hopkinson Family Papers (Collection 1978), the Historical Society of Pennsylvania.

At the beginning of March Donald H. Mugridge, "The United States Sanitary Commission in Washington," *Records of the Columbia Historical Society, Washington, DC* 60/62 (1960/62), 136.

She heard stories Jon Meacham, *American Lion: Andrew Jackson in the White House* (New York: Random House, 2008), 61–62.

She kept all LCA to CFA, March 19, May 3, 1829, AFP; Mona McKindley, e-mail to author, October 7, 2013. For the billiard table controversy, see editorial from the Steubenville, Pennsylvania, *Ledger,* May 17,

1827, reprinted in Arthur M. Schlesinger Jr., Fred L. Israel, and William P. Hansen, eds., *History of American Presidential Elections 1789–1968* (New York: Chelsea House, 1985), 452.

Since leaving the glare LCA to CFA, January 18, February 1, April 16, April 3, 1829, LCA to GWA, April 8, 1829, AFP.

A letter arrived LCA to GWA, April 1, 1829, LCA to JA2, July 16, 1827, AFP.

On April 8 LCA to GWA, April 8, 1829, LCA to CFA, April 16, 1829, AFP.

She expected him DJQA, May 2, 1829.

Over the next few days DJQA, May 3, 4, 1829.

His corpse would JQA to LCA, June 13, 1829, AFP; DJQA, May 3, 1829; LCA, undated statement after the death of GWA [1829], AFP.

To Charles, she LCA to CFA, May 7, 1829, AFP; DJQA, May 6, May 21, 1829.

What story she constructed LCA to Thomas Hellen, May 17, 1827, LCA to CFA, July 5, 1829, AFP.

Louisa remained alone LCA to CFA, May 19, 1829, LCA to JQA, June 22, 1829, AFP.

Her focus turned LCA to JQA, July 2, 17, 1829, AFP.

She missed her husband LCA to JQA, June 22, July 7, 1829, CFA to LCA, June 28, 1829, AFP.

She had wanted to accompany CFA to

LCA, April 18, 1829, JQA to LCA, June 18, 1829, AFP.

He probably also DCFA 2: August 20, 1829.

Whatever John Quincy "Report of a Trial: Miles Farmer, versus Dr. David Humphreys Storer," Court of Common Pleas (Suffolk County), Massachusetts, Supreme Judicial Court, Miscellaneous Pamphlet Collection, LC; DCFA 2: May 13, 28, July 16, June 18, 1829.

He dreaded telling DCFA 2: August 22, 23, 1829.

Back in Washington LCA to JQA, August 28, September 27, 1829, AFP.

In May 1830 DJQA, May 2, 1830; DCFA 3: June 19, 1830.

She had never taken Ibid.; Karen Yourell at the Adams National Historical Park showed me and told me about the yellowwood tree.

2

She may have read JQA to JA2, September 15, 1830, AFP; DJQA, September 18, 1830.

She wanted nothing LCA to JA2, September 27, 1830, JQA to JA2, October 27, 1830, AFP.

The election took place DJQA, November 7, 1830.

His wife made LCA to JA2, November 14, 1830, AFP.

Her rage, though LCA to JA2, August 29,

November 14, 1832, AFP.

She reached Washington LCA to CFA, January 5, 1831, AFP.

Her thoughts often LCA to JQA, June 21, 1832, AFP; "Diary," DLCA 2:693.

Her mood, though LCA to Abigail Brooks Adams, January 29, 1831, AFP; LCA to Anna Maria Thornton, July 23, 1844, William Thornton Papers, LC; Benjamin Waterhouse to LCA, January 14, 1833, AFP.

Her sharp edge "Diary," DLCA 2:691.

As usual, she disclaimed LCA to CFA, February 6, 1835, January 3, 1833, LCA to JA2, August 22, 1832, AFP.

She set herself up LCA to JQA, May 18, 1832, LCA to CFA and Abigail Brooks Adams, January 26, 1848, LCA to CFA, February 21, 1831, AFP.

But family was her LCA to Abigail Brooks Adams, January 29, 1831, LCA to CFA, November 29, 1834, LCA to Abigail Brooks Adams, June 9, 1836, AFP.

No one blinked For the Second Great Awakening, see Gary Dorrien, *The Making of American Liberal Theology: Imagining Progressive Religion, 1805–1900* (Louisville, KY: Westminster John Knox Press, 2001), 1–179.

That atmosphere affected LCA to JQA, August 21, 1826, AFP; "Diary," DLCA 2:737; LCA to CFA, December 13, 1839, LCA to JQA, May 29, 1837, AFP; "Diary,"

DLCA 2:738.

She was sure LCA to Mary Hellen Adams, July 14, 1841, AFP.

She had watched LCA to JQA, June 21, July 14, August 17, 1832, July 22, 1834, [April 21?, 1831], AFP.

3

She had outbursts LCA to JQA, July 19, 1834, JQA to LCA, July 24, 1834, LCA to JQA, July 29, 1834, AFP.

John was only twenty-nine DCFA 5:143.

Living with him LCA to CFA, December 7, 1833, LCA to JQA, July 16, 1834, AFP.

John Quincy listened JQA to JA2, July 23, 26, 1834, AFP.

Faced with few alternatives LCA to JA2, July 31, 1834, LCA to Mary Hellen Adams, August 10, 1834, AFP.

"Then came the" DCFA 5:405.

John Quincy left DJQA, October 18–23, 1834; JQA to LCA, October 23, 1834, AFP.

By the time DCFA 5:409–10.

A year later "Diary," DLCA 2:688–89, 692–93, 696, 694. The alternative translation to the epigram is proposed in the footnote on 689.

It took something heroic "Diary," DLCA 2:705.

It occurred to her "Narrative of a Journey," DLCA 1:375; William Lee Miller, *Arguing About Slavery: The Great Battle in the United*

States Congress (New York: Knopf, 1996), 206–12.

"Narrative of a Journey" "Narrative of a Journey," DLCA 1:375, 406.

Part Ten: In My Own Name

1

There was more Due to limited data, estimates of life expectancy before the twentieth century, especially for women, are uncertain and disputed, but best estimates for a white female in the United States between 1830 and 1839 typically have it at around forty. The figure is slightly higher for women who survived childhood. J. David Hacker, "Decennial Life Tables for the White Population of the United States, 1790–1900," *Historical Methods* 43 no. 2 (2010): 45–79.

Louisa had not planned LCA to CFA, February 10, 1837, AFP.

Had Louisa mentioned Miller, *Arguing About Slavery;* Howe, *What Hath God Wrought,* 512–15. Kenneth S. Greenberg, ed., *Nat Turner: A Slave Rebellion in History and Memory* (New York: Oxford University Press, 2003).

John Quincy was not Miller, *Arguing About Slavery,* 206–12; JQA to CFA, December 15, 18–21, 1835, AFP; Michael O'Brien,

Henry Adams and the Southern Question (Athens: University of Georgia Press, 2005), 161.

When they arrived LCA to CFA, February 10, 1837, AFP.

That morning he had Miller, *Arguing About Slavery,* 343–48; Joseph Wheelan, *Mr. Adams's Last Crusade: John Quincy Adams's Extraordinary Post-Presidential Life in Congress* (New York: Public Affairs, 2008), 130–33.

John Quincy was indeed Oliver, *Portraits of John Quincy Adams and His Wife,* vii; Miller, *Arguing About Slavery,* 297.

His wife was different LCA to CFA, February 10, 1837, AFP.

The feeling of a fight Ibid.; "Diary," DLCA 2:694; LCA to JQA, November 5, 1840, AFP. For more on Rachel Clark, see LCA to CFA, January 1, 1832, LCA to JQA, May 12, 1837, AFP.

Louisa wasn't afraid LCA to Mary Hellen Adams, May 30, 1833, AFP; "Diary," DLCA 2:696.

She could imagine LCA to CFA, February 2, 1838, AFP; "Diary," DLCA 2:696–97.

Unlike most white Americans Mann, "Slavery Exacts an Impossible Price," 50–230; LCA to CFA, February 7, 1838, AFP.

Even as John Quincy LCA to Abigail Brooks Adams, May 14, 1847, January 29,

1848, AFP.

As he had for years John Quincy Adams, "Misconceptions of Shakespeare upon the Stage," *New-England Magazine* 9 (December 1835): 435–40; DJQA, January 25, 1843.

If Louisa learned LCA to CFA, March 19, 1843, AFP; Miller, *Arguing About Slavery,* 306.

2

At times, she was LCA to CFA, February 24, 1837, AFP.

The ne plus ultra Zagarri, *Revolutionary Backlash,* 145.

Despite her battle cry JQA to LCA, September 29, 1837, LCA to CFA, December 27, 1837, AFP.

That was another joke The series of letters "On the Province of Women" was originally published in the *New England Spectator* and then republished as a pamphlet. Sarah Grimké, *Letters on the Equality of the Sexes, and the Condition of Woman* (Boston: Isaac Knapp, 1838); Miller, *Arguing About Slavery,* 315.

But when Louisa read "Diary," DLCA 2:713–14; LCA to CFA, February 7, 1838, AFP.

"Although I have not" LCA to Sarah Grimké, January 11, 1838, Sarah Grimké to LCA, February 6, 1838, AFP. The interpretation of the equality of the sexes that Louisa had offered to Grimké, in which Adam and Eve were intellectually equal but Eve was spared from labor due to her beauty, came from a reading of Genesis that borrowed from a common interpretation of Milton's *Paradise Lost*. Milton's Eve was a paragon — "Grace was in all her steps. / Heaven in her eye. In every gesture dignity and love" — and the Victorian woman, the angel of the hearth, was her descendant. Louisa tried even to excuse Eve of the fall. It was *Adam's* fault, she wrote. His love of Eve had turned into a *"Passion"* for her, and had led him to sin. In Louisa's account nowhere does she mention that Eve bit the apple first. Nowhere does she account for Eve's desires.

Grimké replied sympathetically Sarah Grimké to LCA, August 8, 1838, AFP.

So many women Caroline Frye to LCA, September 24, 1845, Sarah Grimké to LCA, February 6, April 13, April 20, August 8, 1838, AFP.

Even Grimké's response JQA to LCA, November 15, 1838, AFP.

There was no groundswell Miller, *Arguing About Slavery*, 317. For women and petitioning, see Susan Zaeske, *Signatures of Citizenship: Petitioning, Antislavery, & Wom-*

en's Political Identity (Chapel Hill: University of North Carolina Press, 2003), and Susan Zaeske, " 'A Nest of Rattlesnakes Let Loose Among Them': Congressional Debates over Women's Antislavery Petitions," in *In the Shadow of Freedom,* 97–124.

It stood to John Quincy Miller, *Arguing About Slavery,* 318, 322.

When a woman Bemis, *John Quincy Adams and the Union,* 372.

In early September DJQA, September 3, 1838.

What must it have LCA to CFA, March 26, March 8, 1838, LCA to Abigail Brooks Adams, January 12, 1836, AFP.

She defended herself LCA to CFA, May 30, 1841, AFP.

Her thoughts about gender LCA to Abigail Brooks Adams, November 27, 1840, August 7, 1846, AFP.

Essays like one Zagarri, *Revolutionary Backlash,* 16, 170.

Nothing less than LCA to JA2, December 23, 1821, AFP.

Where did that leave Heffron, *Louisa Catherine,* 333; "Diary," DLCA 2:732–34.

It wasn't only "Adventures," DLCA 1:247, 175.

How hard it was Bemis, *John Quincy Adams and the Union,* 375–76.

When she did JQA to CFA, April 14, 1841, AFP.

He must have LCA to Abigail Brooks Adams, April 3, 1841, AFP.

She kept to her "Diary," DLCA 2:753; "Adventures," DLCA 1:64; "Diary," DLCA 2:747.

Even as she struggled "Adventures," DLCA 1:63–64.

On July 1, 1840 Ibid., 355.

Many historians and biographers Quoted in Zaeske, " 'A Nest of Rattlesnakes Let Loose Among Them,' " 109; Bemis, *John Quincy Adams and the Union,* 7.

Louisa's voice in LCA to [illegible], April 9, 1849, Everett-Peabody Papers, Massachusetts Historical Society.

3

"Among the many" LCA to Abigail Brooks Adams, January 15, 1844, AFP.

It amazed her LCA to Mary Hellen Adams, January 22, 1847, AFP.

Her eyes and voice LCA to CFA, March 16, 1841, January 8, 1846, AFP.

Every New Year's Day LCA to CFA, January 2, 1848, AFP.

In 1843, Louisa's LCA, "Rough Draft of my Will," October 23, 1843, AFP; Linda K. Kerber, *Women of the Republic: Intellect and Ideology in Revolutionary America* (Chapel

Hill: University of North Carolina Press, 1980), 9.

When she needed cash Henry Adams, *The Education of Henry Adams,* ed. Ernest Samuels (Boston: Houghton Mifflin, 1974), 16–19; Garry Wills, *Henry Adams and the Making of America* (Boston: Houghton Mifflin, 2005), 16. Wills convincingly argues that Henry drew on Louisa, as well as his wife, Clover, as a model for the female protagonists of his novels.

On July 11, 1847 DJQA, July 30, 1847.

Their old quarrels LCA to Abigail Brooks Adams, May 14, 1847, AFP; Adams, *The Education of Henry Adams,* 14.

Both of them DJQA, November 18, 1838.

She had felt "Diary," DLCA 1:84.

The previous November LCA to Mary Hellen Adams, November 25, 1846, AFP.

Louisa sat with him LCA to Mary Hellen Adams, November 29, 1846, February 3, 1847, AFP.

John Quincy knew DJQA February 11, 1847; "Diary," DLCA 2:702; LCA to Mary Hellen Adams, December 1, 1846, AFP.

The Adams house Mary Cutts, *The Queen of America: Mary Cutts's Life of Dolley Madison,* ed. Catherine Allgor (Charlottesville: University of Virginia Press, 2012), 174–75.

Louisa had lost LCA to Abigail Brooks Adams, February 6, 1848, AFP. For political chatter, see, for instance, LCA to CFA, January 13, January 27–February 7, 1848, AFP.

On February 21 Kaplan, *John Quincy Adams,* 568; Wheelan, *Mr. Adams's Last Crusade,* 248.

By the time LCA to Harriet Boyd, April 8, 1848, Herbert Battles Tanner Family Papers, 1790–1972, Wisconsin Historical Society, Library-Archives Division.

Louisa spent the next months "Diary," DLCA 2:770.

She would live John Adams III to Abigail Brooks Adams, January 11, 1852, AFP.

But she looked Abigail Brooks Adams to CFA, February 27, 1852, Elizabeth C. Adams to CFA, May 6, 1852, Elizabeth C. Adams to Abigail Brooks Adams [ante May 15, 1842], AFP.

On May 15 DCFA, May 15–16, 1852, AFP.

Louisa's funeral was *Baltimore Sun,* May 19, 1852; *National Intelligencer,* May 19, 1852.

Charles was later DCFA, May 18, 1852, AFP.

That December, her body DCFA, May 23, 1852, AFP.

ABOUT THE AUTHOR

Louisa Thomas is the author of *Conscience: Two Soldiers, Two Pacifists, One Family — a Test of Will and Faith in World War I*. She is a former writer and editor for Grantland and a former fellow at the New America Foundation. Her writing has appeared in *The New York Times*, *Vogue*, *The Paris Review*, and other places.